Canada-U.S. Tax Comparisons

A National Bureau
of Economic Research
Project Report

Canada-U.S. Tax Comparisons

Edited by John B. Shoven
and John Whalley

The University of Chicago Press

Chicago and London

JOHN B. SHOVEN is professor of economics at Stanford University.
JOHN WHALLEY is professor of economics at the University of Western
Ontario, where he is also director of the Centre for the Study of Interna-
tional Economic Relations.

The University of Chicago Press, Chicago 60637
The University of Chicago Press, Ltd., London
© 1992 by the National Bureau of Economic Research
All rights reserved. Published 1992
Printed in the United States of America

01 00 99 98 97 96 95 94 93 92   1 2 3 4 5 6

ISBN (cloth): 0–226–75483–9

Library of Congress Cataloging-in-Publication Data

Canada-U.S. tax comparisons / edited by John B. Shoven and John Whalley.
        p.   cm.—(A National Bureau of Economic Research project re-
port)
    Includes bibliographical references and indexes.
    1. Taxation—Canada. 2. Taxation—United States.   I. Shoven,
John B.   II. Whalley, John.   III. Title: Canada-US tax comparisons.
IV. Series.
HJ2449.C27   1992
336.2′00971—dc20   92-13915
                                                                  CIP

Relation of the Directors to the
Work and Publications of the
National Bureau of Economic Research

1. The object of the National Bureau of Economic Research is to ascertain and to present to the public important economic facts and their interpretation in a scientific and impartial manner. The Board of Directors is charged with the responsibility of ensuring that the work of the National Bureau is carried on in strict conformity with this object.

2. The President of the National Bureau shall submit to the Board of Directors, or to its Executive Committee, for their formal adoption all specific proposals for research to be instituted.

3. No research report shall be published by the National Bureau until the President has sent each member of the Board a notice that a manuscript is recommended for publication and that in the President's opinion it is suitable for publication in accordance with the principles of the National Bureau. Such notification will include an abstract or summary of the manuscript's content and a response form for use by those Directors who desire a copy of the manuscript for review. Each manuscript shall contain a summary drawing attention to the nature and treatment of the problem studied, the character of the data and their utilization in the report, and the main conclusions reached.

4. For each manuscript so submitted, a special committee of the Directors (including Directors Emeriti) shall be appointed by majority agreement of the President and Vice Presidents (or by the Executive Committee in case of inability to decide on the part of the President and Vice Presidents), consisting of three Directors selected as nearly as may be one from each general division of the Board. The names of the special manuscript committee shall be stated to each Director when notice of the proposed publication is submitted to him. It shall be the duty of each member of the special manuscript committee to read the manuscript. If each member of the manuscript committee signifies his approval within thirty days of the transmittal of the manuscript, the report may be published. If at the end of that period any member of the manuscript committee withholds his approval, the President shall then notify each member of the Board, requesting approval or disapproval of publication, and thirty days additional shall be granted for this purpose. The manuscript shall then not be published unless at least a majority of the entire Board who shall have voted on the proposal within the time fixed for the receipt of votes shall have approved.

5. No manuscript may be published, though approved by each member of the special manuscript committee, until forty-five days have elapsed from the transmittal of the report in manuscript form. The interval is allowed for the receipt of any memorandum of dissent or reservation, together with a brief statement of his reasons, that any member may wish to express: and such memorandum of dissent or reservation shall be published with the manuscript if he so desires. Publication does not, however, imply that each member of the Board has read the manuscript, or that either members of the Board in general or the special committee have passed on its validity in every detail.

6. Publications of the National Bureau issued for informational purposes concerning the work of the Bureau and its staff, or issued to inform the public of activities of Bureau staff, and volumes issued as a result of various conferences involving the National Bureau shall contain a specific disclaimer noting that such publication has not passed through the normal review procedures required in this resolution. The Executive Committee of the Board is charged with review of all such publications from time to time to ensure that they do not take on the character of formal research reports of the National Bureau, requiring formal Board approval.

7. Unless otherwise determined by the Board or exempted by the terms of paragraph 6, a copy of this resolution shall be printed in each National Bureau publication.

(Resolution adopted October 25, 1926, as revised through September 30, 1974)

Contents

Preface

This volume contains eleven papers which together explore and compare both features of and experiences with tax policy in the United States and Canada. The papers are the result of a project on comparative U.S.-Canada tax policy executed as part of the program on U.S.-Canada comparative social policy of the William H. Donner Foundation, New York.

The project involved six prominent public finance scholars from each side of the border, along with two more senior scholars. The objective was to explore jointly the similarities and differences in tax structures, the reasons for any differences identified, the contrasting experiences with tax reform (especially in the 1980s), and whether the tax systems are converging or diverging, and why. The papers have been commissioned with these objectives in mind and are reproduced here along with the commentaries of the two senior scholars (one paper, by John Whalley, formed the basis for part of the introduction and so is not published separately here).

What emerges is a picture of both similarity and differences. Corporate tax structures, following the reforms of the 1980s, are similar across the border, and income taxes have many similarities (but with differences). But Canada has a national sales tax, while the United States does not; the United States has sharply higher social security taxes; Canada has much more revenue sharing and, generally, a more decentralized federal structure. And while there are similarities in the tax reforms both countries entered into in the 1980s, both the extent of policy convergence in the area, and the degree to which tax changes in the United States automatically trigger similar changes in Canada, remain topics of debate. The reader will see alternative points of view in the papers, reflecting the fluid state of debate in this field.

We would like to thank the William H. Donner Foundation for supporting this project under its comparative social policy program and the Alfred P. Sloan Foundation for providing financial support for the project. The Ford

Foundation also contributed support. We are especially grateful to William T. Alpert of the William H. Donner Foundation for his help and encouragement in seeing the project through, and to James Capua of the William H. Donner Foundation and Art Singer of the Alfred P. Sloan Foundation for further encouragement. At the National Bureau of Economic Research, Robert Allison and Geoffrey Carliner have provided strong support, and Ann Brown has done an outstanding job in seeing the volume through to publication. At Stanford, Rosannah Reeves has provided sterling support, while at Western Ontario, Leigh MacDonald provided initial support with Connie Nevill seeing the project through in its final stages. To all we are grateful.

John B. Shoven and John Whalley

Introduction

William T. Alpert, John B. Shoven, and John Whalley

1. Background to the Project and Its Wider Context

Traditionally, social scientists, and economists in particular, have limited their investigations of social policy issues to analyses with a single-country focus. While useful, such studies do not provide the full richness of perspective that comes from analyzing more than a single jurisdiction. Certainly there have been studies comparing economic systems, but until quite recently many of the studies of different jurisdictions relied on provincial or state comparisons for their variation.

This book offers a series of studies focusing on one particularly promising area for cross-national comparison—the harmonization and comparative tax reform experiences of Canada and the United States. Cross-national research requires recognition of the policy environment or context in which social programs are established and carried out. This context includes the property rights established in a society, the incentive structures, the degree and kinds of economic freedoms, and the systems of private and public decision making and their relationship. In the case of Canada and the United States, general similarities exist with respect to these matters.

This was true in the Canada-U.S. case long before the passage (in 1987) of the Canada-U.S. free-trade agreement and the latest Canadian constitutional reform (in 1982) establishing the Charter of Rights and Freedoms (Bill of Rights). The United States and Canada therefore provide a natural joint labo-

William T. Alpert is associate professor of economics at the University of Connecticut and the senior program officer at the William H. Donner Foundation, New York. John B. Shoven is professor of economics at Stanford University and a research associate of the National Bureau of Economic Research. John Whalley is professor of economics at the University of Western Ontario, Canada, where he is also the director of the Centre for the Study of International Economic Relations. He is a research associate of the National Bureau of Economic Research.

1

ratory for comparing the effects of differing social and economic policies. The countries share political, legal, cultural, and constitutional inheritances, federal structures, remarkably similar standards of living, and pluralistic societies. Both are advanced industrial nations with important primary and manufacturing sectors, and large and rapidly growing service sectors.

Despite these similarities, differences exist—the melting pot in the United States versus the mosaic in Canada as metaphor for society, a universal health care system in Canada with no counterpart in the United States, a broad-based national sales tax in Canada with no such tax in the United States, a larger federal role in the United States and a smaller one in Canada. There are numerous other differences, ranging from the structure of urban areas to the official status of minorities. Recognition of these differences is critical in cross-national research.

The evaluation of social policies must consider the historical circumstances of the country under analysis. Is the society's history one that would lead it to consider certain taxes rather than others? It might be argued, for example, that the U.S. public would not consider a national value-added or consumption tax for historical and social reasons that do not exist in Canada or Europe. Such a tax may pose problems of implementation and acceptance in the United States that would not arise in Canada or Europe.

The work in this volume offers support for two competing themes. The first is that social policies of the countries are essentially different. In Canada, social policy forms a middle ground between the extremes of U.S. individualism and European collectivism. Relative to the United States, Canada has established a set of social programs that provides a higher minimum level of support for its citizens. Canadian social policy also has a tradition of universality—in health care, retirement programs, family allowances, and so on. This is not so in the United States, where the tradition is much more individualistic and less collectivist. Thus, Canada has a heritage more reminiscent of European social democracies.

The alternative view is that the social policies of the two countries are fundamentally similar. While differing in detail, they both spring from British historical roots. More importantly, the framework for policy is alike. The problems of income maintenance, employment standards, aging, pay and employment equity, equal tax treatment, immigration, and so on, are defined in similar terms in both countries. Additionally, social programs depend upon public and private components, as in the area of pensions.

In the tax policy area, both countries have federal and provincial/state tax systems with graduated personal and corporate taxes. Both rely on a diverse mixture of taxes, which include property, payroll, excise, and corporate and personal income. Furthermore, they depend on means testing for many social programs, although such testing is more common and stringent in the United States. Finally, the two countries devote significant shares of budget expenditures to social programs. Thus, in this view Canada and the United States fall squarely within a common Anglo-Saxon tradition, with similarities in policies and outcomes that overwhelm any differences that appear.

In this volume the authors find that certain aspects of the tax systems of the two countries are converging in important ways, while in other respects there is a surprising independence in their policies. For example, Canada's adoption of a national value-added tax does not promise quick replication in the United States. Neither is the United States likely to follow and eliminate mortgage interest deductibility any time soon, despite the fact that some steps have been taken to limit this tax expenditure. A second generalization from this collection of work is that although policies differ, outcomes are often surprisingly similar. For example, although the tax systems differ in many important ways (see table 1), they generate approximately the same amounts of revenue, produce similar costs of capital, and produce comparable distributions of income.

2.   The U.S. and Canadian Tax Systems and Their Evolution in the 1980s

The 1980s have witnessed major tax changes in the United States and Canada. These have come in the form of both ongoing change (such as steady increases in the social security payroll taxes in the United States in the first half of the decade, and several rate increases in the federal sales tax in Canada later in the decade) and dramatic, comprehensive tax change packages (in 1981 and 1986 in the United States and in 1987 in Canada).

In the United States, rate reductions at the personal level and sharp acceleration in depreciation allowances at the corporate level characterized change in 1981. Unwinding this acceleration, eliminating the investment tax credit, consolidating brackets at the personal level, and increasing revenue at the corporate level characterized the 1986 changes. In Canada, moves to reduce both corporate tax rates and the acceleration in depreciation allowances in the 1985 budget were developed into a broad reform package in the summer of 1987. The package included further rate reductions at the personal and corporate level, bracket consolidation at the personal level, elimination of both the investment tax credit and the acceleration in corporate depreciation allowances, conversion of most existing personal-level exemptions and deductions into credits, and a commitment (since implemented) to replace the existing manufacturers' sales tax with a value-added (or goods and services) tax.

An outside observer looking only at the 1986 U.S. changes and the 1985–87 Canadian changes might well think that many of the elements involved were a reflection of two economies moving in tandem. In both countries, corporate and personal tax rates were reduced, the number of tax brackets was sharply reduced, the investment tax credit was eliminated, and depreciation deductions were decelerated. The conclusion might be drawn that these changes represent clear evidence that the tax systems of the two economies were converging, driven in part by increasing integration in the form of larger

Table 1   Major Similarities and Differences between Canadian and U.S. Tax
                 Systems

Similarities	Differences
1. Both have federal tax systems.	1. Canada has a broadly based federal sales tax (MST, since replaced by GST); the U.S. has none.
2. Both have graduated personal income taxes and corporate taxes with a standard and small-business rate.	
	2. U.S. collects proportionately more revenue through the social security tax. Old age support in Canada is largely funded from general revenue.
3. The configuration of reliance on personal income, corporate, sales and excise, social security, and property taxes is similar. Resource taxes are more prominent in Canada (since resource industries are more important).	3. There is considerably more revenue sharing in Canada than in the U.S. The Canadian federal government collects a majority of revenues, but directly spends only a minority.
	4. Excise taxes (gasoline, tobacco, alcohol) are considerably higher in Canada.
	5. Canada has more generous tax treatment of savings (tax-sheltered pension contributions, capital gains.)
	6. Canada has integrated personal and corporate taxes, through a dividend tax credit.
	7. The tax unit in Canada is the individual, while there is both joint and separate filing in the U.S.
	8. Tax incentives and special allowances of various kinds are more widely used in Canada.
	9. Tax deductions for mortgage interest are available in the U.S.

Sources: Tax News Service (various issues); Pechman (1987).

trade and investment flows between the two economies. The similarity of change and the timing might also be taken to reflect that, being the smaller economy, Canada has had to follow the policy actions of the United States; otherwise Canada would lose tax base and revenue, and other undesirable effects could follow.

Differences in Tax Structure

Before examining further the connections between the Canadian and U.S. tax reforms of the 1980s, it may be helpful to compare the broad structure of the two tax systems. Table 1 lists their major similarities and differences. Canada has a federal structure with ten provinces responsible for the majority of public sector expenditure, particularly in education and health care. Under this structure, there is a multilevel tax system with individual, corporate, and sales taxes levied by the provincial and federal governments, and property taxes levied by the municipalities.

After the tax reforms of the 1980s, the Canadian system featured marginal federal income tax rates ranging from 17 to 29 percent on income net of deductions, with a provincial surcharge of 14–16 percent; federal corporate tax rates ranging from 12 to 28 percent, with additional provincial tax rates of 10–17 percent; and a federal manufacturers' sales tax with rates of 13.5 percent, since replaced with a goods and services tax (the GST) with a rate of 7 percent. This combined system collected federal, provincial, and local taxes amounting to around 33.5 percent of GDP in 1986/87.

The U.S. tax system is related in that it also embodies a federal structure. As table 1 points out, however, there is distinctively less revenue sharing between the U.S. federal and state governments than between the Canadian federal and provincial governments. Like Canada, there are federal and state personal income and corporate taxes, but unlike Canada, there is a large social security tax and no federally operated, broadly based sales tax.

After the tax reform of 1986, the U.S. system contained marginal personal income tax rates of 15 and 28 percent, and corporate tax rates of 20 and 34 percent. Retail sales taxes at the state level varied from 0 to 7.5 percent, with excise taxes being levied on such items as alcohol, tobacco, and gasoline. Federal, state, and local government revenues accounted for almost one-third of GNP; this figure is almost identical to its Canadian counterpart (see Pechman 1987, p. 1).

Tax Changes in the 1980s

Tables 2 and 3 document the major U.S. and Canadian tax changes during the 1980s. The first change of the decade in the United States occurred in June 1981 with the Reagan administration's Economic Recovery Tax Act. This tax package reduced individual rates, which previously had ranged from 14 to 70 percent, to 11 to 50 percent by 1983, with a corresponding reduction in the maximum capital gains tax rate from 28 to 20 percent. It also introduced a new accelerated depreciation system, termed the Accelerated Cost Recovery System (ACRS). Substantial debate followed these reforms, reflecting earlier debates in the United States on tax structure in the 1970s. This led to the 1984 U.S. Treasury tax reform proposals and eventually to the Tax Reform Act of 1986.

The main features of the 1986 Reform Act are by now well known.[1] At the personal level, the previous multibracket rate structure, with marginal rates ranging from 11 to 50 percent, was replaced by a two-rate structure of 15 and

---

1. See, for instance, Deloitte, Haskins, and Sells (1986), Pechman (1987, 1988), and Herber (1988).

Table 2   Major U.S. Tax Changes During the 1980s

1981   *Economic Recovery Tax Act (ERTA)*

- Acceleration in depreciation allowances increased; three asset lives of 15, 5, and 3 years
- Rate cuts at personal level and bracket consolidation (minimum tax reduced from 14 to 11 percent; maximum tax reduced from 70 to 50 percent)
- Changes in Individual Retirement Accounts (IRAs; tax-sheltered pension contributions)

1984   *Tax Reform Proposals*

- Proposal to raise about $50 billion in revenue
- Three-tier system of taxation of life insurance companies and life insurance proceeds replaced by single-taxation system at corporate rate
- Other restrictions on deductions

1986   *Tax Reform Act*

- Investment tax credit eliminated (was 10 percent)
- Acceleration in depreciation largely removed
- Cut in corporate tax rate (maximum rate reduced from 46 to 34 percent; minimum rate reduced to 20 percent)
- Reduction in number of personal tax brackets (from 14 to 5 in 1987, to 2 in 1988)
- Cuts in personal tax rates (maximum rate reduced from 50 to 38.5 percent in 1987, to 28 percent in 1988; minimum reduced to 15 percent in 1988; the rates to be indexed)
- Full taxation of capital gains
- Increase in revenue collected at corporate level
- IRA use limited

Throughout Decade

- Steady increase in ceilings and rates in the Social Security tax
- Steady attempt to close tax loopholes
- Base-broadening measures

Source: Tax News Service (various issues).

28 percent, with a 5 percent surcharge for some higher-income taxpayers. There were also increased personal and dependent exemptions. An expanded tax base was achieved through the elimination of several deductions, including those for sales taxes, the $100 dividend exclusion, and consumer interest expense, and an increased inclusion rate for capital gains.

At the corporate level, the 46 percent top rate was reduced to 34 percent. There was a substantial reduction in investment incentives, with an elimination of the investment tax credit and a sharp deceleration in depreciation allowances. In addition, a number of industry-specific tax preferences were eliminated, including those for oil and gas producers and for financial institutions. The alternative minimum tax was increased, with a 20 percent rate applying to corporations and a 21 percent rate for individuals.

Table 3   **Major Canadian Tax Changes During the 1980s**

1981   *Budget*

   • Loophole plugging
   • Cut in top marginal personal rates (reduced from 65 to 50 percent)

1984   *Budget*

   • Major planned changes in pension tax rules announced, to be phased in in future
     years (increase in tax deductions for contributions)

1985   *Budget*

   • Announcement of $500,000 lifetime capital gains exemption
   • Corporate Tax Discussion Paper announces planned rate reduction and limiting of
     use of investment incentives

1986   *Budget*

   • Announcement of plan to study VAT as possible replacement for MST

June 1987   *Tax Reform Package*

   • Corporate rate further reduced
   • Investment incentives eliminated (investment tax credit, acceleration in depreciation
     allowances)
   • Personal rates reduced and brackets consolidated
   • Exemptions in personal tax converted to credits
   • Capital gains provisions substantially curtailed
   • VAT replacement of MST confirmed, and three options spelled out

April 1989   *Budget*

   • Confirmation of GST as replacement for MST by 1991
   • Increase in federal surtax
   • MST increases: construction materials from 8 to 9 percent; alcohol and tobacco
     from 18 to 19 percent; telecommunication services from 10 to 11 percent; other
     goods from 12 to 13.5 percent
   • Excise taxes on gasoline increased

January 1991   *Budget*

   • Implementation of GST/MST switch
   • Credit-invoice VAT will apply to the final sale of goods and services, with certain
     items classified as tax-free (can claim input tax credits) and tax-exempt
   • Tax-free items: basic groceries, agricultural and fishery-related products,
     prescription drugs
   • Tax-exempt items: existing housing, charities and nonprofit organizations (with
     certain restrictions)

Sources: St-Hilaire and Whalley (1985), Government of Canada (1985, 1989), Fretz and Whalley
(1990, ch. 7).

Tax changes in Canada during the 1980s had different origins from those in the United States. In May 1985, a discussion paper on corporate tax reform was released along with the budget of that year (see Government of Canada 1985). It suggested a reduction in statutory rates and an elimination of investment incentives. In January 1986, a minimum personal tax was introduced. In the February 1986 budget, the corporate tax rate was reduced from 36 to 33 percent and the general investment tax credit was eliminated. In late 1986, a planned release of a discussion paper on sales tax reform was shelved, ostensibly because of the passage of the U.S. tax reform legislation and because of the argument that Canadian tax reform should consider a wider range of reform options, including income tax reform (see the discussion in Bossons 1987). The result was a 1987 White Paper on tax reform, which proposed further changes in individual, corporate, and sales taxes (see Government of Canada 1987a–d for more details).

The resulting legislation in December of 1987, like the 1986 U.S. tax reform, consolidated personal rate brackets and enacted the changes in personal and corporate taxes mentioned above, with a further lowering in the corporate tax rate to 28 percent. The lowering of corporate rates was clearly seen as needed, since with lower U.S. corporate rates, increased debt financing in Canada by cross-border integrated multinationals would erode the Canadian tax base. Changes in personal taxes were also seen as following the U.S. pattern, but the arguments made were based on individual incentive (effort), rather than on tax-competitive effects. Distinctive Canadian elements, such as the conversion of deductions and exemptions into credits, were also consciously included in the reform package.

In January 1988, changes were also proposed in the then-existing federal manufacturers' sales tax that came close to shifting the tax from a manufacturing-level tax to a wholesale tax for a limited range of products. The April 1989 budget reiterated plans to introduce a value-added tax to replace this tax, with the details subsequently following on its introduction in 1991 (see Government of Canada 1989).

Objectives of Tax Reform in the 1980s

The stated objectives for tax reforms in Canada and the United States in the 1980s reflected a range of concerns: economic neutrality, lower tax rates, equal treatment of equals, fairness for families, fairness across income classes, simplicity and perceived fairness in the tax system, and inflation-proof tax law.

But, at the same time, there were differences between the countries. In the Canadian case, tax changes were less the outcome of a consciously designed strategy for improving the Canadian tax system than they were a response to various emerging pressures on the system. One was the need for revenue, in the future as well as currently. The idea was to put in place a tax system with the broadest possible base and lowered rates, not only for the resulting efficiency gains but also for the increased ease of raising rates for future revenue requirements. Another was the perception that the Canadian tax system had undermined Canada's international competitiveness and needed to be changed.

In the U.S. case, public sentiment for tax change was already present in the late 1970s in the form of attempts to limit taxes. Thus, in 1978, Proposition 13 emerged in California followed by widespread constraints upon state and local taxes, especially on property taxes. In the late 1970s and early 1980s, high inflation rates were a major further concern because of bracket creep in the federal income tax. By the early 1980s, the view had become widespread that the income tax was unfair. The congressional response to these concerns was evident in the early 1980s in the introduction of several comprehensive income tax bills, each bill advocating a substantially broadened personal income tax with sharply lower marginal rates and fewer brackets.

Beyond these factors, there was a feeling that the U.S. tax system had become overly complex, with a proliferation of exclusions, adjustments to income, deductions, and other complexities. These, in turn, were perceived to have led to substantial erosion of the tax base through loopholes, which violated principles of vertical and horizontal equity and, in addition, distorted resource allocation. This lack of a comprehensive tax base was felt to distort saving and investment, asset and financing decisions, work effort, and invention and innovation. The system, in particular, encouraged investment in socially unproductive tax shelters.

There was also a view that the tax system had created unfair treatment for families, since tax burdens increased relatively more for large families with many dependents than for other taxpayers. In the early 1980s, high inflation rates and the interaction of inflation and taxes were felt to create further inequities and distortions. In neither country did the tax system of the day accurately measure real income from capital in most cases.

3.   Separate Development or Interdependent Convergence?

Perhaps the central issue in evaluating the similarities in tax reform experience during the 1980s between the two countries is the extent to which tax changes in the smaller country (Canada) were driven by earlier change in the larger country (the United States). Have the incentive mechanisms linking policy between the two economies become so strong that failure to follow change in the larger country inevitably results in large penalties on the smaller one, such as loss in tax base through migration, loss in revenue, opportunities for tax arbitrage, and other effects?[2]

2. This issue of foreign response to the 1986 U.S. tax reforms is also discussed in Tanzi (1987) and Whalley (1990). Tanzi, writing soon after the reforms and without having the full range of foreign responses available to him, suggested that the similarity of outcome reflects common intellectual forces more than direct cross-country harmonization pressures. Bossons (1987), in

There is no doubt that during the 1980s some of the tax changes introduced in Canada reflected these concerns. In 1987, reducing the Canadian corporate tax rate was rationalized, in part, by the argument that otherwise Canada would suffer base (and revenue) erosion. However, Canadian-specific issues, such as the large number of corporations that did not pay tax because they were in a net loss position for tax purposes, also were important influences on the reform. The 1987 Canadian personal income tax changes also clearly mirrored some of the features of the U.S. changes by consolidating brackets and lowering rates. The Canadian policy debate at this time unambiguously involved arguments to the effect that unmatched rate reductions in the United States might generate an outflow of professional and other higher-income labor from Canada (see Government of Canada 1987a, p. 21, and Dodge and Sargent 1988, p. 52).

At the same time, the strength of the role of tax changes in the United States in generating comparable changes in Canada remains very much in doubt, even in these cases. While the interactions involved were discussed in Canadian government circles, these changes were at the same time reflective of general directions that nearly all OECD countries were moving in during this period (see Whalley 1990). As table 4 clearly shows, rate reductions at personal and corporate levels, along with personal bracket consolidation, occurred not only in Canada and the United States but also in other OECD countries—the United Kingdom, Japan, Sweden, Australia, and New Zealand. This raises the question of whether common intellectual influences, shared by countries other than Canada and the United States, were behind these changes. Indeed, it is arguable that the 1984 corporate changes in the United Kingdom had more influence on policy in Canada and the United States, by demonstrating the resolve of at least one major government to move in this direction, than subsequent effects through direct links between the two economies. It is quite clear, for instance, that the U.K. initiatives were influential in stimulating consideration of corporate tax reform in Canada.

Other factors also enter into any evaluation of how strong tax policy interdependence between the two countries actually was in the 1980s. While there are clearly elements of similarity in tax change, as we stress above, the more fundamental differences in tax structure between the countries, detailed in table 1, have persisted throughout the 1980s (considerably higher indirect taxes in Canada, considerably higher social security taxes in the United States, much larger revenue sharing in Canada, and other features). If increasing integration between the economies generates an incentive structure for more tax similarity, why have only a subset of similar changes occurred in the

---

contrast, emphasizes the importance of cross-border pressures from the United States into Canada as far as corporate taxes are concerned and emphasizes the role played by the U.S. income taxes in redirecting Canadian reforms.

Table 4   Corporate and Personal Tax Changes in the 1980s: U.S., Canada, and Other OECD Countries

	U.S.	Canada	U.K.	Japan	Sweden	Australia	New Zealand
Personal Taxes							
Bracket Consolidation	14→2	10→3	13→6→2	15→5	11→4	5→4	5→2
Rate Reductions (top marginal rate)	50→28(+5)	34→29 (federal only)	80→40	70→50	80→50 (by 1991)	60→49	66→33
Corporate Taxes							
Rate Reductions	46→34	36→28 (federal only)	52→35	42→37.5	58→30 (by 1991)	46→49→39	45→42→28→33
Change in Investment Incentives	ITC eliminated; Accelerated depreciation withdrawn	ITC eliminated; Accelerated depreciation withdrawn	Accelerated depreciation withdrawn	Accelerated depreciation withdrawn	Limits on writeoffs	Accelerated depreciation withdrawn	Accelerated depreciation withdrawn
Dates of Major Changes	1986	1985/87	1984	1987/88	1984	1988	1988

Source: Adapted from Whalley (1990).

1980s, with other larger differences in tax structure between the two countries left unchanged?

A further issue in disentangling links between U.S. and Canadian tax changes in the 1980s is the question of timing. Who moved first, and with what effect? Dating tax reforms and determining their underlying intent is a difficult exercise in any case, and comparing across countries makes it even more so. One of the complexities of trying to determine whether the United States changed its tax system first and, if so, whether its actions predated actions in Canada, is that what constitutes a major tax change is often hard to determine. In the U.S. congressional system, because of the need for eventual consensus, a date of agreement and a concrete act can be taken to date the reform. Under the Canadian parliamentary system, a number of tax measures through a series of budgets cumulatively constitute reform over a much longer period of time.

Despite the difficulty in dating tax reform efforts, it does appear that Canada was considering and instituting corporate-level changes simultaneously with or even prior to the tax reforms in the United States. This claim is particularly damaging to the theory that Canadian tax policy simply must follow U.S. changes, because corporate capital is probably the most mobile of factors across the border. It is also true that many other countries were also moving in the same direction on corporate tax reform. On the other hand, once the United States moved, Canada clearly began to modify its position. In some cases, Canada went further in directions it was already moving, but in others, the policy directions were reversed. Thus, Canada modified its corporate tax reform in 1987 through deeper cuts in rates, in light of the U.S. actions of 1986, even though Canada had been moving in the same general direction from 1985 onward. At the personal level, it seems reasonable to claim the United States moved first. But the U.S. personal tax changes of 1986 seem not to have triggered the same kind of direct Canadian response that corporate tax measures did.

Two alternative interpretations of these events offer themselves. One is that change in the larger country drives the response in the smaller country. The other is that what similarities there are in the changes largely reflect common intellectual influences at work.

Our conjecture is that the common intellectual influences may well have been the primary reason for the similarity of result, rather than the strength of direct links between the two countries. This in no way negates the importance of direct linkages, but suggests that because of many impediments to the movement of factors between countries (such as immigration restrictions and trade barriers), only in the corporate capital area did these linkages dominate.

The broader implication seems to be that concerns in Canada over wider and deeper integration between Canada and the United States, particularly following the Canada-U.S. free-trade agreement—that policy autonomy in Canada will progressively weaken—do not seem to be strongly borne out by experience with tax policies in the two countries in the 1980s. This appears to have been the case for a number of reasons: large and persistent differences in tax structure remain despite the common elements in the tax changes; there is surprisingly limited effect on tax policy from direct economic integration between the countries; and a strong role is played by ideas and intellectual influences in policy formation in both countries. When ideas are jointly shared, similar policies result; when they are not, dissimilar outcomes occur.

4.   Summaries of the Studies

The 1980s were clearly a decade of dramatic changes in the tax structures of Canada and the United States. The two economies are undoubtedly still adjusting to those changes. The goal of this volume is to evaluate the forces behind the changes, their consequences, and the likely evolution of tax policy for both countries. We now provide brief summaries of each of the contributions in the volume.

Tax Harmonization

The first two papers deal explicitly with the pressures for harmonization of the personal and corporate tax systems in Canada and the United States. In the first of them, Robin Boadway and Neil Bruce begin by clarifying the definition of tax harmonization and discussing its advantages and disadvantages. Harmonization's primary disadvantage is that it may constrain each country's ability to pursue different objectives using different tax policies. The advantages of tax harmonization lie in the areas of efficient allocation of mobile factors across boundaries, reduction in tax arbitrage possibilities, and more sensible treatment of transactions and institutions involving overlapping or multiple tax jurisdictions.

Boadway and Bruce describe the differing fiscal structures of the Canadian and American economies. First they examine the broad fiscal differences between the countries and then focus on the detailed differences in the personal and corporation income tax systems. In general, Boadway and Bruce find that the corporate tax systems are far more similar than the personal income tax structures. They attribute this observation to stronger pressures for harmonization in the taxation of highly mobile capital.

Boadway and Bruce also examine the harmonization of state-and provincial-level taxes with the national tax systems in the two countries. They find that the Canadian subnational tax systems are almost completely integrated or harmonized with the federal-level tax, whereas the individual states in the United States follow widely varying tax policies. The authors examine how cross-border income flows are currently treated by each country.

Finally, the authors analyze the extent to which pressures for income tax harmonization are likely to impinge on independent income tax policy making in the two countries as a result of increasing economic integration. They also consider the advantages of extending the formal harmonization provisions that exist to varying degrees within the countries to their cross-border taxation policies. The authors consider the specific issue of taxing income to capital, which is distinguished from factors such as labor and land by its high degree of mobility across the international border. Specifically, they analyze the difficulties in using the corporation and personal income tax systems in conjunction with each other (such as with an integrated income tax system) in order to tax income to capital as it accrues. The difficulties arise because of the cross-border investments of multinational corporations. Boadway and Bruce conclude by discussing the ideal system of tax harmonization from a worldwide point of view.

Roger H. Gordon's paper examines the issue of tax harmonization in light of increasing integration of the Canadian and American economies and the recent free-trade agreements between the two countries. Gordon notes that the mobility of goods and capital between the United States and Canada is already substantial and will increase as a result of the free-trade agreements. The impact of mobile goods and factors on tax design and policy has already been studied in the local public finance literature. The findings indicate that the mobility of taxed activity will drive a community's tax structure toward benefit taxation, in which people pay in taxes an amount appropriate to cover the costs they impose on the public sector. This suggests that the increasing mobility between the two countries should cause each country's *national* tax structure to evolve toward benefit taxation. Where this pressure will be greatest depends on the degree of mobility of each type of taxed activity.

Gordon, as is discussed in several other papers in this volume, notes that the mobility pressures are probably greatest when dealing with taxes on capital income. Taxing the return on capital located within the United States (or Canada) simply drives capital elsewhere, until the resulting capital shortage within the country brings the net-of-tax return to capital back up to the return available elsewhere in the world. But this capital shortage results in lower wage rates, or lower land rents—the tax is ultimately paid by immobile factors. Corporate income taxes then effectively result, not in taxes on capital, but in an arbitrary pattern of taxes on these immobile factors. Corporate income taxation of multinationals suffers from the further problem that these firms can easily manipulate their financial accounts so as to transfer profits to subsidiaries located in tax havens. It is thus very difficult to collect any taxes from such firms, regardless of who ultimately pays these taxes.

While mobility of individuals between the two countries is not great in terms of numbers, the pressures created may not be negligible. High-income individuals, or those facing high estate taxes, may have a lot to gain by relocating. Since such individuals are often retired, relocation is particularly easy. Mobility of these individuals makes redistribution of income through the tax system more difficult. While the pressure of migration is probably minor at this point for the United States and Canada, it is likely to become very important within the European Community as all barriers to migration of individuals among the member countries are eliminated.

Gordon argues that even though tax competition will push each country's fiscal structure toward that of a benefit tax, such a tax system may not be mutually advantageous; in fact, both countries may well gain through explicit or implicit coordination of fiscal policies. In many cases the appropriate form of coordination involves equalization of tax rates. If, for example, the United States and Canada agree to impose equal estate tax rates, then retired individuals will not be able to escape the tax simply by moving between the two countries. Similarly, equalizing corporate income tax rates eliminates the incentive on a firm to relocate. It is equalization of net tax rates, however, not statutory tax rates, that matters. If only the latter are included in an agreement, then each country has an incentive to attract activities that are taxed on net by giving them, for example, extra public services or tax subsidies not covered by the agreement. Unless the governments are willing to make such agreements comprehensive enough to include all the factors entering into the net tax rate, agreements are unlikely to be very effective.

The world economy has become far more integrated in recent years. Remaining barriers to the mobility of goods, capital, and individuals are dropping at a rapid pace, particularly in the European Community but almost as quickly between the United States and Canada. Gordon argues that once the implications of these changes for national taxes are recognized, national tax structures are likely to look very different than they do now.

Income Security and Tax Incidence

The third and fourth papers in the volume deal with income security and tax incidence in Canada and the United States. Jonathan R. Kesselman's paper notes an important exception to the trends toward harmonization in the two countries' tax codes. He finds that the income-security systems of the two countries have shown remarkably little convergence either in stand-alone provisions or tax-based provisions. Unlike many other areas of economic policy where Canada has imitated the United States, income security faces few competitive pressures for harmonization. This lack of harmonization pressure is at least partially due to immigration laws that make it difficult to move from one country to the other. Unskilled and low-wage workers may be particularly immobile.

Kesselman's paper provides a detailed description of the income-support policies of Canada and the United States. He finds that while each country has made many recent changes to policies affecting income security, these changes have usually been made without taking advantage of the experience with similar policies of the other country. Despite the general lack of coordination or even information sharing, the income-support systems of both countries have some common shortcomings. Three problem areas discussed by Kesselman are the high effective tax rates faced by beneficiaries due to phaseout provisions; the complexity of income-support programs in both countries (particularly due to the simultaneous use of multiple programs in each country); and the failure to achieve horizontal equity and vertical equity.

Kesselman concludes his paper by speculating about the future evolution of income-security programs in the two countries. He suggests that reforms would build upon refundable credits or income guarantees for those unable to work, including dependent children. Employable persons would be assisted mainly through work-related benefits; the choice will hinge on administrative and compliance factors as much as on pure economic considerations. Kesselman also hints that the increasingly severe competitive pressures from the rest of the world may ultimately result in pressure to harmonize and rationalize income-support policies in both countries.

The contribution of James B. Davies to this volume asks what is known about overall tax incidence and recent changes in incidence in Canada and the United States. There is a popular notion that Canada has a more egalitarian income distribution than the United States. Davies examines whether there is truth to this notion, and then attempts to assess how differences in the tax systems affect the relative degree of income inequality on the two sides of the border.

For the most part, previous estimates of tax incidence have been made in an annual framework. There has been a long-expressed dissatisfaction with this arbitrary time period, however. Recently there has been some interest in generating estimates of the lifetime, as opposed to the annual, incidence of taxes. Important insights are gained, which are relevant to the comparison of tax structures in Canada and the United States. For example, general sales taxes look considerably less regressive over the lifetime than they do in annual data, since consumption is approximately proportional to permanent income. Since Canada relies much more heavily on sales and excise taxes as a revenue source than does the United States, this finding implies a significant difference in the comparison of overall tax progressivity in the two countries, depending on whether an annual or a lifetime framework is used.

Davies's study concentrates on changes in the income distributions and the tax progressivity in the two countries over the 1970s and 1980s. In the early 1970s, the overall incidence of taxes appears to display a similar degree of progressivity, if one uses annual data in the analysis. However, if one accepts the conclusion from the studies of lifetime tax incidence that sales and excise taxes are significantly less regressive than social insurance contributions, then from a longer-term viewpoint the overall tax system was probably more progressive in Canada than in the United States, even in the early 1970s.

Since 1970 the major causes of changes in the relative progressivity of taxes have likely been changes in rate structures and overall tax mix. The absence of bracket and exemption indexation through most of the period reduced the progressivity of the U.S. federal income tax sharply. Canada, in contrast, had indexation throughout the subperiod with highest inflation and introduced measures such as child and sales tax credits, which reduced tax burdens on low-income families significantly. Finally, the shift in tax mix in the United States has been toward rising social insurance contributions, whereas in Canada the shift has been toward increasing the personal income tax. Hence, the United States has seen a buildup of one of the least progressive forms of taxation, while Canada has seen an increase in the importance of one of the most progressive forms of taxation. The conclusion is that, over the last two decades as a whole, the overall Canadian tax system has become more progressive than the American system.

The significance of the overall divergence in progressivity trends between Canada and the United States is all the greater due to the contrasting changes in inequality of pretax income between 1970 and 1990. Inequality in pretax income (which includes transfer payments) has been trendless in Canada, but has increased steadily year-by-year since about 1975 in the United States. The combination of rising underlying inequality and a decreasingly progressive tax system overall in the United States (until 1986) forms a sharp contrast with Canadian experience.

Davies argues that the relative trends in progressivity and inequality may have been reversed since 1986. The 1986 U.S. tax reform unambiguously increased overall progressivity; the Canadian reforms were probably less progressive. Further, the United States now has fully indexed bracket amounts for inflation, while Canada now adjusts the figures at the inflation rate less 3 percent. Thus, the Canadian tax system may become gradually less progressive relative to the U.S., reversing its traditional trend.

Effective Tax Rates and the Cost of Capital

The fifth and sixth papers deal with the effective rate of tax on capital investments in the two countries and the comparative cost of capital. The study by Kenneth J. McKenzie and Jack M. Mintz compares effective corporate income tax rates for companies operating in the United States and Canada. The effective tax rates are calculated for a number of specific cases that allow for differences in assumptions regarding risk, financial arbitrage, the use of tax losses, and the tax treatment of multinational investments. The McKenzie-Mintz "base case" assumptions are open economy arbitrage (i.e., only corporate-level and not personal-level tax differences are considered), an absence of risk, fully taxpaying firms, and no multinational investment. In that case, the authors find that the aggregate Canadian effective corporate tax rate (29 percent) was substantially higher than the aggregate American tax rate (20 percent) in 1990.

McKenzie and Mintz disaggregate by sector their calculations of the effective corporate tax rates for the two countries. They also compute the rates for 1975, 1980, 1985, and 1990. The authors conclude that the difference between Canadian and U.S. effective corporate tax rates was even larger in the earlier years. Thus, the combination of the tax measures adopted in the 1980s and the lower rate of inflation experienced in both countries by the end of the period examined has caused some convergence in the effective tax rates.

McKenzie and Mintz find that their conclusions are fairly insensitive to most of the assumptions imbedded in their base case. However, their conclusions are overturned when they incorporate into their analysis companies experiencing tax losses. Assuming that tax losses confer an advantage to companies in sheltering future income from taxation, McKenzie and Mintz find that the 1990 difference in effective corporate tax rates on capital in Canada and the United States is virtually eliminated. Their final assessment, therefore, is that Canadian and U.S. corporate tax rates are very similar in aggregate, although this conclusion masks considerable differences between the two countries for specific industries, investment activities, and tax-loss experience.

The paper by John B. Shoven and Michael Topper examines the cost of capital in the United States and Canada, rather than concentrating on effective tax rates. The cost of capital is the hurdle rate faced by potential new investments. In general, the cost of capital is determined by the terms available in financial markets as well as by tax considerations. For comparative purposes, the Shoven-Topper paper includes calculations on the cost of capital in Japan.

Shoven and Topper pay considerable attention to the role of risk premia and the interaction of risk premia and taxes in determining the cost of capital. They feel that most previous work on the cost of capital has relied too much on the real interest rate as a measure of the terms available in financial markets. In fact, financial market returns exhibit a great deal of risk aversion, with risky assets having much higher average rates of return than safe ones. The paper asserts that the hurdle rate on new investments should similarly differ depending on the riskiness of the venture.

One of the conclusions of Shoven and Topper is that risk premia are extremely important components of the cost of capital, at least as important as the interest rate or taxes. They also find that the corporate and personal tax systems of Canada and the United States (and Japan) magnify risk premia. That is, the tax systems cause the extra return demanded on risky undertakings to be larger. The key finding of the authors relevant to the theme of the volume is that the cost of capital is very similar for Canada and the United States. This similarity occurs because financial terms appear to be almost identical in the two countries and because the corporate tax systems are effectively quite similar. The authors conclude that the cost-of-capital figures are so similar in the United States and Canada that the location of investments between the two countries is not distorted. Shoven and Topper find that both of these countries suffer a large cost-of-capital disadvantage relative to Japan. While this is partially due to tax features, it is mostly a result of the segmented Japanese financial market, which exhibits a substantially smaller risk premium.

International Spillover of Taxation

The seventh paper, written by Joel Slemrod, deals with the impact of the U.S. tax reform on Canadian stock prices. Slemrod examines one potential channel of international spillover of taxation. The issue addressed is how Canadian businesses were affected (as reflected by the stock market) by U.S. tax reform. His analysis is an event study of the impact of the Tax Reform Act of 1986 on the abnormal stock market returns of publicly traded Canadian corporations. The paper's premise is that the U.S. tax reform induced changes in the prospects for Canadian enterprises that were promptly reflected in their stock market valuation.

Slemrod proposes that there are at least three possible avenues of influence of the U.S. tax reform on Canadian companies. First, there is the "My enemy's enemy is my friend" model, which asserts that anything that is bad for U.S. firms will therefore be good for their Canadian counterparts. Second, there is the "As the U.S. goes, so goes Canada" logic, which suggests that whatever changes are taking place in the United States will also soon be made in Canada. Finally, there is the "But I'm half American" story, which suggests that multinationals are so important that both Canadian and U.S. firms are directly affected by changes in U.S. tax laws.

Slemrod's event study examines stock price behavior around four key dates in the evolution of the 1986 U.S. tax reform. In general, he finds that Canadian stocks had negative abnormal returns around these dates, when the U.S. tax reform presumably became more likely. However, when he examines the cross-industry correlation of abnormal Canadian and U.S. returns, he finds it to be negative. That is, those industries that fell in value on the U.S. market around the key dates tended to be those that rose in value in Canada. This lends some support to the "My enemy's enemy is my friend" theory. However, there was no evidence that this negative correlation was particularly strong for industries with a high degree of competition between the two countries. Slemrod concludes his paper suggesting that further investigations into the spillover effects of one country's tax policies would be profitable.

Demographics and Fiscal Policy

The eighth paper, written by Alan J. Auerbach and Laurence J. Kotlikoff, examines how demographics and fiscal structures are likely to interact over the next several decades in Canada and the United States. They predict how these influences will affect each country's rate of capital accumulation and identify the implications of differences in projected saving for patterns of trade and capital flows. The consequences of demographic changes are particularly interesting in a Canada-U.S. comparison because Canada's population is aging even more rapidly than the United States's; the governments of the two countries offer significantly different packages of social services (such as social security, health care, and education) to their citizens; the respective public pension systems are financed quite differently; and the two countries obviously differ sharply in their size and openness.

Auerbach and Kotlikoff's study uses a general equilibrium dynamic simulation model of the United States and Canada, which takes account of the interrelated behavior of households, firms, and government during the process of demographic transition. Their model projects the behavior of each economy from 1990 to 2050 under a variety of assumptions about the fiscal response to the financial pressures imposed by aging populations.

Among the interesting findings is the prediction that rising real wages (due to the smaller relative size of the working-age population) should more than offset any added payroll tax burden to finance public pensions. Their model predicts a continuing decline in the U.S. saving rate over the next sixty years, while it forecasts that Canadian saving rates will rise until 2010 and then decline quite sharply. The different demographic patterns are behind the different evolution of saving rates. The Canadian current account is predicted to follow the same pattern as saving—increasing surpluses until 2010 followed by declining surpluses and eventually deficits.

Taxes and Housing

In the ninth paper, James M. Poterba compares the relative tax burdens on owner-occupied housing in Canada and the United States. One reason why this is an important topic is that widespread concern arose in the 1980s about international competitiveness. This concern led to calls for policies to encourage investment in plant and equipment. The net effect of the tax code on investment in a particular part of the economy depends on the relative tax treatment of investment in different sectors. Consequently, one way to encourage industrial investment is to discourage housing investment, and vice versa.

The two countries differ sharply in their tax treatment of owner-occupied housing. The U.S. tax system allows households to deduct mortgage interest payments in computing their taxable income. Further, housing capital gains are fairly lightly taxed. The Canadian tax system does not permit mortgage interest deductions and thus makes the tax treatment of housing less favorable. There are many additional ways in which the tax treatments differ.

Poterba's research shows that the net incentives for housing investment in Canada are in fact smaller than those in the United States, but that the disparities between the two nations have narrowed over time. In 1980, for example, the effective cost of purchasing owner-occupied housing was only one-third as great for a high-income U.S. household as for its Canadian counterpart. The net effect of the last decade's declining marginal tax rates in both nations, however, has been a fall in the relative U.S. tax subsidy to housing. Poterba estimates that by 1989 the cost of owner-occupied housing services for top-bracket households was nearly two-thirds as great in the United States as in

Canada. For households with lower incomes, and hence lower marginal tax rates, the disparities were even smaller.

The narrowing of tax incentives for housing investment in the two nations may explain the converging ratios of housing capital relative to GNP. In 1960, for example, the stock of owner-occupied housing in Canada was 18 percent of GNP, compared with 26 percent in the United States. In 1989 the housing stocks in both nations were 27 percent of GNP. Similarly, while in 1970 the home-ownership rate for most age groups was higher in the United States than in Canada, by the mid-1980s the rate among younger age groups in Canada was higher than that in the United States.

Poterba notes that harmonizing tax policies across countries requires attention to more than just policies related to the investment and financial transactions of international firms. It requires broad-based attention to the structure of taxation, including the treatment of nontradable assets such as housing. The last decade has witnessed convergence in this aspect of the U.S. and Canadian tax codes, but disparities remain. The Canadian tax code still provides a smaller incentive for investing in owner-occupied housing than does the U.S. tax system.

Sales Taxes

The tenth paper, authored by Charles E. McLure, Jr., discusses the lessons for the United States from the Canadian debate on sales tax reform. The United States has been looking for ways to reduce its federal deficit for nearly a decade now, and the possibility of introducing a value-added tax (VAT) or a national sales tax is often mentioned as a potential major new source of revenue. On the other hand, Canada has had a manufacturers'-level sales tax (MST) since 1924 and has just replaced it with a VAT. If the United States seriously considers some form of a national sales tax, then it seems only prudent for U.S. policy makers to learn from the Canadian experience.

McLure briefly describes the basic mechanics of three retail-level sales taxes (the credit-method VAT, a subtraction-method VAT, and a retail sales tax). He also evaluates two pre-retail taxes, the manufacturers' sales tax and the wholesale-level business transfer tax. Although ideal versions of the three retail-level taxes have identical effects, McLure notes that the credit-method VAT offers several advantages in practice. He also argues that a sales tax that stops short of the retail level distorts economic choices and creates severe administrative difficulties.

McLure summarizes the policy debates concerning sales and value-added taxes in the United States and Canada. He also elaborates on particular key issues, including intergovernmental issues, low-income relief, and economic neutrality. Special attention is devoted to the taxation of food, housing, agriculture, financial institutions, nonprofit institutions, and small businesses.

Subnational Taxes

The eleventh paper, written by François Vaillancourt, deals with the question of harmonization of subnational tax systems (state, provincial, and local) across Canada and the United States. Vaillancourt asserts that when U.S. and Canadian tax systems are compared, it is usually at the federal level, with little attention paid to subnational—provincial/state and local—tax systems. But subnational tax systems collect an important share (40–50 percent) of overall tax revenues in both countries and are, therefore, likely to have an impact on economic choices. The author describes the subnational tax systems of the two countries and examines the degree of harmonization within and between countries for 1976 and 1986. This examination is of interest since there has been little, if any, comparative quantitative assessment of the degree of harmonization of subnational tax systems in Canada and the United States.

Among the empirical findings of Vaillancourt's study are that there is a greater level of harmonization across subnational governments in Canada than in the United States, on a tax-by-tax basis. However, the overall effective tax burden is more uniform in the United States than in Canada, indicating a greater degree of tax-instrument substitution in the United States. Vaillancourt also notes that the elimination of the sales tax deduction in the U.S. federal income tax system has made subnational taxes more important in location decisions.

Evolution of Tax Policy in Canada and the United States

In addition to the eleven research papers just summarized, there are the reflections of two senior public finance figures—Richard A. Musgrave and Thomas A. Wilson—on the evolution of tax policy on both sides of the border. Their comments offer a glimpse into the future for tax policy, as well as an assessment of the current state of fiscal policy. The comments of these two eminent scholars add a unique perspective to the volume.

References

Bossons, John. 1987. The Impact of the 1986 Tax Reform Act on Tax Reform in Canada. *National Tax Journal* 40(3): 331–38. .

Deloitte, Haskins and Sells. 1986. *The Tax Revolution: A New Era Begins.* New York: Deloitte, Haskins and Sells.

Dodge, David A., and John H. Sargent. 1988. Canada. In *World Tax Reform: A Progress Report,* ed. J. A. Pechman, 43–69. Washington, D.C.: Brookings.

Fretz, Deborah, and John Whalley. 1990. *The Economics of the Goods and Services Tax.* Canadian Tax Paper no. 88. Toronto: Canadian Tax Foundation.

Government of Canada, Department of Finance. 1985. *The Corporate Income Tax System: A Direction for Change.* Ottawa: Department of Finance (May).

————.1987a. *Tax Reform 1987: The White Paper.* Ottawa: Department of Finance (June 18).

————.1987b. *Sales Tax Reform.* Ottawa: Department of Finance (June 18).

————.1987c. *Tax Reform 1987.* Ottawa: Department of Finance (December 16).

————.1987d. *Supplementary Information Relating to Tax Reform Measures.* Ottawa: Department of Finance (December 16).

————.1989. *Budget '89: Budget Papers.* Ottawa: Department of Finance (April 27).

Herber, Bernard P. 1988. The Federal Income Tax Reform in the United States: How Did It Happen? What Did It Do? Where Do We Go From Here? *American Journal of Economics and Sociology* 47(4): 391–408.

Pechman, Joseph A. 1987. Tax Reform: Theory and Practice. *Journal of Economic Perspectives* 1(1): 11–28.

————, ed. 1988. *World Tax Reform: A Progress Report.* Washington, D.C.: Brookings.

St-Hilaire, F., and J. Whalley. 1985. Reforming Taxes: Some Problems of Implementation. In *Approaches to Economic Well-Being,* vol. 26 of the Macdonald Commission Report, ed. D. Laidler. Toronto: University of Toronto Press.

Tanzi, Vito. 1987. The Response of Other Industrial Countries to the U.S. Tax Reform Act. *National Tax Journal* 60(3): 339–55.

Tax News Service. Various issues. Vols. 14–19 (Australia, Canada, Japan, Mexico, New Zealand, Sweden, United Kingdom, United States). Amsterdam: International Bureau of Fiscal Documentation.

Whalley, John. 1990. Foreign Responses to U.S. Tax Reform. In *The Economic Impact of the Tax Reform Act of 1986* ed. J. Slemrod. Cambridge: MIT Press.

1 Pressures for the Harmonization of Income Taxation between Canada and the United States

Robin Boadway and Neil Bruce

1.1 Introduction: The Question of Tax Harmonization

The determination of tax policy is among the most sovereign functions of governments. The choices to be made include of the level of tax revenues to be collected (and hence the level of public sector spending), the economic activities to be taxed (the tax bases and the tax mix), the distribution of the tax burden over different groups and income classes in the country, and the distribution of the tax revenues to different levels of government in the country. From an economic point of view, there are a number of criteria that might be used in formulating tax policy. These include minimizing the burden on the population of raising the given amount of revenue, minimizing the administrative costs of the tax system both to the government and to the taxpayers, achieving the desired amount of income redistribution, increasing the stability and predictability of the revenue base, and using tax policy as an instrument of industrial and regional policy. These objectives are conflicting to some extent. The way in which the conflicts are resolved is through the political process of the country.

The question of tax harmonization concerns the conflict between the demand for different tax policies across countries and the pressure for tax uniformity that arises because economies are highly integrated due to international mobility of capital, goods and services, and, perhaps, labor. The question would not arise if economies were segregated so that differences in the tax systems were irrelevant (except perhaps through a "demonstration effect"), nor would it arise if there were no incentives for countries to have different tax systems. (But countries with identical policy objectives might

Robin Boadway is professor of economics at Queen's University, Kingston, Ontario. Neil Bruce is professor of economics at the University of Washington, Seattle.

The authors would like to thank John Shoven and John Whalley for comments on an earlier draft of this paper.

still attempt to differentiate their tax structures, in order to shift the burden of taxation to other countries.) However, economies are becoming increasingly integrated in terms of the cross-border flow of goods, services and, especially, capital. Although there are still substantial barriers to the free movement of labor, these too are likely to fall—in Europe in 1992, and possibly between Canada and the United States as their economies become more tightly entwined as the free-trade agreement is phased in.

Despite this trend toward economic integration, national governments maintain the viewpoint, possibly an illusion, of setting independent tax policies, although the constraints imposed on such policy making by international considerations have been increasingly recognized. Among the most important pressures for tax harmonization in the presence of economic integration are the following:

i. *International mobility of factors and income.* In the presence of different tax burdens, which are not compensated by equivalent benefits (that are somehow conditional on taxes paid), factor owners will locate their factors across tax jurisdictions so as to minimize the tax burden. Moreover, such international "tax planning" may not require the physical movement of factors. Multinational corporations can readily shift capital income across international borders through accounting procedures.[1]

ii. *Overlapping tax jurisdictions.* The fact that the residence of a factor owner may differ from the factor's location gives rise to the possibility that more than one country will perceive itself as having taxing authority. This is particularly likely if countries adopt, as most do, the world income of their residents as the appropriate income tax base. It also arises because of the existence of multinational corporations that operate in both tax jurisdictions.

iii. *International tax avoidance and tax arbitrage.* While tax avoidance and arbitrage can occur within a country, the scope for such activities is expanded greatly when economies are highly integrated. The ability of residents in a country to locate income-generating activities abroad reduces the ability of the domestic tax authority to monitor taxable income and therefore to enforce taxation, since it is a general rule of law that one country does not take cognizance of the revenue laws of another country. Also, differences in the tax rates and bases of different countries open tax arbitrage opportunities, perhaps beyond the ability of a single country to close, especially where there are multinational corporations whose activities span the different tax jurisdictions.

iv. *Strategic considerations in the setting of tax policies.* With integrated economies, the best tax policies chosen by an individual country depend on the tax policies chosen by other countries or, in the case of policy "leadership," the policy reactions of the other countries. Thus, different tax policy instruments may be "strategic substitutes" (i.e., involve positive spillovers)

---

1. Gordon (ch. 2 in this volume) looks more closely at the economic pressures for tax harmonization arising from the mobility of goods and factors.

or "strategic complements" (negative spillovers) in the setting of tax policies by other countries. A special example of such strategic considerations is the temptation facing the individual country to try to shift the tax burden to foreigners. This may occur either through the standard tax incidence channels, whereby each country attempts to choose its tax policy so as to improve its terms of trade, or through "Bertrand competition" in tax rates, in which each country tries to attract taxable income from other countries (and hence revenue from other countries' treasuries) by offering lower tax rates. These types of policies are of the "beggar-thy-neighbor" sort and more often than not lead to a situation in which all countries are worse off.[2]

It should be apparent that these same issues arise to some extent within a country that has multiple levels of government, each having taxing powers, such as within a federation. Internal harmonization, however, is more likely to be accomplished through coordinated arrangements, since the scope for cooperation is greater. Not only are the powers of the governments involved separated or subordinated constitutionally, but the ability to make intergovernmental transfers exists. In contrast, harmonization of tax systems across countries is more likely to come about through actions taken by countries individually with limited amounts of cooperation. Among the issues to be addressed in this paper are the extent to which such "noncooperative" harmonization is sufficient for countries to obtain their tax objectives, and the extent to which further benefits can be gained through extending the cooperative harmonization arrangements that prevail internally to the international sphere.

We focus on harmonization issues related to the corporate and personal income tax systems of the United States and Canada. An essential distinction, which is made necessary by the openness of a national economy, is between income taxes levied on the basis of *residence* of the recipient and income taxes levied on the basis of the *source* of the income, that is, the jurisdiction in which the income is generated. The issues involved are not unlike those raised by the distinction between indirect (sales) taxes levied on a destination basis and on an origin basis. However, the income tax systems of countries typically contain elements of both residence and source bases, unlike sales taxes, which tend to be one or the other.

The ultimate objectives of the paper are to assess the extent to which interdependencies between the Canadian and U.S. economies impose pressures on the governments to adopt similar income tax systems and to consider whether coordinated measures could be desirable. On the first question, we conclude that the pressures for harmonization exist largely at the level of the corporate tax. Given the limited degree of labor mobility across countries, residence-based taxes like the personal income tax can be, and are, considerably different across the two countries. Nor are there likely to be great pressures to change this. At the corporate level, pressures for harmonization are consider-

---

2. Strategic considerations are only important if countries have market power. It could be argued that they are not important for the Canada-U.S. case.

ably stronger. These arise from the free mobility of capital across countries, the fact that firms can operate simultaneously in several jurisdictions, the difficulty in taxing corporations on the basis of residence, and the existing method of crediting foreign tax liabilities of corporations. These imply that corporations are effectively taxed on a source basis and that there will be strong pressures for countries, especially small capital-importing ones, to design their tax systems to conform with those of their creditor nations. In the case of Canada, there is considerable pressure to adopt a corporate tax system close to that of the United States. While the United States might seem to have more leeway, the fact that it operates in a wider world economy implies that its independence in setting corporate tax policy is also limited. Not surprisingly, the corporate tax systems of the United States and Canada are much more similar than are the personal tax systems, and are unlikely to become less so in the future. Given this, and given the difficulties of implementing a coordinated system of tax harmonization between sovereign countries, it is not likely that the gains from a more explicit form of corporate tax harmonization between the two countries would be sufficient to warrant instituting it. Further substantive gains might only be accomplished if the entire world changed the basis for taxing corporations. We document these arguments more fully in the rest of the paper.

We begin in the next section by discussing the advantages and disadvantages of tax harmonization. We then describe the differing fiscal structures of the Canadian and American economies in section 1.3. We first examine the broad fiscal differences between the countries and then focus on the detailed differences in the personal and corporation income tax systems. We also examine differences in the internal tax harmonization arrangements between the two countries, and finally we examine how cross-border income flows are currently treated by each country. In section 1.4 we analyze the extent to which pressures for income tax harmonization are likely to impinge on independent income tax policy making in the two countries as a result of increasing economic integration. We consider the specific issue of taxing income to capital, which is distinguished from factors such as labor and land by its high degree of mobility across the international border. Specifically we analyze the difficulties in using the corporation and personal income tax systems in conjunction with each other (say, as an integrated income tax system) in order to tax income to capital as it accrues. The difficulties arise because of the cross-border investments of multinational corporations. In section 1.5 we offer some brief conclusions and recommendations and extend the discussion to the broader perspective of worldwide corporate tax harmonization.

1.2   The Costs and Benefits of Tax Harmonization

It will be useful at the outset to define what we mean by harmonization, since it is a fairly general term whose meaning can vary from one context to another. Harmonization is a qualitative term which refers generally to the degree of uniformity of the tax system across jurisdictions—here, countries.[3] Departures from uniformity could be in terms of the tax base or the rate structure, or both. As well, harmonization may involve jurisdictional and enforcement provisions. The jurisdictional provisions involve how to divide the tax base among jurisdictions when the same tax unit is operating in both jurisdictions. For example, if income is to be taxed on the basis of source, a common means for determining the source of income must be adopted. Similarly, if taxation is based on residence, an agreed-upon means of determining the residence of the taxpayer must be established. These agreements reduce the possibility of the double taxation of income, or its zero taxation; to do so fully may require agreeing to a common base as well. Enforcement involves agreeing to enforce each other's laws and to exchange information.

Tax harmonization can come about through cooperative or noncooperative means. Cooperative harmonization involves an agreement between jurisdictions to adopt certain measures of uniformity, such as a common base, rate structure, allocation rules, and exchange of information for enforcement. This is the form of harmonization in existence in many federal states, including Canada, and to a lesser extent, the United States. The European Economic Community, as part of the attempt to remove fiscal frontiers within Europe, is trying to agree to some measures of tax harmonization, particularly in the VAT area. In the case of Canada and the United States, income tax harmonization has been largely noncooperative. That is, the countries decide their own tax policies in a decentralized fashion, taking as given the tax policies of other countries (or, in the case of a "leader" country, taking as given a reaction function of others). Competitive pressures may nonetheless induce some uniformity in the tax systems. And some agreement on the taxation of cross-border income flows exists in the form of the tax treaty provisions.

Evaluating the benefits and costs of tax harmonization requires distinguishing among objectives. From a worldwide perspective, it could be argued that a single tax system with a single tax collecting authority would be optimal. However, for a decentralized world in which different countries have different sizes of public sectors and place different weights on equity versus efficiency objectives, a fully uniform tax would not be optimal. There will always be a conflict between worldwide objectives and national objectives of tax systems.

In the context of a decentralized world with separate tax collection systems, it is possible to enumerate several beneficial effects of tax harmonization. The main ones are as follows:

3. Defining harmonization with reference to the degree of uniformity in tax structures achieved is not the only possibility. One could instead define harmonization in terms of the behavior of governments. For example, Mintz and Tulkens (1991) define tax harmonization "as any agreements undertaken by jurisdictions to correct, in a cooperative way, the effects of fiscal externalities resulting from noncooperative behavior". We wish to use the concept in a way that allows for noncooperative harmonization, so we have chosen to define it in terms of the results achieved.

i. *Production efficiency.* Reductions in the differential tax treatment of different factors of production will reduce production inefficiency in the allocation of resources across countries. Differential effective tax rates across countries, ceteris paribus, may provide an incentive for factors to move to lower-taxed jurisdictions. The economic costs of this will be higher the more mobile are the factors of production. Given the fact that capital tends to move freely among countries while labor does not (e.g., because of immigration laws), this problem is more serious for capital than for labor. Thus, the benefits from harmonizing personal taxes levied on a residence basis (including personal capital income) are relatively low, except perhaps for certain categories of persons who may be internationally mobile. For indirect taxes levied on a destination basis, the benefits from harmonization may be somewhat larger. The reason is that the destination principle may be difficult to enforce for certain types of transactions, such as services and cross-border shopping. To the extent that these can be controlled, the benefits from harmonizing are low. The real problems arise in the taxation of corporations. There are serious difficulties in attempting to tax corporations on a residence basis, whether residence is defined on the basis of the owners of the corporation or not. Thus, in practice, corporation income, at least equity income, is taxed on an origin basis. Since corporate capital is internationally mobile, different effective tax rates in different jurisdictions will lead to productive inefficiency, or international inefficiency in the allocation of capital. Much of our discussion in this paper will focus on the issue of harmonizing of the corporation income tax.

ii. *Avoidance of tax arbitrage.* The more harmonized are corporate tax bases and rates, the fewer are the opportunities for avoidance of tax by international tax arbitrage by corporations operating in more than one jurisdiction. This can take many forms. One is via transfer pricing in vertically integrated firms. Related to this is setting up subsidiaries or residence in low-tax jurisdictions and arranging to have much of taxable income taken in that jurisdiction. Another is by purely financial transactions, such as raising debt in countries of high tax rates to take advantage of interest deductibility provisions. The use of formula apportionment for determining the origin of tax bases avoids some of these problems, especially those involving financial transactions, since the formulas are typically based solely on real variables such as location of sales, wages, and capital assets.

iii. *Simplicity of administration and compliance.* Tax harmonization can lead to savings in the cost of tax collection and compliance. This is especially true if jurisdictions use a common tax base and formula apportionment rules. Then a single set of accounts will suffice, rather than separate accounts for each jurisdiction. Even greater savings can be obtained if there is a single tax collection authority, as is sometimes the case among jurisdictions in federal countries (e.g., Canada).

iv. *Avoidance of double taxation.* Another advantage of tax harmonization arrangements that include tax base allocation rules is that the same income will not be taxed twice, or not taxed at all. To avoid fully the possibility of double taxation or nontaxation requires both a common base and a common allocation formula. Of course, it will still be the case that income will be taxed at different rates in different jurisdictions, but it will not be taxed by two jurisdictions at the same time (or by none).

v. *Avoidance of tax competition.* Different jurisdictions setting their tax systems in a decentralized manner will naturally be in a competitive situation, if only implicitly. If income is taxed on a source basis, there may be an advantage to each from reducing its tax rate to increase its tax base, given the behavior of the other. Since each will be acting in the same manner, the net effect will be to compete tax rates to a suboptimal level, to the detriment of both. If the countries are of different sizes, the gains may accrue more to one country than to another. Of course, some tax competition may be a good thing, in the sense that it leads to more uniform rates. However, if it also leads to rates that are too low for the purposes of fulfilling the withholding function of the corporation income tax or if it eliminates the taxation of economic rents, that will be a disadvantage. The seriousness of this problem clearly depends upon the role of the corporate tax. If the world consisted of nations levying personal taxes on consumption, so that the corporation income tax was not needed for domestic withholding purposes, and if there were no economic rents or profits, it might be desirable for nations to compete the corporate tax away entirely.

These beneficial effects, whether they come about cooperatively or noncooperatively, must be set against the costs of harmonization. The latter are simply the constraints imposed on the ability of nations to pursue their own independent tax policy objectives. For example, as we argue below, a corporate income tax designed purely for domestic reasons might be viewed primarily as a withholding device for the personal income tax. In this case, its base and rate structure would be chosen to complement that of the personal tax, and the two taxes would be integrated by a method such as imputation. However, in an open economy, there are good reasons why the corporate tax might be forced to conform with corporate taxes levied elsewhere, even in a noncooperative setting. This will constrain the use of the corporate tax as a domestic withholding device and may also compromise the design of the personal income tax. Thus, the pressures for harmonization, where they exist, will compromise domestic policy objectives. In other cases, harmonization may not conflict with domestic policy. This is especially the case where cooperative harmonization schemes are negotiated to reduce tax competition and evasion. In these cases, there are net gains to be shared among the parties to the agreement. In the end, any conflicts between the benefits and costs of harmonization will have to be resolved by political judgment, since value judgments about tax policy will be involved.

1.3   Differences in the Fiscal Systems of the United States and Canada

The problem of harmonizing tax systems arises because countries want to pursue different tax structures and policies. Different tax structures and policies in turn may reflect differences in the amounts of government spending desired, the types of government spending, and the levels of government responsible for the spending. In this section we briefly examine the different fiscal environments of the United States and Canada and describe in some detail how the income tax systems and internal harmonization measures differ between the two countries. We also examine the existing provisions governing the taxation of cross-border income flows. This will serve to put our analysis into perspective.

1.3.1   The Differing Fiscal Environments: Some Stylized Facts

Although both the Canadian and U.S. governments are federal in nature, they differ in many key respects. The roles that the governments have assumed, the division of responsibilities between federal and state or provincial governments, the fiscal relations between the two levels of government, and the tax systems all differ considerably across the two countries. From an economic perspective, responsibilities are far more decentralized in Canada than in the United States, as reflected by greater relative spending by the provinces as compared with the states. For example, as seen in tables 1.1 and 1.2, the fraction of total spending by all levels of government in Canada accounted for by provincial and local governments averaged 60% during the period 1980–89, while for the United States the comparable fraction is 38%. Moreover, this fraction has been growing steadily in Canada, whereas it has remained relatively constant in the United States since the 1960s.

In Canada, the provinces assume responsibility for basically all health, education, and welfare expenditures. They finance these with a combination of their own revenues and substantial transfers received from the federal government. The exceptions are public pensions and unemployment insurance, for which the federal government has acquired responsibility by constitutional amendment. The federal government also makes extensive redistributive transfers to the needy provinces, and is now obliged by the constitution to continue to do so.[4] In the United States, a larger proportion of health and welfare expenditures is federally financed, although, of course, the level of public intervention remains much smaller in the United States than in Canada in the areas of health, education, and welfare. Surprisingly, transfers to persons are slightly more important than spending on goods and services by the U.S. government relative to the Canadian. In the United States, transfers to persons as a percentage of total expenditures averaged 35% for all govern-

---

4. Section 36 of the Constitution Act, 1982, imposed such an obligation formally, essentially writing the existing practice into law.

Table 1.1   **U.S. Tax and Expenditure Structure**
                     (Decade Averages)

Years	(1)	(2)	(3)	(4)	(5)	(6)
1950–59	.68	.31	.10	.19	.32	.22
1960–69	.68	.22	.14	.22	.38	.25
1970–79	.72	.16	.19	.32	.43	.29
1980–89	.74	.11	.21	.35	.38	.35

Notes: (1) Total income taxes/total revenues, all levels of government; (2) Corporate income taxes/total income taxes, all levels of government; (3) Total income taxes (state and local)/total income taxes (all); (4) Transfers to persons/total expenditures, all levels of government; (5) State and local expenditures/expenditures all levels; (6) State and local income taxes/total state and local revenue. "Total income taxes" include personal income taxes, corporate income taxes, and social insurance contributions.

Table 1.2   **Canadian Tax and Expenditure Structure**
                     (Decade Averages)

Years	(1)	(2)	(3)	(4)	(5)	(6)
1950–59	.35	.54	.05	.18	.45	.05
1960–69	.33	.41	.17	.20	.53	.13
1970–79	.38	.26	.33	.31	.59	.21
1980–89	.37	.20	.39	.33	.60	.23

Notes: (1) Total income taxes/total revenues, all levels of government; (2) Corporate income taxes/total income taxes, all levels of government; (3) Total income taxes (provincial and local)/total income taxes (all); (4) Transfers to persons/total expenditures, all levels of government; (5) Provincial and local expenditures/expenditures all levels; (6) Provincial and local income taxes/total provincial and local revenue. "Total income taxes" include personal income taxes, corporate income taxes, and social insurance contributions.

ments combined over the decade 1980–89, while for Canada the comparable figure is 33%. This is true despite the larger component of defense spending in the U.S. budget. In both countries, the percentage of expenditures accounted for by transfer spending has grown rapidly during the postwar decades.

Governments in both countries obtain their revenues from a tax mix that includes both indirect and direct taxes. Direct taxes, including personal and corporation income taxes plus payroll tax contributions to the public pension plan, averaged 37% of combined government revenues in Canada over the decade 1980–89. In the United States, the comparable share was 74%. Thus, the U.S. government is much more dependent on income taxes for revenues than is Canada. The relative importance of total income taxes in both countries has risen over the postwar decades. Despite this, the corporation income tax has declined in relative importance in both countries. In the decade 1950–59, the corporation income tax accounted for 54% of total income tax revenues of all governments in Canada and 31% in the United States. By the 1980s, this fraction had declined to 20% and 11%, respectively. This trend is remarkably similar for both countries, suggesting that harmonization pressures with respect to corporation income taxes may be considerable. Income taxes on persons have accounted for the growth in direct taxation in both countries. However, in the United States growth in the social security payroll tax has been much greater than in Canada, particularly in the past decade.

The U.S. federal government uses only direct taxes as major tax sources, while the Canadian federal government also levies an indirect sales tax, the manufacturers' sales tax, which was replaced with a 7% value-added tax in January 1991 (the so-called Goods and Services Tax). The provinces and most states use both direct and indirect taxes, the latter being a retail sales tax. Income taxes are a more important source of revenue for the provinces than for the states, with income tax revenues collected by provincial governments averaging 39% of total income taxes over the 1980s; in the United States, state and local governments collected 21% of total income taxes over the same period.

1.3.2 Differences between the Canadian and U.S. Income Tax Systems

While the Canadian and U.S. personal and corporate income tax systems have many features in common, they also have some important differences, both in the tax base and the tax rate structure. The personal income tax systems in both countries are accurately described as "hybrid" annual income and consumption taxes, although some features are inconsistent with either pure base. Both countries tax at least some components of capital income accruing to households, and both have well-developed corporation income tax systems, which act as backstops for the personal tax systems. Canada follows a modified imputation approach, which allows for some integration between the personal and corporate tax systems, while the United States has a classical system in which no credit is given to shareholders for corporate taxes paid. In this part, we discuss the major differences between the income tax systems of the two countries. These differences are summarized in table 1.3.

Differences in the Personal Income and Payroll Tax Systems

The Tax Base and Unit. Both countries tax annual employment income, broadly defined to include most cash market transactions. In Canada, most payments in kind, such as employer-paid fringe benefits, are included in taxable income. The main exception is contributions to pension plans. In the United States, many fringe benefits remain tax exempt. Government transfer payments are, for the most part, fully taxed in Canada.[5] Most transfer receipts were untaxed in the United States until the second half of the 1980s, when unemployment insurance benefits and half of social security benefits to high-

---

5. The exception is the Guaranteed Income Supplement paid to low-income persons aged 65 and over, which is nontaxable. However, persons receiving it are unlikely to be taxable in any case.

Table 1.3   Notable Differences in the Canadian and U.S. Federal Income Tax Systems

	Canada	U.S.
Pertaining to the Tax Unit:		
Personal		
Liability	Resident and deemed resident persons	Citizens and resident persons
Rate Structure	Individual income	Family income
Dependents	Tax credits	Tax exemptions
Child Care Expenses	Deductible to limit	Declining tax credit
Capital Gains on Bequests	Realized at death	Stepped up
Income Splitting	Subject to regulation	"Kiddie tax"
Corporate		
Liability	Incorporated in Canada	Incorporated in U.S.
Consolidation	No	Affiliated domestic corporations and foreign branches permitted
Intercorporate Dividends	Exempt	Exempt between affiliated corporations, 20% included otherwise
Pertaining to the Tax Base (Receipts):		
Personal		
In-kind Compensation (Employer paid)	Taxable, except employer-paid pension contribution	Most employer-paid fringe benefits exempt
Private Pension Benefits	Taxable with credit	Taxable
Social Insurance Benefits	Taxable	Unemployment benefits and ½ Social Security benefits taxable
Income Accruing on Pension Funds	Exempt (including RRSPs)	Exempt
Interest	Taxable	Taxable, except qualifying state and local bonds
Capital Gains (Realized)	¾ included with $100,000 life-time exemption and unlimited exemption for residence	100% included with exemption for residence (limited)
Lottery Winnings	Exempt	Taxable
Gifts	Exempt	Taxable over $600,000
Corporate		
Foreign Income	Exempt from active income of controlled foreign affiliate	Taxable when repatriated with FTC (controlled foreign affiliate)
Intercorporate Divs.	Exempt	Exempt from controlled affiliate, 20% included otherwise
Capital Gains (Realized)	¾ taxable	Taxable

(continued)

Table 1.3 (continued)

	Canada	U.S.
Pertaining to the Tax Base (Deductions and Credits):		
Personal		
	Itemized deductions and credits	Standard or itemized deductions
Mortgage Interest	No	Deduction (large limit)
State and Local Taxes	No	Property and income tax deductions
Medical Expenses	Credit in excess of 3% net income	Deduction in excess of 7.5% of AGI
Charitable Donations	Credit	Deduction
Social Insurance Contributions	Credit	No deduction
Private Pension Plan	Deduction to limit	Deduction if through 401(k); IRA limited to low-income taxpayers
Dividends	Credit if from domestic corporations	No credit or deduction
Corporate		
State/Local Taxes	Property taxes deductible; resource allowance	Income taxes, property taxes, and royalties deductible
Depreciation	40 classes, elective, "in" ½ year rule	8 classes, mandatory, "in" and "out" ½ year rule Switch to straight line
Inventory Cost	FIFO	LIFO or FIFO
Depletion Allowance	None	Cost for large oil and gas firms, percentage for other
Investment Tax Credits	R&D, qualifying investment in Maritimes	Incremental R&D
Loss Carryover	Backward 3 years, forward 7 years	Backward 3 years, forward 15 years
AMT	No	Yes
Pertaining to Tax Rates:		
Personal		
Graduation	3 brackets, flat after $55,605 (1989)	3 brackets with "bubble"; flat after $200,000 (1989)
Highest Rate	29% in top bracket	33% in bubble
Indexation	Above 3%	Full
Surtax	4% and 5.5%	None
Social Insurance payroll Tax	9.4% (combined) to a maximum contribution of $3,000	15.3% (combined) to a maximum contribution of $7,000 (1990)
Corporate		
Tax Rate, Most Firms	28%, 23% on manufacturing and processing income	34%
Rate Concessions to Small Businesses	Smaller than $200,000	Smaller than $200,000, with 39% bubble midsize

income persons were subjected to income tax. In Canada, the tax unit is the individual, but there are tax credits based on family size, and some tax reliefs are based on family income. In the United States, the tax unit is the family, and income tax schedules depend on the taxpayer's marriage status. There are fixed exemptions for other dependents.

There are also significant differences between the countries in their taxation of the capital income of persons. Apart from that accruing in tax shelters, nominal interest income is fully taxed in Canada as it accrues. This is also true in the United States, except for the exemption on interest from state and local bonds. Nominal capital gains are fully taxed upon realization in the United States, but in Canada only three-quarters of realized gains are taxable and the individual taxpayer has a C$100,000 cumulative lifetime exemption (higher for small businesses and family farms). Capital gains on a taxpayer's personal residence are effectively exempt in both countries, although in the United States the exemption can only be taken once in a lifetime, can be taken only by taxpayers aged 55 or over, and is limited to $125,000 of gains. Dividends are fully taxed in both countries, but Canada allows a dividend tax credit (see below).

There are notable departures from the Haig-Simons definition of comprehensive income in both countries. Income to owner-occupied housing, nonrealized capital gains, and the accruing earnings on pension funds are exempt in both countries (and in Canada, Registered Retirement Savings Plans, known as RRSPs). Gifts and lottery winnings are excluded in Canada, but the United States taxes lottery winnings and gifts and inheritances over $600,000.

The tax systems of the two countries differ notably with regard to deductions from income. Expenses incurred in earning income and interest payments on money borrowed to make taxable investments are deductible in both countries. In Canada, all persons can deduct (from earned income only) contributions to RRSPs up to a specified total less pension plan contributions. Less generous deductions for contributions to IRA plans are available to low-income households in the United States. Employee contributions to pension plans are not deductible in the United States, although effectively the same thing can be arranged through 401(k) plans. Limited child care expenses are deductible in Canada, but are creditable at a declining rate of 30% to 20% in the United States. Moving expenses are deductible in Canada and in the United States, but only as an itemized deduction in the latter (see below).

The United States allows a choice between a standard deduction and an itemized deduction for mortgage interest, state and local taxes (except sales taxes), medical expenses in excess of 7.5% of adjusted gross income, moving expenses, casualty losses, and charitable donations. Canada allows tax credits for medical expenses in excess of 3% of net income and for charitable donations. Canada Pension Plan contributions, unemployment insurance premiums, university tuition, and C$1,000 of pension income are also creditable. The United States allows exemptions for dependents. In Canada, personal, spousal, and dependent tax credits are given, and there are also some "vanishing" tax credits available to lower-income taxpayers. The tax credit rate is equal to the lowest tax rate (17% federal), except for charitable donations over C\$250, which are credited at 29% federal. These credits are matched at a corresponding rate under the provincial income tax systems, which also contain some province-specific tax credits.

Canada has a dividend tax credit to provide relief from double taxation at the personal and corporate levels on dividends. The dividend tax credit of approximately 22% (federal) is available on taxable dividends (received dividends grossed-up by one-quarter) from corporations resident in Canada against personal income taxes payable on dividends in Canada. Since provincial taxes are applied on federal tax liabilities, this is effectively increased by a further 52–62%, depending on the province, when provincial taxes are applied. The dividend tax credit rate supposedly is set so that the system is integrated "on average." However, it is underintegrated for dividends from a fully taxpaying corporation and overintegrated on dividends from nontaxpaying corporations. The implications of a dividend tax credit in the context of an open economy are discussed further in section 1.4.

The Tax Rate Structure. Canada and the United States both have graduated income tax structures with three brackets. The top rate in the United States is nominally 28% (federal), although it is actually 33% for incomes above \$74,850 (married, filing jointly in the 1989 tax year) until the advantages of the lower initial tax bracket and the personal exemptions have been recaptured (at around \$200,000, depending on taxpayer circumstances). The rate structure, including brackets, exemptions, and the standard deduction, is fully indexed to the previous year's inflation rate. State income tax rates vary widely, but the top rate in many states is around 10%. Since the state income tax is deductible from federal income tax, the combined top marginal rate is about 35% (nearly 40% in the phaseout bracket). For the purposes of cross-country comparison, we consider the state of New York, which has a top personal rate of 8.75%, yielding a combined top rate of around 34% (39% in the phaseout bracket).[6]

In Canada, the highest marginal rate is 29% (federal) on income above C\$55,605 (1989 tax year) but there is also a "temporary" surtax of 4% (5.5% for high incomes). All provinces except Quebec set their income tax as some fraction of the federal income tax owing. In Ontario, it was 52% in 1989, rising to 53% in 1990. The highest gross-up occurs in Newfoundland, at 62%. There are also provincial surtaxes on high incomes (10% in Ontario). The combined top rate in Ontario (including federal and provincial surtaxes) in 1989 was 47%. Thus, it is clear that even after Canadian tax reform, the high-

---

6. In some states, federal income taxes are also deductible from state income taxes, so the combined rate is lowered still further.

est marginal income tax rate in Canada remains substantially higher (at least 8 percentage points in the case of Ontario versus New York) than that found in the United States. This reflects a higher average level of taxes on personal income in Canada, as revealed in tables 1 and 2. The tax structure is indexed in Canada as in the United States, but only by the excess of the previous year's inflation over 3%. Therefore, there is some degree of bracket creep operating for taxpayers below the top bracket in Canada.

Offsetting the higher Canadian tax rates to some extent are the higher social security taxes in the United States. In the United States, the Old-Age, Survivors, and Disability Insurance (OASDI) tax is 15.3% for the employee and employer combined, to a maximum contribution of around $7,000 (1990). The OASDI tax is deductible as a business expense for employers but is not deductible against income for employees. In Canada, the combined Canada Pension Plan and unemployment insurance contributions (employee and employer) are at 9.4%, up to a total of about C$3,000, but these taxes are deductible to employers and creditable at 17% for employees. There are also payroll taxes (approximately 2% in Ontario) or compulsory hospital plan premia at the provincial level to fund public health insurance programs that exist in all provinces. In making these comparisons, it should be recognized that public pension and unemployment insurance contributions are viewed, to some extent, as benefit taxes. To the extent that an offsetting benefit is perceived, these taxes are less likely to act as a disincentive than general income taxes are.

The other offsetting factor with respect to capital income is the partial integration measure in Canada, as compared to the classical corporate income tax system in the United States. When the combined top corporate and personal tax rates on dividend income are compared between New York and Ontario, taking into account the dividend tax credit, the rates are approximately equal (lower in Ontario if the 33% rate is used for New York). The rate is clearly lower in Ontario if the capital income is earned in manufacturing and processing, where the corporate tax rate is lower. It should be kept in mind, however, that the integration measures are available only to resident Canadians. Moreover, the impact of such measures may not be those expected (see section 1.4).

Differences in the Corporate Income Tax Systems

Differences between the Canadian and U.S. corporation income tax systems (CITs) are perhaps the most relevant for the purposes of harmonization, since capital is highly mobile between the two countries. Furthermore, many corporations are residents of both countries and can exercise some degree of discretion as to where they take their income.

The Tax Base. The CITs in both countries are similar in overall structure. Both are accrual taxes on what is essentially shareholders' income accruing within the corporation. Accruing revenue from both business and financial sources is included in the tax base. In Canada, intercorporate dividends from domestic corporations are tax exempt. In the United States, the dividend tax exemption applies only to dividends from controlled domestic affiliates, with a 20% inclusion for dividends from noncontrolled corporations. Three-quarters of realized capital gains are included in Canada, whereas there is full taxation of realized capital gains in the United States.

Current expenses such as wages, fees, rents, and losses due to fire and theft are deductible as they accrue. Current expenses include employer payroll taxes and private pension plan and social insurance contributions. Interest on debt is expensed but may be capitalized in both countries. In some cases in Canada (e.g., real estate development), interest capitalization is required. In the United States, state corporate taxes, local property taxes, and royalties are deductible, whereas in Canada only property taxes, including the provincial corporate capital taxes, are deductible. There is a fixed abatement of tax points for the provincial corporate income tax, and a resource allowance equal to 25% of net profit is given in lieu of a deduction for provincial royalty payments and mining taxes. In the United States, there is a cost depletion allowance for large oil and gas firms and a percentage depletion allowance for small oil and gas firms and mining. Charitable donations are deductible in both countries within limits. In the United States, donations of appreciated capital property are deductible at assessed market value; in Canada the deduction is limited to the adjusted cost base.

Some capital costs are effectively expensed. In Canada, there is 100% write-off for resource exploration and development expenses in mining, exploration expenses in oil and gas, and all R&D expenses except land and buildings. In the United States, there is 100% write-off for mining and small oil and gas producers, 70% for large oil and gas producers, with the remainder capitalized. These write-offs are not elective, unlike the CCA in Canada (see below). Also, in some cases the fast write-off cannot be used to create a net operating loss. In the United States, exploration and development expenses for mining must be amortized for calculating the alternative minimum tax.

The tax depreciation provisions differ significantly between the two countries. Perhaps most significantly, the Canadian CCA is an elective deduction, whereas the U.S. deduction is mandatory. The Canadian regulations set maximum declining-balance recovery rates for around forty asset classes. In the United States, the postreform modified accelerated cost recovery system rates apply to eight recovery period classifications set out in the asset depreciation range classifications. On average, U.S. recovery rates are higher than in Canada (accelerated depreciation was reduced by less in the United States than in Canada under recent corporate tax reforms). Also, the United States allows the switch to straight-line depreciation when it becomes favorable to do so. On the other hand, the put-in-use rule in the United States is more effective than the pending Canadian rule, and the United States has half-year rules upon purchase and disposition of a capital asset, unlike Canada's purchase half-year rule. There are recapture provisions in Canada. Recapture in the United States is automatic, since capital gains are fully taxed.

Another significant difference is in the costing of inventory. The United States allows firms to choose between FIFO and the more favorable LIFO conventions. In Canada, FIFO is mandatory. Further, the partly compensating inventory deduction of 3% was abolished in Canadian tax reform, so there is no compensation for purely inflationary changes in inventory valuation.

Both countries allow carryover for net operating losses. In the United States, they can be carried back three years and forward fifteen, while in Canada, the carryover is three and seven years, respectively. However, the elective CCA permits additional scope for loss carryover in Canada.

Another major difference between the corporate tax systems is the importance of the alternative minimum tax (AMT). In the United States, AMT income includes one-half of book profit, with the remainder based on taxable income adjusted to reduce various tax preferences. A significant factor is that foreign tax credits can be used to offset no more than 90% of the AMT liability, so for firms subject to the AMT there may not be full relief from international double taxation. In Canada, there is no AMT for corporate income, but the recently introduced large-corporation capital tax is credited against corporate income surtaxes and acts as a minimum tax. The base of this alternative tax is unrelated to corporate income and therefore immune to erosion because of income shifting by transnational corporations.

The Tax Rate Structure. In the United States, there is a graduated rate structure at the federal level. Nominally, the top rate is 34% for corporate income in excess of $75,000, but firms in the range of $100,000 to $335,000 pay 39%, as the benefits of the lower rates on corporate income below $75,000 are phased out. Forty-five states and the District of Columbia levy a local corporate income tax, and some follow the federal method of reporting income. The state tax rates are usually graduated and range from 1% to a high of 12% in Minnesota and Iowa. The major industrial states may have relatively low rates (2.5% in Illinois) or higher rates (9% in New York). Since the state tax is deductible, the combined top rate is about 41% (45% in the phaseout range) and about 40% in New York.

There are two main tax credits available to U.S. corporations—the R&D incremental tax credit of 20% on qualifying spending in excess of the average of the past three years, and the foreign tax credit (discussed in the next section). Also, there are some special investment tax credits for energy conservation investments and the like at the state level.

In Canada, the combined corporate tax rates are slightly higher, except on income derived from manufacturing and processing. The basic federal rate is 28%, with a lower rate of 23% on income derived from manufacturing and processing (when fully phased in by 1991), plus a corporate surtax of 3%. There are special low rates on the first C$200,000 of business income for

Canadian-controlled private corporations. All provinces levy a corporate income tax, basically using the federal definition of corporate income. The provincial rates are higher than the state rates in the United States and are not deductible from the federal tax. The Ontario basic rate is 15.5%, giving a combined basic rate inclusive of the federal surtax of 44.3%. On income derived from manufacturing and processing, the Ontario rate is 14.5%, so the combined rate on this type of income (1991) is 38.2%. The top rate is higher in some provinces. Overall, the rates are much closer to those in the United States than is the case for the personal income tax.

There are three main tax credits available to corporations in Canada—the investment tax credit of 15% for qualifying investments in the Atlantic region, the R&D tax credit of 20% (30% in Atlantic Canada), and the foreign tax credit.

1.3.3   Internal Income Tax Harmonization in the United States and Canada

In both the United States and Canada, the personal and corporate income taxes are co-occupied by the federal government and the states or provinces. Differing amounts of harmonization occur between the two levels of government in the two countries. In Canada, harmonization exists to a high degree, largely owing to the fact that the existing system evolved from a wartime situation in which the federal government was the sole occupant of income taxation and funded provincial expenditures through transfers. Starting in 1962, the federal government began turning over income tax revenue-raising capacities to the provinces. At the same time, it offered the provinces the opportunity to join tax collection agreements with the federal government, under which the federal government collects taxes on behalf of the provinces. These tax collection agreements are still in effect and form the basis for harmonizing the corporate and personal income tax systems in Canada.

Under the tax collection agreements, participating provinces agree to abide by the tax base used by the federal government but may set their own tax rates. In the case of the personal tax, the rate they choose is applied to federal taxes payable, thereby guaranteeing that the federal rate structure applies to both levels of government. For the corporate tax, provinces apply their tax rates to the federal tax base. As well, the federal government will administer provincial tax credits for a small fee, provided they are judged to be simple to administer and do not discriminate against residents of other provinces or distort investment decisions. The federal government for its part collects all taxes on behalf of the agreeing provinces and pays over to the provinces assessed tax liabilities. The federal government bears the cost of bad debts but retains all interest earned on the funds. For the corporate tax, the provinces agree to a formula apportionment method for allocating revenues among provinces. The formula is a simple one: the share of a firm's taxable income accruing to a province equals the average of its share of revenues of the firm and its share of the wage bill.

All provinces except Quebec have signed a tax collection agreement with the federal government for the personal income tax, while all except Alberta, Ontario, and Quebec belong for the corporate income tax. Despite this lack of universal coverage, all provinces, agreeing or not, have virtually the same corporate income tax base as the federal government and follow the same allocation formula. The personal tax system for Quebec does diverge somewhat from that in the rest of the provinces. Thus, there is a fairly high degree of harmonization among income tax bases, the main differences being in the levels of tax rates. Even here the differences are not great, owing to the extensive system of interprovincial fiscal equalization that exists in Canada. Presumably the historical evolution of the system has had an important impact on the degree to which harmonization has been achieved and maintained. The fact that the system was operated by the federal government alone during the war meant that a fully harmonized system was the starting point. Once a uniform system was in place, arbitrary deviations from it were unlikely to occur.

Nevertheless, there are increasing signs of strain and discontent among the provinces. The federal government retains unilateral control of the income tax bases and changes them from time to time on its own initiative. As the provinces come to occupy more and more of the tax room, they naturally would like to have more and more influence on their own tax structures. The main way open for them to exercise this desire is to implement provincial tax credits of various sorts. There has been a proliferation of provincial tax credits and rebates administered through the agreements in recent years, and this has fragmented the system somewhat. More significantly, the principle of maintaining a common base has been violated in three provinces with the introduction of flat-rate income taxes at the personal level alongside the ordinary income taxes. These are administered through the agreements. The basic legislation governing the agreements has remained unaltered since its inception. It may be reviewed and changed as the federal government enters the retail sales tax field and attempts to negotiate analogous agreements with the provinces for harmonization in this area.

The Canadian case is somewhat interesting from a broader perspective, since it is similar in form to the system of harmonization being proposed for the European Economic Community. We return to the pros and cons of this type of harmonization in a later section of the paper.

Income tax harmonization in the United States is much less structured than in Canada. Indeed, it is virtually nonexistent, in the sense that there are no formal tax collection agreements and all states collect their income taxes separately from the federal government. This is the case despite the fact that the Federal-State Tax Collection Act of 1972 empowers the federal government to enter into agreements with the states not unlike those that exist in Canada. No states have chosen to do so. The implicit harmonization that does exist involves states voluntarily adopting some aspects of the federal tax structure, such as the base. There is the additional complexity in the United States that many local governments also levy an income tax at the personal level, while some states levy none. Only forty states levy a general personal income tax, while three others levy a tax on capital income only. As well, local income taxes are used by many local governments in eleven states.

The nature of state personal income taxes and their relation to the federal tax differ widely over states. Four states actually collect personal taxes as a percentage of federal tax liabilities (as in Canada). Eight states adopt the federal tax base as the state tax base but choose their own rate structures. Both of these systems obviously reduce compliance and collection costs for the states and the taxpayers. However, the states still maintain their own independent collection and audit machinery. Twenty-six states use the same definition of gross income as the federal government, but then apply their own systems of deductions and exemptions as well as tax structure. Finally, six states set their entire tax structures essentially independently of the federal government.[7]

The other difference between the Canadian and U.S. systems of personal taxation is that, whereas the Canadian tax system is based on the residency principle as regards income earned in different provinces, the U.S. system typically involves personal taxation at source. That is, states usually tax all income earned in the states by residents and nonresidents alike and then provide credits for tax paid in other jurisdictions. (Many states also provide a deduction for taxes paid at the federal level.) However, not all states apply the same rules, so there may be double taxation of personal income, or none, depending on the states involved. In any case, the system is considerably more complex than the Canadian one.

Forty-five of the states also levy a corporation income tax. All collect their own, and only six adopt the federal corporate tax base. As well, different states use different methods for allocating taxes to their jurisdictions. Most states use formula apportionment to do so, with the formulas typically involving proportions of sales, payroll, and property. Not all states use the three factors with equal rates. For example, some states give larger weight to sales, especially states for which sales are large compared with production. As with the personal tax, the possibility exists for double or under taxation of some sources of income. Also, because of the absence of a system of interstate fiscal redistribution, tax rate differentials may be higher across states than across provinces.

1.3.4   Taxation of Cross-Border Income Flows

While the United States and Canada have varying degrees of internal tax harmonization, there are no official arrangements for harmonizing their national tax systems, except through the provisions of the Canada-U.S. Tax Convention (1980), henceforth referred to as "the treaty." The tax laws in each

---

7. A more detailed analysis of tax rate differences across states and provinces may be found in Vaillancourt (ch. 11 in this volume).

country contain provisions determining whether a taxpayer is resident or not and provisions determining whether a particular income receipt is from a domestic source or not ("source rules"). These provisions are chosen independently in each country, with tax treaty provisions taking precedence over them in the event of a conflict, but only to the extent of the conflict.

Both Canada and the United States adopt the same general conventions regarding cross-border income flows. Residents (persons and corporations) in each country are taxed on the basis of their world income (i.e., domestic and foreign source income), while nonresidents are taxed only on the basis of income originating in the country (i.e., source income only). In Canada, residence of persons is determined mainly on the basis of the taxpayer living in the country, although persons may be "deemed residents" when some permanent attachment exists, even if they are not physically residing in the country. Corporations are considered resident if they were incorporated in Canada. The United States taxes its citizens on their world income irrespective of where they reside, although there is a $70,000 exclusion of foreign earned income for qualifying individuals residing abroad. Corporations are residents of the United States if incorporated there.

Source rules apply in both countries, but are more developed in the United States. Generally, income is considered to be from a domestic source if it is income derived from employment within the country, business income from "carrying on business" in the country (or "effectively connected" within the United States), rent and royalties from real property located within the country, interest from a domestic payer, or dividends from a firm incorporated within the country. Capital gains are considered domestic source only if they result from the disposition of real estate. Both countries exempt interest paid by domestic governments (the United States also exempts interest paid by U.S. chartered banks). Social insurance payments from the domestic government are also considered as domestic source income. In determining business income, expenses are deductible, but in the United States regulations governing the allocation of expenses apply where the taxpayer has both domestic and foreign source income. Among the most important of these regulations are those governing the allocations of interest and R&D (or other intangibles) expenses. In Canada, a thin-capitalization rule puts an upper bound on interest expenses, while in the United States interest expenses are allocated according to asset shares by location. In the United States, R&D expenses are allocated partly on the basis of where the research took place and partly on the basis of the location of sales. Canada allows for deductions for R&D conducted abroad if "related to Canadian business."

The taxation of domestic source income of nonresidents is essentially schedular in both countries. Employment income is taxed in the same way as it would be taxed in the hands of a resident, but with a more limited set of deductions, exemptions, or credits. Likewise, business income is taxed in the same way as for a resident, under the personal or corporate tax systems as applicable. Gross-basis-type (i.e., no deductions) taxes are imposed by both countries on interest, dividends, royalties, and fees paid to nonresidents. The basic tax rate is 30% in the U.S. and 25% in Canada, but these rates are reduced by treaty. These taxes are enforced by withholding by the payer. Both countries have branch profit taxes at the same rate applying to nonretained earnings of branch firms (which replicate the dividend withholding taxes applying to dividend repatriations from subsidiaries).

The tax codes of both countries contain provisions designed to alleviate the double taxation of cross-border income flows, although the actual provisions differ. The U.S. allows a foreign tax credit up to the domestic tax liability for income-type taxes levied on foreign source income in the source country. A "deemed-paid" credit is allowed against U.S. corporation income taxes for foreign corporation income taxes paid by a controlled subsidiary (10% or more share ownership). In general, to be creditable, the foreign taxes must be net income taxes and similar to the U.S. taxes against which they are credited, although gross-basis withholding taxes are creditable under special rules. Resource royalty type taxes are explicitly excluded. Foreign tax credits may be extended to dissimilar foreign taxes under treaty. Where foreign tax credits are not applicable, a deduction can be taken. The foreign tax credit is subject to an overall limitation equal to the ratio of foreign source income to world income times the U.S. tax liability and also to ten different "basket" limitations according to type of income (active, passive, dividend, interest, etc.). From 1986 on, foreign earnings and taxes have been calculated on a cumulative basis in determining the foreign tax credit limitation. This is intended to prevent the acceleration of foreign tax credit eligibility through the use of the "rhythm method" of repatriation, which is possible when foreign depreciation deductions are optional, as in Canada.

In contrast, Canada employs a mixed system of exemptions, credits, and deductions to alleviate double taxation. Dividends paid out of "exempt surplus" (essentially the active business income of controlled foreign affiliates located in listed—mainly tax treaty—countries where Canadian ownership exceeds 50% or more) are exempt from the Canadian corporation income tax, while foreign tax credits of foreign corporation income taxes and gross-basis withholding taxes up to the Canadian corporation income tax liability are permitted against dividends received from foreign corporations in which the Canadian parent has ownership of 10%-50%. Foreign tax credits against Canadian personal income taxes are also allowed for personal income taxes and withholding taxes levied in the source country. Again, where foreign tax credits are not applicable, deductions of foreign taxes paid are usually allowed. The overall limitation is calculated in the same way as for the United States, although there are only two "basket" limitations—"business" and "nonbusiness" income.

Canada and the United States both adopt a "separate accounting" approach to determining the income of resident corporations and their foreign subsidiaries. This implies two things. First, foreign source income is not subject to taxation (if at all) in the residence country until it is received by the parent ("repatriated"). Thus, the parent-country taxes (if applicable) are said to be "deferred." Second, scope is opened for international tax planning by the multinational corporation because of its ability to manipulate the source of income. The tax laws in both countries contain provisions designed to prevent international tax avoidance made possible by the separate accounting approach coupled with the existence of "tax havens." These provisions take two forms: transfer pricing regulations enforcing arm's length prices on transactions between related corporations and provisions requiring what is effectively unitary tax treatment for passive income and other "tainted forms" accruing to controlled affiliates of resident corporations. Section 482 of the U.S. tax code allows the authorities to scrutinize transactions between related corporations and impute arm's length prices where feasible or attribute "commensurate income" to intangibles. Section 69(3) of the Canadian Income Tax Act allows the authorities to deem payments received from nonresidents that would have been reasonable in an arm's length transaction when inadequate compensation is found.

Passive income of controlled personal corporations and sales and service income passing between controlled subsidiaries in other countries is included in the current income of the U.S. parent under the Subpart F provisions (with a corresponding foreign tax credit and subsequent tax-free disposition). The equivalent Canadian provision is the so-called FAPI (foreign accrual property income) rule, which requires income from property and business income, other than from active business of a controlled foreign affiliate, to be included in the income of the Canadian parent. There is nothing equivalent under FAPI to the U.S. inclusion of sales and service income among related foreign affiliates, although income from services that would otherwise be active business income will be included in FAPI if the income is charged as a deductible expense to the controlling parent (or in some cases to an unrelated party).

Many of the above provisions are modified under the Canadian-U.S. tax treaty. The treaty contains "tie-breaker" provisions for determining residence in the case of dual residence persons and corporations. An important one is that a corporation resident in Canada may be taxed only on its Canadian source income (i.e., treated as a nonresident) if it was incorporated earlier in the United States. Both countries also agree to determining the source of business income on the basis of it being attributable to a "permanent establishment." There are also limits on gross-basis withholding tax rates. Nonresident withholding taxes on royalties, fees, and dividends paid to related corporations in the other country are limited to a maximum of 10%. A maximum withholding rate of 15% applies to interest and to dividends paid to unrelated corporations in the other country. Also, the branch profits tax rate is limited to a maximum of 10% in the case of branches of corporations resident in the other country. Pensions and annuities originating in one country and paid to a resident of the other are subject to a maximum withholding tax of 15% by the source country, to the extent that such income would be included in taxable income of residents of that country.

The tax treaty also extends certain deductions and exemptions available to resident persons to nationals of the other country, prohibits discriminatory taxation of the other country's persons and corporations, mandates double-taxation relief through credits and exemptions, and authorizes competent authorities to alleviate individual cases of double taxation. The latter may arise through ex-post application of the transfer pricing regulations of each country.

1.4   General Analysis of Income Tax Harmonization between Countries

In this section we examine some general issues associated with income tax harmonization. Primarily we are concerned with how similar the income tax structures must be for countries whose economies are highly integrated, and the extent to which the need for similarity limits the pursuit of national tax policy objectives. Our discussion will be restricted to the case of two countries, though similar principles apply more generally. In the next section, we investigate in more detail the constraints imposed on tax-policy making in an individual economy. We begin here with a preliminary discussion of the way pressures for harmonization impinge on tax policy objectives.

1.4.1   Harmonization and the Objectives of Tax Policy

As mentioned in the introduction, there are several major objectives of tax policy. First and foremost is the revenue objective. A country's tax system must yield a predictable and stable source of revenue sufficient to finance planned government spending. In particular, the revenue base must be protected from widespread erosion due to tax avoidance and the shifting of the tax base into low-tax jurisdictions. Second, there is the distribution objective. The burden of the tax revenue obtained should be distributed across the population in some desired manner. While the distributive objective may be based on principles of vertical equity across income groups, regional factors also play an important role, especially in Canada. A third objective is to minimize the economic cost or burden of raising the desired level of revenue. This requires both administrative efficiency, meaning that the collection and compliance costs of obtaining the revenue are minimized, and economic efficiency, meaning that the deadweight costs of the distortions imposed by the tax system on the allocation of the economy's productive resources among competing uses are minimized. Finally, for our purposes, there is the industrial policy objective, whereby the government seeks to use the tax system to reallocate production to achieve noneconomic goals. Again, an important element here may be regional policy. Obviously, this last objective will usually conflict with the neutrality objective. Typically these objectives will conflict with one another; a fully efficient tax system will not be equitable, nor will it be administratively feasible. Regional policy objectives will conflict directly with efficiency. Because of this, a judgment must be made about the optimal way to trade off these objectives, and this will differ from country to country.

While Canada and the United States undoubtedly share the broad objectives outlined above, section 1.3 indicated that there are important differences between the two countries. The combined levels of governments raise a proportionally larger amount of revenue in Canada than in the United States. Also, the distributional objectives of tax policy appear to be pursued more vigorously in Canada, both in terms of vertical redistribution and regional redistribution. The result is substantially higher top marginal tax rates in Canada than in the United States. The regional objectives of tax policy also contribute to the (perhaps) greater extent of production non-neutralities in the Canadian tax structure, since these are partly achieved by region-specific investment tax credits. Also, Canada continues to maintain a preferential corporate tax rate on corporations engaged in manufacturing and processing activities. On the other hand, the personal income tax in Canada appears to contain fewer consumption non-neutralities than that of the United States, mainly because mortgage interest and lower-level government taxes are not deductible, while most fringe benefits and transfer payments are included in taxable income.

The implications of economic integration for the tax policy choices made by a government may be significant. For one thing, the free flow of goods and factors across international borders may alter the desirability of certain objectives. For example, distributive objectives that require a high marginal tax rate on upper-income persons may be unattractive if labor markets for skilled and entrepreneurial persons are integrated across international borders, so that such individuals may leave the country in search of lower tax rates. Similarly, the taxation of capital income may be tempered by the mobility of capital between jurisdictions. In addition, the best method of achieving a policy objective may be altered by economic integration. Where it is possible, the burden of taxation on the population of an individual country can be reduced by actions that attempt to shift the burden to foreigners. While these beggar-thy-neighbor policies may appear efficient from the individual perspective of a country, they are not likely to be so from the collective perspective of all of the countries involved. Even when such policies are excluded, the best method of achieving a policy objective may be altered by openness. For example, attempts to pursue industrial policy objectives through corporate tax incentives may be ineffective if multinational corporations are very important in the production sector and tax relief simply transfers tax revenue to foreign treasuries rather than provides incentives for the taxpayer. Instead, a direct subsidy that does not alter the foreign tax liability of the corporation may be a more effective instrument. Similarly, if high-income persons are very mobile internationally while low-income persons are not, the negative income tax solution of using higher marginal tax rates to fund universal lump-sum tax relief may be less desirable than income maintenance programs targeted on the (immobile) poor through the use of high "claw-back" rates.

Economic theory might suggest that the objectives of tax policy could best be achieved through direct taxes on persons or households, since the ultimate burden of all taxes falls on them in any case. The optimal tax literature has shown that if certain separability conditions are satisfied, indirect taxation is unnecessary. Given that these conditions are not unreasonable ones and that, in any case, we do not know in which way preferences actually vary from them, there is not a strong efficiency or equity argument for having a separate indirect tax system. The personal income tax would presumably be on a residence basis. The chosen base could be either consumption or income or, possibly, some hybrid. The residence income tax rate structure could be chosen to achieve domestic distribution objectives if persons are immobile across international borders. Otherwise, the caveats mentioned above apply.

Unfortunately, things are not so simple outside the world of pure theory. There are several reasons why governments may want to supplement the personal income tax with other forms of taxes. Direct taxes on corporate income fulfill several objectives. First, if accruing income to capital is to be included in the personal tax base, a corporation income tax is more or less necessary as a "withholding" tax against undistributed income accruing to shareholders within corporations. Second, it may be desirable to tax differentially pure profits or rents, where they exist. This can be done with a business income tax of correct design or, in the case of resource properties, by auctioning off property rights or levying severance taxes (or equivalently, charging royalties). Such taxes may be sector-specific, but need not be restricted to corporations. They might also be origin-based rather than residence-based. Another reason for levying a corporation income tax (and for similar provisions applying to business income of unincorporated businesses under the personal tax) is that such a tax is most useful as an instrument of industrial policy, since it applies at the level of the producer. Again, this objective suggests that an origin-type business income tax would be desirable if it were possible. Finally, a country that is host to a substantial amount of foreign-owned capital may wish to levy such a tax simply to capture revenue that would otherwise accrue to foreign treasuries. This is the case when the home country offers a foreign tax credit for corporation income taxes paid in the host country by the subsidiaries of its domestic corporations. Of course, this objective alone requires only that the host country tax income accruing to foreign-owned capital and not domestically owned capital. But singling out foreign capital would appear discriminatory and is likely to be ineligible for the foreign tax credit offered by the home country. For that reason, the corporate tax system would likely have to apply identically to both domestic and foreign-owned firms. Its design must take account of all the objectives of corporate taxation in a single tax system. We return in the next section to the specifics of the design of a corporate tax in an open economy.

In addition to direct taxation, governments also tend to levy broad-based indirect sales taxes. Such taxes are widely used by governments around the world, including state and provincial governments in the United States and Canada and the Canadian federal government. From a purely economic perspective, the effect of broad-based indirect taxes can be replicated by direct taxes. For example, as Shibata (1967) showed in his pioneering work on tax harmonization, destination-based general sales taxes on consumption are ultimately equivalent to residence-based direct taxes on consumption. Similarly, direct taxes on income are equivalent to sales taxes on consumption and net investment. Thus, despite popular arguments to the effect that destination-based sales taxes are useful because they avoid imposing barriers to trade, they are essentially redundant from a purely economic point of view.

Nonetheless, there is a compelling reason based on tax avoidance and evasion for a government to levy a broad-based sales tax in addition to a direct tax. Income that goes untaxed under the direct tax system due to avoidance or evasion can be taxed as it is spent by the means of broad-based sales taxes. Furthermore, the higher the personal income tax rate, the greater is the incentive to evade. This may be particularly important if residents of the country can "hide" accruing income by investing abroad. The existence of a general sales tax both brings the expenditures from evaded income into the tax net and lowers the incentive to evade by lowering the level of direct taxes. Of course, this may be at the expense of other (equity) objectives.

Two major economic differences between broad-based direct and broad-based indirect taxes are that the former are more commonly levied on income (though hardly on a comprehensive basis) while the latter are typically levied on consumption, and that direct tax rates can be made taxpayer-specific and therefore can be chosen in accordance with ability to pay while the latter are levied on transactions and are therefore "anonymous" (i.e., must be levied at the same rate on all taxpayers regardless of ability to pay). The first distinction seems artificial, since direct taxes can be levied on consumption by allowing saving to be deducted, while indirect taxes can be levied on an income basis by including in the tax base the sale of capital goods (net of depreciation) to producers. The second distinction seems more important, in that direct taxes appear to be better suited for achieving a government's distributional objective. Although the indirect tax could achieve some types of redistribution through the use of differentiated tax rates across commodities, there is not a great economic case for so doing, and it may prove to be a "blunt instrument" in use.

Despite the possible equivalences between direct and indirect taxes, a major consideration from the Canadian perspective is that the U.S. foreign tax credit is allowed for income taxes only and explicitly excludes indirect taxes. Thus, even if the objectives of Canadian governments could be achieved with indirect taxation, there are good revenue reasons for relying on income taxes to the extent that governments of creditor countries do, because of the substantial

presence of foreign-owned capital. In the remainder of this paper, we will
focus on harmonization problems solely as they relate to income taxation.

1.4.2   Noncooperative Harmonization: How Similar Must the
Tax Systems Be?

It is commonly thought that the pressures for tax harmonization resulting
from economic integration inevitably lead to highly similar tax structures. Yet
the income tax systems of the United States and Canada, and even the income
tax systems of different states in the United States, do differ from one another
in significant ways. The point is that economic integration does not necessarily force uniformity in fiscal systems. This is the case for several reasons.
First, to the extent that tax differences are matched by fiscal benefit differences, there is no incentive for factors to move unless the benefits can be
retained while the taxes are reduced by such movements. This is particularly
true for persons who are likely to make fiscally induced migration decisions,
not on the basis of their marginal tax rates or even their average tax rates, but
rather on the basis of their appraisal of the net fiscal surplus (positive or negative) associated with living in a taxing (and spending!) jurisdiction.

A second reason why different income tax structures can be sustained is
that there is considerable immobility of persons across international borders.
Thus a government can levy its income tax on the world income of its taxpayers as determined by residence. Except for any differences in the ability to
evade taxes on foreign and domestic income, the tax system exhibits "factor
export neutrality," and there is no incentive for taxpayers to locate their factors
on the basis of differing tax systems between countries, because they are subject to the same domestic taxes on all income. By the same token, because
labor is free to migrate across jurisdictions within a country, personal tax systems should be less diverse within a federation than across countries, though
even here, different tax levels may be offset by different levels of benefit from
expenditures.

Third, even if a factor is taxed on the basis of the source of its income and
even if it is perfectly mobile between different tax jurisdictions, different tax
rates can still be imposed in different jurisdictions—they just may not have
effects intended. Different tax rates can be imposed at source on the income of
an internationally mobile factor if the before-tax factor return compensates for
the tax differential. What is altered here is not the ability of a country to set a
different tax rate, but the incentive for it to do so. Thus, for example, Canada
(or a U.S. state) can differentially tax income to capital, say by levying a
higher corporate tax rate, but the before-tax return to such capital must rise to
compensate. Thus, if the purpose of the difference is to place a higher tax on
owners of capital, the tax difference does not achieve its objective, despite
its being fiscally possible, because the tax is shifted to noncapital (and non–
internationally mobile) factors. Only if the before-tax return cannot change,
so all of the factor is driven from the country by a positive tax differential,

would the country or state perceive itself as being forced into fiscal uniformity with the other. The point here is that the pressures for uniformity should be understood in terms of the way they alter the desirability to governments of choosing similar tax systems as much as the extent to which they are forced to do so.

Of course, the return to a highly mobile factor can rise so as to compensate for a jurisdictional tax difference only to the extent that returns to other immobile factors can fall. We are talking about real returns here, so returns can fall as a result of output prices in the country rising. Even in the case of traded goods for which world prices are fixed, domestic money prices and the exchange rate can rise while the money prices of immobile factors remain fixed so real returns decline. If the monetary authority resists pressure for depreciation, the price of nontraded goods can rise, shifting the burden to domestic consumers of such goods who own immobile factors. Thus there are several channels through which differential taxation of the income to mobile factors can be achieved.

The above discussion suggests the extent to which economic integration forces harmonization on the countries involved. As long as persons remain relatively immobile across the border, the residence-based personal income tax systems can be quite differentiated. We see this to be the case between the United States and Canada at the present time, and there is little reason to think that these differences cannot continue. However, one probable pressure for harmonization that is important on the personal income tax side is the pressure on Canada to keep the average tax rate on high-income persons from increasing any more relative to those that prevail in the United States.

Similarly, differences in benefit-related taxes, such as social insurance taxes, levied on a residence basis, are unlikely to pose problems of disharmony. Even where imposed on employers, such taxes are ultimately borne by households who, on average, enjoy equivalent value in benefits. It seems reasonable, however, that it would not be possible to try to "make the foreigner pay" by levying such taxes on foreign-owned capital income.

If pressures for uniformity exist anywhere, it is almost certainly with respect to corporation income taxes. The residence of a corporation is far more flexible than that of persons. As a result, corporation income taxes are likely to be more like source taxes. Since the source of income can be manipulated by the corporation, both in actuality and according to accounting records, differences in the corporate tax systems are likely to give rise to considerable cross-border tax shifting.

Indeed, the pressures for uniformity in corporation income taxes should be greater as a result of the 1986 reforms in the United States. Prior to these reforms, a Canadian subsidiary of a U.S. multinational could utilize elective deductions such as the CCA so as to arrange to pay more Canadian corporation income taxes in years when repatriations of dividends to the U.S. parent occurred—the so-called rhythm method. The upshot of this method was that harmonization pressures served mainly to equalize average corporation tax rates, but not necessarily statutory tax rates. A higher statutory rate could be offset by more generous deductions, since those deductions could be taken in years when dividends were not repatriated. As long as the average corporation income tax in Canada did not exceed the U.S. rate, the Canadian corporation income taxes could be fully credited, even though the deemed-paid corporation income taxes in Canada were (and still are) determined using a broad U.S. definition of taxable income that does not allow for the generous deductions in the host country. The method of calculating the deemed-paid corporation taxes in the host country was changed by the United States in 1986 to preclude widespread use of the rhythm method. As a result, higher statutory tax rates in Canada are likely to result in "excess" foreign tax credits for subsidiaries of U.S. multinationals. With excess foreign tax credits there is an enormous tax incentive for the multinational corporation to shift income from Canada to the United States. Thus, there will be great pressure for Canada to keep statutory corporate tax rates close to U.S. levels.[8]

There is also an important way in which the pressures to harmonize corporation income tax rates feed back on the personal income tax system. As mentioned, an important function of the corporation income tax is to act as a withholding tax for the personal income tax. It is no accident that the corporation income tax rate in both countries is approximately the same as the highest personal rate. If this were not the case, there could be widespread tax avoidance through corporate retentions. Thus, pressures to keep the Canadian corporation income tax rate no greater than the U.S. rate add to the pressures to keep the highest personal tax rate no higher as well.

The main conclusion we can draw here is that in the absence of high mobility of persons across the Canada-U.S. border, both countries should be able to pursue a fair amount of independent tax policy with respect to residence-based taxes. Source-based taxes on the income of highly mobile factors are another matter. Existing arrangements are likely to force a fair amount of uniformity, perhaps to the detriment of each country's ability to pursue its own tax policy objectives.

However, the corporation income tax need not be the source-based tax it has become. To convert it back into a residence-based tax may require modification of existing tax treaty arrangements. The main feature of the corporation income tax that makes it a source-based tax is the provisions used to relieve double taxation. In particular, home countries have offered tax credits on taxes paid abroad by their corporations. Consider the following alternative residence-based corporation income tax system, in which no foreign tax credit is offered. In this hypothetical scenario, the host-country corporation income tax is credited when distributions are made to foreigners. That is, dividends

---

8. For a complete discussion of how the deemed-paid corporation income tax is calculated and the implications for crediting Canadian taxes in the U.S., see Bruce (1989).

paid to nonresident owners are deducted from the corporate tax base. (Measures would have to be taken to prevent credits from being given to domestic-owned foreign "shell" corporations, if a classical separate-entity corporation income tax arrangement is desired with respect to domestic residents. If an imputation system is desired, dividends paid to domestic shareholders would be deductible from the corporate tax base as well.) Under this system, the local corporation tax is eliminated as far as the foreigners are concerned. If the foreign recipients are corporations, the income may then be subject to corporation income taxes in the home country. In this scenario, the corporation income tax is designed exactly like the personal income tax: it applies to resident recipients only (at least once the income is distributed). No double taxation occurs, and no double-taxation relief measures are needed.

In the absence of the foreign tax credit provision by the capital-exporting country, there is little cost to the host country from implementing such an arrangement, assuming that it has no market power in capital markets. Without a foreign tax credit, the cost of capital is increased to the capital-importing country by the amount of its corporation income tax, so eliminating the corporation tax on income distributed to foreign shareholders has distributive consequences only within the host country. All countries in the world would have to eliminate the foreign tax credit for this residence-based corporate tax system to be feasible. If the capital-exporting country allows a foreign tax credit for host-country corporation taxes paid, the capital-importing country would be silly to credit its own corporation income tax to foreigners, at least up to the level that is eligible for the foreign tax credit abroad. The elimination of the host-country corporation tax on income to foreigners will not lower its cost of capital, because the tax is paid in the home country anyway: it simply transfers the revenue to the home country.

Thus, if the desired corporation income tax rates are the same in the two countries, the foreign tax credit simply acts as a lump-sum transfer from the capital-exporting country to the capital-importing country, and no harmonization problems occur. The difficulty arises if the countries want to impose different tax rates. This would pose no problem if the differential part of the tax rate could be made residence-based. For example, if the capital-importing country wants to impose a higher corporate tax rate, no problems would occur if it credited the excess tax on distributions to foreigners. This would allow it to collect the revenue transfer from the capital-exporting country and follow an independent tax policy. It would also be complex and appear discriminatory if distribution credits were given only to foreigners or if distribution credits for the full corporation tax were given to domestics (i.e., an integrated domestic system) with partial credits to foreigners.[9] This topic is developed further in section 1.5.

---

9. Of course, the existing tax system in Canada, which gives a dividend tax credit to domestic shareholders but not to foreign shareholders, is even more discriminatory.

1.4.3   Spillovers in Determining Tax Rates

As long as some income taxes in a country are imposed on the basis of source or as long as there is some degree of mobility of persons across international borders, the setting of tax policy instruments in a country will involve spillovers into other countries. As a result, the independent (i.e., noncooperative) setting of tax policies in different countries may fail to achieve objectives that could be achieved if the countries were to coordinate (i.e., cooperatively harmonize) the setting of their tax policies. We illustrate this point in terms of the objective of taxing different activities in a manner that is economically efficient.

When the government of a country sets its tax policy instruments independently, it is unlikely to take account of any benefits or costs it imposes on the other countries with which it trades. Spillovers may arise through changes in external prices (the terms-of-trade effects that are analyzed extensively in the trade literature) or through the shifting of economic activity, actual or by accounting measures, between jurisdictions. In this section, we argue that such spillovers are likely to lead to tax rates imposed on the income of internationally mobile factors being too low rather than too high. Ironically, much of the tax harmonization literature focuses more concern on the danger of double taxation or discriminatorily high tax rates on cross-border income flows than on tax rates that are too low (except for the problem of outright tax avoidance through the use of tax havens).

The argument is developed in figure 1.1, where the domestic supply of an internationally mobile factor F to domestic production uses is given by the upward sloping supply curve labeled S. The supply curve S is drawn for given tax rates abroad. For simplicity, it is assumed that S is not perfectly elastic and that the before-tax return to the factor in domestic use is fixed at W_o. The return to the factor is taxed at rate t so the after-tax return to the factor in domestic use is $W_o(1 - t)$ and tax revenue $abcd$ is collected.

Consider now the domestic government's decision as to whether to raise the tax rate on this type of factor income. If it raises the tax rate marginally, domestic tax revenue will rise by the rectangle $cfhg$ (the increase in the tax rate cg times the amount of the factor still employed in domestic use cf) and fall by the rectangle $ebdf$ (the preexisting tax rate ef times the amount of the factor that leaves domestic taxable uses eb). The latter is approximately equal to the area $ebdh$. Obviously, in order for the government to want to raise the tax rate, the area of $cfhg$ must exceed $ebdf$. If the quantity of the factor leaving domestic employment (eb) goes into nontaxable uses (household production or leisure), the area $ebdf$ (or $ebdh$) will also be the marginal "deadweight loss" incurred by raising the tax rate on income to factor F. Taxes would be set optimally (from an economic efficiency perspective) when revenue-increase rectangles (like $cfhg$) are the same multiple of the marginal deadweight-loss rectangles (like $ebdh$) across all factors of production.

Suppose rather than escaping to untaxed uses, factor F locates in another

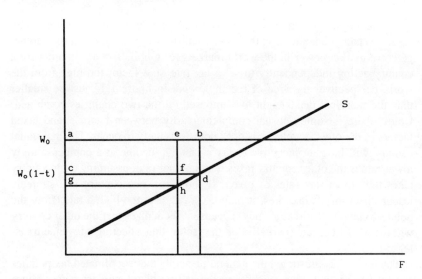

Fig. 1.1 Spillovers in the taxation of a mobile factor F

tax jurisdiction, which maintains the lower tax rate on its income. In this case the rectangle *ebdf* is not a deadweight loss to the world as a whole. Rather it is an increase in the tax revenue of the other country, which does not increase its tax rate on F. But the domestic economy in deciding on whether to raise the tax rate ignores the revenue increase in the other jurisdiction. It treats the loss of *ebdf* in the same way as it would if the factor escaped to untaxed uses. If the factor is in fixed supply to taxable uses in all jurisdictions, it could be a good thing to tax it from an efficiency perspective. But high factor mobility between tax jurisdictions is likely to make F appear a bad candidate to the individual country. Another factor of production which is immobile across international borders, but which has a less elastic supply curve to domestic taxable uses (the alternative use being untaxable), appears to be more attractive to tax from the point of view of the individual country. This is the case even though from the perspective of all countries combined, it may not be a good factor to tax at a higher rate.

What is being described here is the potential inefficiency of "tax competition" where a particular form of income is highly mobile between two tax jurisdictions. In the extreme case, a factor may be in perfectly elastic supply to each country but in perfectly inelastic supply to all countries combined. Bertrand-type competition in tax rates may eliminate the taxation of such a factor, desirable as it may be from a world perspective. Moreover, tax competition does not require that the factor actually be internationally mobile in a physical sense. Instead, income to that factor may simply be moved across borders to seek the lowest tax rate by the accounting procedures of multinational firms.

Surprisingly, there is far less of an incentive for countries setting tax rates independently to end up taxing the income of a factor too much, as long as all countries take the tax rates in the other countries as given and countries do not perceive market power in the world markets for mobile factors. In order for a country acting independently to set a tax rate on a factor too high from the world perspective, the area of rectangle *ebdf* in figure 1.1 must be smaller than the marginal deadweight loss imposed on the two countries combined. Unless there is some unusual complementarity between factor F and taxed factors in the other country, this does not seem likely to occur. The individual country will have an incentive to tax a factor's income at a compensatingly lower rate if the other country taxes it at a higher rate, assuming each country takes the others' tax rates as given. If, however, one country is a strategic leader in setting its tax rates, it may tax a factor at too high a rate (from the point of view of world efficiency) because it recognizes that the other country will reduce its tax rate (partially) on the factor, thus affecting a revenue transfer to itself.

The above has illustrated the general principle that coordinated tax policies can lead to mutual improvements in the setting of tax policies across countries, even when economic pressures would otherwise force the tax structures toward uniformity. However, a recent article by Kehoe (1989) has identified a case in which the opposite may be true. Coordinated (or cooperative) setting of tax policies across countries may yield an outcome that is inferior to the noncooperative case. The example involves the time inconsistency involved in setting taxes on capital or income to capital. Fischer (1980) showed in a closed economy framework that the tax rate on capital that a government would choose (and therefore like to promise) before the private sector has made its saving decision is not the same as it would choose once the decision has been made. This is the case even if a government is motivated by economic efficiency, because once saving is committed it is in fixed supply and hence a good thing to tax. This time-consistent tax rate on capital income is inferior to the lower tax rate that would be imposed if the government could somehow commit itself.

Kehoe's point is that if capital is internationally mobile and its income can be taxed only at source, then tax competition results in a much lower tax rate than if countries cooperate in setting such rates. Suppose the optimal tax rate on capital income (with commitment) is zero or close to it. This outcome may be achievable with tax competition but not with cooperation. With cooperation, countries would agree to tax the fixed capital stock in the integrated economies at a higher (time-consistent) rate. This higher rate would be anticipated by the private savers and a less efficient level of capital accumulation would result. We return to the issue of cooperative harmonization between Canada and the United States after exploring in more detail the ways in which income tax policies are constrained by international pressures.

1.5 Some Implications of the Openness of the Economy for the Design of the Income Tax System

In this section, we consider the issue of income tax policy in an open economy, drawing on the principles that have been discussed above. The openness of an economy to the rest of the world, particularly to capital flows, imposes some constraints on policy and provides some opportunities as well. The objective of this section is to discuss how open economy considerations influence a country's independent choice of an income tax system, particularly the tax base. These considerations could be thought of as applying independently to the United States and Canada. Our discussion proceeds by first recalling the open economy setting and the constraints it imposes on attaining the objectives of tax policy, given the stylized facts about the existing circumstances. Then, the implications for tax design in a single country are discussed. In the next section, we will extend the analysis to consider the case for coordinating (integrating) the tax systems of the two countries, where they are taken to operate in a wider world economy.

1.5.1 The Open Economy Setting

The key defining feature of an open economy is the cross-border flow of goods and capital. For our purposes, it is the flow of capital that is most relevant. The flow of goods, tax-free or otherwise, is of limited relevance for the design of direct tax systems. We will assume that the economy's capital markets are fully open to the rest of the world, and that the economy can be viewed as essentially a small open economy on world capital markets. This implies that rates of return on capital are exogenous to the country, subject perhaps to country-specific risk differentials. We presume in our discussion that this is true for rates of return on unincorporated business capital as well as corporate capital, although in practice it might be argued that capital market imperfections might at least partly segment unincorporated businesses (and private corporations) from public capital markets. That is ultimately an empirical question, and one for which an answer is difficult to verify. While capital flows freely between countries, its owners need not. In fact, we assume that there is very limited international mobility of persons, so for all intents and purposes, residency of households can be taken as fixed.

Our interest is in the direct tax policies of an open economy such as Canada. The country takes personal and corporate tax policies as given elsewhere. What is important for our purposes is to recognize that the common practice in the rest of the world is for corporate taxes to be levied on an origin basis. Given that countries want to tax corporation income, taxing it on an origin basis seems to be the only alternative.[10] This is achieved in a variety of ways

10. The reasons for this are discussed, for example, in Kay and King (1990, ch. 14). Essentially, residency of corporations is quite arbitrary; they can choose to establish residence where

in different countries. For example, a country may tax the worldwide income of its resident corporations, including repatriated earnings of subsidiaries operating abroad, and the income of foreign firms operating within its boundaries. A credit is then granted for taxes paid in foreign countries. Alternatively, repatriated earnings may be allowed to flow tax-free into the domestic economy without credit. The effect in either case is that corporate income is approximately taxed on an origin basis.

At the same time, the personal tax is typically levied on some notion of income and on a residence basis.[11] Different countries apply widely differing personal tax rates to differing bases. However, given the relatively low degree of labor mobility between most countries, this is not a significant constraint. Countries are relatively free to set their own personal tax systems as they wish.

The real constraints arise in the treatment of capital income and particularly from the fact that while personal income is taxed on a residence basis, corporate income is taxed on an origin basis. As mentioned in section 1.4, the ideal tax from an economic point of view might be a tax on persons levied on a residence basis (perhaps supplemented by a consistent system of indirect taxes). If the personal tax base is to be income, it is useful to supplement it with a corporate tax for withholding purposes. In an open economy, a further withholding role for the corporate tax is implied by the existence of origin-based corporate taxes elsewhere in the world. Thus, the income tax system becomes one of residence-based personal taxation combined with origin-based corporate taxation.

It is this conflict between the use of residence and origin bases in the same system that leads to constraints in tax policy. The small open economy assumption effectively segments the savings side of capital markets from the investment side (i.e., savings and investment are independently determined and need not be equal in any given year). The implication of this mixture of residence and origin principles is that tax measures operating through the personal tax system affect only the savings side of the market, while corporate tax measures affect only the investment side. This makes it very difficult to implement the ideal personal tax system.

Suppose that income is the desired personal tax base. One would like to include in the base as many types of capital income as are feasible. This basically means income from business capital assets, since income from personal

---

they prefer. An alternative view has been put forward by Musgrave (1990), that some notion of "internation equity" provides countries with a right to tax income earned by corporations within their jurisdictions. In the concluding section of this paper we suggest that a residence-based system has certain advantages over a source-based system of corporate taxation, but that some international cooperation would be required to achieve it.

11. Again, this is only partially adhered to, given the system of withholding taxes and the practice of some countries (e.g., the U.S.) of taxing citizens on a worldwide basis regardless of residence.

assets such as human capital and consumer durables are difficult to tax. The tax should be levied on an accrual basis, which is difficult to do in the case of capital gains, so capital gains are typically taxed when realized. A corporate tax can then be supported as a means of taxing retained earnings as they accrue within the corporation, so that taxes cannot be postponed indefinitely by keeping them within the corporate sector.[12] The existence of origin-based corporate taxes elsewhere in the world further supports the use of a corporate tax as a withholding device.

The corporate tax will typically apply on all equity income in the corporation and not only retained earnings. Otherwise, the objective of withholding from foreigners would not be satisfied. In the absence of further measures, the tax system would still discriminate systematically in favor of retained earnings and against new share issues because of the so-called trapped equity effect. To avoid this, it has been argued, for example by the Carter Commission in Canada, that the corporate tax should be integrated with the personal tax. This would undo the discriminatory double taxation of equity income from new share issues under the two taxes and would put corporate and unincorporated income on a par. As a practical necessity, the integration must be done at the personal level. That is, it cannot discriminate between domestic and foreign corporations, since to do so would entail the loss of tax crediting by foreign governments and the consequent loss of the tax transfer from foreign treasuries.

However, integration of the two taxes by a measure such as the dividend tax credit at the personal level would affect primarily the savings side of the capital market. While full integration would eliminate the discriminatory treatment of new share issues relative to retained earnings (as well as unincorporated business income), it can be shown that it would do so by effectively removing the taxation of capital income on equity income at the personal level altogether.[13] The upshot would be a personal tax system in which only interest income is taxed, and a corporate tax system that serves to distort the investment side of the market by taxing equity income at source. In fact, the corporation would have a tax incentive to finance its investments by debt, while taxes would favor households holding equity.

Thus, it seems to be difficult to tax capital income properly at the personal level in an open economy, at least in the absence of accrual-based capital gains taxation. If the latter could be implemented, then a classical corporate income tax system might be used for withholding from foreigners. However, the differential tax treatment of corporate and unincorporated business income

---

12. Note that keeping funds within the corporate sector does not imply keeping them within the same corporation. Thus, a corporation with excess funds on hand could keep them in the corporate sector for the shareholders by, for example, acquiring shares of another corporation or even taking it over. Given the intercorporate tax-free flow of dividends, the funds can continue to accumulate free of additional tax. This is just the trapped-equity effect mentioned below, and it provides a strong incentive for takeovers by mature firms.

13. This is analyzed in detail in Boadway and Bruce (in press).

would remain. As well, debt would still be favored at the corporate level because of the interest deductibility provisions of the tax. This would be the case independent of the personal tax treatment of interest income, again because of the separation of the savings and investment side of the capital market.

1.5.2 Income Tax Policy in an Open Economy

What does all this imply for tax policy in a small open economy? Consider first the personal tax base. Fundamentally, the choice is between an imperfect income base and a consumption base. Equivalently, the issue can be put in terms of what types of asset income should be included in the tax base.[14] A consumption base would effectively include no asset income. It is well known how that can be achieved in a fairly exact and administratively feasible manner. An income base will typically include only some forms of asset income. Consumer durables and human capital income are typically excluded, as are many forms of assets yielding imputed returns (cash balances, insurance, etc.). That leaves mainly business assets in their many forms. These include real interest income on debt (with payments and receipts treated symmetrically) and all forms of accrued equity income (dividends, real capital gains, unincorporated business income, rents, royalties, etc.). Of course, in practice even many business assets go untaxed at the personal level, since they are financed from tax-sheltered pension funds.

Administratively, the full and proper taxation of income on business assets is difficult to achieve under a personal tax alone. Apart from the requirement to index capital income, there is the need to measure accrued capital income. This is difficult to do properly for unincorporated business income. It is also difficult to do for capital gains, so capital gains must for practical purposes be taxed on realization.

That being the case, in the absence of complementary tax devices, a significant part of capital income could accumulate in tax-sheltered form within the corporation by retaining and reinvesting earnings.[15] As discussed, one of the functions of the corporate tax is to act as such a complementary device for the personal tax. In the closed economy, it can do so more or less perfectly. A corporate tax on equity income of the corporation, with its rate set to the top marginal rate of the personal tax and fully integrated with the personal tax by means of a dividend tax credit with the same rate, will serve the purpose. It will succeed in taxing retained earnings on the same basis as new equity issues and will fully remove the differential tax treatment of new equity issues, retained earnings, debt, and unincorporated business assets. It was for this reason that the Carter Commission recommended such a system for Canada in

---

14. It is important to note that we are dealing only with the choice of base here. In principle, the rate structure can be chosen independently of the base. Therefore, whatever the base, a more or less arbitrary degree of progressivity can be achieved by appropriate choice of the rate structure.

15. Note that the reinvestment can take the form of purchasing shares in other corporations, or of keeping the funds within private corporations. As long as the funds are not taken out of the corporate sector as a whole, they are sheltered from personal taxation.

the mid-1960s. Note that with a fully integrated personal and corporate tax system, the need to tax capital gains disappears altogether, at both the corporate and the personal levels. If capital gains continue to be taxed, they too should be fully integrated with the personal tax. [16] The tax-free flow of intercorporate dividends should remain.

Even this seemingly simple system is complicated to administer in its ideal form. For one thing, capital income should ideally be included in the tax base on an real accrued basis. This implies that the base should be indexed. It also means that accrued equity income would have to be measured for both corporations and unincorporated businesses. As is well known, this is difficult to do. For another, the interest deductibility provision gives rise to certain anomalies. The fact that businesses (both corporate and noncorporate) need only be taxed on their equity income means that interest should be deductible from the tax base, at least in real terms. The unlimited ability of firms to deduct interest, combined with integration achieved via a dividend tax credit (and the absence of a capital gains tax), implies that there is a tax arbitrage opportunity that must be closed off, involving the ability of a shareholder to use the corporation as a device for tax arbitrage by using the interest deductibility provision. If the corporate tax rate exceeds the personal tax rate on interest income, shareholders can be made better off if the corporation borrows to pay out dividends.[17] Naturally, there will be a limit to the firm's ability to do this. Creditors may impose restrictions on the borrowing of the firm for this purpose because of the absence of collateral or the risks of bankruptcy. The arbitrage may be less direct than the above. For example, the borrowed funds may be used indirectly for the buying of shares of other corporations, as in the case of takeovers financed by debt. This tax advantage of takeovers is quite separate from that arising due to the trapped equity effect mentioned above. In the latter case, the takeover arises from the fact that the firm has excess funds on hand in the corporation already, while debt-financed takeovers (leveraged buyouts) may be viewed as pure tax arbitrage operations using outside funds.

This tax arbitrage opportunity arises because the debt the firm is issuing is not being used to purchase business capital-producing revenues for the firm, but is being used simply to pay out funds either directly or indirectly to equity holders. One obvious way to close it off would be by limitations on the deductibility of interest. For example, firms might be restricted to deducting interest on debt used to acquire business capital only, though presumably this might be difficult to enforce. Alternatively, there might be some restriction imposed

16. This is demonstrated analytically in Boadway and Bruce (in press).

17. For example, suppose the corporation borrows $100 in perpetuity at an interest rate i and immediately pays out the proceeds as a dividend. If the effective personal tax on dividends is τ, shareholders receive $\$(1 - \tau)100$ after tax. In the future, dividends must fall each period by $\$i$ $(1 - u)100$, where u is the corporate tax rate and interest deductibility is assumed. Thus, shareholders' dividends fall by $\$i(1 - u)(1 - \tau)100$ each period. From the point of view of the shareholder, the present value of this financial transaction is $\$(1 - \tau)100[1 - (- u)/(1 - t)]$, where t is the personal income tax rate. As long as $u > t$, shareholders will be better off. Similar principles apply if the firm is able to repurchase shares using the initial funds.

on the use of the dividend tax credit. For example, dividends might only be eligible for the dividend tax credit if they were paid from after-tax profits. Again, this might be difficult to administer. The Carter Commission (1966) recommended a similar scheme, whereby the total tax credited to shareholders would be restricted to taxes actually paid at the corporate level. This was rejected partly for administrative reasons. It could also be rejected for other reasons in an open economy, as discussed below.

Another, related, difficulty in integrating personal and corporate taxes with the dividend tax credit in the personal tax system concerns the fact that different corporations are liable to differing tax rates. Statutory tax rates differ for firms of different size, for firms in different industries, and for firms in different provinces (or states). To the extent that these differing tax rates are implemented explicitly for industrial policy reasons, the granting of a uniform tax credit is appropriate. To do otherwise would effectively undo the preferential treatment (at least in a closed economy; see below). However, in the case of differential rates across provinces, different dividend tax credit rates might be desired in an ideal world. Also, if firms face different effective tax rates because some are in a nontaxpaying position, full crediting would not seem to be sensible. This situation could be avoided by full loss offsetting in the tax system.

Finally, the use of corporate taxation by more than one level of government increases the complexity of integrating the corporate and personal tax systems, even in a system as highly coordinated as that of Canada—or even in a closed economy. The problem is that while the corporate tax is levied at source, the dividend tax credit is applied against personal taxes, which are levied on a residence basis. To the extent that shareholders in one province own corporate shares in another, the crediting will come at the expense of a different province, which collected the corporate taxes. Provinces that are net corporate capital importers from other provinces will benefit, and vice versa.[18] This is an unavoidable consequence in a system of integration applying to personal taxes. In a closed economy, it can probably be avoided by applying dividend relief at the corporate level, that is, by allowing firms to deduct dividends from their corporate tax base, with the so-called dividend-paid deduction. In an open economy such a remedy would not be available, as discussed below.

The upshot of this discussion is that even in a closed economy the task of designing a reasonable corporate and personal income tax system is not a straightforward one, even given that at the outset certain types of asset income are necessarily excluded (i.e., basically nonbusiness asset income). The problems of properly accounting for capital income and of using the corporate tax effectively as a withholding device are significant. It is partly for this reason

---

18. This will be at least partly offset by the system of equalization, which operates on both the personal and the corporate tax collections across provinces.

that many economists have argued in favor of using personal consumption or its equivalent as the tax base.

In an open economy, the problems are even greater. Suppose a country wants to tax its residents on their income, including accrued capital income. In addition, it wants to exploit any tax transfers from foreign treasuries that international tax crediting arrangements permit. If the personal tax system cannot tax capital gains on accrual, a corporation income tax is required for the purposes both of withholding at source against domestic residents and transferring taxes from foreign treasuries. The corporate tax will have to be a tax on equity income defined, not as the policy maker might ideally define it for domestic withholding purposes, but to conform with the tax systems of creditor nations. In the absence of integration provisions, the corporate and personal tax systems will favor retained earnings at the expense of new share issues, and will favor unincorporated businesses relative to corporations. An attempt to integrate must involve a dividend tax credit applied at the personal level. The dividend-paid deduction would not be a desirable instrument here, since it would apply to dividends paid both to residents and to foreigners, and that would effectively negate any withholding against foreign treasuries. Furthermore, assigning the dividend tax credit on the basis of corporate taxes paid (as suggested by Carter) would not be desirable in an open economy for the same reason.

All the problems mentioned above for designing an integrated corporate and personal tax system for the closed economy would continue to apply. In the open economy, there would be more. A fully integrated corporate and personal tax system achieved using the dividend tax credit would succeed in removing the differential tax treatment of new equity issues and retained earnings and would remove the differential tax treatment of corporate and noncorporate equity, but it would do so by removing the tax on equity income at the personal level altogether. Only personal interest income would remain taxed.

This system hardly constitutes taxing persons on an income basis. To do that would involve foregoing integration altogether (as in the U.S. case), plus taxing capital gains on accrual. Failure to do the latter would allow persons to shelter retained earning within the corporate sector. Given that it is difficult to tax capital gains on an accrual basis, the alternatives for personal taxation in an open economy would seem to be as follows:[19]

i. Tax capital income to the extent possible, which means in practice roughly the way it is taxed now. Interest, dividends, rents, and royalties are all taxed as received (with full loss offset). Unincorporated business income is taxed on accrual, albeit imperfectly. Capital gains are taxed on realization. The corporate tax is integrated with the personal tax. As mentioned, such a

---

19. In all these options, we presume that a corporate tax is in effect. Because of the segmentation of the savings and investment sides of the market, what is done at the personal level can be evaluated separately from what is done at the corporate level. We return to the corporate level below.

system effectively means that equity income goes untaxed at the personal level, while interest is taxed. Persons have an incentive to hold equity income, while firms have an incentive to finance with debt. There is no differential treatment of corporate and unincorporated forms, nor of these forms and personal assets. However, this outcome is achieved by essentially removing much of capital income from the personal tax base. (The Canadian system is like this, except that integration is not full, and pension and RRSP funds are sheltered.) The dividend tax credit provision does not apply on funds invested in sheltered form; that is appropriate in the open economy setting. It would, of course, be desirable to index capital income for inflation. As well, the problems with unlimited interest deductibility, mentioned above, remain.

ii. Tax capital income as in (i), but do not integrate the personal and corporate tax systems. In this case, part of equity income is taxed (i.e., new equity issues), but retained earnings are not. Persons have an incentive to accumulate wealth within the corporation rather than to hold debt or acquire new equity. As above, firms prefer to finance by debt because of the interest deductibility provisions. Corporate equity is discriminated against vis-à-vis unincorporated equity. The result is a tax system much like the U.S. system. It is far from an ideal income tax system, since it includes many interasset distortions.

iii. Use consumption as the base for the personal tax by following the prescription of the U.S. Treasury *Blueprints* (1977) as adopted for Canada by the Economic Council of Canada (1986). The corporate tax should not be integrated with the personal tax in this case. Unincorporated business assets are taxed on a cash-flow basis or its equivalent, as outlined in Boadway and Bruce (1984). This would avoid all the interasset distortions at the personal tax level as outlined above, leaving only the distortions caused by the corporate tax. Given the extent to which assets are currently sheltered in the Canadian personal tax system, this would not require a major departure from the present system.

Given these options for personal taxation, it could be said at the least that considerations of an open economy nature strengthen the case for consumption, as opposed to income, taxation at the personal level. Ultimately, the decision involves weighing these considerations against other equity and efficiency objectives of taxation.

Next, consider the corporate tax. In a closed economy, the main argument for a corporate tax follows from its role as a withholding device against earnings retained within the corporation. This role is considerably weakened in the open economy because of the segmentation of the investment side of the market from the savings side. In a small open economy, the corporate tax essentially distorts the investment decision without affecting the savings side at all. However, in an open economy, the corporate tax acquires another withholding role, against foreign corporations that can credit taxes at home (or are exempt from taxes at home on foreign income). This becomes the main role for the corporate tax in an open economy.

The exact design of the corporate tax for this purpose depends on two opposing considerations (from the perspective of the small open economy). On the one hand, the desire to extract as large a tax transfer as possible from foreign treasuries would suggest mimicking foreign tax regimes to the extent possible. On the other hand, taxing foreign corporations means unavoidably taxing domestic ones as well. This consideration implies that a distortion is imposed on domestic firms' investment decisions. It would support as low a tax rate as possible. Some judgment must be made as to the balance between these opposing objectives. Presumably, the greater the proportion of assets held by foreign-owned firms, the higher the corporate tax rate would be, and vice versa.

1.6   Cooperative Income Tax Policies between Two Open Economies

The above discussion concerned tax policy for an economy whose capital markets are open to international capital flows. Tax harmonization involves coordinating the taxes of more than one country. The question addressed now is whether there are any significant advantages to be gained from two countries, both operating in a wider world economy, coordinating their tax systems, given that each of them has its own tax policy objectives. We have already seen that there are certain pressures for a single country's tax system to conform in certain ways with those of other nations, even when it operates independently. The issue is whether there are additional gains to be had from further cooperation between two such countries.

The analogy with tax harmonization in a single country with a federal system of government might seem to be apt here. The Canadian case is instructive. In Canada (as in the United States), the federal and the provincial governments use both the personal and the corporation income taxes. Residents are subject to taxes at both levels of government. Furthermore, residents are free to move from one province to another. In these circumstances, explicit income tax harmonization makes a lot of sense. On the administrative side, harmonization can allow for a single tax collection authority and thereby reduce collection and compliance costs significantly. At the personal level, harmonization of the base and the rate structure reduces the possibility of inefficiencies in the allocation of labor across provinces by reducing the ability of the provinces to use the tax structure to attract desirable types of persons. However, the use of a common base and rate structure necessarily implies some loss of sovereignty of different units of government in tax policy. This is resolved in Canada heavily in the federal government's favor, though it is not clear that this situation will continue indefinitely, given the growing relative importance of the provinces in the collection of personal income tax revenues.

Harmonization of the personal tax structure also allows for a system of imputation applying across provinces, whereby tax credit is awarded for corporate tax revenues collected anywhere in the federation. As mentioned, since the corporate tax is collected on a source basis, imputation at the personal level involves some interprovincial redistribution of tax revenues. However, this is likely to be offset considerably by the extensive system of interprovincial redistribution that occurs through the grant system, especially the system of equalization and Established Programs Financing transfers. Indeed, it is this system of equalizing transfers that also reduces the use of the personal tax system for tax competition.

At the same time, the fact that integration occurs at the personal level means that the rate of imputation is the same across provinces, despite the fact that corporate tax rates may vary from one province to another. This seems to be an unavoidable consequence of having to integrate at the personal level rather than the corporate level. Even if different provinces could select their own rates of imputation (and there is probably no reason why they should not be allowed to), there is no ideal rate. If the Canadian economy were a closed one, it would be better to apply the imputation at the corporate level, say, by a dividend-paid deduction against corporate taxes paid. But this is not a sensible alternative in an open economy, because it would effectively undo any withholding against foreigners whose own corporate tax systems operate on an origin basis.

Harmonization of the corporate tax also entails the potential benefits of a single tax collection authority (although three provinces take no advantage of it). The main advantage of tax harmonization is the use of a common base. In addition to reducing compliance costs, the use of a common base facilitates the use of formula apportionment for allocating corporate income to province of origin. The use of a formula, though to some extent arbitrary, limits the ability of a firm to engage in tax arbitrage activities, especially those involving financial transactions designed simply to change the province in which the firm takes its profits. Of course, since no allocation formula will be perfect, there will remain some incentives for conducting operations in one province relative to another. Those incentives will depend upon the differential in tax rates across provinces. Again, the system of federal-provincial transfers minimizes these differentials, though presumably it does not eliminate tax competition altogether.

When we move to the Canada-U.S. setting, there are several institutional differences that considerably weaken the case for extending a form of tax harmonization. First, there is no single higher level of government with a mandate to implement a tax policy according to a single objective. That is, there is no analogy with the federal government in a federal country. Second, though residents are mobile internally within a federation, they are essentially immobile internationally, unless the nations have agreed to a common market; this is not the case for Canada and the United States. Third, there is no system of redistributive grants between nations such as exists within a federation (e.g., Canada). These can reduce the pressures for tax competition and otherwise offset the anomalies that can occur from the fact that while corporate taxes are levied at source, personal taxes are levied on a residence basis. Taken together, these considerations imply to us that the two countries are unlikely to benefit greatly from tax harmonization of the sort used in the Canadian federation.

Given the immobility of labor across the two countries, taxation of personal incomes on a residency basis allows each country to pursue its own domestic tax policy objectives with minimal constraints. Thus, the openness of the economy seems not to constrain one country from imposing a substantially different personal tax base or rate structure from the other. Canada could, for example, adopt a personal consumption base independently of the United States. Similarly, the decision whether or not to impute corporate tax liabilities against personal taxes could be taken independently by each country — as has been done. We have seen that this decision is effectively the same in an open economy as the decision as to whether to tax equity income fully at the personal level or not.

It is at the level of the corporate tax that international harmonization becomes more of a possibility, especially given the ability of capital to flow between countries more or less unrestricted. As mentioned, international capital mobility will already induce some harmonization in the tax system, since it will be in the interest of a given country to adopt a tax system similar to those operating abroad, under international tax crediting arrangements. Any further harmonization that can be achieved by agreement would involve at the least a common base. Since there is no natural ideal base for the corporate tax, this would remove the discretion that otherwise exists at the national level, thus reducing a country's independence to conduct tax policy with domestic objectives in mind. Similar arguments might be applied to the rate structure. There is already considerable pressure for harmonization of rates. It is not obvious that there is much to be gained from further explicit agreement.

Beyond this, the two countries may prefer to harmonize their integration systems. If this could be done at the corporate level by, say, a system of dividend-paid deductions, the ideal integration system could be achieved. Unfortunately, it would be difficult to do, since it would require treating firms resident in one of the two countries in a different manner from other foreign firms. Such discrimination would presumably not be compatible with existing international treaty conventions. Either the dividend deduction would have to apply to all firms, which would not be desirable from an international tax transfer perspective, or the integration would have to occur at the personal level, in which case there is little to be gained from harmonization of the corporate bases. We have already seen that when integration is applied at the personal level, there is no reason why different countries cannot pursue independently different policies, one integrating and the other not.

It might be thought that administrative gains could be had from coordination, especially in the form of reduced compliance and collection costs. Significant benefits would probably require implementing some form of formula apportionment system for allocating the tax base between jurisdictions. However, for this to be of real value, agreement on common base would be required. Then only one set of accounts would need to be compiled for the two countries. Of course, the need for separate accounting with other countries would not be avoided. A common base with formula apportionment would simplify the system for taxpayers, remove some incentives for wasteful tax planning, and avoid double-taxation problems within the two countries. At the same time, it would involve considerable loss in sovereignty to the agreeing governments, since both would have to accept the same tax base.

The chances of this outcome being achieved are remote indeed as far as Canada and the United States are concerned. While Canada's corporate income tax system is highly harmonized within the country among the various jurisdictions, the same is not true of the United States. A prerequisite to international harmonization is harmonization within each country. In the absence of this, the chance for adopting formula apportionment with a common base is limited. Of course, it would still be possible to apportion without using a common base, but many of the advantages would be lost.

Nevertheless, there are some partial measures that could be adopted to the mutual advantage of both countries. A good example of cross-border "complementarity" between measures undertaken to improve compliance is the use of withholding taxes on investment income. As mentioned earlier, a major disadvantage for the individual country in imposing such withholding taxes on domestic financial institutions is that residents can easily shift their savings abroad. Thus, the attempt to improve compliance may be counterproductive. If, however, the United States and Canada both impose withholding taxes on investment income, compliance is improved in both countries, providing savings cannot be shifted to third countries. Note that in this regard, tax treaty provisions that specify special low withholding-tax rates for partner countries would be undesirable.

Another potential area of cooperation is the use of the corporation income tax system to offer economic incentives to certain activities; for example, a corporation income tax credit for R&D spending could be offered. Under the existing system of taxation for cross-border income flows, the impact of such an incentive is blunted for R&D activities carried on by U.S. multinationals in Canada, because of the U.S. foreign tax crediting arrangements. Rather than offering these corporations tax relief for carrying out R&D expenditures, these arrangements mean that revenues are transferred to the U.S. Treasury. From the firm's perspective, lower taxes paid in Canada simply imply higher taxes paid when the income is repatriated to the United States. However, if the repatriation is far enough in the future, the Canadian tax relief can have some incentive effects. It is expected that the 1986 reforms in the U.S. taxation of foreign source income are likely to reduce the effects of Canadian tax incentives. [20]

The United States could enable Canada to better use its corporation income tax to pursue industrial policy objectives by also adopting an exemption system, or by allowing qualifying Canadian tax incentives to reduce U.S. corporation income taxes on repatriated incomes (so-called tax sparing). The latter would be difficult to do on a bilateral basis, since the United States has steadfastly refused to offer tax sparing to developing countries, unlike some other capital-exporting industrial economies. This refusal is supported by the belief that unless a compelling market-failure rationale for the incentive exists, the incentive could cause an inefficient allocation of capital between countries, with the cost being borne by the United States. Also, it is believed that coupling the present deferral advantage with tax sparing will offer excessive relief.

The main argument against replacing the U.S. foreign tax credit with an exemption system is that the latter invites the capital-importing countries to attract income from the United States by offering a lower corporate tax rate— the typical negative spillover policy. However, this could be mitigated by allowing the exemption to apply only to particular forms of income in listed countries, such as Canada does. The main problem with this solution is that the Canadian system seems inordinately complex and is perhaps unmanageable for U.S. multinationals that operate in numerous countries. Also, as long as Canada and the United States each maintain certain corporate tax preferences that are perceived as working against the other country's interests, such as the special tax rate for manufacturing and processing income in Canada and the Foreign Sales Corporation provisions in the United States, agreement to recognize each other's corporate tax incentives will be difficult to obtain.

The market pressures for a high degree of uniformity in the corporation income tax structures of Canada and the United States probably constrain the abilities of both countries to pursue national tax policies, even when those policies do not interfere with the other country. It is less obvious that the disadvantages are so great that the two countries will find it desirable to adopt a coordinated approach to the taxation of multinational corporations operating in both countries.

1.7   Concluding Remarks: Worldwide Tax Harmonization

The previous discussion was predicated on the fact that Canada and the United States operate in a broader world context, in which certain tax institu-

---

20. A similar situation does not apply to the impact of U.S. corporate tax incentives on the activities of Canadian foreign affiliates operating there, because Canada exempts most income repatriated from the U.S. from corporate taxation. Thus, U.S. corporate tax reliefs act as tax incentives to the firms affected.

tions are taken as given. In particular, it has been assumed that, while personal tax systems adhere to the residence principle, corporate tax systems use the origin or source principle. That is, foreign tax liabilities of home country corporations on their income earned abroad is credited against domestic tax liabilities. In such a system, an ideal income (or consumption) tax system is impossible to achieve. The corporate tax becomes partly a device for withholding against foreign treasuries. The combination of the residence principle for personal taxation and the source principle for corporate taxation makes it impossible to avoid distortions on capital markets. For example, it is not possible to implement a proper imputation system so as to ensure that equity income is taxed only once and is treated equivalently to interest income.

If a way could be found to tax corporations on a residence basis, these problems could be avoided. In principle, such an outcome is possible; in this final section, we explore it briefly. Essentially all that is involved is for countries to adopt a deduction system for foreign tax liabilities, rather than a credit system. Under such a system, provided all countries behave as if they have no market power in international capital markets, the incentive would exist for them to adopt a residence-based corporate tax system.

Consider first a capital-importing country, in which capital imports come from countries in which a deduction system is used. In such a system it can easily be demonstrated that the transfer of revenues from the treasury of the creditor country is not possible. Any attempt to extract tax revenues from foreign corporations will result in an outflow of foreign capital until the tax is fully shifted back to the residents of the taxing country. In such a setting the home country could follow several different tax policies. If it wishes to tax income comprehensively at home, but is unable to tax capital gains on accrual, it could levy a general corporate tax on all corporations. Then, to impute the tax it could offer a dividend-paid deduction to corporations as dividends are paid out. It would want to do so both for domestically owned and foreign corporations. Not to do so for foreign corporations would simply drive out capital and impose a tax burden on domestic residents.[21] The income tax system would be properly integrated, and income would be taxed once in the hands of residents. Furthermore, there would be no incentive for capital to be misallocated internationally on account of the corporate tax system applying at source. Note also that no further withholding taxes would be desired, again assuming that the deduction system applied to them as well.

It would be somewhat more difficult to operate a classical corporate tax system, as discussed in section 1.4. To do so would require giving a dividend-paid deduction only to foreigners, and this would be difficult to administer. Furthermore, it would seem to provide incentives for evasion by domestic corporations.

21. One might think an alternative would be simply to levy that tax on domestic corporations alone. However, this would be difficult to administer, since it would be necessary to identify and treat properly corporations with some (or all) foreign owners.

If the country wishes to tax residents on a consumption tax basis, it could do away with the corporate tax as a withholding device altogether. There would be no need to withhold against domestic residents, since capital income would not be taxed. And because it is not possible to transfer tax revenues from foreign treasuries, it is unnecessary to withhold against foreigners. The role of business taxation would be reduced to that of collecting pure profits. For that some form of cash-flow tax or its equivalent would suffice.

From the point of view of creditor countries, such a system would seem to be preferable to the existing one, since it eliminates the transfer of tax revenues they now face under the credit system. Creditor-country tax policies could be constructed exactly as above. They could operate an integrated tax system by imposing a corporate tax and imputing at the corporate level by a dividend-paid deduction. Or they could operate a consumption tax system by avoiding the use of the corporate tax for withholding purposes at all. Again, a classical system is somewhat more difficult to administer for the same reason as above.

If both creditor and capital-importing countries adopted such a residence-based corporate tax system, international production inefficiencies could be avoided and all countries could adopt the residence-based tax structure that most accorded with their policy objectives. Bringing about such a system would seem to be difficult, since it apparently involves agreement by all countries simultaneously. However, it is not obvious why explicit agreement would be required. It would seem to be in the interest of creditor countries to move to a deduction system. If they did so, even one by one, capital-importing countries would be induced to follow suit. One of the great unsolved questions of international tax theory is why creditor countries continue to use the credit system, when it seems clearly to be in their interest to use the deduction system instead.

References

Boadway, R., and N. Bruce. 1984. A General Proposition on the Design of a Neutral Business Tax. *Journal of Public Economics* 24(July): 231–39.
————. In press. Problems with Integrating Corporate and Personal Income Taxes in an Open Economy. *Journal of Public Economics.*
Bruce, N. 1989. The Impact of Tax Reform on International Capital Flows and Investment. In *The Economic Impact of Tax Reform,* ed. J. Mintz and J. Whalley. Toronto: Canadian Tax Foundation.
Canada. 1966. *Report of the Royal Commission on Taxation* (The Carter Report). Ottawa.
Economic Council of Canada. 1986. *The Taxation of Income From Capital.* Ottawa.
Fischer, S. 1980. Dynamic Consistency, Cooperation and the Benevolent Dissembling Government. *Journal of Economic Dynamics and Control* 2: 93–107.

Kay, J. A., and M. A., King. 1990. *The British Tax System*. Oxford: Oxford University Press.

Kehoe, P. 1989. Policy Cooperation among Benevolent Governments May be Undesirable. *Review of Economic Studies* 56(April): 289–96.

Mintz, J., and H. Tulkens. 1991. The OECD Convention: A "Model" for Corporate Tax Harmonization? In *Public Finance with Several Levels of Government* (Proceedings of the 46th Congress, International Institute of Public Finance), ed. R. Prud'homme, 298–314. The Hague: Foundation Journal Public Finance.

Musgrave, P. 1990. International Coordination Problems of Substituting Consumption for Income Taxation. In *Heidelberg Congress on Taxing Consumption,* ed. Manfred Rose, Berlin: Springer-Verlag.

Shibata, H. 1967. The Theory of Economic Unions: A Comparative Analysis of Customs Unions, Free Trade Areas, and Tax Unions. In *Fiscal Harmonization in Common Markets,* vol. 1, ed. C. S. Shoup. New York: Columbia University Press.

U.S. Treasury Department. 1978. *Blueprints for Basic Tax Reform*. Washington, D.C.

2 Canada-U.S. Free Trade and Pressures for Tax Coordination

Roger H. Gordon

The economies of the United States and Canada are closely linked—trade between the two countries is substantial, their capital markets are highly integrated, and even movement of individual workers between the two countries is nonnegligible. The U.S. and Canada have now agreed to eliminate all remaining tariff barriers between the two countries during the next few years. To what degree does this increasing economic integration create pressure on the two countries to change their tax systems? Which aspects of the systems will be most affected? Will their tax systems inevitably become more alike, as each country finds it in its economic interest to choose tax provisions resembling those in the other country? When will explicit coordination and harmonization of tax provisions be called for?[1] Addressing these questions is the objective of this paper.

The effects of mobility of goods and factors between jurisdictions on their fiscal systems has been explored at length in the local public finance literature, stimulated by Tiebout (1956). These models assume that everything and everyone is mobile without cost—implicitly, even community boundaries can adjust. The basic conclusion of this literature is that competition among communities drives the tax system toward one in which each individual's or firm's tax payment closely matches the cost of the services received from the com-

Roger H. Gordon is professor of economics at the University of Michigan and a research associate of the National Bureau of Economic Research.

Much of this paper was written while the author was visiting the Universidade Nova de Lisboa. He would like to thank the other participants in the Canada-U.S. Tax Comparisons project, and especially John Shoven and John Whalley, for comments on a previous draft.

1. By "coordination," I will mean negotiation to internalize fiscal externalities. "Harmonization," in contrast, will refer to equalization of tax rates and tax bases, whether this occurs through agreement or as a result of market forces.

munity (or the costs imposed on the community, from pollution or congestion for example), a tax system known in the literature as *benefit* taxation.[2] With any other tax structure, decisions in one community clearly affect welfare in other communities, creating the potential for mutually beneficial coordination of fiscal policies.[3]

The existing tax systems in the U.S. and Canada differ substantially from a benefit-tax structure.[4] To what extent can these differences continue to survive, given the increasing openness of the two economies? Of course, economic mobility between the U.S. and Canada, while substantial, is hardly costless. In this paper, I attempt to assess the pressures created by current and prospective levels of mobility between the two countries. In section 2.1, the implications of existing levels of capital mobility are examined: What implications does capital mobility alone have on domestic tax policies and the need for tax harmonization? Section 2.2 examines the further pressures created by free trade in the full range of outputs. Finally, in section 2.3, the pressures created by labor mobility, to the extent that it exists between the U.S. and Canada, are assessed.

There are three key conclusions of the discussion. First, taxes on capital income are unlikely to survive for long, even under existing levels of international capital mobility, without explicit coordination of capital income tax policies among all major countries; an agreement between just the U.S. and Canada would accomplish little. While existing double-taxation conventions may have led in the past to implicit coordination of capital income taxes, the increasing complexity of international capital markets will make any coordination in the future much more difficult. Second, unrestricted trade between the two countries will force them either to "level the playing field," by eliminating any tax or regulatory distortions to the relative prices of traded goods, or else to agree on a common set of tax distortions (e.g., agricultural price supports) with a common set of trade barriers to support these internal price distortions. Finally, to the extent that labor mobility is allowed, redistribution through the tax system becomes more difficult. Under existing levels of mobility, however, this pressure is not yet very important.

Inevitably, the analysis is somewhat abstract, attempting to forecast the broad direction of change in the tax structures in each country. Boadway and Bruce (ch. 1 in this volume) examine in much more detail how these pressures are currently being felt and the likely short-term responses to them.

---

2. To the degree to which a community's taxes deviate from benefit taxes, other communities have the incentive to bid to attract those individuals or firms who on net pay more than they impose in costs on the community. For further discussion, see Buchanan and Goetz (1972).

3. See Gordon (1983) for an exploration of the various possible sources of externalities.

4. See Boadway and Bruce (ch. 1 in this volume) for a detailed description of the existing tax structures in the two countries.

2.1   Tax Implications of Capital Mobility

How does capital mobility affect the design of tax policy? To explore this question, assume for simplicity that only one good is traded among countries. Trade therefore simply takes the form of some of this good being imported now, in return for an acceptable amount of this good being exported back as return payment in a later period. To shorten the discussion, I will ignore the implications of risk or inflation.

Without taxes, capital would flow between countries until the rate of return from investing in each country is the same. Let i_j^a represent the rate of return on asset a in country j. Without taxes and uncertainty, the return on all assets would be equalized in equilibrium, so that $i_j^a = i_k^b$ for any asset a in country j and asset b in country k. Given this, investors would be indifferent between investing in domestic or foreign capital and between investing in different types of financial securities.

The equilibrium ownership structure of securities, and the equilibrium allocation of capital, can be affected in many ways by taxes. The existing tax treatment of capital income is quite complex. To begin with, a corporation's income is directly subject to tax in the country in which it is located, under the corporate tax.[5] If the owners of a corporation reside in the same country, then they are taxed as well on the income they receive from the investment under the personal income tax.[6] For foreign owners of the firm, however, the tax treatment is more complicated. Payments may first be subject to a withholding tax in the source country. If the owner is an individual, the pre–withholding-tax income is then taxable in the home country, but with a credit for any withholding tax. If the owner is a corporation, the pre–corporate-tax income underlying the payments is subject to tax in the home country, but with a credit for any corporate income and withholding taxes already paid on this income.[7] Finally, payouts to the ultimate individual owners are also taxed.

What pressures does capital mobility create, given the existing tax system? To simplify the discussion, I will initially assume that income from capital is subject to corporate taxation only in the source country, and that income to individuals from capital is taxable only in the country where the individuals reside. In effect, these assumptions ignore withholding taxes and corporate surtaxes on repatriated income.[8] The discussion will start by examining the implications of capital mobility for residence-based taxes, such as the per-

5. For simplicity, the discussion ignores noncorporate firms.
6. In Canada, there is a dividend credit, which reduces the extent of the double taxation inherent in this tax structure.
7. In all cases, the credit is not refundable, so is limited to the amount of taxes due in the home country on that income. For further detail on U.S. and Canadian provisions, see Boadway and Bruce (ch. 1 in this volume).
8. This last assumption may not be that unreasonable. Hines and Hubbard (1990) provide evidence that U.S. multinationals, at least, pay little or no U.S. taxes on their repatriated earnings.

sonal income tax, then will turn to source-based taxes, such as the corporate tax. Finally, the discussion will return to explore the implications of capital mobility for withholding taxes and corporate surtaxes and to explore the implications of Canada's dividend-credit scheme.

2.1.1 Capital Taxation under the Residence Principle

In principle, under a residence-based tax each country taxes the capital income of its own residents at accrual, regardless of where this income is earned, but does not tax the income of nonresidents, even when they invest in local securities or in local real capital. Let the effective tax rate for residents of country j on income from asset a in country k be t_{jk}^a. Then, equilibrium for investors residing in country j requires that $i_j^a(1 - t_{jj}^a) = i_k^b(1 - t_{jk}^b)$, while equilibrium for investors residing in country k requires that $i_j^a(1 - t_{kj}^a) = i_k^b(1 - t_{kk}^b)$. As emphasized in Slemrod (1988), these two equilibrium conditions cannot hold simultaneously unless

(1)
$$\frac{1 - t_{jj}^a}{1 - t_{jk}^b} = \frac{1 - t_{kj}^a}{1 - t_{kk}^b}$$

for all assets a and b. Given equation (1), investors will again be indifferent between investing in any of the available financial securities. Firms will then seek the cheapest form of financing, given the resulting pretax rates of return on different financial securities.

If equation (1) does not hold for all asset pairs, however, then tax arbitrage possibilities exist enabling investors to rearrange their portfolio holdings to reduce tax payments. Each investor has the incentive to reduce his holdings of assets that are taxed relatively heavily in his country and increase his holdings of assets that are taxed relatively lightly. In the process, investors save on taxes. If investors can own negative amounts of some assets and can deduct the required payments,[9] then this rearrangement of portfolios can in principle continue without limit,[10] though risk considerations presumably limit the extent of this arbitrage.

Of course, similar arbitrage possibilities can arise even in a closed economy.[11] In fact, Gordon and Slemrod (1988) found that in 1983 in the U.S., as a result of such arbitrage, the attempt to tax the return to saving and investment resulted in a slight net loss in tax revenue; interest deductions more than offset the taxable income generated by both real and financial investments. Countries in practice seem to recognize arbitrage opportunities gradually, and

9. For example, borrowing implies a negative holding of bonds, and interest payments are normally deductible.

10. Technically, this requires that each investor be able to "go short" in at least one asset, deducting the payments from taxable income, and that each investor be taxed relatively more heavily on the asset he goes short in.

11. See Stiglitz (1985) for a number of examples.

then attempt to eliminate them case by case. For example, in the U.S. individuals are not allowed to deduct interest when they borrow for the purpose of buying a tax-exempt bond. But this is just an example of a wide variety of possible forms of tax arbitrage, and enforcement of even this restriction is very difficult. Under the 1986 tax reform in the U.S., a broader attempt was made to limit arbitrage possibilities by restricting interest deductions, except for businesses, and restricting taxpayers' ability to deduct losses more generally.[12] When this arbitrage takes place across borders, detecting and dealing with it is that much more difficult.

If investors in each country can "go short" in the appropriate asset, then capital income taxation collects significant revenue only if these arbitrage possibilities are closed off, which requires that equation (1) be satisfied for all pairs of assets. An agreement between the two countries on relative tax rates could occur implicitly as well as explicitly. Neither country would want to deviate from a common set of relative tax rates, since doing so would open up arbitrage opportunities for investors in both countries—*any* set of relative tax rates would be a Nash equilibrium. However, both countries may gain by jointly agreeing on a particular set of relative tax rates. The normal presumption has been that a "neutral" tax system, under which income from all assets is taxed at the same rate, is the most attractive.

If no deductions are allowed for payments on debt or other "short" positions, then a country would never lose revenue from taxing capital income, even without agreeing with the other country on the relative tax rates on different assets. Equilibrium portfolio holdings in each country would still depend on the tax policies in both countries, however, making welfare in the two countries interdependent. Coordination of relative tax rates would still in principle be justified. However, as shown formally in Gordon (1986), each country acting in isolation would have the incentive to set its tax rates so that its residents invest in the security paying the largest amount pretax. This is accomplished simply by equating the tax rates on all assets, so that $t_{jj}^a = t_{jk}^b$, regardless of the tax policy chosen in the other country. Therefore, a "neutral" tax system may well be the Nash equilibrium as well as the optimal policy chosen after full coordination.

Given any agreement on relative tax rates on different assets, each country could then choose independently the absolute level of its tax rates without opening up arbitrage opportunities. Each country's policies affect the welfare in the other country only through any resulting changes in the market interest rate. If each country is small relative to the world capital market, then these changes will be small, implying no important externalities when choosing the absolute level of residence-based capital income tax rates. The U.S., however, is not plausibly small relative to the world capital market. It has the incentive

12. One apparent response has been an increase in corporate borrowing, since corporate interest deductions are still allowed.

to reduce its borrowing from foreigners in order to reduce the market interest rate, thereby reducing the interest payments on its existing debt. Given that Canada is a net debtor in the world capital market, a reduction in the market interest rate would be a benefit for Canada, a benefit ignored by the U.S. in designing its own policies.[13] In particular, under optimal policies the U.S. would be indifferent to borrowing still less, but Canada would gain from the resulting fall in the interest rate. This creates the potential for mutually beneficial agreements on tax policy.

Use of a residence principle for capital income taxation leads to a major problem with tax enforcement, however. Within a country, firms and institutions that pay dividends and interest can be required to report the names of the recipients, and how much they receive, to the local tax authorities. A country has no direct way to require foreign firms and institutions to make such reports. But if the tax authority receives no information directly about the capital income received by its residents from foreign sources, then it will find it extremely difficult to enforce the taxes due on this income. Reporting income from assets owned abroad in effect becomes voluntary, and normally investors do not knowingly make voluntary tax payments. If in practice savings invested abroad are tax free, then *all* savings become tax free, because investors can invest through a foreign financial intermediary in all assets, including domestic assets. In fact, they may be able to borrow domestically, deduct the interest, then invest the funds abroad tax free.

Can this enforcement problem be solved through suitable cooperation between the two countries? The countries could, for example, agree to share information provided by firms and institutions regarding the names of recipients of capital income. Any such agreement would allow each country to tax the capital income of its residents and so would appear to be mutually beneficial. However, given the disparity in the sizes of the U.S. and Canada, Canada might have an incentive to refuse to cooperate. Without the agreement, the relatively huge number of U.S. investors could flock to Canada hoping thereby to evade U.S. taxes. The resulting gains to the Canadian economy, whether or not the gains were taxed, might well more than offset the losses to Canada from not being able to tax the capital income of Canadian residents. If so, the U.S. would need to compensate Canada in order to secure any such agreement.

Such an agreement would be futile, in any case, given that a third country (e.g., Switzerland) could agree to facilitate the tax evasion of U.S. or Canadian investors. Such a country could open its own financial intermediaries to foreign depositors and refuse to share information with other countries. The income to foreign investors working through these financial intermediaries

---

13. Changes in the market interest rate have further effects on efficiency to the degree to which choices were not efficient initially due to distorting taxes. In particular, if income from savings is taxed, then any resulting decrease in savings reduces welfare. A change in the market interest rate also has distributional consequences which may be of concern to the government.

would again be exempt in practice from residence-based taxes. This third country could tax away some of the gain that investors receive from evading their domestic taxes and still attract funds.[14] By refusing to cooperate with other countries, it might not be able to tax the capital income of its own residents, but if the country were small enough that would be a minor consideration.[15]

Taxation at Repatriation

Even if a country cannot independently detect capital income earned abroad by its residents, it may be able to detect income as it is repatriated, through monitoring all deposits in domestic financial intermediaries or through auditing individuals whose expenditures clearly exceed their cash flow. What happens if a country simply taxes capital income at repatriation? If repatriated income is taxed at the same rate, regardless of the date of repatriation, then the effective tax rate on capital income is reduced the longer repatriation is postponed; if repatriation can be postponed indefinitely, then the effective tax rate goes to zero. Economic repatriation may even be possible without triggering the repatriation tax. For example, the investor may be able to borrow at home, possibly using the foreign assets as collateral. The borrowed funds could be used to finance any desired expenditures at home and in fact could lead to further tax savings through interest deductions. The U.S. tax law has evolved over time, trying to close off such devices for avoiding the repatriation tax, but doing so is very difficult.

2.1.2 Capital Taxation under the Source Principle

Under a source-based tax, each country would tax the return to real capital located within its borders, with rates perhaps varying by type of real capital.[16] If in country j the returns to asset a are taxed at rate t_j^a, then in equilibrium $i_j^a(1 - t_j^a) = i_k^b(1 - t_k^b)$ for all assets a and b. Since this condition is the same for investors in each country, allowing for capital mobility does not create additional complications when characterizing the equilibrium.

What can be said about the optimal source-based capital income tax rate? Diamond and Mirrlees (1971) argued that when all excise taxes can be used flexibly, and when there are no pure profits, then the optimal tax system will lead to efficient production. In particular, if a country is a price taker in the world capital market, then efficient production means that investment occurs until the marginal rate of return equals that prevailing on the world market. Therefore, in such a setting, the optimal source-based capital income tax rate should be zero. The intuition underlying this result is very simple: In a small open economy, a source-based tax on capital cannot be borne by capital, since

14. Competition among such countries would drive any tax down to zero, however.
15. See below, however, for a discussion of use of source-based taxes to help enforce residence-based taxes.
16. Tax rates might also depend on the form of the financial claim to the real capital income.

capital owners will not invest in the country unless they earn the same return as they earn elsewhere. Therefore, the tax ultimately must be paid by immobile factors, presumably land and labor. But in that case, a direct tax on these factors would dominate, since it would have the same incidence yet not distort the international flow of capital.

What if firms can earn a rate of return above the world rate? Within a closed economy, a tax on pure profits, as occurs under a cash-flow tax, does not distort allocations, and so is attractive on efficiency grounds.[17] In an open economy, however, pure profits may also be mobile. For example, if the profits are tied to technology rather than to location, then the firm will locate production based on economic conditions in the available countries. An open economy would then be able to extract rents from the firm only to the extent to which the country provides locational advantages greater than exist elsewhere. A small country presumably provides at best small advantages; the implication, based on the same reasoning as before, is that the optimal tax on these pure profits is close to zero.[18]

The Diamond-Mirrlees argument also implies, however, that a large open economy will wish to equate the domestic marginal product of capital to the marginal cost to the country of extra funds on the world market. As a result, a country such as the U.S., which is large relative to the world capital market, has the incentive to take advantage of this market power by restricting net capital flows. Given that the U.S. has recently been a net borrower in the world capital market, this would imply taxing investment in order to reduce net borrowing. Before the 1980s, when the U.S. was a capital exporter, the incentives would instead have been to subsidize investment to restrict capital exports. Canada does not plausibly have market power in the world capital markets, so should not attempt to change investment incentives.[19]

Except as a means to take advantage of monopoly power, are there any other ways of explaining the continued though relatively minor role of corporate taxes in the U.S. and Canada? One traditional rationalization for the corporate income tax is that it is necessary to prevent wholesale avoidance of a residence-based tax on equity income, given the favorable treatment of accruing capital gains under existing tax systems. This argument is appropriate only in a closed economy, however, where domestic shareholders can be taxed indirectly on their accruing capital gains through imposing a corporate tax on domestic corporations. In a small open economy, the rate of return earned by

17. See, for example, Mirrlees (1972).
18. If the profits arise from control of a patent, then the patent right itself can be relocated to a tax-free country, and the pure profits paid in the form of a tax-deductible license fee to this country, with no change in the location of production.
19. See Gordon and Varian (1989), however, for an argument that even a small country may have market power with respect to equity issued in the country, due to its idiosyncratic risk. See also Gordon (1988), who argues that when each country produces a distinct good, each country has market power and the optimal use of this market power will lead it to restrict net capital flows.

domestic residents on their savings, before personal taxes, is set by the world market and so is unchanged by a domestic source-based tax.

A related argument is that the corporate tax prevents avoidance of the domestic tax on *labor* income, at least in closely held corporations. Without the corporate tax, shareholder-employees in such firms have the incentive to leave their labor earnings in the firm, thereby allowing their shares to increase in value. When they need cash, they can simply sell some of their shares in the firm, paying tax on the accumulated gains at the more favorable capital gains rate. A cash-flow tax on corporate income at the same rate as the labor income tax would eliminate this opportunity, though it might discourage firms earning pure profits from locating in the country. A better alternative, at least in theory, would be to shift from a labor income tax to a consumption tax. Given the appropriate treatment of bequests, both have the same lifetime incidence, but the consumption tax is not vulnerable to the above evasion strategy.

Certainly if a firm imposes costs on the public sector through use of public services and facilities, then user fees would be appropriate, even in the Diamond-Mirrlees setting. It is difficult to justify a tax on capital *income* based on this reasoning, however.

These arguments together suggest that at least a small open economy should not make use of source-based capital income taxes. However, source-based capital income taxation in one country imposes clear externalities on other countries, suggesting that countries may gain by jointly agreeing to use source-based taxes. In particular, when one country raises its source-based capital income tax, capital flows to other countries, raising wage rates in the other countries and raising tax revenues if these countries also use source-based capital income taxes. In fact, a uniform capital income tax at source is equivalent to a uniform tax based on residence. While a residence-based tax is very difficult to enforce, given the government's lack of independent information about capital income earned abroad by its residents, enforcement of a source-based tax in theory should be much easier, since any activity within the country can be monitored by the tax authorities. Therefore, countries may well find it attractive to jointly tax capital income at source as a means of taxing indirectly the capital income earned by their residents.[20] The U.S. and Canada together, however, are not much larger relative to the world capital market than the U.S. alone, suggesting that the room for Pareto-improving gains between these two countries alone may be quite limited.

Furthermore, source-based taxation, at least of multinational firms, has its own enforcement problems. There are many ways in which a multinational can shift accounting profits toward the country with the lowest statutory tax rate, even without changing the location of real activity. The easiest approach

20. See Giovannini and Hines (1990) for a discussion of how transfers might be made between governments so that the allocation of revenue among countries would be equivalent to that arising under a residence-based tax.

is probably through manipulation of the transfer prices assigned to goods and services moving between firms within the multinational. Similarly, the multinational can locate patents for new technology in the country with the lowest tax rate. Yet another approach is to do the bulk of the debt financing for the multinational in the country with the highest tax rate, using perhaps as collateral the assets located in other countries. Governments have little ability to monitor the diverse nature of transactions within a firm and can effectively challenge only a small fraction of these schemes.

Given that multinationals can quickly and easily shift taxable income toward those countries with the lowest statutory tax rate, each country has a strong incentive to cut its statutory tax rate in order to benefit from this process. Tax competition then drives statutory tax rates towards zero, even if the location of real activity is not very sensitive to relative tax rates.

The above discussion of optimal tax policy assumes that capital is fully mobile in response to differences in rates of return. Once capital is invested in a country, however, it is difficult to move even in response to high tax rates. Therefore, while the amount of new investment may be very sensitive to tax rates, the amount of existing capital may be virtually fixed. As a result, at any date a country has an incentive to seize any existing capital but then to promise never to do so again, in order not to discourage new investment.[21] Assuming it could make such a binding promise, then by the above arguments it would choose never to tax new investment. But governments have no way to precommit their future tax policy. If no commitment has been made, then once new investment occurs and the capital has become immobile, the country again has the incentive to seize the capital. This is known as the "time consistency" problem. Perhaps reputation effects inhibit even the initial seizure of capital. Alternatively, the country can subsidize initial investments to compensate for the taxes that inevitably will be collected from these investments at a later date, regardless of what may have been promised.

2.1.3   Capital Income Taxation under the Current Law

So far, we have ignored the incentives created by existing double-taxation conventions. Given these conventions, how does the forecasted behavior of each government change? What joint tax structure would be forecasted to arise? Comparing this tax structure with that which arises without this convention, can we explain why countries choose to adopt it? Existing double-taxation conventions affect the taxation in the home country of both portfolio income earned abroad by domestic investors and corporate income repatriated from foreign subsidiaries by a domestically based multinational. In each case,

---

21. The same incentives can exist even with taxation based on residence. For example, if foreigners have large holdings of domestically issued bonds, then a government has the incentive to inflate the currency unexpectedly, thereby wiping out its debt to foreigners.

the home country allows a tax credit for particular taxes paid abroad, whereas our previous discussion assumed that foreign tax payments were deductible.

One further complication ignored in the previous discussion was the use of a dividend-credit scheme in Canada. The incentives created by this scheme are complicated enough that they merit a separate discussion.

Withholding Taxes on Portfolio Income

Let us begin by examining the equilibrium use of withholding taxes on portfolio income earned by foreign investors. Existing double-taxation conventions allow a tax credit in the home country for withholding taxes paid on portfolio income accruing in the host country, with a maximum credit equal to the taxes due on the income in the home country. If tax treaties did not also specify the rate of withholding tax, how would each country respond?

Assume first that tax evasion is not a problem, so that each country can effectively tax income earned by domestic residents from foreign portfolio holdings. Consider first the incentives faced by a small host country. Since a withholding tax does not affect the net-of-tax earnings of foreign investors, as long as the withholding tax rate remains below the domestic tax rate faced by these foreign investors on their portfolio income, the tax produces revenue without any loss to domestic residents. Therefore, the host country should choose to raise this tax rate at least up to the foreign tax rate.[22] If the tax rate is raised further, however, it does discourage capital inflows, and the Diamond-Mirrlees reasoning still implies that a small open economy would not choose to impose such distortions.[23]

How would the home government behave, given this foreign withholding tax rate? In Gordon (1992), I find that the home country, taking the foreign withholding tax rate as given, would never choose a tax rate on the portfolio income of domestic residents equal to this foreign withholding tax rate; the optimal tax rate could in principle be either higher than this rate or zero.[24] When the tax rate is below this point, raising the tax rate affects the net-of-tax rate of return only of domestic investments, and so acts like a source-based tax. Within this range, a tax increase is therefore undesirable. When the tax rate is above the foreign withholding tax rate, however, a tax increase affects foreign and domestic holdings equally, making tax increases just above the foreign rate more attractive than tax increases just below the foreign rate. This implies that there is no Nash equilibrium set of tax rates.[25]

---

22. With a diversity of foreign tax rates, the story becomes a bit more complicated, since the country is no longer a price-taker in the world capital market.

23. As noted before, a large open economy would set its taxes to take advantage of this market power.

24. Bond and Samuelson (1989) find, under different assumptions that allow each country to tax domestic and foreign income at different rates, that the optimal tax rate must be higher.

25. Gordon (1992) shows that there will be a Stackelberg equilibrium, however.

Without tax evasion as a problem, I argued above that residence-based taxes should create few externalities, implying little gain from coordination. Therefore, even if the treaty led to a clear outcome, it would be very unlikely that both countries would prefer this outcome to the situation without the treaty.

What if investors can evade domestic taxes without any cost or risk by investing through foreign financial intermediaries? Then domestic investors can always avoid tax by investing abroad, so a withholding tax is simply a source-based tax, and by the same arguments used above we conclude that a small open economy should not impose a source-based tax.

If evasion is costly enough, however, then Gordon (1992) shows that host countries will again impose a withholding tax at a rate equal to the home country rate, rather than act as a tax haven. If the home country acts as a Stackelberg leader, then an equilibrium exists under the double-taxation convention. From each nation's perspective, this equilibrium Pareto-dominates the equilibrium without the double-taxation convention, in which there are no capital income taxes. In principle, further welfare gains should be possible through explicit coordination of withholding tax rates; capital income tax rates are lower in the above equilibrium than would be jointly optimal. However, successful coordination must be done on a worldwide basis; if Canada and the U.S. alone increased their tax rates, then their investors would simply invest elsewhere, where tax rates remained low.

Another possible explanation for why countries impose withholding taxes is that each country's equity is a unique asset, if only because it provides risk diversification not available elsewhere. In that case, each country has the incentive to take advantage of its monopoly power by, for example, imposing a withholding tax on payments to foreign equity holders.[26] What if those paying this tax include domestic investors buying through a foreign intermediary to evade domestic taxes? Imposing a withholding tax remains attractive as long as taxing capital income is part of the desired tax system.[27]

If the only motivation toward imposing withholding taxes is to take advantage of market power, then there would be a joint efficiency gain from reducing these trade distortions by jointly setting a low ceiling for withholding tax rates. In theory, Canada should gain more from such an agreement, given the much greater market power of the U.S.[28] Note that the agreement in this case reduces withholding tax rates from those chosen in the Nash equilibrium,

---

26. For further discussion, see Gordon and Varian (1989).

27. The withholding tax also reduces the incentive to use foreign financial intermediaries, leading to potential efficiency gains if domestic intermediaries are more efficient at handling domestic investments.

28. Such an agreement could require coordination of withholding tax rates with respect to third countries. Otherwise, the optimal Canadian withholding tax rates toward third countries would presumably be low, given the limits on its market power. As a result, third parties could then purchase U.S. equity through Canadian financial intermediaries, paying two rounds of low withholding tax rates as the funds traveled from the U.S. to Canada and then to the third country, rather than paying the higher U.S. withholding tax rate that applied to that third country.

whereas the treaty would jointly raise withholding tax rates when its objective is to stem tax evasion.

Corporate Taxation of Repatriated Earnings

Previously, I argued that source-based tax rates would be at or near zero in a Nash equilibrium. How do existing double-taxation conventions dealing with repatriated corporate earnings change the equilibrium behavior of the two governments? Let us ignore initially the effects of taxation at repatriation rather than at accrual and assume that all capital flows are direct investments by multinational corporations.

Under the provisions of the tax treaty, a source-based tax assessed just on foreign direct investment does not affect investment incentives as long as the source-based tax rate is below the corporate tax rate in the multinational's home country. Therefore, each country has the incentive to set its source-based corporate tax rate on foreign direct investment equal to the corporate tax rate prevailing in the other country.[29]

The incentives faced by the host country do not end here, however. Since a multinational pays the same tax rate regardless of the location of an investment, the before-tax rate of return on investments in the two countries would be equated. However, when one country acquires funds from the other country, it pays the net-of-tax rate of return on these funds, as a result of the source-based taxes. A small open economy would therefore want to equate the value of the marginal product of capital with this net-of-tax rate of return paid for funds acquired from abroad, or earned on funds invested abroad. In order to induce firms to equate the marginal product of capital with the net-of-tax cost of funds, the government could provide a suitable direct subsidy to new investment.[30] This subsidy produces the desired result as long as it is treated as extra income, rather than as a reduction in the creditable tax payment under the tax treaty.[31]

What are the incentives faced by the home country? As before, given the tax rate imposed in the host country, the home country would set its corporate tax rate either to zero or to some rate above the host country's tax rate. When its rate is below the host country's tax rate, the tax is simply a source-based tax and so is undesirable. When the rate is higher than the source country's tax rate, then the tax at the margin is a residence-based tax and so is potentially desirable. The fact that the host country receives some of the revenue makes the tax *more* attractive at the margin, since less is lost from any drop in investment due to a tax increase.

Given that multinationals are based in both countries, each country is both

---

29. I assume here that if the resulting tax rate on domestic investors is higher than is desired, then the government can rebate the excess through, for example, a dividend-credit scheme.

30. The appropriate subsidy rate would be $tf'/(1 - t)$, where t is the residence-based tax rate, and f' is the marginal product of capital.

31. For further discussion, see Findlay (1986).

a home country and a host country for some investment. A Nash equilibrium may or may not exist. If not, one country, the U.S. for example, could act as a Stackelberg leader. As before, the resulting equilibrium should provide higher welfare in each country than exists in the equilibrium without the double-taxation convention, in which capital income taxes are not used. Further gains from worldwide coordination exist, but not much can be accomplished on a bilateral basis.

How do the results change if we take into account that investments made through a foreign subsidiary are taxed only at repatriation rather than at accrual? As Jun (1987) shows, postponement of realization drives the effective tax rate on the initial equity investment down toward (and in the limit equal to) the tax rate in the host country, while Hartman (1985) argues that for investments financed by retained earnings, the effective tax rate is simply the host country tax rate. But if the effective tax rate is the host country tax rate, then a small open host country would not choose to impose such a tax.

What happens if capital flows to foreign firms can take the form of portfolio investments, rather than just direct investment by foreign subsidiaries? Funds can flow from the home country to the host country either by direct investment by a multinational, which itself is owned by home country individuals, or else by purchase of equity in host country firms by home country individuals. In either case, the same host country corporate taxes are paid, and home country individuals owe tax at the same rate on the net income they receive.[32] The key difference is that with direct investment by a multinational, supplementary taxes might be owed to the home country. If so, portfolio investment is preferred for tax reasons. If there are no nontax reasons favoring direct investment, then supplementary taxes would never be paid at repatriation, and a small open host country would therefore not impose a source-based tax.

Dividend-Credit Schemes

What incentives are created by the presence of the dividend-credit scheme in Canada? Most of the discussion of the effects of such a scheme assume a closed economy. But as Boadway and Bruce (1989) emphasize, the effects of the scheme are very different in an open economy. For simplicity, assume that the scheme provides full integration of the corporate and personal tax systems, and assume to begin with that the Canadian corporate tax rate is below the U.S. corporate rate.

When Canadian corporations invest in the U.S., they must pay U.S. corporate taxes on their foreign earnings. When the earnings are repatriated, no corporate surtax is due, but shareholders still receive a dividend credit based on the difference between their personal tax rate and the Canadian corporate tax rate. If the corporate tax rate exceeds the personal tax rate, then on net

---

32. This ignores the dividend-credit scheme available in Canada for income from domestic corporations. See below for further discussion.

Canada provides a subsidy for direct investment by Canadian multinationals in the U.S. and thereby raises the return to savings in Canada above the return available in the world market.[33] This subsidy is not available when Canadian individuals buy shares in U.S. corporations, so this scheme favors direct investment over portfolio investment.

How does its presence affect the equilibrium corporate tax rates? As a home country, when Canada raises its corporate tax rate it increases the subsidy it gives to investments by Canadian investors in the U.S., making it more likely that the optimal tax rate is zero rather than above the U.S. rate. As a host country, however, Canada would still wish to set its corporate tax rate equal to the U.S. rate. Therefore, on net Canada would more likely prefer a tax rate below the U.S. rate.

The U.S., as Stackelberg leader, would now have to take into account that Canada would more likely keep its corporate tax rate below that of the U.S. This would certainly affect the optimal tax rate in the U.S.

2.2 Tax Policy, Given Free Trade

Based on recent agreements, all tariffs and most nontariff barriers to trade between the U.S. and Canada will be eliminated by 1998. What implications will this policy change have for the domestic tax structure in each country?

Assume to begin with that each country is free to use tariffs, but that trade is not otherwise restricted. As noted above, Diamond and Mirrlees (1971) showed that a small open economy that imposes excise taxes on all goods would choose to produce efficiently under an optimal tax system. This implies that it would choose not to distort trade patterns. As emphasized in Gordon and Levinsohn (1990), however, this does not necessarily imply that a country would avoid use of tariffs. In particular, the effects of an excise tax on a particular good can be duplicated by a production tax and an import tariff or export subsidy on that good. It may be that it is easier to administer a combination of a tariff and a production tax, at equal rates, on some goods than to administer an excise tax on these goods. Both have the same economic effects, and neither distorts trade patterns.[34] To the degree that tax or other policies distort relative output prices, then optimal policy would involve undoing these distortions at the border through suitable export taxes and subsidies.

Of course, if a country does have market power in a particular good, then it

33. Specifically, under the dividend-credit scheme, shareholders receiving a dollar of dividends are credited with earning $1/(1 - T_c)$ in pre–corporate-tax profits, where T_c is the corporate tax rate. On this income, they owe personal taxes at rate t_c, but receive a credit for corporate taxes already paid, implying a net tax liability of $(t_c - T_c)/(1 - T_c)$. By assumption, $t_c < T_c$. If income Y is repatriated from foreign earnings and generates no corporate surtax at repatriation, then net tax payments in Canada on these earnings are $(t_c - T_c)/(1 - T_c)Y < 0$, implying a subsidy to foreign investment.

34. Trade distortions are present in this argument when the tax law favors purchases of goods produced in a particular location.

will want to take advantage of this market power, as shown in the optimal tariff literature. However, doing so does not require use of explicit tariffs, since again the combination of a production tax and a consumption subsidy has the same effects.

One of the main source-based taxes in the U.S. and Canada is the corporate income tax. This tax raises the prices of corporate relative to noncorporate goods, and alters relative corporate prices due to differences in capital-output ratios and due to idiosyncracies in depreciation and other detailed provisions in the tax law. Under optimal tariff policy in a small country, these distortions would be offset at the border.

Domestic regulations may also distort relative prices, creating the incentive to use tariffs to offset these distortions. For example, agricultural price supports lead food prices to be above marginal costs, justifying export subsidies on these products. Similarly, the U.S. lumber industry may face a below-market price for use of the National Forests, leading lumber prices to be below marginal costs and thereby justifying export taxes.

The Canadian sales tax also creates nontrivial distortions to the relative prices of imported and domestically produced goods, as reported in Dodge and Sargent (1987). Since the tax is imposed at the wholesale rather than the retail level, the amount of tax collected on a finished product depends on the number of transactions that occur between firms at the wholesale stage. To some degree, industries can change how they organize their production in order to minimize the total sales tax payments that are incurred, but doing so has its own costs.

What will be the implications for source-based taxes, and for regulatory distortions, of the free-trade agreement between the U.S. and Canada? This agreement will have no economic effect if each country can costlessly offset the change through a suitable modification to its domestic tax structure as it applies specifically to income flows between the two countries. To compensate for the drop in tariff or nontariff barriers for a particular good, each country could compensate by cutting the domestic tax (increasing the subsidy) on production of that good and increasing the sales tax rate on consumption of that good. To avoid any economic changes, tariffs between the U.S. or Canada and third countries would need to be suitably readjusted.

These compensating adjustments in the domestic tax system, to neutralize the effects of the free-trade agreement between the U.S. and Canada, are substantial and awkward. If they cannot be made, then source-based taxes on production will become more costly from each country's perspective, since the resulting distortions to the trade pattern between the U.S. and Canada could no longer be neutralized by suitable border distortions. Given the large volume of trade between the two countries, these distortions will be important, creating significant pressure to cut distortions to the relative prices of different goods to maintain an efficient composition of trade. Similarly, regulations that distort relative output prices become much more costly.

Various responses to these pressures are possible. For one, policy distortions to the relative prices of domestic output can be reduced by "leveling the playing field" by eliminating differences in the effective tax rates on different industries. If the tax system raises the prices of all domestically produced goods by the same percentage, then the exchange rate between the Canadian and the U.S. dollars would simply readjust, leaving trading incentives unchanged. Such a shift in the tax system in each country has been occurring recently in any case, whether or not connected to the U.S.-Canada free-trade agreement. To the extent that regulations create price distortions (e.g., various agricultural programs designed to raise crop prices artificially), then each country would face competitive pressure to redesign these regulations to "level the playing field" between affected sectors and other domestic industries.

From the perspective of the two countries together, however, as long as any particular industry is *equally* favored or disfavored by the tax and regulatory system in both countries, no policy distortion to trade patterns is created. In some cases, harmonizing the relative tax rates on different industries in the two countries may be easier or more desirable than allowing competitive pressures to undermine rate differences across industries, which each country might in principle have desired. Tariffs between the U.S. or Canada and third countries can then be used to neutralize these distortions.

Coordination between the two countries can also affect the size of tariff barriers with respect to the rest of the world. Together the two countries have more market power than either country has in isolation, particularly in goods such as lumber or wheat. Coordination would therefore lead to increased restrictions on their combined trade with the rest of the world.

Coordination of policies between the two countries, whether concerning policies with respect to each other or with respect to the rest of the world, does not require a written treaty. A country that deviates from an implicit agreement could incur "punishment" from the other country in some form. As long as the threat of "punishment" is a sufficient deterrent, the implicit agreement will be sustainable.[35] This use of threats to enforce an implicit agreement is commonly seen with regard to tariff policy, and may well occur with regard to tax policy as well.[36]

2.3 Tax Policy, Given Mobility of Individuals

So far, the discussion has ignored tax and expenditure pressures created by the movement of individuals across borders. Yet travel between the two countries is extensive, taking the form of tourism and business trips as well as

35. There is a large literature in cooperative game theory on the sustainability of such a cooperative outcome.
36. Since tariffs can be duplicated through use of a suitable set of domestic taxes, the two policy areas are not really distinct in any case.

changes in the location of employment or even of citizenship. The U.S.-Canada free-trade agreement reduces some restrictions on the movement of individuals across the border. What pressures are created by such movement of individuals?

This is in many ways the key question examined in the local public finance literature. As argued by Buchanan and Goetz (1972) and many others, mobility of individuals imposes externalities on jurisdictions, which depend on the degree to which an individual pays an amount in taxes that differs from the costs the individual imposes on the jurisdiction, whether in the form of increased costs of public services or increased congestion. This applies in both the sending and the receiving jurisdiction. When a community gains on net from the presence of an individual, because tax payments exceed the costs the individual imposes on the community, the community has an incentive to encourage immigration; the converse is also true. This competitive pressure pushes the tax system toward a benefit-tax structure in which the net gain to the jurisdiction from acquiring or losing an extra individual is competed down to zero. At that point, individuals simply pay for the costs they impose on the community.

What implications does this story have for tax policy at the national level? Consider first the pressures created by temporary migration, such as tourism. Through such migration, countries trade in services as well as in goods.[37] Therefore, tax and regulatory policies potentially can distort the relative trade in services versus goods, as well as distort the composition of trade in goods that physically cross the border. Countries would face competitive pressure to reduce or eliminate policy distortions to the composition of trade, which now includes services as well as "tradables."

When individuals cross the border, however, they also normally increase the costs of public services, since they make use of roads, police protection, and other services. A country would want to encourage immigration if tax payments exceed the net costs imposed by immigration, as well as the converse. By the Diamond-Mirrlees reasoning, a small open economy would simply charge for the services obtained, whether directly or indirectly, and so would design tax policy to increase the cost of goods used by migrants above the cost of goods that are physically exported. The playing field would be intentionally "tilted" to compensate for the costs imposed on the public sector when certain goods are purchased. Countries with relative market power in, for example, tourist-related services, would attempt to charge even more to take advantage of this market power.

Individuals who change their country of employment create more extensive changes in the tax revenue and public service costs in each country. Presumably, the relocation of higher-paid individuals creates larger relative gains, since their tax payments are relatively large compared to the cost of the public

37. Migration is not even needed for trade in financial services.

services they require. Similarly, each country has an incentive to discourage the immigration of those who impose net fiscal costs, be they the poor, the sick, or the elderly.

Competition for individuals who provide a net fiscal gain to the jurisdiction therefore reduces the degree to which the fiscal system redistributes from rich to poor and again pushes toward a benefit-tax system. But the resulting tax structure cannot simply equate benefits and tax payments in present value over the lifetime, since individuals can remain in the country during those periods when they gain on net, and leave when they lose on net. Therefore, even the *timing* of taxes would be pushed to coincide with the timing of benefits. As a result, national debt would be discouraged, since it creates the incentive to emigrate during those periods when the debt is repaid. Similarly, redistributive policies such as social security would come under pressure, since those who work for a short period under existing law gain substantially from the system. Since nonworkers do not pay labor income taxes but do make use of public services, and often more extensively than workers do, even labor income taxes may not easily be sustainable. A country that relies heavily on a labor income tax would become a haven for nonworkers, such as students or the retired. Public services such as subsidized college education or free medical care would attract residents of the other country who hope to take advantage of these subsidies.[38] All of these are examples of pressures towards a benefit-tax structure. Which tax system most resembles a benefit-tax structure depends on the composition of public expenditures. If consumption of public services roughly corresponds with consumption of private goods, then a consumption tax or a VAT may most closely approximate a benefit tax. User fees certainly approximate a benefit tax.[39]

This evolution towards a benefit-tax structure would occur even if both countries desired a redistributive fiscal policy. Based on this reasoning, the conventional wisdom in public finance has always been that redistribution should be done at the national rather than at the local level. Retranslated to this context, the analysis suggests that policies regarding redistribution should be coordinated between the two countries. Of course, coordination must cover *both* tax and expenditure policies, otherwise each country can make use of its remaining flexibility to attract those who pay more than they receive.

The Tiebout literature argues, however, that expenditures financed by benefit taxes should not need coordination; competition among jurisdictions pushes them to offer an efficient composition and level of public services.[40]

---

38. Of course, countries may impose residency requirements for these benefits, to some degree lessening the pressures.

39. The recent shift from a property tax to a head tax in financing public services in the United Kingdom could be interpreted as a response to this type of pressure.

40. Given that a VAT should roughly correspond to a benefit tax, at least relative to other taxes used at the national level, it is ironic that the EC has focused its tax coordination efforts on this particular tax. For discussion of various limitations of the Tiebout argument, see, for example, Stiglitz (1983).

How can jurisdictions choose the composition and level of services financed by benefit taxes without coordination, however, and yet agree to restrictions on their expenditure policies to prevent undermining of interjurisdictional agreements on redistribution? In a federal system, these contradictory pressures are avoided by having redistribution done at the national level. Competition among communities then leads to a local benefit-tax structure. In this case there is no fiscal gain to a community from attracting those who pay relatively more to the *national* government. Without a federal structure, however, coordination of at least some expenditure policies may be necessary to preserve redistributive policies, even though this coordination undermines the ability of each government to provide the composition or level of public expenditures desired by its citizenry.

At this point, these various pressures will be much more important within the EC, where all restrictions to migration are being eliminated, than in the U.S.-Canadian context. The pressures are still there, however, and will surely increase over time.

2.4 Conclusions

When analyzing the fiscal implications of unrestricted mobility among jurisdictions, the local public finance literature concludes that the fiscal system will be driven toward a benefit-tax structure, in which people pay in taxes an amount appropriate to cover the costs they impose on the public sector. Yet existing national tax systems in the U.S. and Canada differ substantially from benefit-tax structures. As a result, the increasing mobility of output, capital, and even labor, between the two economies will create a variety of pressures pushing the tax system towards a benefit-tax structure.

Where this pressure will be strongest depends on the degree of mobility of particular types of goods, services, and people across the border. This paper explored in turn the types of pressures created by mobility of capital, unrestricted trade in all outputs, and mobility of people.

Even though tax competition will push each country's fiscal structure toward that of a benefit tax, such a tax system may not be mutually advantageous; in fact, both countries may well gain through explicit or implicit coordination of fiscal policies. In many cases the appropriate form of coordination involves equalization of tax rates. Where, for example, the local public finance literature calls for the national government to handle redistribution, given the degree to which individual mobility undermines any one community's efforts at redistribution, the same logic calls here for coordinating redistributive policies between the two countries. A number of other examples of fruitful areas for policy coordination are discussed.

Ultimately, the implications of the increasing interdependence of the two economies for their national fiscal structures should be substantial. Fortunately, the two countries can watch the European experience after 1992 to learn better how to redesign the existing fiscal systems in the two countries.

References

Boadway, Robin, and Neil Bruce. 1989. Problems with Integrating Corporate and Personal Income Taxes in an Open Economy. Queen's University. Manuscript.

Bond, Eric W., and Larry Samuelson. 1989. Strategic Behavior and the Rules for International Taxation of Capital. *Economic Journal* 99 (398):1099–1111.

Buchanan, James, and C. Goetz. 1972. Efficiency Limits of Fiscal Mobility: An Assessment of the Tiebout Model. *Journal of Public Economics* 1 (1):25–43.

Diamond, Peter, and James Mirrlees. 1971. Optimal Taxation and Public Production: II—Tax Rules. *American Economic Review* 61, no. 3, pt. 1:261–78.

Dodge, David A., and John H. Sargent. 1987. Canada. In *World Tax Reform: A Progress Report,* ed. Joseph Pechman. Washington, D.C.: Brookings.

Findlay, Christopher. 1986. Optimal Taxation of International Income Flows. *Economic Record* 62 (June):208–14.

Giovannini, Alberto, and James R. Hines, Jr. 1990. Capital Flight and Tax Competition: Are There Viable Solutions to Both Problems? Columbia University. Manuscript (March).

Gordon, Roger H. 1992. Can Capital Income Taxes Survive in Open Economies? *Journal of Finance* 47(3).

———. 1988. Comment on "Tax Policy and International Competitiveness," by Lawrence H. Summers. In *International Aspects of Fiscal Policies,* ed. Jacob A. Frenkel. Chicago: University of Chicago Press.

———. 1986. Taxation of Investment and Savings in a World Economy. *American Economic Review* 76 (5):1086–1102.

———. 1983. An Optimal Taxation Approach to Fiscal Federalism. *Quarterly Journal of Economics* 98 (4):567–86.

Gordon, Roger H., and James Levinsohn. 1990. The Linkage Between Domestic Taxes and Border Taxes. In *Taxation in the Global Economy,* ed. Assaf Razin and Joel Slemrod. Chicago: University of Chicago Press.

Gordon, Roger H., and Joel Slemrod. 1988. Do We Collect any Revenue from Taxing Capital Income? In *Tax Policy and the Economy,* vol. 2, ed. Lawrence H. Summers, 89–130. Cambridge: MIT Press.

Gordon, Roger H., and Hal Varian. 1989. Taxation of Asset Income in the Presence of a World Securities Market. *Journal of International Economics* 26 (314):205–26.

Hartman, David. 1985. Tax Policy and Foreign Direct Investment. *Journal of Public Economics* 26:107–21.

Hines, James R., Jr., and R. Glenn Hubbard. 1990. Coming Home to America: Dividend Repatriation Decisions of U.S. Multinationals. In *Taxation in the Global Economy,* ed. Assaf Razin and Joel Slemrod, 161–200. Chicago: University of Chicago Press.

Jun, Joosung. 1987. Taxation, International Investment and Financing Sources. Yale University. Manuscript.

Mirrlees, James A. 1972. On Producer Taxation. *Review of Economic Studies* 39 (1), no. 117:105–11.

Slemrod, Joel. 1988. Effect of Taxation with International Capital Mobility. In *Uneasy*

Compromise: Problems of Hybrid Income-Consumption Tax, ed. Henry Aaron, Harvey Galper, and Joseph A. Pechman, 115–48. Washington, D.C.: Brookings.

Stiglitz, Joseph. 1985. The General Theory of Tax Avoidance. *National Tax Journal* 38 (3):325–37.

———. 1983. The Theory of Local Public Goods Twenty-five Years after Tiebout: A Perspective. In *Local Provision of Public Services: The Tiebout Model after Twenty-five Years.* New York: Academic Press.

Tiebout, Charles M. 1956. A Pure Theory of Local Expenditure. *Journal of Political Economy* 64 (5):416–24.

3   Income Security via the Tax System: Canadian and American Reforms

Jonathan R. Kesselman

3.1 Harmonization of Income Security?

Many aspects of Canadian economic policy, particularly in the taxation arena, can be viewed as imitating policy developments in the United States. Yet this has not been the case with respect to most income security policies in Canada, including those delivered through the tax system. Canadian and American income security policies have evolved in substantially different ways over the course of this century. There has been surprisingly little imitation beyond the implementation of unemployment insurance following the shared experience of the Great Depression. For example, the contributory Canada and Quebec Pension Plans were introduced only in 1966, more than thirty years after Social Security was implemented in the United States, and with quite different structures and goals. There are no Canadian counterparts to the American food stamp program or the earned-income tax credit. Not only has there been little imitation by Canada of U.S. income security policies, but there is also comparatively limited knowledge in the United States about Canadian developments. U.S. income security policy has drawn virtually nothing from the Canadian experience. Canadian demogrant programs of Family Allowance and Old Age Security, as well as several types of personal tax credits and benefit clawbacks, have no close parallels in the United States.

What accounts for the lack of harmonization of Canadian income security

Jonathan R. Kesselman is professor of economics at the University of British Columbia.

The author acknowledges with thanks the helpful discussions and comments on earlier drafts from Åke Blomqvist, Dennis Guest, Derek Hum, Tony Scott, John Shoven, John Whalley, and participants in the Canada-U.S. Tax Project. Elizabeth Wakerly provided skillful research assistance, and Sheila Kesselman gave expert editorial assistance. The author is solely responsible for all views and any remaining errors.

policies with those in the United States?[1] It contrasts strikingly with Canada's imitation of the United States in many other areas of economic policy, including personal and corporate taxation, deregulation of industry, and privatization of public services. One could cite fundamental cultural and historical differences, such as the stronger and more recent British and continental European ties of Canadians, both personal and intellectual. The two countries also differ in their constitutional allocation of responsibilities for the provision of income security within confederation. For example, the federal government in Canada has required constitutional amendments to pursue three of its major income security programs.[2] The United States, in contrast, has never been impeded by constitutional factors in its income security policies, though the income tax required an amendment. These varied factors are undoubtedly important. One might also consider that the economic pressures are less for Canada to conform to U.S. policies in the income security field than for other areas that are more directly affected by competitive forces.

3.1.1   Economic Reasons for Nonconvergence

It remains to be explained why there are no strong competitive pressures for Canada to imitate the income security policies of the larger neighboring U.S. economy. Such pressures might operate through any of three possible channels: 1) the tax burdens needed to finance income security and the associated pressures on business costs; 2) the incentives for international migration from a heavy tax burden and an attractive income security regime; and 3) the impact of income security provisions on the operations or costs of particular markets or industries. We shall examine each of these three possible channels of influence to see why they have not posed major constraints on Canadian income security policies.

First, there is the cost of financing income security programs and the resulting tax pressures on Canadian businesses competing with American firms in overlapping markets. The total cost of government is relevant here, not the cost of income security provisions alone. Canada has more budgetary leeway than the United States because of its lesser share of national income spent on defense. However, this surplus is more than consumed on a variety of uniquely Canadian concerns: the transport and communication costs of running a large, sparsely populated country, bilingualism and other cultural con-

---

1. For income security, the term "harmonization" could refer to either the total scale of such programs or their structure. Given the much larger relative size of unemployment insurance and public health insurance in Canada than the U.S., it is clear that income security has not been harmonized in the sense of total scale. The present study focuses on the structure of income security, and it is found that neither the expenditure programs nor the tax-based provisions of the two countries have been harmonized.

2. The affected programs were unemployment insurance, Old Age Security, and the Canada Pension Plan. These constitutional barriers arose because the programs were contributory-financed (OAS was initially financed by earmarked taxes). The federal government is much less constrained in providing income security through general-revenue financed programs, provisions in the tax system, and federal cost-sharing of provincial programs. See Blomqvist (1985).

cerns, and regional objectives. Health care and hospitals are almost fully in the public sector in Canada, but this also relieves businesses from the cost of providing private medical insurance.[3] Canada has less extensive urban poverty than the United States and enjoys greater equality in the pretax, pretransfer distribution of incomes.[4] Hence Canada has less need for income security provisions, even if Canadian social values might tend to promote more adequate income security. A country can pursue more ambitious distributional or other social goals through programs financed by taxes that reduce real net incomes, rather than inflate export costs. Even if some of the incremental tax burden were to fall upon export costs, flexibility of exchange rates should compensate for any competitive disadvantages.

Second, there is the possible flow of migrants into Canada, from the United States or elsewhere, if income security becomes relatively attractive on the Canadian side of the border. Similarly, Canadian workers or business people may wish to emigrate if they feel their tax burdens have become excessive. Migration flows have been a concern—regardless of whether objectively warranted—in the setting of Canadian personal income tax rates, or for that matter all taxes impinging upon real after-tax incomes of Canadian workers. Because of immigration barriers in each country, the most relevant workers are highly skilled, highly paid workers such as physicians and other professionals, star athletes and public performers, and business entrepreneurs and upper managers. These groups might be induced to migrate based on relative tax burdens but are irrelevant for most income security issues. Even the Canada-U.S. free-trade agreement has eased mobility barriers for only a select list of professions and occupations. The primary beneficiaries of most income security programs—the elderly and poorly paid, low-skilled persons—simply do not qualify under the general classification for immigration to Canada. Under the sponsored family-reunification classification, many such lesser-skilled persons may be admitted, but they are restricted from obtaining welfare payments by the required sponsor's guarantee of financial support.[5] As a result of these institutional factors, any migration-based pressures for harmonization of the general levels of income security between Canada and the United States have been quite limited to date.[6]

Third, there are the possible effects of income security programs or similar

3. This issue came up in the context of the free-trade debate of 1988, where critics claimed that free trade would place extreme pressure on Canada to abandon universal health coverage. Yet the total percentage of GDP devoted to health care costs is less for Canada than for the United States.

4. For Canadian figures see Vaillancourt (1985a); for comparative Canadian-American analysis, see Hanratty and Blank (1992).

5. They are excluded from Social Assistance for a period of years, but they may still qualify for unemployment insurance after sufficient employment and for health insurance coverage after minimal residence requirements set by the provinces.

6. Hum (1988) and Boadway and Bruce (ch. 1 in this volume) agree with this general assessment. See Sinn (1990) and Gordon (ch. 2 in this volume) for an analysis of how perfect international mobility of labor could undermine the ability of any country to pursue independent redistributive policies.

tax provisions upon economic behavior related to international competitiveness. Some income security provisions might have an impact upon particular markets or industries in Canada in ways that either handicap them or favor them in their competition with businesses on the other side of the border. They may handicap an industry by reducing the supply of workers through relatively generous levels or terms of benefits. Or they may favor the industry by tying benefits to working in the industry, even if only sporadically or seasonally, such as the Canadian unemployment insurance provisions with respect to the fishing and forestry industries. Competitive pressures will tend to inhibit Canadian policy from pursuing the former types of policies too far. Political pressures, including GATT-based and free-trade-related litigation, may be invoked when Canada pursues the latter types of policies to extremes. These industry-specific provisions of income security are most commonly contained in unemployment insurance, workers' compensation, training subsidies, and regionally directed grants to business, rather than in the income security provisions of the personal tax system.

It appears that the pressures for future harmonization of Canadian and American income security are limited primarily to areas affecting specific markets or industries.[7] Canadian policies are more likely to be constrained in this respect than are American policies. This follows both because of the relative scale of the two countries' markets and the greater power of the United States in situations of policy conflict. The most relevant programs are regional or industry-oriented provisions of unemployment insurance and possibly training offered in conjunction with income security. It could also apply to direct or subsidized employment programs having a particular impact on specific markets or industries, although these are not a significant part of the current policy landscape. Harmonization pressures are much less likely to arise with respect to tax-based provisions, such as those aimed at relieving or supplementing low incomes or differentiating tax burdens by family size. Our study proceeds with a comparative description and analysis of income security in the two countries, with a special emphasis on provisions embodied in their tax systems. Perhaps greater familiarity will encourage policy makers in each country to adopt those elements of the other country's income security system that are effective and would make sense in the home-country setting.

3.1.2   Organization of the Study

Our study first reviews the basic features of income security provided independently of the tax system, income security provisions of the personal tax system, and the interface between the tax system and independent transfer provisions. Sections 3.2 and 3.3 provide a broad-brush account of these institutions for Canada and for the United States, with more detailed treatment of selected areas reserved for the later analysis. The main part of the study as-

---

7. See Hum (1988) for an earlier expression of this conclusion.

sesses and compares the income security features embodied in the two countries' personal tax systems. At lower incomes, our major interest is the adequacy of benefits and their incentive effects. Tax-relieving provisions are also relevant at lower incomes. At middle and higher incomes, our major interest lies in horizontal equity and incentive effects. Particular attention is given to provisions relating to family size and characteristics such as age, disability, and marital and dependency status. In addition to the labor market incentives that are paramount for the working poor, our analyses also touch on other incentives: aggregate savings and composition; notches and poverty traps; reporting of income and evasion; timing and bunching of income; and family formation and disintegration.

The analyses are organized in terms of the structural design issues facing income security provisions. Since our central focus is on income security delivered via the tax system, we follow the main features used to design a personal tax. Section 3.4 examines the choice and definition of the tax and transfer unit. In section 3.5 we assess the appropriate tax and transfer base, that is, the measure of ability to pay taxes and need for transfers. Section 3.6 investigates important timing issues, such as payment frequency and responsiveness, and their implications for horizontal equity. Section 3.7 is an assessment of the effective marginal tax rates implied by various income security provisions in the tax system. Section 3.8 considers program simplicity and possible reasons for the undue overlap and complexity of existing income security and taxation provisions. In section 3.9 we speculate about the future evolution of income security systems in Canada and the United States and the potential role for tax provisions. We consider further the outlook for future harmonization of income security across the two countries.

3.2   The Canadian Income Security System[8]

Income security in Canada consists of general cash transfer programs, in-kind provisions and subsidies, personal tax provisions, features of other taxes, and the finance of social insurance. These various types of provisions have numerous linkages, often through their treatment in the personal tax system. We will review the primary provisions, lumping social insurance benefits under the category of general cash transfers. Some important cash transfers, such as the demogrants, will be discussed under the personal tax heading, where they can be treated under the categories of "children" and "the elderly." Only the most general descriptions are offered in this section; more detailed, but selective, analyses of particular provisions are provided in sections 3.4 through 3.8. Overview descriptions of the comparable U.S. income security provisions are provided in section 3.3. A summary of the key income security programs and related tax provisions for both countries appears in table 3.1.

---

8. This section draws on CCH Canadian Limited (misc. years), Canadian Tax Foundation (misc. years), and government documents describing taxation and income security programs.

Table 3.1   Summary of Key Income Security Programs and Tax Provisions, 1990

Program or Provision	Canada	United States
General Cash Transfers		
Income-tested	Social Assistance (SA)—categorical; provincial programs with federal cost-sharing Guaranteed Income Supplement (GIS), Spouse's Allowance—for elderly; federal; some provinces supplement	Aid to Families with Dependent Children (AFDC), Public Assistance—categorical; state programs with federal cost-sharing Supplemental Security Income (SSI)—for elderly and disabled; federal; most states supplement
Demogrants	Family Allowances (FA), Old Age Security (OAS)	None
In-kind Transfers		
Health Care	Public medical and hospitalization insurance; universal comprehensive coverage; provincial with federal block cost-sharing	Medicare—for elderly and some disabled, limited coverage, federal. Medicaid—for the poor; state with federal sharing
Housing	Limited provision of subsidized public housing, tax credits for low-income renters, provincial and municipal	Subsidized public housing, tax incentives for private construction of low-income housing
Food	None	Food Stamps—income-tested subsidies
Child Care	Limited provision of income-tested subsidies	Limited provision of income-tested subsidies
Personal Income Tax		
Filing Basis for Couples	Individual, except that very low-income spouse is included on taxpaying spouse's return	Joint return for married couples; income fully aggregated, wider tax brackets for couples
Allowance for Filer	Nonrefundable tax credit	Personal exemption, phased out at very high incomes; also a standard deduction for filers who do not itemize their deductions
Dependent Spouse	Nonrefundable tax credit, offset by part of spouse's income; income attribution rule to deter income-splitting	Personal exemptions, phased out at very high incomes
Dependent Children	Nonrefundable tax credits	Personal exemptions, phased out at very high incomes
	Equivalent-to-married tax credits for single parents	Head-of-household tax filing status for single parents
	Tax deductibility of child-care costs	Income-related tax credits for child care costs
	Income attribution rule to deter income-splitting	Some attribution of child's income to parent's tax return (kiddie tax)
Elderly Status	Nonrefundable tax credit	Increment to the standard deduction

Table 3.1   (continued)

Program or Provision	Canada	United States
	Tax credit for $1,000 of private pension income	Nonrefundable tax credit for those with little Social Security benefits
	Registered Retirement Savings Plans and Registered Pension Plans—to tax-shelter savings for retirement	Individual Retirement Accounts—and employer-based pension plans to tax-shelter savings
Disabled Status	Nonrefundable tax credit and deduction for expense of part-time attendant needed in order to work	Increment to the standard deduction for blindness
	Tax credit for medical expense above threshold	Itemized deductions for medical expense above threshold
Refundable Credits	Refundable child tax credits and refundable sales tax credits, both income-tested	Earned-income tax credits—based on earned income and presence of child in tax unit
	Low-income, property-tax, renters, or cost-of-living tax credits, some provinces	Sales tax credits, some states
Taxability of Transfers	Taxable: FA, OAS, CPP/QPP, unemployment insurance (UI)	Taxable Social Security (half-taxable above lower-middle-income levels), UI
	Nontaxable: SA, GIS, workers' compensation, in-kind benefits	Nontaxable: AFDC, public assistance, SSI, workers' compensation, in-kind benefits
Clawback of Benefits	FA and OAS clawback above middle incomes	None
	UI partially clawed back above middle incomes	
Other Taxes		
Property Taxes	Provincial homeowners' grant or seniors' grant	State "circuit-breaker" tax reliefs
Social Insurance and Finance		
Unemployment Insurance	National program, comprehensive coverage, no experience rating; employer and employee premiums; tax credits for employee premiums	State programs, limited coverage, experience rating; entirely financed by employer premiums
Workers' Compensation	Provincial public programs, limited experience rating	State and private provision, experience rating
Retirement	Canada and Quebec Pension Plans (CPP/QPP)—retirement benefits modest, supplemented by OAS and GIS; benefits closely linked to individual's lifetime contributions; no earnings test on beneficiaries; tax credits for employee premiums	Old Age, Survivors, and Disability Insurance (OASDI) provisions of Social Security—substantial redistributive tilt to the relation between an individual's benefits and lifetime contributions; earnings test on beneficiaries

3.2.1   General Cash Transfers

Welfare payments are delivered by the individual provinces under programs of "social assistance" (SA). There are significant interprovincial variations in the eligibility requirements for social assistance, as well as the benefit levels. Some provinces, such as those in the Atlantic region, severely restrict access to benefits by single persons without dependents. Others, including Quebec, offer much lower benefit rates for young singles. However, national legislation provides for federal cost-sharing of SA programs (and related services) and also limits provincial discrimination against nonresidents and the use of waiting periods for benefits.[9] Benefits are not taxable under the personal tax due to special relieving provisions but are almost always below the levels at which income would be taxable in any event. Asset tests as well as income tests are typically applied to claimants and beneficiaries. Most provinces will disregard modest amounts of earnings but will otherwise reduce SA benefits dollar-for-dollar with increased earnings.

The most common reasons for persons receiving SA are: unemployment, if jobless benefits are low or exhausted; single parenthood or inadequate income relative to family size; and various forms of disability. Persons with disabilities may also qualify for benefits under two social insurance programs not subject to asset tests. Every province offers a program of worker's compensation for injuries incurred on the work site. These plans are financed by employer contributions, and the benefits are not taxable due to special relieving provisions. There are also limited benefits for disability under the Canada Pension Plan (CPP) and the Quebec Pension Plan (QPP), which are primarily earnings-linked contributory public pension schemes. Some of the elderly also receive supplements to their receipts from federal programs under adjuncts to the SA programs in several provinces.

Unemployment insurance is the single largest income security program in Canada. Its expenditures account for 1.7 percent of the country's GDP even in periods of high employment. The program is national in scope, but contains eligibility and benefit duration provisions that are regionally graduated. Coverage of the program is nearly universal, except for the self-employed and persons working very short hours. After a two-week jobless period, insured claimants who have worked sufficient weeks over the previous year receive weekly benefits equal to 60 percent of their average insured earnings. The maximum level of insurable earnings is somewhat above the average full-time industrial wage. Benefits are fully taxable and subject to partial clawback at higher incomes. The duration of benefits can range up to fifty weeks and hinges upon the claimant's period of insured employment and the unemploy-

---

9. From the inception of the Canada Assistance Plan in 1966, costs of most SA benefits and social services have been 50 percent shared by the federal government. The 1990 federal budget imposes spending restraints on CAP that may affect the sharing of costs for the three wealthier provinces. See Hum (1983) for analysis of CAP.

ment rate in the region. The UI program also encompasses benefits for sickness and maternity, as well as some work-sharing and training provisions.

3.2.2   In-kind Provisions and Subsidies

The primary forms of in-kind provision for lower-income Canadians are public insurance for hospitalization and most health care expenses; these services are in fact provided to all Canadians, irrespective of income. They are delivered by the provinces and partially financed by block transfers from the federal government. Federal legislation prevents the provinces from imposing user charges or coinsurance rates on users. Coverage under these schemes is virtually universal across the population. Only the two westernmost provinces still charge premiums for participation in their medical-care insurance schemes; Ontario abandoned such charges just in 1990 and replaced them with a payroll tax. Persons receiving SA obtain a waiver from paying premiums, and almost no one is denied service even if uninsured. The financial pressures of such an open-ended arrangement have forced provinces to limit the range of covered services and have led to significant waiting periods for some medical and surgical procedures. Many provinces also reimburse a portion of prescription drug costs above a threshold; most provinces reduce or waive the deductible for SA recipients and the elderly.

Outside of health care, Canadian in-kind public provisions and subsidies are less extensive than in the United States.[10] Public supply of housing and child care is quite limited, even for low-income families. There is somewhat greater reliance on private nonprofit groups to supply day care, and on cooperative societies and subsidized private builders to supply low-income housing. SA recipients may receive additional benefits or subsidies to help pay unusually high rental costs or to cover day care costs to facilitate their employment. Many provinces will also provide discretionary amounts under Social Assistance for special needs such as children's winter clothing. Some provinces provide income-tested subsidies for day care expenses to persons who are not SA beneficiaries. Nonprofit day care centers may receive capital grants or other provincial funding. Several provinces provide income-tested tax credits to renters as part of the personal income tax. As previously noted, Canada has no food stamp program, although volunteer-run food banks have grown in recent years.

3.2.3   Personal Tax Provisions

The Canadian personal income tax is imposed at both the federal and provincial levels, with nine of the ten provinces piggybacking their taxes onto the

---

10. This study does not examine public education or higher education, despite their obvious links with poverty and income security. Public education in Canada is more uniform in quality across low- and high-income neighborhoods and municipalities than public education in the U.S., on account of extensive provincial financing. College and university tuitions are significantly lower in Canada than in most of the United States, although attendance is more limited and probably more biased toward students with higher class origins than in the U.S.

federal tax; only Quebec imposes its provincial income tax separately. The individual is the basic unit for taxation in all jurisdictions, with adaptations to include in a tax filer's return the low earnings of a dependent spouse and children. Spouses and children whose incomes exceed modest levels are accountable for their own personal tax returns. Canada has pioneered many types of tax credits that serve income security objectives for the poor and horizontal equity goals for the broader taxpaying population. The 1987 tax reforms further extended the use of nonrefundable tax credits to replace personal exemptions and many items that were formerly deductible (see Cloutier and Fortin 1989). Because provinces apply their taxes at 47 to 62 percent of the taxpayer's basic federal tax, the total value of the nonrefundable credits is correspondingly magnified.[11] Our review of these provisions and related income transfer programs is classified by four demographic groups—nonaged adults, children, the elderly, and the disabled.

Nonaged Adults

Every person who files a tax return in Canada can claim a nonrefundable tax credit. These personal tax credits replaced personal exemptions in the country's major tax reforms of 1987, which first became effective with the 1988 tax year.[12] A nonrefundable credit for the filer can be made equivalent to a personal exemption through appropriate adjustments to the income-break points for the progressive tax rate schedule. The Canadian reforms made the conversion from exemptions to credits more valuable for low-income tax filers and less valuable for high-income filers. The nonrefundable credits for filers also replaced a deduction intended to cover employment expenses. Hence, the credits now are the sole tax-relieving device for low-income filers in Canada; there is no standard deduction or other such provision. In 1988 the basic filer's tax credit was set at $1,020; the basic tax exemption for a filer would have been about $4,270 if the previous system had been continued. (All amounts for Canadian tax and spending provisions in this study are given in Canadian dollars; all amounts for U.S. provisions are in U.S. dollars.) The levels of the two provisions are not directly comparable because the federal tax rate schedule was also collapsed from ten brackets to three—17, 26, and 29 percent. Still, the taxable income threshold was increased by the reforms. Tax credits and boundaries on the rate brackets are indexed annually for inflation, to the extent that it exceeds 3 percent.

---

11. Basic federal tax is an amount prior to reduction by the *refundable* federal credits. Hence, the refundable federal credits do not assume additional value with provincial taxation.

12. In the tax years from 1965 through 1985, Canada also had a wide variety of nonrefundable tax credits provided as "general tax reduction." These were usually a stated percentage of federal tax otherwise payable, with a minimum and/or maximum amount of credit; in some years there was a flat amount per filer and spouse, and in 1977 and 1978 an amount per child was added. See Kesselman (1979) for analysis of these credits and the refundable child tax credits.

Married persons with relatively low incomes are claimed on their spouses' return but must file separate returns if they have a taxable level of income. The filing spouse can claim a marital tax credit, which is a maximum amount ($850 in 1988) reduced by a portion (17 percent) of the dependent spouse's income above a disregard level. This marital credit phases out to zero at an income at which the dependent spouse must file a separate return. A single parent can also claim an "equivalent to married" credit on behalf of the first child. Many deductible or creditable expenses in the income tax can be transferred to a spouse or supporting parent when the spouse or child is unable to claim the full amount on account of insufficient taxable income. Hence, there is a limited degree of income-splitting for low-earning spouses and children, in a variety of circumstances. However, there are extensive income attribution rules to inhibit the splitting of investment incomes for tax purposes through intrafamilial transfers of assets.

Refundable sales tax credits are offered to offset a portion of the federal manufacturers' sales tax, which enters the prices of many consumer goods. These credits predated the 1988 reforms by several years. They can be claimed by lower-income tax filers, or a short tax return can be filed by nontaxable persons to claim their credits. The RSTC is specified as a given amount per adult plus a given amount per child in the household; this maximum total is reduced by 5 percent of the couple's combined net income exceeding a threshold ($18,000 in 1990). The maximum will be enriched and the phaseout threshold greatly increased in 1991, when the credits will be renamed the Goods and Services Tax (GST) credits. The goal is to offset the increased federal sales tax burdens at lower incomes when the tax is converted to a value-added tax format. Indexation for inflation above 3 percent annually will be applied to the credit amounts and phaseout threshold.

Dependent Children

The Canadian tax and transfer treatment of dependent children is a web of overlapping and interacting provisions. First are the nonrefundable child tax credits for children, claimable by a supporting parent and reduced by a portion of a child's income above a disregard level. The credits assume different values for the first two children under 19, other children under 19, and infirm dependents 18 and older. These credits replaced tax exemptions for dependent children in the 1988 tax year. Second are the child credits within the RSTC, which will be enlarged with their replacement by refundable GST credits in 1991. Third are the refundable child tax credits (RCTC), which were introduced in 1978 and formed the model for the later RSTCs. Fourth are the Family Allowance demogrants, monthly payments of about $33 for each child, irrespective of family income. The FA payments have been taxable to the higher-income parent for many years. Beginning in the 1989 tax year and fully implemented by the 1991 tax year, FA payments are further subject to complete clawback as either parent's income rises above $50,000. There are also tax deductions for child care expenses of working parents and a recently introduced small tax credit for minding one's own child at home.[13]

Quebec uses both tax and spending powers to operate the continent's only pronatal policy. This reflects the province's desire to maintain its Francophone population in the face of low birth rates. Following the national tax reforms, Quebec converted from personal exemptions to nonrefundable personal credits in reforming its own tax in 1988. However, in Quebec the credit per child is nearly 40 percent of the filer credit, whereas federally the child credit is only 6 to 13 percent of the filer amount. Quebec provides provincial family allowances in addition to the federal payments, and it gears these payments to favor larger families. The province further supplements its family allowances with "availability allowances" paid to families with children under age six; these increase sharply with the family's number of children of all ages. Quebec also provides lump payments, in installments, for newborn children. In late 1989 these were $500 for the first child in a family, $1,000 for the second child, and $4,500 for the third and each subsequent child. None of these provincial payments is taxable or subject to clawback.

The Elderly

The elderly also face a combination of tax and transfer provisions aimed at income security. First is the nonrefundable tax credit for persons aged 65 and over, which replaced a comparable tax deduction for age. This amount ($550 in 1988) is in addition to the basic filer's credit and can also be claimed for an elderly spouse. Second is the federal demogrant program of Old Age Security, which makes payments to all elderly Canadians who have met a minimal residence requirement. Monthly benefit levels in 1990 are over $340 per elderly person. OAS payments are taxable and have further become subject to clawback, beginning in 1989, for recipients with incomes above $50,000. Third is the federal Guaranteed Income Supplement, which acts like a guaranteed income for the elderly. Maximum monthly benefits are over $400 per single person and $520 per couple; payments are reduced by 50 percent of the recipient's other income (excluding OAS). Fourth, many provinces supplement GIS payments for very low income seniors, and their phaseout rates can increase the total effective marginal tax rate to 75 or 100 percent, depending upon how they are combined with the GIS benefit reduction rate.

Other tax and social insurance provisions are aimed at savings for retirement. The first $1,000 of a taxpayer's annual pension income from private sources obtains a credit at the bottom-bracket rate; prior to the 1988 tax year there was a deduction instead. Consumption tax treatment is given to specified

---

13. Child care expenses are deductible against earned income of the lower-income parent in the federal and most provincial income taxes; in the Quebec income tax, they can be deducted by the higher-income parent.

amounts of savings through employers (Registered Pension Plans) and through private trusteed accounts (Registered Retirement Savings Plans). Reforms originally announced in 1986 and now being implemented will provide a more balanced treatment of permitted amounts of savings through these two vehicles, as well as between defined-benefit and money-purchase pension plans. Tax deferral will be allowed on 18 percent of a taxpayer's earned income up to an annual limit of $15,500 of savings in 1995, which will be indexed for subsequent growth of average wages. The Canada and Quebec Pension Plans are mandatory contributory public pension schemes. CPP/QPP benefits are roughly proportional to the contributor's lifetime contributions. Benefits are paid without any earnings test but are fully taxable. The schemes are partially funded, with most assets in the form of loans to the provinces.

The Disabled

In addition to the Social Assistance payable to most unemployable disabled persons, there are also tax provisions to relieve the position of the taxable disabled. An additional tax exemption amount was converted to an additional credit of $550 for disability in 1988. The definition of disability for this credit has been broadened from a narrowly prescriptive one (blindness or confinement to a wheelchair or bed) to a much broader functional one ("markedly restricted in activities of daily living"). Disability must be certified by the claimant's physician. Disability credits are nonrefundable but can be transferred to the tax return of the disabled person's spouse or supporting parent. Medical expenses exceeding 3 percent of the taxpayer's net income can be claimed for a nonrefundable credit computed at the bottom-bracket rate; this provision replaced the former tax deduction for such expenses. The medical expense credit is available to all taxpayers and can be claimed by the lower-income spouse with respect to the entire family's medical expenses. In 1989 the working disabled were granted a deduction of up to $5,000 for the expenses of a part-time attendant required to enable an individual to work.

3.2.4   Other Taxes and Social Insurance Finance

Some of the provinces offer tax relief for persons at lower incomes through income-conditioned credits to offset sales taxes, property taxes, or the presumed property tax component of residential rents. Others offer grants to offset part of the property tax, in some cases with an additional amount for elderly homeowners. Many U.S. states provide similar "circuit-breaker" relief of property taxes to elderly or poor homeowners through refundable income tax credits. The provincial share of financing for hospitals and medical care comes out of general revenues, but several provinces have imposed payroll taxes on employers earmarked for health spending. Provincial programs of workers' compensation are financed by levies on employers; some provinces apply different rates by industry or even a limited form of experience rating by firm. Several provinces also relieve individuals from paying any income tax at a somewhat higher level of income than the tax threshold for the federal personal tax. Quebec parallels many of the nonrefundable credits from the federal income tax in its provincial tax.

The federal social insurance programs are almost fully premium-financed. Although the UI program had substantial general-revenue financing in the early 1970s, this was reduced in the later 1970s and eliminated in 1991. Employer premiums are 1.4 times employee premiums; both are based on insurable earnings up to a ceiling that somewhat exceeds the average full-time industrial wage. Finance of the Canadian UI program utilizes no experience rating, although the idea has periodically been entertained (see Kesselman 1983; Cousineau 1985). The Canada Pension Plan is financed by premiums applied equally to employers and employees. In 1990 the rates were 2.2 percent for each party on annual earnings between an exempt level of $2,800 and a ceiling of $28,900. Premium rates are scheduled to rise steadily over the next generation to maintain the program's financial viability. Still, the overall Canadian income security system for the elderly relies much more heavily than the U.S. system on general-revenue financed programs, such as OAS and GIS. This balance tilts the Canadian system sharply toward a pay-as-you-go basis, despite the partial degree of funding of the CPP/QPP programs.

Although receipts of UI and CPP benefits are taxable, benefits from workers' compensation programs are not. For UI recipients whose annual income exceeds 1.5 times the program's maximum annual insurable earnings, benefits are subject to a clawback of up to 30 percent through a provision in the income tax. This provision predates the clawbacks recently imposed on FA and OAS receipts at higher incomes. The employee's UI and CPP premiums receive nonrefundable credits at the bottom-bracket tax rate. Prior to the 1988 tax year they were deductible in the personal income tax. Employers' shares of these premiums are fully deductible from personal and corporate income taxes.

3.3   The U.S. Income Security System[14]

3.3.1   General Cash Transfers

The individual states provide welfare payments under programs of public assistance, particularly for families with dependent children. Federal rules establish the general requirements for eligibility under Aid to Families with Dependent Children, including income and asset tests and prohibition of residence requirements for citizens. The federal government matches state welfare costs, with the federal share inversely related to a state's financial resources. As in Canada, there are significant interjurisdictional variations in the benefit levels. Most welfare recipients are also eligible for Medicaid, food

14. This section draws on Commerce Clearing House, Inc. (misc. years), U.S. Advisory Commission on Intergovernmental Relations (1990), Rejda (1988), MacDonald (1977), and government documents describing taxation and income security programs.

stamp, and social service benefits; where locally available, public housing, energy assistance payments, and reduced-price or free school lunches may also be obtained. The states typically impose work requirements on employable beneficiaries, ranging from work tests to subsidized employment to community service. For an initial period, a beneficiary may keep $30 plus one third of monthly earnings; after that period, any earnings reduce benefits dollar-for-dollar.

Disability and old age are other conditions that the states cover in their income security provisions. Every state has a workers' compensation law for employment-related injuries. Unlike the monopoly operation of workers' compensation by the Canadian provinces, most states allow employers to purchase policies from a private insurer or to self-insure. Some states also allow the purchase of insurance from a competitive state fund, and a few make coverage elective for firms. Most of the states provide income-tested benefits to supplement federal programs for impoverished elderly and disabled persons. Social Security has two major cash benefits: the earnings-related Old-Age, Survivors, and Disability Insurance program, and the income-tested Supplemental Security Income program. These federal programs are reviewed later in this section, along with relevant taxation provisions for the elderly and disabled.

Unemployment insurance is delivered as a series of state programs with partial financing through federal tax rebates to the states against a federal payroll tax on employers. Receipt of these rebates by a state is contingent upon meeting certain federal minimum standards and the use of experience rating in the UI payroll taxes imposed on individual firms. The states use several experience-rating methods, most of which set upper and lower bounds on the rates paid by any firm, regardless of how high or low its layoff rate has been. During some years the federal government has also enacted special programs to extend the period of regular unemployment benefits, based on high unemployment. Few states require any employee contributions. Coverages of the state plans are typically less comprehensive than the Canadian scheme. Average benefit rates are somewhat lower, as are benefit durations, and most states will completely deny benefits to workers who have voluntarily left their jobs. Total expenditures on UI in the United States account for just 0.3 percent of GDP, less than one-fifth of the corresponding figure for Canada.

3.3.2 In-kind Provisions and Subsidies

Limited health care insurance is provided to the aged, disabled, and poor under two governmental programs. The federal Medicare program covers all of the elderly and the disabled who have drawn long-term Social Security benefits. It provides partial insurance for inpatient hospital care and limited home health-care services; it also offers a voluntary, supplementary medical insurance plan for doctors' services and outpatient care. None of these benefits is income tested, but there are various deductibles and coinsurance charges. The supplementary plan has monthly charges for participation. Medicaid is a series of state programs with federal cost-sharing inversely related to a state's per capita income. It covers most of the health care costs of welfare recipients and of most persons drawing income-tested benefits under the federal Supplemental Security Income program for the aged and disabled. States may also extend coverage to medically needy persons who are not beneficiaries of welfare or SSI.

Although general welfare benefits are quite low in many states, they are usually supplemented by access to several in-kind benefits and subsidies. In addition to the cited health care benefits for the poor, these include food stamps, public housing, child care subsidies, energy assistance, and free or reduced-price school lunches. All these benefits are provided on an income-tested basis; often the person must be eligible for welfare to obtain the other benefits. The linkage of benefits and sequencing of income tests can create very high cumulative effective marginal tax rates, or what has been called the "poverty trap." None of these benefits nor the public health care benefits constitute taxable income, as they are already income-tested. Note, however, that most welfare recipients do not receive all of these in-kind benefits. Some are not available in every state or locale; and some, such as public housing, may be rationed by waiting lists as well as income tests. Many persons who do not qualify for welfare are still eligible for food stamps.

3.3.3 Personal Tax Provisions

The 1986 Tax Reform Act constituted a major rewriting of the U.S. code for personal income taxation. Some of its provisions were first operative in the 1987 tax year, with others phased in over several years. Forty states also impose broad-based personal income taxes that they administer themselves. Many state tax provisions are linked to the federal tax concepts and therefore were automatically recast with the federal reforms. Other states have explicitly redrafted their laws to conform with the broadened taxable base in the federal tax. Several state income taxes use nonrefundable credits instead of personal exemptions. The federal tax collapsed its rate structure to two positive rates of 15 and 28 percent; there is also a 5 percent surtax at upper-income levels.[15] While the federal reforms were primarily aimed at broadening the taxable base to facilitate the rate reductions, a number of the changes have an impact upon income security and horizontal equity. We will review these changes for the same four demographic groups as we did for the Canadian tax reforms. Income transfer programs aimed at the elderly and disabled are also covered.

15. In 1989, only a few states had top marginal tax rates as high as 10–12 percent. Because state income taxes are an itemized deduction in computing an individual's federal tax, only a handful of people faced total federal-state marginal rates exceeding 40 percent.

Nonaged Adults

Personal exemptions are allowed for each tax filer, spouse of the filer, and dependent child.[16] The reforms raised the amount of the per capita exemption from $1,080 in 1986 to $1,900 in 1987, with phased increases to $1,950 in 1988, $2,000 in 1989, and indexation to consumer prices for later years (yielding $2,050 in 1990). A 5 percent surtax is imposed above specified income levels to tax back first the benefits of the 15 percent rate bracket and then the benefits of personal exemptions. This surtax creates an additional effective rate bracket, of 33 percent, in the middle of the 28 percent bracket.[17] The tax further allows a standard deduction for filers who choose not to claim itemized tax deductions for allowable expenses. For the 1990 tax year, the standard deductions were $3,250 for single filers, $5,450 for married couples filing jointly ($2,725 if filing separately), and $4,750 for household heads. The standard deductions are a vital element in setting the minimum taxable threshold at lower incomes.

Four distinct rate schedules apply to the following groups: single persons, married persons filing jointly, married persons filing separately, and heads of households. After the 1986 reforms, all filers face the same rates (15 and 28 percent), but the applicable income brackets differ by group. Joint filing is most common among married couples and confers tax savings when the incomes of the two differ substantially. For couples with similar incomes, the system imposes a higher tax burden than the two would face if unmarried. Prior to the 1986 reforms there was a second-earner deduction (10 percent of the lower-earning spouse's earnings up to $30,000) to mitigate this "marriage penalty." It also served to moderate the higher marginal tax rate facing the lower-earning partner under joint filing. The 1986 reforms eliminated the second-earner deduction, on the rationale that married couples would be compensated by adjustments to the standard deduction and the rate schedule. Unmarried heads of household enjoy a larger standard deduction and a more favorable rate schedule than single persons.

Dependent Children

As already noted, a dependent child generates an exemption of $2,050 that can be claimed by a supporting adult. This is subject to the 5 percent surtax to

16. From 1975 to 1978, the U.S. provided a "general tax credit," which in 1978 equaled the greater of $35 for each personal exemption or 2 percent of the first $9,000 of taxable income. The credits were nonrefundable and in addition to the $750 per-capita personal exemptions. In 1978 the president proposed to replace all of these provisions with nonrefundable per-capita credits of $240, but Congress instead raised the personal exemptions to $1,000 in 1979. For background analysis, see Danziger and Kesselman (1978).

17. Benefits of the 15 percent bracket are recovered above 1990 taxable incomes of $47,050 for a single filer, $67,200 for a head of household, and $78,400 for joint married filers. The personal exemptions are recovered only above taxable incomes of $97,620 for a single filer, $134,930 for a head of household, and $162,770 for joint married filers.

recover the tax savings at very high family incomes. The 1986 reforms precluded a child from claiming a personal exemption on the child's own tax return if he or she could be claimed as a dependent on another's return. Such a child may still use up to $500 of his standard deduction to offset his unearned income, and his full standard deduction to offset his earnings. Unearned income over $1,000 of children under age 14 has become taxable at the parents' marginal tax rate—the "kiddie tax." The 1986 tax act included sweeping changes to the taxation of trusts, in particular grantor trusts and generation-skipping trusts. These reforms have severely curtailed the ability of families to shift taxable incomes to members in lower rate brackets. They also have increased the tax filing requirements for children and the number of children who have to pay taxes on their earned incomes.

Two U.S. tax credit provisions are linked to the presence of dependent children. These predate the 1986 reforms and survived with minor changes to their credit and phaseout levels. First is the earned-income tax credit, which is a refundable tax credit based on earnings of tax units with at least one dependent child (see Steuerle 1990). For the 1990 tax year the EITC could be claimed by a supporting adult at a rate of 14 percent on the first $6,810 of earned income (for a maximum credit of $953). The credit is phased out at a rate of 10 percent for incomes between $10,730 and $20,264 in 1990. Claimants can file certificates with their employers to have an advance portion of the EITC added to their paychecks throughout the year. Second is the provision of nonrefundable credits for dependent-child-care expenses of working parents. The credit rates decline with increase in the adjusted gross income of the claiming tax unit. In 1990 the credits were 30 percent of allowable expenses for filers with incomes of $10,000 and less, declining to 20 percent of expenses for filers with incomes above $28,000. As in Canada, these tax provisions for child care expense are applied to the earnings of the lower-earning parent.

The Elderly and the Disabled

Several of the key U.S. tax and transfer provisions are similar for the elderly and the disabled. For persons who are elderly or blind, extra amounts can be claimed along with the standard deduction. For the 1990 tax year these increments were $800 for age or for blindness ($1,600 for age *and* blindness) for a single filer and $650 for each person over 65 or blind for joint married filers (that is, $2,600 where both are blind and aged). Prior to the 1986 reforms, age and blindness were handled with personal exemptions. The earlier approach benefited even very high-income filers, who typically itemize their deductions rather than take the standard deduction. There is also a nonrefundable tax credit for the elderly receiving little or no Social Security benefits and for the totally disabled receiving disability income. The credit is 15 percent of specified base amounts, depending upon the claimant's filing status, reduced by the nontaxable Social Security and pensions received.

Certain tax deductions are potentially available to all filers but have particular relevance to the situation of the elderly and the disabled. Deductions for
medical care expenses can be claimed along with other itemized deductions in
lieu of the standard deduction. The 1986 reforms raised the threshold for medical care claims to 7.5 percent of the filer's adjusted gross income, from the
former 5 percent floor. The reforms also severely limited the tax deductions
available for savings in Individual Retirement Accounts. Now such deductions are confined to low- and moderate-income taxpayers; upper-income taxpayers can deduct up to $2,000 of IRA contributions in a year only if neither
the taxpayer nor the spouse is an active participant in a qualified pension plan.
Tax-sheltered treatment remains on saving undertaken within qualified
employer-based pension plans.

The Social Security program provides two major types of cash benefit programs for the elderly and the disabled, one contributions-related and the other
needs-based. Old Age, Survivors, and Disability Insurance offers benefits related to a claimant's insured earnings over his or her working life.[18] The benefit formula for OASDI is highly skewed in favor of persons whose "average
indexed monthly earnings" over their working lives were quite low. A special
minimum benefit for low-income workers with long coverage lends a further
redistributive tilt to the program. Beneficiaries under age 70 face an earnings
test, which reduces benefits by 50 percent of earnings above a threshold; in
1990 the earnings offset was reduced to one-third for beneficiaries between
ages 65 and 69. Supplemental Security Income provides income- and assets-
tested benefits for the aged, blind, and disabled. Payments can be made irrespective of the claimant's work history. The maximum benefits are quite low
and are further reduced by 50 percent of earnings above a small disregard
level. Most states supplement the federal SSI payments.

3.3.4   Taxation of Benefits and Social Insurance Finance

None of the income-tested cash benefits, such as welfare and SSI, and no
in-kind public benefits or subsidies constitute taxable income in the United
States. This avoids the compounding of effective marginal tax rates that would
result by taxing benefits that had already been subject to an income test. Workers' compensation benefits are similarly nontaxable, even though they are not
subject to an income test.[19] If these benefits, or any of the others, were to be
made taxable, some upward adjustment of benefit rates would be required to
maintain their adequacy on an after-tax basis. The 1986 reforms made all
unemployment insurance benefits received taxable. Previously, there had been

18. The original 1935 act covered retirement benefits for the aged; benefits for survivors, disability, and Medicare were introduced over the following thirty years. Medicare was discussed
earlier, and we do not review the survivors' benefits here (as in the CPP, benefits may be paid to
survivors of insured persons under certain circumstances).

19. Most disability pensions financed by employers are taxable in Canada and the U.S. Note
that both countries exclude from tax the receipt of damages for physical injury or death.

an exclusion from tax of jobless benefits for persons with incomes below specified thresholds ($12,000 for single filers and $18,000 for joint filers). Since 1984, OASDI Social Security benefits have been partially taxable to households with incomes above specified thresholds ($25,000 for single filers and $32,000 for joint filers; neither has been indexed). Taxable income includes the lesser of one-half of benefits or one-half of income (including half of benefits and all of nontaxable interest income) above the threshold. One justification for the half-inclusion rate was that beneficiaries had never paid tax on the employer share of Social Security premiums.

Finance of UI and workers' compensation was discussed earlier. We now turn to the finance of the other social insurance programs. The SSI component of Social Security is financed out of federal general revenues. Like the Canadian public pension scheme, the U.S. scheme is well short of being fully funded. The OASDHI component is financed by equal premiums on employers and employees. Contribution rates in 1990 for each party were 7.65 percent of a worker's wages and salaries up to $51,300, for a maximum total payment exceeding $7,800 (nearly eight times the comparable maximum for CPP). The employer premiums are deductible under the business's income tax, but employee premiums receive no recognition in the personal tax. Contributions cover both cash benefits of OASDI and the Hospitalization Insurance portion (Part A) of Medicare. The Supplementary Medical Insurance portion (Part B) of Medicare, is financed about one-quarter from the SMI premiums and the balance from general revenues. The United States also enacted a surcharge on the federal income tax of persons covered by Part A Medicare at 15 percent of their tax in 1989 (to a maximum surcharge of $800 per affected person), with scheduled rises to 28 percent in 1993. This "Medicare tax" would have been used to finance coverage for catastrophic illness and prescription drugs, but it was repealed before coming into effect.

3.4   The Tax and Transfer Unit[20]

Defining the benefit unit for income security serves many of the same objectives as choosing the tax unit for personal taxation. The primary goal is to choose groups across which relative well-being can be assessed, so that income support or tax relief can be appropriately targeted. Achieving this horizontal-equity goal is inextricably linked with the measure of well-being (usually some variant of income) and timing and accounting issues; these topics are treated in the following two sections. A benefit unit is usually taken as a group of persons across which there is some presumption that income and

20. For the analytical foundations of this and the following two sections, see Kesselman (1982, 1990b) and the references cited therein. Danziger and Kesselman (1978) and Kesselman (1979) are relevant to the present section; Pechman and Engelhardt (1990) also overlaps with some issues in this section.

other resources will be shared. Typically the group will be residing together, although in some cases separated married persons may be treated together. Once the benefit unit has been defined, it must be determined how income security benefits and tax-relieving provisions should be scaled for different types and sizes of units. In addition to equity objectives, attention must be given to the ease of tracking and aggregating incomes within the benefit unit and coordination with the unit used for personal tax purposes.

3.4.1   Functional Aspects of the Unit

Inconsistency of Tax and Transfer Units

Both Canada and the United States take some version of the nuclear family as the appropriate benefit unit for most income security programs, whether cash or in-kind. Social insurance programs traditionally operate more with the individual as both the contributory and the benefit unit, but there have been many compromises on the benefit side. Some features have been based on concerns over targeting benefits effectively, while others have been justified by a family-need concept of the socially insured contingency. In the early 1970s, the Canadian UI program offered a higher benefit rate for jobless claimants with one or more dependents. OASDI retirement benefits are increased by 50 percent for the spouse of a retired worker, even if the spouse never worked or made payroll contributions. Most survivor benefits under OASDI and CPP also take into account the financial situation of the surviving family. The American food stamp program operates on the basis of an "economic unit" in which there are sharing of common cooking facilities and joint purchasing of food; this sometimes departs from the welfare unit. Federal SSI benefits are reduced by one-third for beneficiaries who live in another person's home and receive support and maintenance there.

As previously noted, the U.S. income tax allows married couples to file jointly. Most of the states also permit some form of joint income tax filing. The Canadian tax allows joint filing only when one partner or a dependent has income below the taxable level. Hence, the taxable threshold in Canada has something of a family basis. Otherwise the Canadian tax uses an individual tax unit. Yet when income support provisions are included in the personal tax system, there are areas in which it uses family rather than individual income. Canadian refundable tax credits for children and for sales taxes each abate above an income threshold, which is applied to the joint incomes of the parents when both are present. In 1990, the thresholds for these phaseouts were $24,750 and $18,000 for the child and sales tax credits, respectively. With conversion of the sales tax credit to a Goods and Services Tax credit in 1991, the threshold increases to $24,800, but it will still be applied to a couple's combined incomes. The phaseout rate on each of these credits for incomes above their thresholds is 5 percent.

Income Aggregation in the Unit

One functional aspect of defining the tax or transfer unit is to determine for which persons income will be aggregated to assess tax liability or benefit entitlement. With a progressive-rate income tax, an individual unit induces persons to split or average their incomes across family members. The use of a family unit may avoid creating these incentives, but it may affect incentives for persons to be married, depending upon the differential tax treatment of single and married persons.[21] Most income security provisions impose income tests with high marginal tax rates on persons at the lowest incomes. When these provisions overlap the personal income tax, they join at the relatively low marginal rates of the bottom bracket. Hence, individuals in a family group would like to segregate all of their income in the hands of one member, so that the others can maximize their benefits. The purpose of a family benefit unit is to track and measure all members' incomes so that they can be counted as joint resources in the computation of need. However, incomes of common-law or more casual partners may be difficult to track and to assess as a family resource for benefit purposes. Common-law relations are most often excluded from the *tax* definition of married status in both countries, based on legal tradition and respect for privacy.

Use of the individual tax unit in Canada places considerable pressure on tax enforcement to prevent the shifting of incomes or income-generating assets between spouses. A variety of income-attribution rules on transferred assets has been used to reduce the opportunities for income splitting. The United States introduced a "kiddie tax" and denied personal exemptions to dependent children on their own tax returns to reduce the opportunities for parents to shift taxable income from assets to their children. One could alternatively expand the U.S. tax unit from the married couple to include children, but doing this would raise the marginal tax rates on the work earnings of many children. Both countries further extend the family tax unit beyond marriage to separated or divorced couples. In most circumstances, court-ordered alimony payments in the United States (and in Canada, maintenance payments as well) are deductible to the payer and taxable to the recipient, thus splitting the income. In the 1988 tax year, Canada extended the same tax treatment for maintenance to separated common-law spouses.

An anomaly arises in the income aggregation for the clawback on Family Allowance and OAS payments introduced in Canada in the 1989 tax year.[22]

21. Income aggregation and the definition of the tax unit also have economic efficiency implications with a progressive tax rate schedule; see Boskin and Sheshinski (1983).

22. The FA and OAS clawbacks were phased in over three years; in 1989 up to one-third of the benefits were clawed back, and by 1991 up to 100 percent of benefits have been recouped. The UI clawback, in contrast, is limited to 30 percent of benefits received; its threshold is just under $50,000 in 1990.

Family Allowance receipts are clawed back at 15 percent of the *higher-income parent's* net income exceeding $50,000 per year. Hence, a two-income family with total net income of $100,000 split equally between the partners will repay none of its FA, whereas a single-income family with net income at all above $50,000 will bear the clawback. This failure to aggregate incomes for the clawback is a departure from the type of aggregation used for determining refundable child and sales tax credits; it would appear to be a violation of horizontal equity, as the concept is normally applied on a family basis for income security. Indeed, the income aggregation for the refundable credits is extended even to the unmarried parents of a child. OAS receipts are also clawed back at a rate of 15 percent, but the clawback applies to net income above $50,000 of the adult receiving the payment.

Scaling of Benefit Provisions

Benefit levels of transfer programs, tax-relieving provisions, and tax-based transfers can be scaled in a variety of ways. The main methods include a per-capita basis, scaling by family size, and recognizing dependency or family relationships. The income-tested transfer programs, including welfare, in both countries use variants of the family-size approach in setting maximum benefit levels. This approach reflects the scale economies of family living and the horizontal-equity notion of equalizing the well-being of different-size family units at the bottom of the income scale. Social insurance programs typically scale their benefits to the contributory earnings level of the beneficiary, although they sometimes make adjustments for family size or need in particular areas, such as survivor benefits. The Canadian demogrant programs of FA and OAS use a per-capita method (in 1990, monthly benefits of about $33 per child and $345 per aged person). However, individual provinces may vary the payment pattern for FA benefits to reflect the number of children in a family or their ages. And there is an income-tested Spouse's Allowance for spouses of OAS recipients and widowed persons aged 60–64.

Tax-relieving provisions are designed to exclude low-income persons from paying personal income taxes. When Canada converted from personal exemptions to personal credits beginning with the 1988 tax year, it kept the scaling based upon age and family size and relationship. In 1990, the levels of these credits were as follows: basic filer, $1,049; married, $874; first two children under age 19, $68 each; other children under 19, $136 each; infirm dependents 18 and older, $257; and elderly or disabled, $566. These credits offset tax that would otherwise be paid; at the bottom-bracket rate of 17 percent, the basic filer credit is equivalent to a personal exemption of $6,169.[23] The United States employs the per capita method for all personal exemptions, with a 1990

23. On tax returns the personal credits are actually specified as exemption-equivalent amounts, and along with other creditable expenses, the filer multiplies their total by the bottom-bracket rate of 17 percent to compute the credit amount.

level of $2,050 per adult or child in the family.[24] As reviewed earlier, the standard deduction plays an important role in setting tax relief for low-income families. The extra exemptions for age and disability were converted to additional amounts of standard deduction under the U.S. reforms.

Both countries provide single-parent households with added relief to reflect their additional needs for living costs. Canada allows single-parent families to claim "equivalent-to-married" credits (equal to marital credits) on behalf of the first dependent child, instead of the much lower child credit amount. The United States allows unmarried heads of household to claim a larger standard deduction and to file under a more lenient tax schedule than single persons. In 1990 these features raised the taxable threshold by $1,500 (plus exemptions for dependents) and reduced taxes due on taxable incomes above $19,450. Note that both countries also extend these provisions to single or separated adults who support an adult relative in their own home.

Transfers delivered through the tax system can also be scaled in various ways. The Canadian refundable tax credits for children and sales tax are both on a per capita basis but differentiated by age. Child tax credits in 1990 were $575 per child. A supplement to the credit of $200 per child under age seven is also available, but this supplement is reduced by 25 percent of deductible child care expenses. The sales tax credits have different values per adult and per dependent child; with their expansion to offset the Goods and Services Tax in 1991, they are scheduled to be $100 per child and $190 per adult.[25] Payment of the earned-income tax credit in the United States is conditional upon the presence of one or more dependent children in the home of the filer. The amount of the credit is proportional to earned income—14 percent of the first $6,810, to a maximum credit of $953 in 1990—and is unaffected by the presence of additional children beyond the first one. The income thresholds for phasing out these refundable credits are fixed amounts in both countries, independent of the family size or type. This fact seems to constitute a minor violation of horizontal equity at income levels where the phaseouts apply.

3.4.2   Tax-Free Income Thresholds

A major distributive aspect of both the Canadian and U.S. personal tax reforms was the increase in tax-free income thresholds and the reduction in the number of low-income taxpayers. The Canada Department of Finance projected that its reform package would increase by 850,000 the number of lower-income tax filers who pay no federal income tax. The U.S. tax reforms

24. Before World War II, personal exemptions in the U.S. departed from a per-capita pattern. Exemptions for children were much less than those for a filer or spouse, and in many years total exemptions for married joint filers were more than twice those of single filers. See Danziger and Kesselman (1978).

25. Single parents will be able to claim an adult credit for one dependent child. In addition, single adults, including single parents, will be able to claim an additional credit equal to 2 percent of net income between $6,169 and $11,169, for a maximum added credit of $100. This latter feature has elements of an earnings subsidy or EITC.

were estimated to relieve 6 million persons who paid federal taxes in 1986 from paying tax in 1988 (1987 was a transitional tax year for reforms). These numbers are quite significant, as they also imply reduced tax liabilities for many taxpayers with incomes somewhat above the new, increased tax-free thresholds. The numbers of persons required to file tax returns were also reduced by the reforms. Still, the availability of refundable tax credits in both countries makes it worthwhile for many low-income persons to file returns even if they are not otherwise required to file. Filing requirements are discussed further in the section on timing and accounting issues.

We can calculate tax-free income thresholds and compare them to the poverty thresholds for selected types of households.[26] For Canada, three types of tax thresholds are constructed: a "tax" threshold which considers only the nonrefundable personal credits; a "tax-credit" threshold which also considers the two refundable credits; and a "tax-credit-FA" threshold which further considers Family Allowance payments. The tax threshold is the highest level of income at which the household pays no federal income tax, ignoring the receipt of refundable credits and demogrants. The tax-credit-FA threshold is the income level (including FA receipts) at which a household's federal income tax, net of refundable credits and including tax on FA, is just offset by gross FA.[27] These figures include only federal personal income taxes. However all provinces except Quebec impose their income taxes as a percentage of the federal tax, so that their tax thresholds are the same, though they are higher in those provinces that provide special tax reductions to relieve low-income taxpayers.[28]

Table 3.2 presents the results of these calculations for Canada in the 1990 tax year for ten groups: aged singles and married couples; nonaged single persons with zero to two children; and nonaged married couples with zero to four children. The tax thresholds, which encompass only the nonrefundable personal credits, exceed the poverty threshold for just one group (married aged couples) and are less than half of the poverty thresholds for several groups (nonaged singles and married couples with two or more children). The tax-credit thresholds, which also include the refundable credits, increase the taxable income level only modestly for units without children, but sharply for those with one or more children. Still, the tax-credit threshold exceeds the poverty threshold only for married aged couples, and even on this basis the single nonaged are taxable at incomes far below their poverty threshold. The tax-credit-FA thresholds affect only units with one or more children; they

26. For both countries, the poverty thresholds do not distinguish between adults and children; the same threshold applies to a two-adult unit and a single-parent unit with one child.

27. The threshold does not consider OAS demogrants for aged taxpayers, since these are an integral part of the Canadian retirement income system. OAS payments are reflected in lower CPP/QPP benefits than the counterpart American OASDI retirement benefits.

28. Because of its own system of credits and rates, Quebec taxes single persons at incomes somewhat below the federal tax threshold. And most provinces impose their taxes at incomes well below the tax-credit and tax-credit-FA thresholds.

Table 3.2   Thresholds in Canada, 1990

	Thresholds			
Household Type	Poverty[a]	Tax[b]	Tax-Credit[c]	Tax-Credit-FA[d]
Aged Head				
Single	$12,459	$9,496	$10,280	
Married	16,891	17,964	19,198	
Nonaged Head				
Single	12,459	6,169	6,953	
Single, 1 Child	16,891	11,310	15,708	$17,949
Single, 2 Children	21,469	11,709	19,344	22,845
Married	16,891	11,310	12,879	
Married, 1 Child	21,469	11,709	16,891	18,885
Married, 2 Children	24,718	12,108	20,268	23,770
Married, 3 Children	27,007	12,906	23,715	28,208
Married, 4 Children	29,314	13,704	26,726	31,409

Sources: Poverty thresholds from Statistics Canada, Household Surveys Division, *Income Distributions by Size in Canada, 1988,* 13-207 (Ottawa: 1989). Tax thresholds computed from taxation provisions and rate schedules for the 1990 tax year.

[a]Poverty thresholds are the Statistics Canada low-income cutoffs for households in urban areas of 100,000–499,999 population; 1988 figures are projected to 1990 based on actual inflation for 1988–89 and a forecast 5 percent rate for 1989–90.

[b]Tax threshold considers only the effects of nonrefundable credits for filer, dependent spouse, children, and age. This and the other thresholds assume one earner per family unit, and all are based on federal taxes (including 5 percent surtax) alone.

[c]Tax-credit threshold considers the effects of tax threshold *plus* the refundable credits for children and sales tax as an offset to income taxes.

[d]Tax-credit-FA threshold considers the effects of tax-credit threshold *plus* the net-of-tax Family Allowance benefits (without provincial variations) as an offset to income taxes.

bring most such units above their respective poverty thresholds (except for married couples with one or two children).[29]

Table 3.3 presents the poverty and tax thresholds calculated for the United States in 1990 for the same ten groups. The country has no demogrant programs, but tax-credit thresholds have been calculated to reflect the earned-income tax credit as an offset to federal income taxes. Note that many states impose taxes at incomes below the federal tax thresholds, although some do have special relieving provisions for low-income taxpayers. The tabulated results show tax thresholds that roughly equal or exceed the poverty thresholds for almost all groups. The only exceptions are single persons, both aged and nonaged, though the gap is quite small for the former. Tax-credit thresholds raise the minimum taxable-income levels only for units with children, and they have their largest effect for smaller families. The tax-credit threshold exceeds the tax threshold by nearly $3,500 for a married couple with one

29. For areas with population above one-half million, the poverty thresholds are 14 percent above those tabulated. In those areas the only group having a threshold (tax-credit or tax-credit-FA) as high as its poverty threshold is married aged couples.

Table 3.3   Thresholds in the United States, 1990

Household Type	Thresholds			Canadian Levels[d]
	Poverty[a]	Tax[b]	Tax-Credit[c]	
Aged Head				
Single	$6,245	$6,100		$8,738
Married	7,878	10,850		16,318
Nonaged Head				
Single	6,774	5,300		5,910
Single, 1 Child	8,759	8,850	$13,416	15,257
Single, 2 Children	10,384	10,900	14,646	19,418
Married	8,759	9,550		10,947
Married, 1 Child	10,384	11,600	15,066	16,052
Married, 2 Children	13,308	13,650	16,296	20,205
Married, 3 Children	15,744	15,700	17,526	23,977
Married, 4 Children	17,774	17,750	18,756	26,698

Sources: Poverty thresholds from Bureau of the Census, Current Population Reports, Consumer Income, *Money Income and Poverty Status in the United States: 1988,* series P-60, no. 166 (October 1989); tax thresholds computed from taxation provisions and rate schedules for the 1990 tax year; last column based on table 3.2.

[a]Poverty thresholds are the average weighted thresholds, with amounts distinguished by age only for households of one and two persons; 1988 figures are projected to 1990 based on actual inflation for 1988–89 and a forecast 5 percent rate for 1989–90.

[b]Tax threshold considers the effects of personal exemptions and standard deductions, including extra deductions for aged filers. This and the other threshold are based on federal income taxes alone.

[c]Tax-credit threshold considers the effects of tax threshold *plus* the earned-income tax credit (available only to units with one or more children) as an offset to income taxes.

[d]These figures are the U.S.-dollar values (converted at 85 cents per Canadian dollar) of the larger of the Canadian tax-credit or tax-credit-FA threshold for each household type.

child, but by just about $1,000 for a married couple with four children. This difference reflects the structure of the EITC. These credits and their phaseout range are independent of the number of children in a family. In 1990, these credits were fully phased out at family incomes just under $20,300.

Both Canada and the United States partially succeed in relieving their poor populations from income tax, if one views the refundable credits and FA as offsets against income tax.[30] One major exception is single persons. Yet, other transfer programs in each country greatly relieve the situation of poor aged single persons, so it is mainly the nonaged single group that is taxable at poverty incomes. Married couples with one or two children also bear net tax at what are deemed poverty incomes in Canada, whereas in the United States these groups and their single-parent counterparts have tax-credit thresholds that substantially exceed the U.S. poverty thresholds. But if a consistent no-

30. Of course, this exercise ignores the indirect and payroll taxes borne by the poor; the former are sizable in Canada, the latter in the U.S. Indeed, the refundable sales tax credits and the EITC were originally intended as partial relief for these other taxes.

tion of poverty is applied to the two countries, Canada goes further than the United States in relieving the poor from taxation.[31] After accounting for the exchange-rate differential, Canadian poverty thresholds exceed those of the United States by 40–80 percent, depending on the household type. Cost-of-living differences between the two countries are not nearly that large. We can compare the two countries by converting into U.S. funds the larger of the Canadian tax-credit and tax-credit-FA thresholds; these are displayed in the last column of table 3.3. Clearly, Canada exempts from tax many people who would not be deemed poor in the United States.

Without indexation or discretionary periodic adjustments, the tax-free thresholds will decline in real value over time and cover a larger proportion of those at low incomes. Beginning with the 1974 tax year, Canada undertook full indexation to the consumer price index; this indexation included both personal exemptions and the income break points for the tax rate schedule. The rate of indexation was reduced to CPI increases above a 3 percent annual floor beginning in 1986, and this limited indexation was continued with the substitution of personal credits for exemptions in 1988. Beginning with the 1985 tax year, the United States undertook full indexation of the tax brackets, standard deductions, and personal exemptions. Personal exemptions were raised by scheduled amounts for each of the tax years 1987 through 1989; their indexation resumed in 1990. Standard deductions and rate brackets were revised by scheduled amounts for 1987 and 1988, after which they have been indexed. The lack of indexation in the U.S. tax through the earlier 1980s made many low-income persons taxable, and the 1986 reforms served to undo that damage.

Indexation is also relevant for the continued effectiveness of income security provisions contained in the personal tax system. Since its inception in 1978, the Canadian refundable child tax credit level and its income threshold for phaseout were indexed. In 1983 its phaseout threshold was frozen, then reduced in 1986, and indexed again for subsequent years. In addition to being indexed, the child credit level has been increased by additional, discretionary amounts in some years. The refundable sales tax credit levels and thresholds for phaseout were not indexed but raised periodically; with their conversion to GST credits in 1991, both will be indexed for inflation above 3 percent per year, as have the parameters of the RCTC since 1988. The $50,000 income threshold for clawing back Family Allowance and OAS payments also will have this limited indexation for 1990 and later tax years. In the United States the EITC has been fully indexed for inflation since 1984, for both the maximum credit and the income range over which credits are phased out. However, the income thresholds above which up to half of OASDI benefits are taxable ($25,000 for single filers, $32,000 for married joint filers) have been un-

---

31. Canadian poverty thresholds are set at the incomes at which a particular household type spends a proportion of its total income on food, shelter, and clothing that is 20 percentage points higher than that for an average-income family of the same type.

changed since their institution in 1984. Like the limited indexation of the threshold for clawing back OAS and FA benefits in Canada, this is a way of gradually implementing greater taxability or income testing on income security benefits.

3.4.3   Tax Differentiation at Taxable Incomes

One can devise a set of personal exemptions and a set of nonrefundable credits that are fully equivalent in terms of their implied tax-free thresholds. Hence, the choice between exemptions and credits reflects mainly value judgments about the appropriate differentiation of tax burdens by family size at *taxable* levels of income. These involve considerations of equity among single adults, married couples, and nonmarried couples. They also concern judgments about whether children are to be treated as consumer goods or as persons with needs as valid as those of adults. These views may be affected by the income level of the family; children's welfare might be viewed as society's responsibility for lower incomes but the family's responsibility at higher incomes.[32] We do not pursue these issues here, but we examine the actual tax differentials by family size embodied in the Canadian and U.S. systems. The degree of rate progressivity affects the tax differentials of credit and exemption approaches. Under a pure flat tax the two would be fully equivalent even at taxable income levels, so the partial flattening of rate schedules in both countries has moderated the differences.

In Canada the conversion of the marital exemption to a nonrefundable credit means that a dependent spouse with no income relieves the supporting taxpayer of a constant amount of taxes. The 1990 federal tax savings are about $920, almost independent of income (the exact value varies slightly because of the way that a two-tier surtax is applied). If the second spouse has a taxable level of income, there are no tax savings to the first spouse; both file separate returns. In the United States there can be much greater tax savings from marriage to an individual with no income. These savings result from the combined effects of the larger standard deduction for married, as against single, filers, the extra personal exemption for the spouse, and the wider tax brackets for married joint filers. In 1990, the resulting federal tax savings from having a spouse with no income were $670 at family adjusted gross income (before claiming deductions and exemptions) of $25,000; $2,880 at $50,000 income; and $4,660 at $100,000 income. At still higher incomes the benefits of the spouse's exemption are phased out, but large total tax savings remain. The U.S. rate schedules are constructed so that a tax penalty arises with marriage for persons with similar incomes.

Tax differentiation by number of children is more complex on account of the variety of provisions. In Canada the nonrefundable credits for dependent children offer the same value in taxes saved independent of the taxpayer's

32. See Brannon and Morss (1973), Pogue (1974), and McIntyre and Oldman (1977).

income.[33] These credits are twice as large for the third and each subsequent child in a family as they are for each of the first two children. But other tax and transfer provisions make the net dollar value of an additional child vary widely by family income. The refundable child tax credits and the child component of refundable sales tax credits are together much larger than the value of the nonrefundable child credits. They are payable to families with no taxable income, as well as to those with incomes up to the thresholds for phase-out. These credits are fully phased out at incomes below $60,000, even for three children. Family Allowance is paid to all families as fixed amounts per child, although some provinces vary payments with the number or ages of children in the family. Payments are taxable and also subject to clawback as either parent's income rises above a $50,000 threshold. At higher family incomes, the only remaining tax differential for a child is the nonrefundable tax credit, which is worth less than $70 in federal tax savings for each of the first two children. The overall pattern of differentials for a child by family income is generally to decline with income. But there are ranges of income over which it rises (income just becomes taxable where the nonrefundable credit assumes value) and has inequities (the clawback is based on the higher-income parent rather than on the parents' combined income).

The tax differentials for children in the U.S. system are simpler due to the number and nature of related provisions. Each extra child gives rise to an additional personal exemption, $2,050 per capita in 1990. The value in terms of federal tax savings from an extra child is proportional to the rate bracket of the taxpayer. In the 15 and 28 percent brackets, the savings per child are $308 and $574, respectively. Moreover, in the income ranges for clawback of the benefits of the 15 percent bracket, each exemption assumes a value of $677 at the effective marginal rate of 33 percent. It appears strange that the clawback of the bottom bracket should raise the tax differential for children at very high incomes. The personal exemptions themselves are clawed back at still higher incomes, so that the tax differential for children fully vanishes. Two other provisions in the U.S. tax can give a substantial tax value to the first child in a family, beyond the extra personal exemption. The presence of a child in a single-parent family qualifies the unit for both the higher standard deduction and the more favorable rate schedule of a head of household. And the presence of a child in a lower-income household usually qualifies the household for the EITC, though for separated or single parents conditions of child custody or household maintenance must be satisfied.

3.5   The Tax and Transfer Base

The base of a tax system measures ability to pay taxes, and the base of a transfer system measures the need for support. Both are measures of the eco-

---

33. This obtains so long as the taxpayer's income is at a taxable level, and the value will vary a bit based on the filer's surtax rate.

nomic resources of the individual or household; typically some variant of income is employed. One might expect a well-designed base to serve equally well for tax or transfer purposes, with individuals moving smoothly from being net taxpayers to net transfer recipients as their measured base declines. Such a uniform base would satisfy horizontal equity, as well as ease the coordinated operation of the tax and transfer systems. However, one often finds different base measures for the two purposes, that is, collecting tax revenues and disbursing income security benefits. The base for transfers is most often a broader one than that for taxes. This may reflect society's more jaundiced view of beneficiaries than of taxpayers, or perhaps the two groups' relative influence on the political process. This section assesses two main aspects of the base for income security issues: the inclusion in the tax base of transfer receipts, and the bases used for income tests, clawbacks, and phaseouts built into the tax system. It also considers the equity aspects of expanding the tax-transfer base to include an imputed return on assets such as housing.

3.5.1   Transfers in the Tax Base

Both countries exclude from their personal tax bases virtually all in-kind public transfer benefits and most income-tested transfers. Canada excludes benefits from Social Assistance, the GIS (and provincial supplements), and workers' compensation, and the United States excludes its benefits from welfare, SSI (and state supplements), and workers' compensation. Because the benefits of these programs (except for workers' compensation) are strongly income-tested, there is little overlap between recipients and taxable persons. But occasionally such a recipient will be taxable in a year when employment, disability, or age status changes so that the individual's income rises or falls sharply. There can be horizontal inequity in the tax-transfer treatment of such an individual compared to others whose employment status has been more stable over the entire year. Yet the tax exemption of such income-tested benefits does simplify the problems of "rate stacking" or coordination to avoid excessive total marginal tax rates.

Canada includes in the personal tax base the benefits of the demogrants (OAS and FA) and the other social insurance programs (UI and CPP/QPP). None of the tax credits themselves are taxable, as they are subject to phaseout provisions. But some provincial welfare schemes may count tax credits and demogrants as part of their recipients' resources. The amounts of demogrants (and UI) clawed back from a taxpayer are themselves tax deductible. This is necessary because FA and OAS are taxable, as well as subject to clawbacks, and would otherwise be taxed at more than 100 percent. The United States includes in the personal tax base certain social insurance benefits—all UI benefits since the 1986 reforms, and up to half of OASDI benefits above specified income thresholds.[34] It does not count the benefits of the EITC as taxable

---

34. See Feldstein (1974) and Munnell (1986) for analysis of the effects of the earlier exclusions and the arguments for including in tax UI and OASDI benefits, respectively.

income, since they are subject to phaseout based on income. But EITC benefits are counted as resources in the income test for AFDC beneficiaries. And the food stamp program includes in income such items as welfare cash benefits, workers' compensation, UI benefits, and farm and training subsidies.

3.5.2 Base for Tax Clawbacks and Phaseouts

Stand-alone income transfer programs usually contain much broader measures of resources, including asset tests, than personal taxes. Sometimes they will start with the tax measure of income and add in other items that are either excluded from or deductible from taxable income. For example, the GIS includes tax-deductible retirement savings, the exempt portion of capital gains, and workers' compensation benefits. The U.S. food stamp program considers AFDC, SSI, and workers' compensation benefits in its computation of benefits. This tilt frequently carries over to personal tax provisions oriented toward income security objectives. In Canada the refundable tax credits are conditioned on the taxpayer's net income *plus* social transfer benefits that are otherwise nontaxable (Social Assistance, GIS, and workers' compensation). In the United States, receipt of otherwise tax-exempt municipal and state bond interest affects the threshold for partial taxation of OASDI benefits; in effect, the interest becomes partially taxable. And disability payments and the value of meals and lodging excluded from gross income qualify as earned income for computing EITC benefits.

3.5.3 Arguments for a Broader Base

Most stand-alone income security programs that are not structured as social insurance contain asset tests. Several income security provisions in the personal tax are conditioned upon a broader base than that used for taxation.[35] Both of these approaches are an attempt to target the limited total available funds more effectively to persons most in need. Yet asset tests are typically a very crude tool, with meager thresholds, above which benefits are completely denied. These tests discourage lower-income people from accumulating much in the way of financial assets, particularly those who expect to need support from time to time. Moreover, the asset tests of most welfare programs in both countries disregard equity in owner-occupied housing (sometimes up to specified limits). This feature biases the composition of savings toward home ownership, exacerbating the distortions of the income tax found in both countries. Other assets such as tax-sheltered savings in RRSPs and IRAs also do not enter into the measure of need, except in years when funds are withdrawn and become taxable.

The cited deficiencies could be remedied by expanding the transfer base to include an imputed return on assets that do not yield current income, such as

35. See studies in Federal Council on the Aging (1977) for analysis of existing U.S. provisions and proposals for broader inclusion of assets in income tests and tax-transfer programs.

home equity and tax-sheltered savings. In effect, this would broaden the base from current taxable income toward potential consumption. One might wish to use such a broadened base for transfers while retaining a somewhat narrower base for personal taxation. Tax-sheltered savings were instituted under the personal income tax precisely to allow tax deferral on the funds. A personal tax on consumption would include net dissavings as part of its base but would not in principle count accruing incomes in tax-sheltered saving accounts. The key reason for using a broader base measure under a transfer than under a tax program relates more to the accounting periods and nonlinear character of the tax-transfer system. An individual can bunch withdrawals from a tax-sheltered saving account so as to obtain large income security benefits in some years, interspersed with years when the individual lives off the withdrawals. The next section examines these timing and accounting issues in greater depth.

3.6 Timing and Accounting Issues

Any tax or transfer program has important timing issues, which are embodied in its accounting and administrative structure. These include the frequency of benefit payment and income measurement and the accounting periods for payments and income measurement. The design of these timing features has major implications for the responsiveness of benefits to the changing needs of households, the horizontally equitable treatment of beneficiaries, and the net budgetary costs of an income security provision. There are further effects on the administrative and compliance burdens of the system, as well as the possible need for recovery of overpayments. While these features may appear as mere technical details in the design of income security, they can vitally influence the efficacy of policies in meeting their prime objectives.

3.6.1 Frequency of Payment

The frequency of income security payments and of tax-based transfer payments affects the ease of household budgeting by beneficiaries. Some observers would argue that frequent payments are important in assisting responsible spending behavior by beneficiaries; others might argue that less frequent but larger payments facilitate the purchase of consumer durables by families who have difficulty in saving and little credit. Regardless of one's view on this matter, the income security objective requires that payments be sufficiently frequent to avoid problems of destitution by those beneficiaries who cannot budget well. Virtually all stand-alone income security programs offer frequent payments, either fortnightly or, at most, monthly. Similarly, some income security provisions of the personal tax system are delivered quite frequently. These include the basic tax-relieving and tax-differentiating provisions that apply to all taxpayers and are integrated into the tax source-withholding tables. Examples are the Canadian nonrefundable personal credits and U.S.

personal exemptions and standard deductions. These are delivered with the same frequency as the individual's pay period.

Other tax-based transfers that are income-tested, such as the refundable provisions, are typically delivered less frequently. The refundable child tax credits were originally paid out just once a year, following the filing of tax returns and based on the filer's previous-year income. In the 1986 tax year, prepayment of two-thirds of a family's RCTC was introduced, with payment in November based on the *previous* year's income.[36] Payment of the balance or recovery of excess advance payments is accomplished with the next tax filing. Upon the conversion of the federal sales tax credits to GST credits in 1991, the payment will be changed from annual to quarterly. If tax-based transfers can be integrated into the tax-withholding mechanism, they can achieve still greater payment frequency. The EITC allows eligible individuals to elect to receive advance payments through their employers.[37] Advance payments are computed by the employer based on the claimant's earnings in each pay period. They are used to offset amounts required to be withheld for the claimant's income tax and OASDHI payroll taxes.

The formal requirements for filing an income tax return differ between the two countries. Canada has no income threshold for requiring individuals to file. Rather, an individual must file only if tax is payable for the year beyond any amounts withheld at source.[38] In the United States, individuals must file a return if their gross income exceeds their tax threshold (as given in table 3.3), even if they have no taxes due.[39] In fact, most of the working poor file returns in both countries to obtain a refund of taxes withheld, or to claim the EITC in the United States. Most other low-income Canadian persons also file returns in order to claim refundable child and sales tax credits. The refundable credits offered by some U.S. states attract additional filers. As a consequence, a great majority of poor and low-income households actually file returns; the proportion is higher in Canada than in the United States despite Canada's less inclusive formal filing requirement.

3.6.2 Responsiveness

Making payments of income security benefits more frequent does not in itself make the programs more responsive to variations in the need of benefi-

36. Advance payments are made to recipients whose net family income for the previous year was less than two-thirds of the credit's phaseout threshold; beginning in the 1990 tax year, advance payments are also made for families with three or more children whose incomes are less than the credit's phaseout threshold.

37. The claimant must file a certificate (Form W-5) with his employer confirming that the claimant is eligible for the credit and has no other certificate in effect with another employer, and indicating whether the claimant's spouse also has a certificate in effect. The tables used to compute advance payments reflect whether the worker has a spouse with a certificate.

38. Individuals also must file if they have received a demand from Revenue Canada, Taxation, to file; if they have received an advance payment of child tax credit for the year; or if they disposed of a capital property in the year.

39. A person who receives advance EITC payments from an employer must file an income tax return, regardless of income level.

ciaries. If a household suddenly drops from an average income to little or no income, policies should provide support with reasonable timeliness, so as to avoid hardship. For example, making the Canadian refundable tax credits payable more often and in advance does nothing to improve their responsiveness. Payments are still based upon the annual filing of tax returns, so that a household with a sudden loss of income might wait up to fifteen months before obtaining any relief. The exact delay will hinge upon the timing and severity of the income drop and upon the unit's income before and after declining, relative to the phaseout threshold of the credit. Other tax-related income security benefits are also linked to the annual filing of returns and therefore suffer similar deficiencies of responsiveness.

Most stand-alone income security programs are more responsive to the changing needs of beneficiaries, because they require income reporting more frequently than once a year. This is true of welfare systems and unemployment insurance.[40] Demogrant programs are highly responsive in their delivery of net benefits; they make universal gross payments and then rely on the withholding system to collect any taxes. Tax-based components of income security can also be somewhat responsive, based on their linkage with the withholding of taxes. Clearly, the personal credits in Canada and the personal exemptions in the United States have their benefits delivered with each pay period for employed persons. However, the current assessment method used in both countries does not allow a worker to catch up for benefits lost when his earnings in a pay period fall below the respective tax threshold; the worker must wait until the next annual tax filing to obtain a refund.[41] Advance payments of EITC are made through employers, based on special credit tables and the worker's earnings in each pay period.

One cost of making income security benefits highly responsive is the need for frequent income reporting. With some added complexities this can be accomplished through tax-withholding devices. Most stand-alone income security programs achieve it by requiring explicit periodic reports of income or employment. It is interesting that the policy most closely approaching a guaranteed income in Canada, the GIS, does not require frequent reporting by beneficiaries. Since the program is confined to the aged, there is much less income variation to be monitored than there would be for a program encompassing the working poor. The GIS requires only one application per year, with monthly benefits based on the claimant's income for the previous calendar year. A person who has just retired or who anticipates a substantial decline in income from specified sources can have benefits computed on estimated income for the current year. However, an *unanticipated* income decline that occurs within a year will not be reflected in higher benefits until the following

40. The food stamp program certifies welfare households for the duration of their welfare grants. Nonwelfare households are certified for three-month periods, but shorter periods can be used, hinging upon anticipated instability of household income or composition.
41. The cumulative assessment method used in Britain ("Pay As You Earn") overcomes this deficiency, but at a considerable administrative cost to employers and the tax department.

year. The counterpart U.S. program, SSI, which covers the disabled as well as the elderly, has monthly reporting, so benefits can respond far more quickly to changes in income.

3.6.3 Timing and Horizontal Equity

Without extensive averaging provisions, departures from linearity in the tax or tax-transfer rate schedule can make a person's net taxes or benefits hinge on the timing of his income receipts. Two individuals with the same long-run average income level could face different taxes or benefits based on the timing of their incomes—a clear violation of horizontal equity. These effects can arise from the benefit schedule in income security programs, the tax rate schedule, tax-transfer provisions, or the interaction between the tax and transfer programs. Both Canada and the United States abolished their provisions for general income averaging with their personal tax reforms of the latter 1980s. The removal of averaging was justified as a simplification measure, and it was further argued that averaging was much less needed on account of the flattening of the tax rate schedules. Yet this view ignores the remaining progressivity of the rate schedules, as well as the nonlinearities introduced by threshold and clawback provisions related to income security and its taxation.

Several examples can be cited to illustrate the horizontal inequities that result from the threshold and clawback provisions; others appear in the next section on effective marginal tax rates. Clawback of FA and OAS payments occurs only above $50,000 of net income in a year. For two persons having average annual net incomes of $50,000, the one with greater year-to-year income variability will have more of his benefits clawed back. Indeed, a person with perfect stability at $50,000 in every year will not face the clawback at all. Similarly, the half-taxability of OASDI benefits arises only above specified annual income thresholds. Hence, income variability around the threshold will raise the filer's taxability of benefits for a given average level of income. The EITC benefit schedule is also nonlinear in earned income; annual benefits first rise with earnings, are flat over a range of earnings, and finally decline with higher earnings. Year-to-year earnings variability either around the level where the maximum EITC benefit is first attained or where the benefit phase-out begins will reduce a worker's total benefits relative to someone with more stable earnings. However, earnings variability around the point where the EITC fully phases out ($20,264 in 1990) will increase the worker's total benefits.[42]

These horizontal inequities result from annual accounting periods for tax-transfer provisions that parallel the period for personal tax accounting. Yet even within the calendar-year period, income variation can lead to the periodic

---

42. The reason that income variability is actually beneficial in this case can be explained in economist's jargon as follows. At the point at which the EITC fully phases out, the tax-transfer schedule becomes convex; all of the other examples of income variability hurting the individual concern ranges at which the tax-transfer schedule is concave.

receipt of benefits that are deemed unwarranted on an annual basis. That is, a person is measured as needy in particular periods of the year, but his entire-year earnings would make him ineligible for benefits. This situation can arise under tax-transfer programs and requires the recovery of excess benefits from the individual. Most stand-alone income security programs avoid this problem by utilizing shorter accounting periods, often coinciding with the benefit payment period. Certain tax-transfer programs, such as the Canadian refundable tax credits, largely avoid this problem by basing their payments on past income. Still, the introduction of advance payments of the refundable child tax credits can produce overpayments. Advance payments of EITC benefits through employers can also yield overpayments that need to be recovered with the annual filing of tax returns. So long as excess payments need to be recovered from households at average or higher incomes, no great difficulties arise. Moreover, the intrayear income variability that creates the excess payments tends to generate overwithholding of income taxes, against which the benefit recovery can be charged.

Nonlinearities of the effective tax-transfer rate schedule also invite individuals to manipulate the timing of their income receipts. Certain types of income can be accelerated, delayed, or bunched so as to maximize the net benefits. The income types that are most open to discretion in timing are the realization of capital gains and the withdrawal of taxable funds from RRSPs and IRAs. Let us illustrate the potential gains to a Canadian retired couple from bunching their RRSP withdrawals, assuming they have funds that would yield $13,000 annually for their life expectancies. We consider the GIS along with provincial supplements in British Columbia, the OAS, and income taxes. The couple's first option is to receive $13,000 annually through withdrawals or annuity payments. This income would disqualify them from the GIS and the provincial supplement, but they would draw OAS benefits of $8,235 per year at mid-1990 rates. The couple's second option is to bunch RRSP withdrawals of $26,000 in alternate years. Because their non-OAS income would be zero every other year, they would receive the full GIS and provincial supplements totalling $7,820 in alternate years. After subtracting out the personal taxes payable in alternate years, their average net transfers would be over 24 percent higher than under the uniform withdrawal strategy.

3.7 Effective Marginal Tax Rates

The total effective marginal tax rate facing an individual includes the explicit marginal rate of personal tax, the clawback or phaseout rates on any relevant tax transfers, and the benefit reduction rates on cash or in-kind benefits that the individual receives.[43] These rates will cumulate additively unless

---

43. Kesselman (1980) assesses these issues for earlier Canadian provisions. Fortin (1985) provides an analysis of effective marginal tax rates in Canadian income security provisions and their distortions and welfare costs.

the benefits of one provision are deductible in the calculation of need, or ability to pay, of the other provision. Most recipients of cash or in-kind benefits from stand-alone income security programs are below the thresholds for personal tax and do not face both marginal rates simultaneously. However, the phaseouts and clawbacks of income security delivered through the tax system confront large numbers of taxpayers who also bear positive rates of tax. Sometimes the marginal rate implications of these provisions are relatively concealed from taxpayers, so that the true effective marginal rates are not always obvious. We illustrate several of these marginal rate effects due to income security provisions in the personal tax system, and then we consider their implications for policy.

The importance of marginal tax rates is well known in the theoretical and policy assessment of taxation; they are equally important for income security issues. Changes in rates may evoke a wide range of behavioral responses by taxpayers and beneficiaries. These include individuals' labor-supply decisions with respect to hours of work, exertion, labor-force participation, regularity of work, industry, occupation, education, training, mobility, responsibility, and joint family decisions. On the labor-demand side, the key choices by business firms include total employment, hours per week versus number of workers, occupational and skill composition, stability of employment, and compensation including fringe benefits. Saving incentives may also be affected with respect to aggregate levels, composition, asset and industry allocation, owner-occupied housing, and entrepreneurial behavior. Other relevant incentives include income reporting, avoidance, and evasion; the timing and bunching of income; and family formation and instability. Many of these effects are the result of "imperfect" definitions of the tax or transfer unit, the tax or transfer base, and timing and accounting principles; but increases in effective marginal rates aggravate the behavioral responses.

3.7.1   Illustrative Marginal Tax Rates

Reducing marginal tax rates was a primary goal of personal tax reform on both sides of the border. Yet both countries previously had, and have retained or expanded, income security provisions in their tax systems that raise effective marginal rates well above the statutory rates. The phaseout provisions in Canada's refundable child and sales tax credits raise effective marginal rates by 5 percentage points for taxpayers with incomes in the phaseout ranges. The 1990 thresholds for the two types of credits are $24,750 and $18,000, respectively. The conversion of the sales tax credit to a Goods and Services Tax credit in 1991 lifts the threshold for phaseout to $24,000. This substantially increases the number of families who face both phaseouts simultaneously and yields a 10-percentage-point increase in their effective tax rates. Added to the middle tax rate bracket for many taxpayers, the increase will create total federal-provincial effective marginal tax rates exceeding 50 percent—at very moderate incomes.

The recently introduced clawbacks on benefits from Family Allowance and OAS add 15 percentage points to marginal tax rates for a range of incomes above the $50,000 threshold. However, since the clawed-back amounts are tax-deductible, the net increase in effective marginal rates ranges from about 7 to 9 percentage points (depending upon the taxpayer's province and income bracket). These increases are added to the rates of the middle and top marginal tax brackets, yielding in some cases total federal-provincial effective marginal rates approaching 60 percent. The clawback on UI benefits, with a 1990 threshold just below $50,000, is applied at 30 percent, so the impact on effective marginal rates is twice that of the other clawbacks.

The conversion of personal exemptions into nonrefundable credits as part of the Canadian tax reforms did have the incidental effect of reducing effective marginal tax rates for a range of income of dependent spouses. In claiming the marital exemption, an initial amount (about $500) of income of the dependent spouse could be ignored, and additional income reduced the net exemption dollar-for-dollar. Hence, a dependent spouse faced an initial 0 percent marginal tax rate, followed by an effective marginal rate equal to that of the spouse (often the relatively high rate of a full-time worker), and finally the bottom bracket rate at income above the basic personal exemption; at this point the spouse filed separately. With personal credits in place of exemptions, a similar arrangement has been retained, namely a small disregard followed by dollar-for-dollar offset of the exemption-equivalent amount of the credit. Since the credits are exemptions evaluated at the bottom bracket tax rate, a dependent spouse with modest income now faces the bottom rate rather than the primary-earner spouse's marginal tax rate.

When the United States reformed its personal tax, it chose to claw back from higher-income taxpayers the benefits of the 15 percent rate bracket and of the personal exemptions. This is done by a 5 percent surcharge for incomes above specified levels, depending upon the type of filer, creating an effective 33 percent marginal rate bracket within the 28 percent nominal rate bracket. Benefits of the bottom bracket are clawed back first and are entirely eliminated at 1990 incomes of $97,620 for single filers and $162,770 for joint married filers. Above those incomes the personal exemptions are clawed back at a rate of 5 percent. The income range for clawing back the benefits of each $2,050 personal exemption in 1990 is $11,480 (the benefit for the 28 percent rate bracket is $0.28 \times \$2,050 = \$574$). Thus the clawback of personal exemptions arises only at very high income levels.

Two other income security features of the U.S. personal tax also raise effective marginal rates. Benefits of the EITC are phased out at a rate of 10 percent for 1990 incomes between $10,730 and $20,264. Many American families in this income range are taxable, and if they qualify for EITC their effective marginal tax rate is 25 percent rather than the nominal marginal rate of 15 percent. Up to half of OASDI or Social Security cash benefits must be included in the taxable incomes of single filers with incomes above $25,000 and married joint filers with incomes above $32,000. This provision operates in such a way as to raise effective marginal tax rates of affected persons by 50 percent of their statutory rates. Most affected persons are in the 28 percent federal tax bracket, so that their effective marginal tax rates jump to 42 percent. Clearly, the addition of income taxes in some states could carry their total effective marginal tax rates above 50 percent.

3.7.2 Policy Issues and Analysis

The notches and poverty traps created by high effective marginal rates, which approach and sometimes exceed 100 percent, are familiar for stand-alone income security programs (see Hausman 1975; Fortin 1985). These result from prohibitions on full-time work for UI beneficiaries, earnings tests for OASDI, and income tests of up to 100 percent for beneficiaries of welfare, GIS (with provincial supplements), and SSI. Income tests on in-kind benefits add directly to the effective marginal tax rates when the programs are not coordinated. The marginal rate effects of income security provisions in the tax system are less severe but also much less recognized. Since these can affect large numbers of people, and those affected have far more earnings than the poor, the potential distortions of economic behavior may be even more important. The use and structuring of such tax provisions raise fundamental issues of policy relating to economic efficiency, vertical equity, and tax administration and compliance.

Clawbacks and phaseouts of income security or tax-based benefits are commonly motivated by the perception that it is "wasteful" for benefits to go to the nonpoor or the well-off. This view cites the poor targeting of public funds, or tax expenditures, for income security objectives. Yet it ignores the economic costs of the clawbacks and phaseouts themselves. These are the economic inefficiencies and behavioral distortions caused by the provisions' increased effective marginal tax rates, along with their administrative and compliance costs. One policy alternative is to have less of such income-testing in the tax system and to raise more gross revenues to finance the more costly but more widely dispersed benefits. That is, one can either raise the marginal effective rates on beneficiaries alone (perhaps within particular income ranges), or one can raise marginal tax rates to a smaller degree for all or most taxpayers. This is a complex choice based upon various trade-offs between efficiency and equity, as well as the administrative and operational aspects.

Optimal tax theory provides general guidance in the decision whether to use clawbacks and phaseouts and, if they are adopted, in the choice of how to structure them.[44] The efficiency cost of raising the effective marginal tax rate in a particular range of income hinges upon the initial marginal tax rate in that income range, how many individuals fall in that range, their total income or

44. For general theory, see Mirrlees (1971) and Atkinson (1982); applications of the theory to a two-bracket rate schedule relevant to design of the tax-transfer system are in Kesselman and Garfinkel (1978) and Sheshinski (1989).

earnings within the range, and the responsiveness of their work effort or tax avoidance activities to higher marginal rates. The efficiency costs rise more than proportionately with increases in the marginal rate, so that one would usually not want to impose clawbacks or phaseouts on top of high rates of income testing in other income security programs. Nevertheless, in some circumstances it may be economically efficient to have very high effective marginal rates, even rates above 100 percent with so-called notches, as a way of concentrating the inefficiencies at lower incomes (see Blinder and Rosen 1985). Since aggregate earnings at those levels are relatively small, this approach can sometimes serve to minimize the total efficiency costs. This analysis may help to explain the existence of poverty traps in the policies of many countries.

More typically, it is efficient to avoid extremely high marginal rates. Income thresholds in tax-based phaseouts are a way to avoid compounding the already high effective marginal rates faced by beneficiaries of stand-alone income security programs. For similar reasons of efficiency cost, one would usually not want to impose high rates of clawback or phaseout on top of high personal marginal tax rates. This suggests that the income thresholds used for such devices be set sufficiently low that the targeted benefits are fully phased out at income levels below those attracting high personal marginal tax rates. Of course, the efficiency goal has to be balanced against the desired distribution of net benefits. A broader view of the policy problem is that the high marginal rates and notches in the separate income security programs need to be assessed and perhaps modified. For reasons of efficiency as well as administration, it may be desirable to undertake such reforms in a way that more closely integrates income security programs and personal taxation.

The flattening of rate schedules with recent tax reforms in both countries suggests that it is now less costly in efficiency terms to apply phaseouts across wide income ranges, including higher incomes. Still, the efficiency costs of providing most income security for employable persons through such income-tested or clawed-back provisions may be excessive. Theoretical and quantitative analyses have found strong efficiency advantages to using alternative policy tools. First, personal "tags" such as disability, old age, and perhaps presence of preschool children can be used to categorize potential beneficiaries as nonemployable (see Akerlof 1978). Higher income-tested benefit rates can be restricted to those who cannot work and those deemed as not expected to work. By reducing the total budgetary costs of universal support programs, this approach can relieve the pressures for higher marginal rates on taxpayers. Second, persons deemed employable can be assisted through a variety of work-related programs, including wage and employment subsidies or similar provisions delivered through the tax system.[45] These programs carry far less

---

45. For elaborations of this categorical approach and of the possible role of government as employer-of-last-resort, see Kesselman (1973, 1985), Mendelson (1986), and Ellwood (1988).

efficiency cost than general income support programs for employable persons, since they sharply reduce the effective marginal tax rates on beneficiaries' work (Kesselman 1976; Ballard 1988).

3.7.3   Application in Canada and the United States

In Canada, the policy debate has centered on the universal demogrants and public health insurance.[46] Universality has been attacked as wasteful, costly, and "inefficient" in its targeting. First the demogrants were made taxable, and more recently they have been subjected to clawbacks up to 100 percent. Several provinces allowed "extra-billing" for physician services and deterrent charges for hospital admissions, but the federal government has thwarted these practices through its control over cost-sharing. Similar moves can be seen in the United States. The legislated but never-implemented Medicare tax (a federal surtax on the income of seniors) is one example. Many other proposals for greater taxability or clawbacks of income security benefits can be found in the Congressional Budget Office's annual report, *Reducing the Deficit: Spending and Revenue Options*. Examples from the 1989 report include: taxing a portion of Medicare benefits; reducing the subsidy for nonpoor children in child nutrition programs; counting energy assistance as income under AFDC, SSI, and food stamps; phasing out the child care credit at higher incomes; taxing the income-replacement part of workers' compensation; and increasing the taxation of OASDI benefits.

All of these policy initiatives and proposals are motivated by the goal of reducing expenditures, recovering part of payments, or improving the targeting of benefits. An underlying objective is to reduce the budgetary deficit or to avoid the need to raise tax rates. Yet all these forms of benefit clawback or income testing act very much like an increased tax on the affected persons. Hence, they invoke the efficiency and equity issues that have already been discussed. Moreover, the notion that benefits of these spending and tax expenditure provisions are not sufficiently targeted on the neediest ignores the fact that they are financed out of general revenues. Even if the tax system were strictly proportional, the payment of universal demogrants or the provision of universal health insurance would be significantly redistributive. And the efficiency costs of such programs may also be minimal, aside from the distortions of the taxes needed to finance them. For example, the OAS demogrants paid to all elderly Canadians may simply substitute for savings accumulated for retirement purposes.[47] Even using coinsurance or deterrent fees for publicly insured health services may provide little effective rationing of demand, and the economic efficiency of these devices is open to question.

---

46. For analysis of the demogrant issues, see Kesselman (1980) and Mendelson (1981).

47. Nevertheless, there may be efficiency gains to recapturing OAS benefits from higher-income recipients on account of the distortions of the taxes needed to finance them. That is, it may be efficient to raise the effective tax rates on the elderly through the OAS clawback so as to reduce the tax rates needed for the general taxpaying population, because the labor-supply responses of the elderly are less than those of the working population.

3.8 Program Complexity and Simplification

It might be deemed acceptable to have very complex taxation provisions affecting primarily businesses and high-income households. Those groups either possess the requisite knowledge or can afford to hire professional advice. Comparable complexity is hardly tolerable for the tax and transfer provisions affecting millions of people at lower incomes, who typically are far less sophisticated in their facility with tax laws, bureaucratic procedures, and paperwork. If the overall tax-transfer system in Canada or the United States is challenging for educated analysts to comprehend, as our study suggests, it must be hopelessly complex for the actual and potential beneficiaries. There may be some legitimate policy objectives justifying limited complications. Examples might include social insurance principles, specific in-kind benefits, work-related benefits, or attempts to refine horizontal equity for persons with differing circumstances. Yet it would be hard to justify many elements of the existing systems or the systems in their entirety.

Undue complexity in transfer programs and tax provisions for income security can undermine their effectiveness. Among the possible results are incomplete take-up by eligible persons, horizontal inequities, errors in computing benefits or taxes due, and uncertainty by beneficiaries about the consequences of various actions on their benefits. The last effect may raise or reduce the disincentives for work and savings behavior relative to a clearer system, but it can hardly be viewed as desirable. Incomplete take-up can be found for both in-kind and tax-transfer programs. About one-fourth of AFDC households do not apply for food stamps, "for unknown reasons," even though virtually all such families are eligible. Significant numbers of elderly Canadians who are eligible for at least partial GIS payments fail to apply for them. Take-up is also less than complete for refundable credits, which require annual filing of tax returns by nontaxable claimants. In contrast, take-up rates are virtually 100 percent for the Canadian demogrant programs, which require just a single registration.

3.8.1 Program Examples

Much complexity arises from the structural features of individual tax or transfer provisions, interactions between provisions, or duplication of function by multiple provisions. The Canadian tax and transfer treatment of dependent children provides a striking example of unwarranted program complexity. The system contains nonrefundable credits, two distinct refundable credits, and demogrants that are both taxable and subject to clawback. The resulting pattern of net benefits per child as a function of family income is hard to justify. Yet the pattern is less haphazard than it was prior to the replacement of child exemptions with nonrefundable credits. At that time the net benefits rose with income because the exemptions were of no value to nontaxable units; they reached a peak at family incomes near the threshold for phaseout of the refundable child credits, which between 1982 and 1985 was $26,330. Hence, the fiscal benefits for a child were larger for nonpoor taxpayers than for poor, nontaxable households. Yet the shift to nonrefundable credits has only partially remedied the pattern, and it has left the multiplicity of provisions.

The Canadian provisions for children could be simplified in ways that would simultaneously rationalize and coordinate them. In 1990 the Family Allowance payment is $400 per child; the exemption-equivalent value of the nonrefundable child credit is $399 for each of the first two children in a family. The FA could be made nontaxable and the nonrefundable credits simultaneously abolished. A revision of the threshold for clawback of FA could offset the lost taxability of FA at middle incomes. In 1991, the threshold for phaseout of refundable credits for the federal sales tax was raised to $24,800 (from its 1990 level of $18,000), almost identical to the phaseout threshold for refundable child tax credits. There is now no reason for keeping the two refundable credits distinct. The two could be consolidated into a single credit, with the credit amount per child equal to the sum of the child amounts under the two existing credits. A more sweeping reform could be instituted that would roll *all* of the child-related provisions into a single child benefit. Perhaps the best approach would be universal child demogrants subject to partial clawback based on family income and beginning at a modest threshold, such as the poverty threshold for the relevant family size. As far as feasible, it would be desirable to integrate this clawback into source withholding of taxes.

The United States has fewer overlaps between tax and transfer systems precisely because it has been less venturesome than Canada on tax-based transfers to the working poor. But food stamps, housing subsidies, and other in-kind and cash transfers do provide many interactions and complexities. Some of these programs count receipts or entitlements from other programs in their computation of benefits. This policy can reduce the problem of high effective marginal rates due to the stacking of benefit-reduction rates from individual programs, but it also complicates program administration and enforcement. Moreover, entitlement to benefits under some programs, such as Medicaid, may hinge upon eligibility for welfare. The only real tax-based transfer in the United States, the earned-income tax credit, has a relatively simple benefit structure because it uses standard tax definitions of earned income and adjusted gross income in computing benefits. Personal exemptions for dependent children are phased out at very high incomes through a 5 percent surtax, which tax expert Joseph Pechman characterized as "bizarre" and "an anachronism that should not be allowed to survive" (1987, p. 22).

In addition to the structural complexity illustrated in the preceding examples, many low-income taxpayers and transfer recipients face serious barriers in simply interpreting their eligibility for particular benefits. Such compliance complexity afflicts a wide range of income security programs, particularly those in which there is scope for administrative discretion. These problems are also found in such commonly used American tax provisions as the dependency exemptions, marital and filing status, the earned-income tax credit, the child care credit, the kiddie tax, and child support payments. For example, an individual's eligibility to claim a tax exemption for a dependent person hinges upon the dependent's relation to the taxpayer, levels of support to the dependent from the taxpayer and from others, and the dependent's income, place of abode, and citizenship or country of residence. For most of these provisions, the qualifying rules could be radically simplified with only minor cost in terms of reduced horizontal equity, potential for abuse, or revenue loss (see suggestions by Schenk 1989). Several Canadian tax provisions affecting low-income taxpayers have similar, often needless complexity in their qualifying conditions. Examples include nonrefundable credits for dependents, deductions for child care expenses, and the tax treatment of alimony and maintenance payments.

3.8.2   Guidelines for Simplification

It is difficult to formulate general principles to guide the simplification of income security, precisely because of the multifaceted objectives of these provisions. In part, complexity is the result of the heterogeneity of the needy population—the elderly, single-parent families, the disabled, the hard-to-employ, and the unemployed. Associated with these various groups is a diversity of concerns regarding work incentives, training, in-kind provision, an income floor, and accustomed living standards. Clearly, the simplest scheme would be a set of demogrants, which would be undifferentiated or based on just a few easily observed characteristics, such as age. Yet this scheme would not satisfy all of the objectives of income security, and its budgetary cost and attendant marginal tax rates would most likely be prohibitive. Some form of categorization, distinguishing between those who are employable and those who are not, would likely be needed for an acceptable demogrant scheme. And the dictates of horizontal equity mean that tax provisions for child care and large medical expenses will not readily be abandoned.

Despite the hazards, let us suggest a few guidelines to be considered in any simplification exercise. The basic definitions used to operate the separate income transfer programs, including in-kind benefits, should be aligned more closely with the definitions of the personal income tax. That is, the unit, the base, and some of the accounting principles should be better coordinated. The creation of a consistent unit for taxes and transfers will require more changes for Canada than for the United States. Coordinated timing will be difficult to achieve, given the annual accounting period for taxation and the shorter periods used for most transfer and social insurance programs. However, the administration and enforcement of income taxes would be aided by the reporting and verification of incomes, earnings, wage rates, and hours over shorter periods of time; reporting of these items would also be required for improved income support devices, including work-related schemes. One can consider which party should be responsible for supplying information needed to operate a program. If this information is relatively complex, the onus should first be on the tax or transfer administrators, then on employers and other payers, and only last on the beneficiaries. The qualifying conditions for income security programs and tax provisions should also be simplified in ways that are consistent with other policy objectives.

3.9   The Future of the Tax-Transfer System

While reforms to tax provisions for income security have been extensive in Canada and the United States over the past five years, the overall tax-transfer systems have not been fundamentally altered. Both countries had previously instituted forms of guaranteed income for their elderly populations. Canada placed a floor under the incomes of the aged through the OAS, GIS, and provincial supplements, and the United States operated through SSI, state supplements, and the minimum-benefit provision of Social Security. Similarly, both countries provided limited, if inadequate, forms of minimum incomes for their disabled: Canada through Social Assistance and CPP, and the United States through SSI and welfare. Almost all of these earlier policies were enacted outside of the personal income tax. Several changes in tax-based provisions for the aged and disabled have been instituted recently. Both countries have attempted to improve the targeting of lower-income persons. Canada converted deductions for private pension income, aged status, and disability into nonrefundable tax credits, while the United States converted its age and disability exemptions into additional deductions restricted to those claiming the standard deduction. Yet the two countries have moved in opposite directions in their provisions for tax sheltering of retirement savings. Canada has expanded and rationalized access to these provisions at the same time that the United States has restricted access.

A more vital question is how the countries have dealt with the nonaged employable poor and their dependent children. Recent tax innovations in this area have been more numerous in Canada than in the United States. A major and largely successful reform goal for both countries was to reduce income taxation of the poor. Canada has been more generous than the United States in setting its thresholds for taxability, particularly when refundable credits and demogrant payments are considered as offsets to personal tax. But both countries still impose income taxes on many poor, nonaged single persons and on smaller proportions of other groups. In the last several years, Canada has reduced the extent of tax indexation for inflation, while the United States has implemented full indexation of its key tax components. The reforms have also increased targeting of tax benefits on lower-income households. Canada has converted personal exemptions and several other deductible items into nonrefundable credits, expanded the scope and generosity of its refundable credits, and introduced a tax clawback at upper-middle incomes on its demogrant payments.[48] The United States has made less extensive changes to augment targeting: increasing standard deductions and limiting itemized deductions, fully taxing jobless benefits, and clawing back personal exemptions at very high incomes. The earned-income tax credit has been fully indexed but not otherwise enriched.

The income security "system" for each country has evolved by piecemeal additions of new programs and tax provisions and by extensions of existing features aimed at improving coverage, scope, or adequacy. It has proven more difficult to remove or rationalize programs and provisions. Even when reforms are justifiable on horizontal-equity or incentive grounds, they create losers unless funds are added to the system. This pattern of evolution has yielded an accretion of programs and provisions, unanticipated interactions, and cumulative complexity. But the hope that these incremental changes are leading toward a streamlined, radically improved system appears elusive. Refundable child tax credits were heralded at their introduction in Canada in 1979 as the basis for a guaranteed income. Again, in 1987, newly enacted refundable sales tax credits were touted as a building block toward a guaranteed income. Similar hopes accompanied the 1964 enactment of food stamps and the later provision of earned-income tax credits, in the United States. Yet none of these provisions offers a promising basis for a broader guaranteed income, even if they have added to the total support for the low-income population.

3.9.1 The Guaranteed-Income Approach

Existing tax provisions do not lead toward a comprehensive income support scheme because of their poor responsiveness to changes in individual needs. In concept, this deficiency could be remedied through frequent periodic income reporting by beneficiaries and corresponding adjustment of their benefits. But this would entail major administrative resources and would not be easily accommodated within the personal tax system. Another major limitation of the move toward a comprehensive income support scheme for employable nonaged persons and their children is the problem of tax-back rates, incentives, and budgetary cost. Consolidation of all existing support programs and provision of an adequate level of guaranteed income, with few or no losers, would carry unacceptable budgetary costs or excessive marginal tax rates. A proposal for a guaranteed income integrated with the personal income tax, detailed in 1985 by a Canadian Royal Commission, displayed all of these difficulties. In order to provide adequate guarantee levels with reasonable

---

48. Part of the expansion of refundable tax credits has been simply to offset the incidence of increased federal sales taxes on lower-income households.

work incentives for beneficiaries, effective marginal tax rates had to rise to 49–65 percent for middle-income earners.[49] Severe disincentives to work and compliance facing the poor under welfare would simply be shifted to the much larger bulk of the taxpaying population.

Recent reforms of personal taxation will further constrain Canada and the United States from pursuing the guaranteed-income or negative-tax approach to reforming income security. Tax reform was motivated largely by a desire to reduce the marginal rates of tax while broadening the taxable base. Adoption of a guaranteed income would substantially raise effective marginal tax rates over a wide range of middle-income taxpayers. These tax rates are still rather high at middle and upper incomes in Canada. Indeed, the use of a variety of clawback provisions and benefit phaseouts in the income tax makes the Canadian effective marginal rate schedule both erratic and higher than the nominal rate schedule. Clawbacks and phaseouts apply above thresholds ranging from $18,000 to $50,000 for Family Allowance, Old Age Security, unemployment insurance benefits, and refundable tax credits. These increments to marginal rates are particularly inefficient because they arise at dense parts of the income distribution. In contrast, the higher marginal rates applied for guaranteed-income benefits to the elderly and disabled pose lesser inefficiencies because they apply to groups with much lower earnings capacity. A similar observation applies to the U.S. method of partially taxing Social Security cash benefits, which raises federal marginal tax rates by half across a range of middle incomes.

3.9.2 Work-Related Subsidy and Employability Approach

The primary policy alternative for income security with respect to employable nonaged adults is to expand the use of work-related subsidies. These subsidies can be delivered through the personal tax system, as with the EITC; through the employer, as with employment subsidies or tax credits; or directly to the worker, as with wage-rate subsidies. All forms improve incentives by effectively subsidizing work, but wage subsidies may be preferred for their superior targeting by beneficiary earnings capacity and their greater work incentives. The extent to which a greater emphasis on work-related support will require categorization of persons who are employable and those who are not remains to be seen. Still, relatively generous provision of benefits for those unable to work will strengthen the economic case for categorization. This overall strategy may also involve the provision of public employment at relatively low wages as a last resort for those unable to find private work. Reforms

49. For the proposal, see Royal Commission on the Economic Union and Development Prospects for Canada (1985); for a critique see Kesselman (1986). Leman (1980) provides a historical account and policy analysis of the failure of earlier proposals for guaranteed incomes in Canada and the U.S.

to UI to improve incentives for reemployment and more stable jobs, particularly in Canada, have an obvious role. Both countries have already made limited moves toward a work-related approach through policies for employment tax credits, wage and training subsidies, work requirements in welfare, and earnings subsidies or tax credits.[50]

Reinforcing the work-related subsidies for employable adults would be a wide range of policies to improve the market earnings capacity of low-skilled, poorly educated workers, and to help their children avoid similar problems when they enter the labor market. This approach to income security reflects an increased emphasis on attacking the causes of poverty and low incomes and a reduced emphasis on alleviating the symptoms. Suitable policies might include improvements in the following areas: institutional and on-the-job training, apprenticeship programs, public education, adult literacy, day care, employment counseling, special public employment, enforcement of support payments, and employment or pay equity. Many policies have been tried previously in these areas; the present challenge is to improve their content and delivery, as well as to find an effective mix of policies. This is an ambitious agenda, and the trade-offs with conventional income support will be difficult. Moreover, these policies have long gestation periods before producing results that ultimately reduce the ongoing costs of providing income security.

Supporting children in lower-income households is another important aspect of income security. Receipt of benefits is tied directly to the presence of children under some provisions (welfare in both countries and the EITC in the United States). Welfare receipt is conditional upon nonemployment in most instances, whereas EITC benefits are tied to earned income. It may be fairer, and simpler, to provide child benefits unrelated to the work-force attachment of the parent, as with Family Allowance and refundable child tax credits in Canada. Any earnings- or work-related subsidies or tax credits would then be provided to adults irrespective of the presence of dependent children. The child benefits could be income tested, either prior to payment or through a clawback device in the income tax. However, it would make sense to target the net benefits on families at low incomes, so that the clawback rates do not affect middle- or upper-income earners. The existing clawbacks on Family Allowance in Canada and on child tax exemptions in the United States affect taxpayers at middle and upper incomes, respectively. With a partial clawback, child demogrants could also serve to differentiate net tax burdens by family size at higher incomes in a simple and nondistorting fashion. Whether one chooses to provide such differentiation hinges on value judgments, as noted earlier in the study.

---

50. Both countries have delivered tax credits through the employing firm. Canada began an employment tax credit in 1978. The U.S. instituted the New Jobs Tax Credit program in 1977 and converted it to the Targeted Jobs Credit in 1979; these provisions were predated by a "work incentive" tax credit for employers of AFDC beneficiaries.

3.9.3   Future Policy Structure and Harmonization

Recent reforms in Canada and the United States reveal a willingness to experiment with tax-based provisions for income security. The extent to which future income security functions are embedded in the tax system, as opposed to spending programs, will hinge upon a host of practical considerations. These include the administrative needs of responsiveness, frequency of payments, the relation between the tax and transfer unit, the relation between the measure of need and the taxable base, publicity costs and take-up rates, and social factors such as the stigma for beneficiaries. Insofar as the policies are structurally tied to training or employment, it is harder to operate them through the income tax, with the exception of an earnings tax credit. Regardless of their exact content, future reforms should ignore the distinction between direct expenditures and tax expenditures. Choices between a tax method and a spending approach should consider only the net revenue costs, vertical incidence, horizontal equity, efficiency costs, incentives, and the delivery aspects cited here (see Kesselman 1990a). It is notable that most recent proposals for reforming income security in both countries, ranging across the ideological spectrum, include tax-based provisions.[51]

Early in this study the main external constraint on the development of the two countries' income security was identified as industry-specific issues. Migration of labor between Canada and the United States was dismissed as unlikely to constrain the levels or structures of each country's income security system, at least as long as steep barriers to immigration remain for most population groups. Yet one could turn the problem around and ask whether the desire for a distinct structure or level of income security in a country such as Canada might inhibit the acceptance of reduced barriers to labor mobility. This would in fact seem to be a realistic proposition. It is hard to imagine Canada, with its universal medical coverage, opening its doors to all American workers. With totally open borders each individual could shop to find the country that maximized his or her income security benefits net of tax burden. Then each country, and particularly Canada as the smaller one, would be severely limited in its ability to pursue independent policies of income security or redistribution. If Canada and the United States wished to integrate their labor markets while still preserving redistributive functions, new institutional arrangements would be required.[52] One approach would be a mutually agreed and coordinated—and perhaps jointly operated—set of income security policies. In other words, the two countries would have to pursue income security policies on a harmonized basis.

While current pressures for harmonizing the Canadian and U.S. income

51. For Canadian examples, see Courchene (1987), Kesselman (1985), and Mendelson (1986); for U.S. examples see Ellwood (1988), Glazer (1988), and Haveman (1988).

52. These issues are discussed in the context of European integration by Sinn (1990). Also see Wildasin (1991), which leads to similar conclusions.

security systems are mostly limited to industry-specific policies, some broader economic forces may also be operative. These pressures do not stem so much from the other country as from the rest of the world and from domestic sources. Both countries face increasingly severe competitive pressures from overseas producers.[53] And both countries face large, continuing budgetary deficits at their federal levels. These considerations and the desire for higher real living standards may incline both countries to devise income security policies that are efficient and promote productivity. They will intensify recent interest in reorienting welfare programs toward work and enhanced employability.[54] They may also lead Canada away from universal programs such as demogrants and health insurance, though such a move would be based on the misconception that universality is inherently inefficient. A wide range of educational, training, child care, and other work-enhancing policies will likely play significant roles in a productivity-oriented approach. The two countries will undoubtedly retain major differences in the institutional manifestations of their income security and related tax policies. Yet one might anticipate a longer-run convergence of Canadian and U.S. policies toward greater efficiency and productivity. One can hope that the policies, with some care in their design and with adequate political support, will also serve well those in need.

References

Akerlof, George A. 1978. The economics of "tagging" as applied to the optimal income tax, welfare programs and manpower planning. *American Economic Review* 68:8–19.

Atkinson, A. B. 1982. The theory and design of income taxation: review and prospects. TIDI paper no. 38. London School of Economics: Economic and Social Research Council Programme on Taxation, Incentives, and the Distribution of Income.

Ballard, Charles L. 1988. The marginal efficiency cost of redistribution. *American Economic Review* 78:1019–33.

Blinder, Alan S., and Harvey S. Rosen. 1985. Notches. *American Economic Review* 75:736–47.

Blomqvist, Å. G. 1985. Political economy of the Canadian welfare state. In *Approaches to economic well-being*, ed. David Laidler, 89–136. Toronto: University of Toronto Press for the Royal Commission on the Economic Union and Development Prospects for Canada.

Boskin, Michael J., and Eytan Sheshinski. 1983. Optimal tax treatment of the family: Married couples. *Journal of Public Economics* 20:281–97.

Brannon, Gerard M., and Elliot R. Morss. 1973. The tax allowance for dependents: Deductions versus credits. *National Tax Journal* 26:599–609.

53. See Courchene (1990) and Osberg (1990) for views on how growing international competition may impinge upon the future development of income security provisions.
54. Gueron (1990) provides a useful review of what has been learned from U.S. initiatives in this area.

Canadian Tax Foundation. Misc. years. *The national finances.* Toronto.

CCH Canadian Limited. Misc. years. *Canada income tax guide.* Don Mills, Ont.

Cloutier, A. Pierre, and Bernard Fortin. 1989. Converting exemptions and deductions into credits: An economic assessment. In *The economic impacts of tax reform,* ed. Jack Mintz and John Whalley, 45–82. Toronto: Canadian Tax Foundation.

Commerce Clearing House Inc. Misc. years. *Federal tax guide.* Chicago.

Congressional Budget Office, Congress of the United States. 1989. *Reducing the deficit: Spending and revenue options.* Washington, D.C.: Government Printing Office.

Courchene, Thomas J. 1987. *Social policy in the 1990s: Agenda for reform.* Toronto: Prentice-Hall Canada for the C. D. Howe Institute.

———. 1990. Commentary on "Distributional issues and the future of the welfare state," by Lars Osberg. In *Perspective 2000,* ed. K. Newton, T. Schweitzer, and J.-P. Voyer, 174–80. Ottawa: Supply and Services Canada.

Cousineau, Jean-Michel. 1985. Unemployment insurance and labour market adjustments. In Vaillancourt (1985b), 187–213.

Danziger, Sheldon, and Jonathan R. Kesselman. 1978. Personal exemptions and per capita credits. In *The President's 1978 tax reduction and reform proposals,* Hearings of the Committee on Ways and Means, 95th Cong., 2d sess., pt. 6, 3558–73.

Ellwood, David T. 1988. *Poor support: Poverty in the American family.* New York: Basic Books.

Federal Council on the Aging. 1977. *The treatment of assets and income from assets in income-conditioned government benefit programs.* Washington, D.C.

Feldstein, Martin S. 1974. Unemployment compensation: Adverse incentives and distributional anomalies. *National Tax Journal* 27:231–44.

Fortin, Bernard. 1985. Income security in Canada. In Vaillancourt (1985b), 153–86.

Glazer, Nathan. 1988. *The limits of social policy.* Cambridge: Harvard University Press.

Gueron, Judith M. 1990. Work and welfare: Lessons on employment programs. *Journal of Economic Perspectives* 4(Winter):79–98.

Hanratty, Maria J., and Rebecca M. Blank. 1992. Down and out in North America: Recent trends in poverty in the U.S. and Canada. *Quarterly Journal of Economics* 107(February):233–54.

Hausman, Leonard J. 1975. Cumulative tax rates in alternative income maintenance systems. In *Integrating income maintenance programs,* ed. Irene Lurie, 39–77. New York: Academic Press.

Haveman, Robert. 1988. *Starting even: An equal opportunity program to combat the nation's new poverty.* New York: Simon and Schuster.

Hum, Derek P. J. 1983. *Federalism and the poor: A review of the Canada Assistance Plan.* Toronto: Ontario Economic Council.

———. 1988. Harmonization of social programs under free trade. In *Free trade and social policy,* ed. Glenn Drover, 25–47. Ottawa: Canadian Council on Social Development.

Kesselman, Jonathan R. 1973. A comprehensive approach to income maintenance: SWIFT. *Journal of Public Economics* 2:59–88.

———. 1976. Egalitarianism of earnings and income taxes. *Journal of Public Economics* 5:285–301.

———. 1979. Credits, exemptions, and demogrants in Canadian tax-transfer policy. *Canadian Tax Journal* 27:653–88.

———. 1980. Pitfalls of selectivity in income security programs. *Canadian Taxation* (Fall):154–63.

———. 1982. Taxpayer behavior and the design of a credit income tax. In *Income-tested transfer programs: The case for and against,* ed. Irwin Garfinkel, 215–81. New York: Academic Press.

————. 1983. *Financing Canadian unemployment insurance.* Toronto: Canadian Tax Foundation.

————. 1985. Comprehensive income security for Canadian workers. In Vaillancourt (1985b), 283–319.

————. 1986. The royal commission's proposals for income security reform. *Canadian Public Policy* 12 (February supp.):101–12.

————. 1990a. Direct expenditures versus tax expenditures for economic and social policy. In *Tax expenditures and government policy,* ed. Neil Bruce, 283–323. Kingston, Ont.: John Deutsch Institute for the Study of Economic Policy, Queen's University.

————. 1990b. *Rate structure and personal taxation: Flat rate or dual rate?* Wellington, New Zealand: Victoria University Press for the Institute of Policy Studies.

Kesselman, Jonathan R., and Irwin Garfinkel. 1978. Professor Friedman, meet Lady Rhys-Williams: NIT vs. CIT. *Journal of Public Economics* 10:179–216.

Leman, Christopher. 1980. *The collapse of welfare reform: Political institutions, policy, and the poor in Canada and the United States.* Cambridge: MIT Press.

MacDonald, Maurice. 1977. *Food, stamps, and income maintenance.* New York: Academic Press.

McIntyre, Michael J., and Oliver Oldman. 1977. Taxation of the family in a comprehensive and simplified income tax. *Harvard Law Review* 90:1573–1630.

Mendelson, Michael. 1981. *Universal or selective? The debate on reforming income security in Canada.* Toronto: Ontario Economic Council.

————. 1986. Can we reform Canada's income security system? In *The future of social welfare systems in Canada and the United Kingdom,* ed. Shirley B. Seward, 117–46. Halifax, N.S.: Institute for Research on Public Policy.

Mirrlees, J. A. 1971. An exploration in the theory of optimum income taxation. *Review of Economic Studies* 38:175–208.

Munnell, Alicia H. 1986. Taxing social security benefits. In *Checks and balances in social security,* ed. Yung-Ping Chen and George F. Rohrlich, 77–93. Lanham, Md.: University Press of America.

Osberg, Lars. 1990. Distributional issues and the future of the welfare state. In *Perspective 2000,* ed. K. Newton, T. Schweitzer, and J.-P. Voyer, 159–74. Ottawa: Supply and Services Canada.

Pechman, Joseph A. 1987. Tax reform: Theory and practice. *Journal of Economic Perspectives* 1 (Summer):11–28.

Pechman, Joseph A., and Gary V. Engelhardt. 1990. The income tax treatment of the family: An international perspective. *National Tax Journal* 43:1–22.

Pogue, Thomas F. 1974. Deductions vs. credits: A comment. *National Tax Journal* 27:659–62.

Rejda, George E. 1988. *Social insurance and economic security.* 3d ed. Englewood Cliffs, N.J.: Prentice-Hall.

Royal Commission on the Economic Union and Development Prospects for Canada. 1985. *Report.* 3 vols. Ottawa: Supply and Services Canada.

Schenk, Deborah H. 1989. Simplification for individual taxpayers: Problems and proposals. *Tax Law Review* 45:121–76.

Sheshinski, Eytan. 1989. Note on the shape of the optimum income tax schedule. *Journal of Public Economics* 40:201–15.

Sinn, Hans-Werner. 1990. Tax harmonization and tax competition in Europe. *European Economic Review* 34:489–504.

Steuerle, C. Eugene. 1990. Tax credits for low-income workers with children. *Journal of Economic Perspectives* 4 (Summer):201–12.

U.S. Advisory Commission on Intergovernmental Relations. 1990. *Significant features of fiscal federalism.* Vol. 1. Washington, D.C.

Vaillancourt, François. 1985a. Income distribution and economic security in Canada: An overview. In Vaillancourt (1985b), 1–75.

———, ed. 1985b. *Income distribution and economic security in Canada.* Toronto: University of Toronto Press for the Royal Commission on the Economic Union and Development Prospects for Canada.

Wildasin, David E. 1991. Income redistribution in a common labor market. *American Economic Review* 81:757–74.

4   Tax Incidence: Annual and Lifetime Perspectives in the United States and Canada

James B. Davies

4.1   Introduction

There is a popular belief that Canada is "more equal" than the United States. As shown in this paper, there is some truth in that notion. The purpose of this paper is to examine the role of differences in the two countries' tax systems in determining the relative degree of income inequality on the two sides of the border. Attention is paid not only to differences at a point in time, but also to how income distributions are changing over time, and to the relationships of these changes to recent tax reform initiatives in the two countries.

What determines the overall impact of taxes on income distribution? Important determinants of the impact of a single tax are its base and rate structure. The incidence of the overall system is in addition affected by the relative reliance on different types of taxes, that is, by the *tax mix*. In analyzing the overall effect of taxes on inequality in Canada and the United States it will therefore be important to look at differences in tax mix, tax bases, and rate structures. Of course, tax effects on income distribution are also affected by how particular taxes are *shifted* in the general equilibrium of the economy. For the most part it is likely that similar taxes would be similarly shifted in the two countries, so that comparisons of shifting are not a major element in the international comparison.

Given the limits of available data, it is not surprising that estimates of the impact of taxes on the distribution of real income have mostly been made in an annual framework. Recently, however, there has been interest in generating estimates of the overall lifetime incidence of taxes (Davies, St-Hilaire, and

James B. Davies is associate professor of economics at the University of Western Ontario and a member of the NBER's Conference on Research in Income and Wealth.

The author would like to thank the conference organizers, Charles McLure, Richard Musgrave, James Poterba, and other conference participants for valuable comments and suggestions. He assumes responsibility for any errors or omissions.

Whalley 1984; Rogers 1988; Poterba 1989). This paper argues that important insights, relevant to the comparison of tax structures in Canada and the United States, can be gained from such work. For example, general sales taxes look considerably less regressive over the lifetime than they do in annual data, since consumption is approximately proportional to permanent income. Since Canada relies much more heavily on sales and excise taxes, a significant difference in the comparison of overall tax progressivity in the two countries is implied, depending on whether an annual or lifetime framework is used.

Section 4.2 presents background evidence on before- and after-tax income inequality, and how it has changed in the last few decades, for the two countries. The impact of transfer payments and other forms of government expenditure is also discussed. Section 4.3 then reviews estimates of overall tax incidence in Canada and the United States for the early 1970s. These estimates are available on a consistent basis for the two countries and provide a useful starting point for the examination of changes in the impact of taxes on income distribution in the two countries over the last two decades, in sections 4.4 and 4.5. Section 4.4 looks at the period up to the recent tax reforms, which are in turn explored in section 4.5. How the conclusions reached in the preceding sections are altered when one takes a lifetime, rather than an annual, viewpoint is examined in section 4.6.

4.2   The Distribution of Annual Income in Canada and the United States

4.2.1   Pretax Distributions

Table 4.1 shows, according to the standard survey data sources, that there is considerably greater inequality in before-tax income in the United States than in Canada, and that the gap has been widening for about the past fifteen years. Income inequality was roughly constant in both countries from the mid-1960s to the mid-1970s. Gini coefficients were in the neighborhood of .32–.33 in Canada and .35–.36 in the U.S.; the bottom 5% had 6.2% of total income in Canada and 5.2–5.4% in the U.S.; and the share of the top 20% was 39–40% in Canada and about 41% in the U.S. Since 1975 there have been only minor changes in the Canadian distribution, but notice that the share of the bottom 20% has risen slightly, to about 6.5%. In contrast, in the U.S. there has been a continuous increase in inequality, which shows no sign of having stopped. The shares of bottom and top 20% are now at 4.6% and 44.0% respectively, and the Gini coefficient has risen to .395, 10% above its 1975 U.S. value, and 20% above the current Canadian value.

While the data shown in table 4.1 provide the best time series on income inequality in the two countries, it is important to realize that they have serious limitations. These estimates come from sample surveys, which are affected by problems of differential response according to income level and by misreport-

Table 4.1   **Quintile Shares and Gini Coefficients for Families (Money Income before Tax)**

Year	Quintile					Gini
	1	2	3	4	5	
1. Canada						
1965	6.2%	13.1%	18.0%	23.6%	39.0%	.319
1969	6.2	12.6	17.9	23.5	39.7	.326
1975	6.2	13.0	18.2	23.9	38.8	.326
1980	6.2	13.0	18.3	24.1	38.5	.323
1981	6.5	12.9	18.3	24.1	38.3	.318
1982	6.4	12.6	18.0	24.0	38.9	.326
1983	6.3	12.4	17.8	24.1	39.5	.334
1984	6.2	12.4	18.0	24.1	39.4	.334
1985	6.4	12.4	17.9	24.1	39.2	.330
1986	6.4	12.4	17.9	24.0	39.3	.331
1987	6.5	12.4	17.8	24.0	39.4	.330
1988	6.5	12.4	17.9	24.0	39.2	.328
2. United States						
1965	5.2	12.2	17.8	23.9	40.9	.356
1970	5.4	12.2	17.6	23.8	40.9	.354
1975	5.4	11.8	17.6	24.1	41.1	.358
1980	5.1	11.6	17.5	24.3	41.6	.365
1981	5.0	11.3	17.4	24.4	41.9	.370
1982	4.7	11.2	17.1	24.3	42.7	.381
1983	4.7	11.1	17.1	24.3	42.8	.382
1984	4.7	11.0	17.0	24.4	42.9	.383
1985	4.6	10.9	16.9	24.2	43.5	.389
1986	4.6	10.8	16.8	24.0	43.7	.392
1987	4.6	10.7	16.8	24.0	43.8	.392
1988	4.6	10.7	16.7	24.0	44.0	.395

Sources: **Canada**— Quintile Shares: Statistics Canada, *Size Distribution of Income in Canada, 1978, 1990* (13-207); Gini Coefficients: Statistics Canada, *Income After Tax Distributions by Size in Canada, 1990* (13-210), and Statistics Canada, *Income Inequality: Statistical Methodology and Canadian Illustrations, 1976,* R. Love and M. Wolfson (13-559). **United States:** U.S. Bureau of the Census, Current Population Reports series P-60, no. 162, *Money Income of Households, Families and Persons in the United States, 1987,* and no. 166, *Money Income and Poverty in the United States, 1988.*

ing (generally underreporting) of income sources. In Canada, the net result of these nonsampling errors is that the survey-based estimates of income aggregates understate transfer income by about 40% and investment income by about 20%. The survey aggregate for wage and salary income, in contrast, is quite close to that in the national accounts. Additionally, these surveys omit capital gains.

While the data shown in table 4.1 may not give an enormously reliable estimate of income inequality for a particular year, it is likely that they capture *trends* in inequality reasonably well. However, the Canadian data miss at least one very interesting trend. The last two decades have been extremely good ones for a small number of Canadian families in the stratosphere of the income distribution. *Fortune*'s 1989 enumeration of the world's billionaires indicated that out of 157 billionaire families worldwide, six were wholly or partly Canadian (see Slovak 1989). Moreover, the Canadians were not at the bottom of the heap. Three of the top eleven families were Canadian. Altogether the six billionaire families had estimated net worth of $29.3 billion (Canadian).

There is a widespread perception in Canada that the reason that a small number of Canadian families have done so well lies in a combination of light taxation and loose regulation. In any case, it may well be that the extreme upper tail of the Canadian income distribution has lengthened considerably over the last two decades. While this would not necessarily increase very much the share of the top quintile, or the Gini coefficient, it is an interesting aspect of the Canadian income distribution.[1]

Part of the reason for the continuing increase in before-tax inequality in the U.S. is no doubt the tendency toward more conservative economic and social programs under President Reagan, including deregulation, declining real minimum wages, and cutbacks in welfare programs. Total government spending on income support, Social Security, and welfare declined from 11.0% of GDP in 1980 to 9.6% in 1988, for example; this decline would by itself account for a little less than half the fall in the share of the bottom 20% (assuming that income maintenance programs all shrank in equal proportion). But note that there had been a significant rise in inequality between 1975 and 1980–81, *before* "Reaganomics" had taken effect. There is likely a "non-Reagan" component of the trend toward greater inequality in the U.S., caused by such factors as changing household structure, large-scale unskilled immigration, technological change, and perhaps declining unionization.[2]

4.2.2   Role of Transfer Payments and Direct Personal Taxes

The standard income distribution figures used as a barometer of the rise and fall of inequality in Canada and the U.S. include cash transfers from government to persons, but make no deduction for taxes paid. They therefore allow partially, and it would seem rather arbitrarily, for the redistributive role of government. Official statistical agencies in both countries are, of course, highly aware of this curious situation, and have published supplementary "after-tax" distributions which deduct some of the important direct personal taxes. While the results still fall far short of a complete analysis of fiscal inci-

1. The aggregate income of the top quintile in Canada, according to the table 4.1 data, would be about $160 billion. Adding several billionaires, each with true economic income of, say, $100–200 million, would not increase this total very much, although it might well "lengthen the upper tail" considerably.

2. Note that any explanation for the secular rise in inequality in the U.S. must identify factors that were not at work in Canada. (This immediately brings the role of technological change into question.) Thus the Canada-U.S. comparison may be very useful in finding out why inequality is steadily rising in the U.S.

dence, they are of some interest. Table 4.2 allows for an instructive Canada-U.S. comparison.

Part 1 of table 4.2 shows the impact of cash transfers and personal income taxes estimated by the Canadian Survey of Consumer Finance (SCF) for families and unattached individuals. The first three lines of part 2 show corresponding data for U.S. households. The U.S. data are only available for *households;* families and unattached individuals are the most closely corresponding category in the Canadian data. However, the difference in family unit definitions has a significant effect on the comparison.[3] Note that for the same income definition as used in table 4.1, total money income (line 2 in both parts of table 4.2), Canada and U.S. appear to be closer together in table 4.2 than in table 4.1. This is likely to be simply the result of the mismatch in family unit definitions in the available data.

Table 4.2 indicates that, without transfer payments, the distribution of money income before taxes in Canada and the U.S. would be much more unequal. In both countries the share of the bottom 20% would decline by over half. Perhaps surprisingly, while the relative importance of transfer payments in the two countries differs by quintile, there is no systematic difference. The introduction of transfers changes income shares, in terms of percentage points, more in Canada than in the U.S. in the second and fifth quintiles, and less in the remaining quintiles. Thus, the great differences in form of transfer payments in the two countries do not lead to one country's transfer payments being systematically more equalizing than the other's. The absence of a systematic difference also reflects the fact that the fraction of national income expended in transfer programs is similar in the two countries. As shown in table 4.3, transfers made up 12.3% of GDP in Canada in 1986, and 11.8% in the U.S.

The income tax comparison made possible by table 4.2 tells a story similar to that for transfers. Like transfers, income taxes reduce income inequality considerably in both countries, although the impact is relatively stronger at high incomes than low. And again, while the comparison of impacts in Canada and the U.S. varies by quintile, there is not a systematically more equalizing impact in one country than the other. U.S. income taxes reduce the share of the top quintile by a greater amount than Canadian taxes do, but they also *increase* the share of the second highest quintile. This absence of a clear-cut difference is somewhat surprising, unlike the finding on transfers, since personal income taxes loom larger in Canada than in the U.S.—12.3% of GDP versus 10.2%, respectively, in 1986. One would perhaps expect Canadian income taxes to have been more strongly equalizing.

Part 2 of table 4.2 also shows what happens to the U.S. distribution when Social Security payroll taxes, as well as income taxes, are deducted from in-

---

3. While the difference in family unit concept affects a comparison of the *level* of inequality between Canada and the U.S. slightly, it may not affect appreciably the comparison of the *changes* in inequality caused by taxes and transfers in the two countries.

Table 4.2   Effects of Transfers and Taxes on Income Distribution, 1986, by Units
                   (Ranked by Total Money Income)

Income Concept		Quintile				
Transfers Included?	Taxes Deducted?	1	2	3	4	5
1. Canada: Families and Unattached Individuals						
No	No	2.1%	8.0%	16.7%	26.2%	47.1%
Yes	No	4.7	10.4	17.0	24.9	43.1
Yes	Yes: PIT[a]	5.6	11.3	17.5	24.8	40.9
2. United States: Households						
No	No	1.1	8.2	16.0	25.6	49.2
Yes	No	3.8	9.7	16.4	24.0	46.1
Yes	Yes: PIT	4.5	11.0	17.4	24.5	42.6
Yes	Yes: PIT & Social Security	4.8	11.1	17.5	24.3	42.2

Sources: **Canada**—Statistics Canada, *Size Distribution of Income in Canada, 1988* (13-207);
Statistics Canada, *Income After Tax Distributions by Size in Canada, 1990* (13-210). **United
States**—U.S. Bureau of the Census, Current Population Reports series P-60, no. 164-Rd-1,
Measuring the Effect of Benefits and Taxes on Income and Poverty, 1986.
[a]Computed using effective tax rates for families of two or more members.

come. U.S. income inequality is further reduced slightly, but the Canada-U.S.
comparison is left ambiguous (even if it were appropriate to neglect social
security payroll taxes in Canada; doing so would be a dubious procedure
since, although smaller than U.S. payroll taxes, they amounted to 4.2% of
GDP in 1986). Overall, after adding transfer payments and deducting income
taxes, both Canadian and U.S. income distributions are much more equal than
the underlying distributions of private income, but there is not a major difference in the degree of redistribution.

Table 4.2 only allows us to scratch the surface of fiscal incidence in Canada
and the U.S. In the next section we discuss the results of taking the entire
panoply of taxes into account, and of modeling the tax-shifting process. However, even this does not allow one to answer the question of which country has
the most redistribution. In order to answer that question one would have to
take into account the many forms of noncash transfers from governments to
persons in the two countries. A systematic study of these transfers is beyond
the scope of the present paper, but table 4.3 allows a few remarks to be made.

Table 4.3 shows the changes in relative importance of different forms of
government expenditure in Canada and the U.S. since 1965. While total expenditures are a larger fraction of GDP in Canada (partly, but not wholly, due
to Canada's relatively larger interest payments), transfer payments and public
expenditures on education are a similar percentage of GDP in the two countries. Where there is a major difference, is in expenditures on national defense
and health. In 1987, Canada spent 1.8% of its GDP on defense and 5.9% on
health. U.S. expenditures in these two categories—6.6% on defense and
1.6% on health—can be obtained, roughly, by reversing the Canadian figures

Table 4.3 **Composition of Government Expenditures**

Year	Total Expenditure	Expenditure Categories				
		Transfers	Defense	Health	Education	Other
1. Canada						
As % of GDP						
1965	25.0%	6.1%	2.7%	2.8%	4.6%	8.8
1970	32.1	8.0	2.1	4.9	6.9	10.3
1975	36.9	10.1	1.8	5.2	6.2	13.6
1980	37.6	9.8	1.5	5.1	5.8	15.4
1981	38.7	9.8	1.5	5.3	5.9	16.2
1982	43.5	11.7	1.8	5.8	6.2	18.1
1983	44.3	12.3	1.8	6.0	6.2	18.1
1984	43.9	12.0	1.8	5.7	5.8	18.5
1985	44.1	12.1	2.0	5.9	6.0	18.1
1986	43.8	12.3	1.9	5.9	5.7	18.0
1987	42.8	12.2	1.8	5.9	5.6	17.5
1988	41.8	11.8	1.7	5.9	5.3	17.0
1989	41.8	11.7	n.a.	n.a.	n.a.	n.a.
As % of Total Expenditure						
1965	100.0	24.2	11.0	11.1	18.5	35.2
1970	100.0	25.0	6.5	15.1	21.4	32.0
1975	100.0	27.5	4.8	14.1	16.8	36.9
1980	100.0	26.2	4.1	13.5	15.5	40.8
1981	100.0	25.4	4.0	13.7	15.1	41.8
1982	100.0	26.8	4.1	13.3	14.3	41.6
1983	100.0	27.8	3.9	13.4	13.9	40.9
1984	100.0	27.4	4.1	12.9	13.2	42.1
1985	100.0	27.5	4.5	13.4	13.6	41.1
1986	100.0	28.0	4.2	13.6	13.1	41.2
1987	100.0	28.5	4.1	13.8	13.1	41.0
1988	100.0	28.4	4.2	14.0	12.6	40.8
1989	100.0	28.0	n.a.	n.a.	n.a.	n.a.
2. United States						
As % of GDP						
1965	27.4%	5.5%	7.2%	1.0%	4.5%	9.2
1970	31.8	7.7	7.4	1.3	5.7	9.6
1975	34.9	11.2	5.4	1.6	6.2	10.5
1980	33.6	11.1	5.1	1.6	5.7	10.2
1981	33.8	11.2	5.3	1.6	5.5	10.4
1982	36.1	12.0	5.9	1.6	5.6	11.0
1983	35.9	12.0	6.1	1.6	5.5	10.6
1984	34.3	11.8	6.3	1.5	5.2	9.5
1985	35.3	11.8	6.5	1.5	5.3	10.2
1986	35.4	11.8	6.6	1.5	5.4	10.1
1987	35.0	11.6	6.6	1.6	5.4	9.9
1988	34.2	11.5	6.2	n.a.	n.a.	n.a.
1989	34.2	11.6	5.8	n.a.	n.a.	n.a.
As % of Total Expenditure						
1965	100.0	20.0	26.3	3.7	16.3	33.6
1970	100.0	24.3	23.4	4.2	17.9	30.2

(*continued*)

Table 4.3   (continued)

		Expenditure Categories				
Year	Total Expenditure	Transfers	Defense	Health	Education	Other
1975	100.0	32.0	15.5	4.6	17.9	30.0
1980	100.0	32.9	15.1	4.7	17.0	30.3
1981	100.0	33.0	15.6 .	4.6	16.2	30.7
1982	100.0	33.2	16.4	4.4	15.5	30.5
1983	100.0	33.3	17.1	4.5	15.4	29.7
1984	100.0	34.3	18.3	4.3	15.3	27.8
1985	100.0	33.4	18.5	4.3	15.0	28.9
1986	100.0	33.3	18.6	4.3	15.2	28.5
1987	100.0	33.1	18.8	4.4	15.4	28.4
1988	100.0	33.6	18.0	n.a.	n.a.	n.a.
1989	100.0	33.8	17.0	n.a.	n.a.	n.a.

Sources: **Canada**—Statistics Canada, *National Income and Expenditure Accounts,* (13-201), various issues (for total expenditures, transfer payments, and defense expenditures); Statistics Canada, *Consolidated Government Finance, 1965, 1970, 1975* (68-202) and Canadian Tax Foundation, *The National Finances, 1988–89,* for other years (health and education expenditures, consolidated, i.e., net of intergovernmental transfers).**United States**—U.S. Department of Commerce, *Survey of Current Business,* various July issues; Department of Commerce, *The National Income and Product Accounts of the U.S., Statistical Tables 1929–76,* September 1981.

for the two items. The U.S. can deter foreign aggressors, but has embarrassing inequities in medical treatment. Canada, on the other hand, cannot deter anyone but has universal, free socialized medicine.

The expenditure figures point to the great difference between Canada and the U.S. in the allocation of medical care, which pushes the balance toward Canada's being more redistributive than the U.S. But these figures do not tell the whole story: they do not call attention to the fact that all postsecondary education available in Canada is heavily subsidized, that many Canadian transfer programs embody the principle of "universality," or that unemployment insurance is more lavish in Canada than in the U.S.[4] What all this adds up to is that Canadians have more *security* in health, education, and income than do U.S. residents. A Canadian citizen is endowed with "cradle to grave" public health care, education, and income security. The system is more extensive, *and* it is more difficult to fall through its cracks than in the U.S. This fact indicates, together with the greater equality in private money income, that there is likely truth in the perception that Canada is "more equal" than the

4. Canada's major "universal" transfer programs are family allowances and old age security (OAS) pensions. While there are slight variations in payments between provinces, in most provinces the family allowance in 1989 was $65.48 per month per child. The OAS pension was $326 per month. Both family allowances and OAS have been part of taxable income for some time. However, in the April 1989 budget it was announced that they would be taxed back at a rate of 15% on individual net income exceeding $50,000. Even such a progressive measure is widely viewed with concern by those who favor a more redistributive government, since it erodes the principle of universality.

U.S. It remains to be seen whether the tax system has any impact on the comparison.

4.3   Comparisons of Tax Impacts on Inequality in the Early 1970s

The previous section looked at simple indications of the effect of taxes and transfers on the distribution of real income in Canada and the United States. The range of taxes considered was limited, and zero tax shifting was assumed. Here we move to a more complete analysis, looking at estimates of overall tax incidence in Canada and the U.S. in the early 1970s. One advantage of proceeding in this way is that it sets the stage for a discussion of changes over the last two decades. But an equally important motivation is that, as we shall see, it is only for the early 1970s that estimates of overall tax incidence have been done on a comparable basis for the two countries.

Attempts to estimate the overall burden of taxes in the U.S. began in the 1940s and 1950s (Colm and Tarasov 1940; Musgrave et al. 1951), and have continued to the present with important contributions from Pechman and Okner (1974), Pechman (1985, 1987), Browning (1978), Browning and Johnson (1979), Musgrave et al. (1974), and others. The situation in Canada is quite different. Irwin Gillespie developed complete estimates of fiscal incidence (i.e., both taxes and expenditures) for Canada for the years 1961 and 1969 (Gillespie 1976, 1980), and Whalley (1984) provided estimates for 1972; but those 1972 estimates are the most recent estimates of *overall* tax incidence available for Canada.[5]

While Gillespie used methods similar to those employed by U.S. authors, a number of differences in procedure—in the income definition, for example, as well as in shifting hypotheses—mean that no direct Canada-U.S. comparison can be made with his 1961 or 1969 results.[6] However, Whalley (1984) replicated the methods used by Pechman and Okner (1974) and Browning and Johnson (1979), using Canadian data for 1972, allowing a direct comparison of estimates of overall tax effects on economic inequality between the two countries at the start of the 1970s.

4.3.1   Comparisons Using Pechman's Approach

Table 4.4 shows Pechman's estimates of the incidence of the overall U.S. tax system, by type of tax, for 1970. The effective tax rates are expressed using a very broad income definition, gross of both transfers and taxes. Both

---

5. A number of authors have, however, looked at the incidence of particular components of the Canadian tax system using more recent data (see, e.g., Vaillancourt and Poulaert 1985; Meng and Gillespie 1986; Maslove 1989).

6. An attractive feature of Gillespie's work is that, in Gillespie (1976) he published all the underlying data series one requires to perform alternative incidence calculations using almost *any* income definition or set of shifting hypotheses. Thus, in the absence of Whalley's work it would be possible to do Canada-U.S. comparisons by applying the shifting hypotheses used by U.S. authors to Gillespie's published data series.

Table 4.4   Pechman's Estimates of U.S. Effective Tax Rates (1970)

Decile	PIT	CIT	Sales and Excise	Property	Social Insurance Contributions	Total
Most Progressive Variant						
1	3.1%	1.9%	7.6%	3.6%	2.2%	18.8%
2	3.5	1.8	7.1	3.4	3.2	19.5
3	4.0	1.5	7.2	2.8	4.8	20.8
4	5.8	1.4	6.9	2.5	6.3	23.2
5	6.8	1.3	6.7	2.2	6.8	24.0
6	7.6	1.1	6.3	2.1	6.7	24.1
7	8.2	1.2	6.0	2.1	6.4	24.3
8	9.1	1.4	5.6	2.2	5.9	24.6
9	10.3	1.6	5.1	2.3	5.4	25.0
10	13.8	5.3	3.5	5.3	2.7	30.7
Total	9.7	2.6	5.3	3.3	4.9	26.1
Least Progressive Variant						
1	3.1	4.0	7.5	7.3	3.5	25.9
2	3.4	3.5	7.0	5.9	3.9	24.2
3	3.8	3.2	7.0	4.8	5.0	24.1
4	5.6	3.0	6.8	4.2	6.0	25.8
5	6.6	2.7	6.5	3.8	6.4	26.4
6	7.3	2.7	6.1	3.7	6.1	26.3
7	8.0	2.7	5.8	3.6	5.9	26.2
8	9.0	2.6	5.5	3.4	5.5	26.4
9	10.0	2.5	5.0	3.1	5.2	26.1
10	14.2	3.4	3.6	3.4	3.0	27.8
Total	9.7	3.0	5.3	3.7	4.8	26.7

Source: Pechman, (1985), table A-2, p. 78.

income totals and the income concept are adjusted to be consistent with the national accounts. Income includes not only the money income reflected in tables 4.1 and 4.2, but also imputed rental income, income-in-kind, and capital gains. The two variants shown in table 4.4 reflect Pechman's "most progressive" and "least progressive" sets of incidence assumptions, which are shown in table 4.5.

Table 4.4 reflects Pechman's well-known result that even in the most progressive variant, the U.S. tax structure as a whole is not very progressive: the tax bite is 18.8% in the bottom decile and 30.7% in the top decile. In the least progressive variant, the overall tax system is approximately proportional at a rate of 25–26%. Strong progressivity of individual income taxes is largely offset by regressivity over some portions of the income distribution in all the other taxes. A further important aspect of this offsetting is that federal taxes are much more progressive than state and local income taxes. This is due, to a large extent, to the greater relative importance of individual income taxes at the federal level.

Table 4.5   **Pechman's Shifting Hypotheses**

Tax	Most Progressive	Least Progressive
PIT	not shifted	not shifted
CIT	½ to capital, ½ to dividends	½ to capital, ½ to consumption
Property:		
Land	capital	landowners
Structures & Improvements	capital	shelter and consumption
Sales and Excise	consumers of taxed goods	consumers of taxed goods
Social Security	labor	labor

Source: Pechman (1985).

Table 4.6   **Whalley's Estimates of Effective Tax Rates for Canada Using Pechman's Methods (1972)**

Income Group (thousands of $)	% of Households	PIT	CIT	Sales and Excise	Property	Social Insurance Contributions	Total
Most Progressive Variant							
<6.5	16.6%	1.4%	2.6%	13.9%	2.5%	2.3%	22.9%
6.5–7.3	3.5	3.7	3.0	12.3	3.3	3.8	26.1
7.5–8.5	6.9	5.7	2.7	12.1	2.8	5.0	28.4
8.5–10	8.0	7.9	2.1	11.7	2.2	4.6	28.6
10–11.5	8.9	9.0	2.1	11.5	2.6	3.9	29.3
11.5–16	24.4	11.4	1.7	10.4	2.1	3.5	29.4
16–25	19.3	13.4	2.4	9.2	2.9	2.6	30.7
>25	8.6	12.5	7.5	5.6	6.6	1.7	33.9
Least Progressive Variant							
<6.5	16.6	1.3	4.1	13.6	5.8	2.6	27.6
6.5–7.5	3.5	3.6	4.0	12.0	6.7	3.5	30.0
7.5–8.5	6.9	5.6	3.8	11.8	5.9	4.4	31.6
8.5–10	8.0	7.7	3.3	11.4	4.6	4.1	31.3
10–11.5	8.9	8.8	3.5	11.3	3.9	3.6	31.4
11.5–16	24.4	11.1	3.1	10.1	3.5	3.3	31.3
16–25	19.3	13.2	3.2	9.1	3.2	2.7	31.5
>25	8.6	13.2	4.6	5.9	3.0	1.9	28.9

Source: Whalley (1984), table 3, p. 662.

Table 4.6 shows the corresponding Canadian numbers for 1972 presented by Whalley (1984). For the overall tax system, the story is quite similar to what Pechman found for the U.S. for 1970. On the most progressive variant there is mild overall progressivity, while on the least progressive variant there is approximate proportionality. The only significant difference between the overall Canada and U.S. incidence patterns is that in the least progressive variant Canada shows slight regressivity at the top of the income scale, while the U.S. shows some slight regressivity at the bottom.

When we examine the individual taxes in tables 4.4 and 4.6, we again find considerable similarity between Canada and the U.S. However, there are some interesting differences, for example with respect to social security payroll taxes. In both countries these are progressive at low-income levels, but become regressive at higher levels. The reason for this pattern lies partly in the fact that a large fraction of income comes from transfer payments, rather than from earnings, for those in the lowest income groups, and partly in the rate structure of these taxes. Tables 4.4 and 4.6 show that in the U.S., social security payroll taxes turned regressive at about the median income level in 1970, whereas in Canada this occurred lower in the distribution—at about the 30th percentile.

A second significant difference revealed by tables 4.4 and 4.6 is that the personal income tax (PIT) is more progressive in Canada than in the U.S. at the bottom of the income scale, and less progressive at the top. American households in the bottom group in 1970 paid 3.1% of their income in PIT in both of Pechman's variants, whereas Canadians in the bottom group in 1972 paid only 1.3–1.4%. The explanation lies with state and local income taxes in the U.S.; the burden of *federal* PIT in the U.S. was only about 1%. At the top of the scale, while the PIT burden jumps from 10.0% to 14.2% from the second highest to the top decile in the least progressive variant, the burden is flat at 13.2% for the top two Canadian groups. In the most progressive variant, Canadian PIT is actually regressive at the top end, whereas U.S. PIT remains significantly progressive.

4.3.2 Comparisons Using Browning and Johnson's Approach

After the range of shifting variants first used in Pechman and Okner (1974) were devised, Browning (1978) and Browning and Johnson (1979) demonstrated a plausible justification for a much more progressive variant of such calculations. Their interest focused on sales and excise taxes. They noted, first, that since transfer payments are largely indexed, to the extent that one's income is derived from transfers one is fully protected against general increases in broad-based sales taxes. This implies that it is not adequate to treat sales and excise taxes as if the burden were entirely on consumers of the taxed items without regard to the composition of their income. In other words, sales and excise taxes have an important sources side, as well as uses side effects. Second, Browning and Johnson argued that the portion of income saved does not escape sales and excise taxes, as assumed in all of the Pechman and Okner variants, since saving provides for future expenditure on consumption, which can generally be expected to be taxed at rates similar to those in force today. The upshot of these two arguments is that the burden of a general sales tax is on factor income, rather than on consumption.

Allocating the burden of sales and excise taxes in proportion to factor income, rather than in proportion to consumption, has a radical effect on estimated overall tax incidence. It also affects the Canada-U.S. comparison, as shown in table 4.7. Table 4.7 reports the result of adopting the Browning and Johnson argument in each country. Part 1 of the table shows the impact for the

Table 4.7   Effective Tax Rates under Forward Shifting and Browning and
                   Johnson Assumptions on Sales and Excise Tax Burdens

1. *United States* (1966)

Decile	Sales and Excise Taxes		Overall Tax System	
	Forward Shifting	Browning & Johnson	Forward Shifting	Browning & Johnson
1	8.9%	2.2%	16.8%	10.1%
2	7.8		18.9	13.3
3	7.1	4.5	21.7	19.1
4	6.7		22.6	20.4
5	6.4	5.1	22.8	21.5
6	6.1		22.7	21.7
7	5.7	5.4	22.7	22.4
8	5.5		23.1	23.0
9	5.0	5.7	23.3	24.0
10	3.2		30.1	32.6
Total	5.1	5.1	25.2	25.2

2. *Canada* (1972)

Income Group (thousands of $)	% of Households	Sales and Excise Taxes		Overall Tax System	
		Forward Shifting	Browning & Johnson	Forward Shifting	Browning & Johnson
<6.5	16.6%	13.9%	3.5%	22.9%	12.8%
6.5–7.5	3.5	12.3	6.6	26.1	21.2
7.5–8.5	6.9	12.1	7.7	28.4	24.4
8.5–10	8.0	11.7	8.7	28.6	25.8
10–11.5	8.9	11.5	9.1	29.3	27.3
11.5–16	24.4	10.4	9.4	29.4	28.6
16–25	19.3	9.2	9.7	30.7	31.4
>25	8.6	5.6	10.0	33.9	37.4

Sources: **United States**—Browning (1978), tables 2, 3, pp. 660, 661. **Canada**—Whalley
(1984), table 3, pp. 662, 663.

Note: The "forward shifting" estimates for the U.S. are from Pechman and Okner's "most progressive" variant calculations. For Canada, they are from Whalley's calculations using Pechman's
"most progressive" variant. Both assume that the burden of sales and excise taxes falls entirely
on the consumers of the taxed items.

U.S., based on Pechman and Okner's original study using 1966 data, while
part 2 uses Whalley's calculations for Canada in 1972. In both countries, sales
and excise taxes become strongly progressive under the Browning and Johnson argument, and the overall progressivity of the tax system is considerably
increased. However, note that the impact on overall progressivity is greater
for Canada, simply because sales and excise taxes are almost twice as large,
overall, as a fraction of income than in the U.S. Thus, going from the Pechman and Okner most progressive variant to the Browning and Johnson case in

Canada reduces the tax bite for the lowest group by fully 10.1 percentage points, and increases the burden on the top group by 3.5 percentage points. The corresponding figures for the U.S. in 1966 are only 6.7 and 2.5 percentage points, respectively. Since, as shown in table 4.8, the gap between Canada and the U.S. in the use of indirect taxes has remained roughly constant since the early 1970s, it remains very much the case today that one's view of the relative progressivity of the U.S. and Canadian tax systems depends on perceptions of the likely incidence of sales and excise taxes.

The second part of the Browning and Johnson argument—the absence of uses side effects of a general sales tax—provides an interesting echo of Pechman's argument for ignoring the spurious uses side effects of property taxes in annual data (see the Appendix to this chapter). In both cases the argument, roughly speaking, is that the uses side effects will largely disappear if we take a longer view than that of a single year. In other words, a lifetime tax incidence argument is being imported into an annual incidence study. The temptation to make such piecemeal adjustments to annual calculations is understandable. However, this approach ignores the fact that many other things will change when we move to a lifetime framework. As discussed in section 4.6, Davies, St-Hilaire, and Whalley (1984) found that not all the changes that occur when explicit lifetime calculations are substituted for annual calculations are in the direction of making the tax system appear more progressive. In fact, there is an approximate offsetting, so that the overall lifetime incidence pattern is not much different from the annual.

4.4   Changes in Tax Effects on Inequality over Time: Prereform Period

Changes over time in the impact of taxes on economic inequality in Canada and the United States have come about due to changes in tax mix, tax bases, and rate structures. For the U.S., we are fortunate in having a consistent series of tax incidence calculations, performed by Joseph Pechman, which sum up the impact of these factors over the period since 1966. This allows the U.S. side of the Canada-U.S. comparison performed in the previous section for the early 1970s to be brought up to date. Unfortunately, on the Canadian side we can only assemble the evidence on changes in tax mix, tax bases, and rate structure, in order to guess what has been happening to the overall impact of taxes on inequality.

4.4.1   Changes in Tax Mix in Canada and the United States

Let us take a look at the evolution of the overall tax mix in Canada and the U.S. in recent years, with the help of table 4.8. Table 4.8 indicates that until the early 1980s, PIT was overall a less important revenue source in Canada than in the U.S., despite the fact that the Canadian provinces rely more heavily on income taxes than do U.S. states. In recent years, however, Canada has come to rely much more on PIT, and the U.S. less. There has been a steady

Table 4.8   **Composition of Government Revenues**

1. *Canada*

			Taxes				
Year	Total Revenue	PIT	Direct Corporate[a]	Indirect[b]	Property	Social Insurance[c]	Other
As % of GDP							
1965	26.4%	6.0%	3.9%	10.1%	3.9%	1.2%	1.7%
1970	32.2	10.1	3.5	10.0	3.8	3.0	1.7
1975	32.8	10.7	4.7	9.6	3.2	3.2	1.4
1980	30.3	10.4	3.9	8.5	2.9	3.1	1.5
1981	32.4	11.0	3.6	9.9	3.0	3.4	1.5
1982	32.9	11.7	3.1	9.6	3.2	3.6	1.6
1983	32.2	11.4	3.0	9.1	3.2	3.9	1.5
1984	32.1	11.2	3.4	9.2	3.1	3.9	1.4
1985	32.3	11.3	3.3	9.2	3.1	4.1	1.3
1986	33.6	12.3	2.9	9.6	3.1	4.2	1.4
1987	33.9	12.8	2.7	9.7	3.1	4.3	1.4
1988	34.5	13.2	2.8	9.8	3.0	4.4	1.4
1989	33.8	13.0	2.4	n.a.	n.a.	n.a.	n.a.
As % of Revenue							
1965	100.0	22.5	14.7	38.3	13.6	4.5	6.3
1970	100.0	31.4	11.0	31.1	11.9	9.2	5.4
1975	100.0	32.7	14.3	29.4	9.6	9.6	4.3
1980	100.0	34.3	12.9	28.1	9.7	10.2	4.9
1981	100.0	34.0	11.1	30.7	9.1	10.5	4.7
1982	100.0	35.7	9.5	29.3	9.8	10.9	4.7
1983	100.0	35.5	9.4	28.4	10.0	12.1	4.5
1984	100.0	34.7	10.5	28.8	9.7	12.1	4.3
1985	100.0	35.1	10.1	28.6	9.5	12.5	4.1
1986	100.0	36.8	8.5	28.6	9.3	12.6	4.3
1987	100.0	37.6	8.0	28.7	9.0	12.6	4.0
1988	100.0	38.2	8.0	28.5	8.6	12.7	4.0
1989	100.0	38.3	7.0	n.a.	n.a.	n.a.	n.a.

2. *United States*

			Taxes				
Year	Total Revenue	PIT	Corporate Profits	Indirect[c]	Property	Social Insurance	Other
As % of GDP							
1965	27.5%	8.1%	4.5%	5.7%	3.5%	4.4%	1.3%
1970	30.8	10.1	3.5	5.8	3.8	5.9	1.6
1975	30.7	9.4	3.3	5.7	3.5	7.2	1.6
1980	32.4	11.3	3.3	5.6	2.7	7.9	1.6
1981	32.9	11.7	2.8	6.0	2.7	8.1	1.6
1982	32.3	11.6	2.0	5.7	2.9	8.3	1.7
1983	31.7	10.7	2.3	5.8	2.9	8.4	1.7
1984	31.5	10.0	2.5	5.8	2.7	8.7	1.8

(*continued*)

Table 4.8   (continued)

2. United States

			Taxes				
Year	Total Revenue	PIT	Corporate Profits	Indirect[c]	Property	Social Insurance	Other
1985	32.0	10.4	2.4	5.7	2.7	8.9	1.8
1986	32.0	10.2	2.5	5.6	2.8	9.0	1.9
1987	32.7	10.7	3.0	5.4	2.8	8.9	1.9
1988	32.4	10.3	2.9	5.4	2.7	9.2	1.9
1989	32.2	10.5	2.5	5.3	2.7	9.2	1.9
As % of Revenue							
1965	100.0	29.5	16.4	20.9	12.7	15.9	4.6
1970	100.0	32.9	11.2	19.0	12.3	19.3	5.3
1975	100.0	30.5	10.8	18.4	11.5	23.6	5.2
1980	100.0	35.0	10.1	17.3	8.3	24.3	5.0
1981	100.0	35.5	8.5	18.2	8.1	24.7	4.9
1982	100.0	35.9	6.2	17.8	8.9	25.8	5.4
1983	100.0	33.6	7.3	18.3	9.0	26.4	5.3
1984	100.0	31.7	8.0	18.3	8.6	27.7	5.7
1985	100.0	32.4	7.6	17.8	8.6	27.9	5.8
1986	100.0	32.0	7.9	17.4	8.7	28.1	5.9
1987	100.0	32.9	9.1	16.6	8.4	27.2	5.8
1988	100.0	31.7	9.1	16.6	8.4	28.4	5.8
1989	100.0	32.7	7.7	16.5	8.4	28.6	6.1

Sources: **Canada**—Statistics Canada, *National Income and Expenditure Accounts* (13-201), various issues. **United States**—Department of Commerce, *Survey of Current Business,* various July issues; Department of Commerce, *The National Income and Product Accounts of the U.S., Statistical Tables 1929–76,* September 1981.

[a]Includes the petroleum and gas revenue tax, levied between 1981 and 1986, and provincial taxes on mining and logging profits, as well as corporate income taxes.

[b]Net of property taxes.

[c]Includes contributions to the Canada and Quebec Pension Plans, unemployment insurance, public health insurance, and workmen's compensation.

rise in the fraction of government revenue coming from PIT in Canada, until in 1988, 38.2% of revenue was from that source, whereas in the U.S. after 1982, PIT revenues fell from 35.9% of total revenue to 31.7% in 1988. The decline in importance of PIT in the U.S. has been made possible by the steady increase in social insurance contributions, which now provide almost as large a fraction of revenue as the PIT—28.6% versus 32.7% in 1989.

Over the longer haul of the last twenty or twenty-five years, both Canada and the U.S. have seen a relative decline of direct corporate taxes, most importantly the corporate income tax (CIT), indirect taxes (i.e., sales and excise taxes), and property tax. The greater buildup of social insurance contributions in the U.S. has been used largely to allow the PIT to keep an approximately level relative position over the last two decades, whereas in Canada the decline in corporate, indirect, and property taxes has required a relative increase in PIT revenues.

Later in this paper it is argued that PIT is the most progressive element in the tax mix, from either an annual or lifetime viewpoint. Social insurance contributions, on the other hand, rank quite low in the progressivity stakes, because their proportional rates only apply on income up to some ceiling. While they are proportional, or mildly progressive in the case of the Canada Pension Plan (CPP), in the lower range of the distribution·they are regressive over a wide upper range. From a lifetime viewpoint, the results of Davies, St-Hilaire, and Whalley (1984) indicate that social insurance contributions are in fact the *most* regressive form of tax. Differences in the trend of the U.S. and Canadian tax mix over the last two decades therefore suggest quite powerfully that overall tax incidence in Canada has likely been becoming more progressive relative to U.S. incidence.

4.4.2   Changes in Tax Effects on Inequality: United States

Table 4.9, taken from Pechman (1985) summarizes changes in overall U.S. tax incidence over the period 1980–85, and can be compared with the numbers in table 4.3 for 1970. Over both the whole period from 1970–85 and over 1980–85, progressivity declined according to either variant of the calculations (most markedly for the most progressive variant). Similar conclusions were reached by others, for example Kasten and Sammartino (1987) of the Congressional Budget Office in a comparison of overall federal tax incidence in the U.S. in 1977 and 1984.

The most important reasons for the overall decline in tax progressivity over the period 1970–85, according to Pechman (1985), were the 1981 PIT cut,

Table 4.9   **Pechman's Estimates of Effective Overall Tax Rates, (1980 and 1985)**

Decile	Most Progressive Variant		Least Progressive Variant	
	1980	1985	1980	1985
1	20.6%	21.9%	28.9%	28.2%
2	20.4	21.3	25.7	25.6
3	20.6	21.4	24.6	24.6
4	21.9	22.5	25.2	25.2
5	22.8	23.1	25.8	25.3
6	23.3	23.5	25.9	25.6
7	23.6	23.7	26.0	25.4
8	25.0	24.6	27.1	26.3
9	25.7	25.1	27.2	26.1
10	27.3	25.3	24.9	23.3
Total	25.2	24.5	26.3	25.3

Source: Pechman (1985), table 5-2, p. 68.

the declining importance of CIT, and the shift toward Social Security payroll taxes. (The 1981 tax cut reduced burdens for those in the top 10% by about one percentage point of income, and was offset among low-income taxpayers by the lack of indexation. See Pechman 1985, pp. 69–70.) Pechman emphasizes that all these changes occurred at the *federal* level. The overall incidence of state and local taxes did not change greatly in any of the variants he considered. These underlying factors can readily be compared with corresponding factors at work in Canada.

4.4.3   Changes in Tax Effects on Inequality: Canada

In 4.8, we see that the changes in tax mix in Canada over the period 1970–85, although qualitatively similar to those in the U.S., were quantitatively different. (The 1965–70 period featured some major changes in the Canadian tax mix, which were quite unlike those in the more recent period.) The most significant difference is that the increase in the importance of social security payroll contributions was much smaller in Canada than in the U.S. Between 1970 and 1985, the fraction of overall government revenue coming from social insurance contributions in Canada rose from 9.2% to only 12.5%, whereas in the U.S. it rose from 19.3% to 27.9%. Some idea of the possible impact can be gained by noting that if the incidence of social security payroll taxes had not changed in the U.S. after 1970, according to Pechman's most progressive variant the tax burden of the lowest U.S. decline in 1985 would have been about 15% of income instead of 22%, and that of the highest decile would have been about 26% instead of 25%.

It should also be noted that, unlike the U.S., Canada introduced full indexation of exemptions and tax brackets in the mid 1970s, so that "bracket creep" effects, such as those reflected in Pechman's estimates for the period 1981–85, were absent. This difference, together with the divergence in payroll-tax trends, strongly suggests that if Canada and the U.S. had about the same overall tax progressivity in the early 1970s, by 1985 Canada likely had a significantly more progressive overall system.

An important footnote on changes in tax mix in Canada is the disappearance of all estate and gift taxes in Canada over this period, which suggests an erosion of the long-run progressivity of the Canadian tax system at very high income levels. This change began with the removal of federal estate and gift taxes when capital gains taxation was introduced in the early 1970s. The provinces then, one by one, removed their succession duties. The absence of estate and gift taxes, the evidence that many rich Canadian families are largely able to avoid PIT, and the lengthening of the extreme upper tail of the Canadian income distribution noted earlier all powerfully suggest that an extremely favorable tax environment has been created in Canada for the genuinely wealthy. This should be borne in mind in interpreting the available evidence on changes in progressivity over time in Canada, which has little to say about taxation of the rich and super-rich.

In Canada there is an important discontinuity in the prereform period. For three years prior to the implementation of tax reform in the 1988 tax year, a series of major changes in federal taxation were put in place by the Conservative government elected in 1984. Although some of the initiatives in this period differed in spirit from those of the 1987 tax reform package, for the most part they were of much the same ilk. Fortunately, there has been some careful study of the incidence effects of at least the PIT changes occuring over this period.

The Conservative government elected in late 1984 faced two difficulties, which have had a major effect on all its tax policy initiatives right up to the present. The first was that towards the end of its predecessor's term a very serious deficit problem had emerged, one considerably more serious even than that faced in the U.S. The other was that a proliferation of tax expenditures under the previous regime had led to a situation in which large numbers of high-income taxpayers were able to escape tax entirely. This created a perception of unfairness in the tax system, which the new government was pledged to remedy. The new prime minister had promised that the rich would pay taxes, and that the taxes would be "handsome" ones.

In the prereform period, the Conservative government anticipated aspects of its June 1987 reform package by broadening the CIT base, lowering CIT rates, and eliminating the general investment tax credit, and by reducing the dividend tax credit and terminating various tax shelters and loopholes in the PIT. However, in addition to these moves, it made some changes which were a good deal less popular. In particular, in the May 1985 budget it announced that it would phase in a $500,000 lifetime capital gains exemption (now reduced to $100,000), and it partially de-indexed the tax system by removing indexation for the first 3 percentage points of inflation each year.[7] Attempts to regain some goodwill included the introduction of refundable sales tax credits and (for the first time in Canada) an alternative minimum tax under the PIT.

The incidence effects of the prereform PIT changes have been studied by Maslove (1989) using an innovative database assembled by Statistics Canada, the Social Policy Simulation Database (SPSD).[8] Maslove compares the distribution of tax burdens for a sample of taxpayers subject to the 1984 and "prereform" 1988 tax law in turn, finding that the burden fell disproportionately

---

7. Fears about the government's intentions were also encouraged by its abortive consideration of removing some of the indexation of Canada's universal transfer payments—old age security payments and family allowances. (The elderly kept their indexed pensions, but family allowances were partially de-indexed, again on the plan of no indexation for the first 3 percentage points of inflation.)

8. This database imputes information from taxation and unemployment insurance administrative data files, as well as Statistics Canada's Family Expenditure Survey (FES), to families and individuals in Statistics Canada's Survey of Consumer Finance (SCF). In addition to putting together many more variables than are available in any single data source, the SPSD uses sophisticated techniques to offset the misreporting and differential response to which the SCF, like any sample survey, is subject.

on middle-income groups. Overall there was a 2.7% decrease in disposable income, but the top 1% of taxpayers saw only a 1.3% decrease (thanks to the lifetime capital gains exemption, for example), and the bottom two deciles had *gains* of 3.7% and 1.7%. In contrast, taxpayers around the $30,000 income mark lost 3.5–3.6% of disposable income.

Thus, while there was a fairly clear preform trend toward less progressivity in the U.S., the Canadian situation is a bit more complicated. Prior to 1985 Canada almost certainly saw less decrease in progressivity than in the United States. However, in the period 1985–87 PIT changes saw the middle lose out to bottom and top income groups, in relative terms. While it still seems likely that Canada at the immediate preform point had a significantly more progressive overall tax system than the U.S., the changing incidence of PIT suggests that the gap might have closed somewhat, at least in the top half of the income distribution, over the last few years before reform.

4.5   The Effects of Tax Reform

In analyzing the effects on income distribution of the recent tax reforms carried out in the U.S. and Canada, it is important to keep in mind the starting point. An easily overlooked aspect of the initial situation is that both countries' PIT systems had important *consumption tax* aspects (as shown by the relatively light taxation of capital gains, generous sheltering of pension funds, etc., in both countries). However, Canada was positioned significantly more toward the consumption tax end of the spectrum than the U.S., with its $1,000 investment income deduction, dividend tax credit, more liberal RRSP/RPP contribution limits, and lack of consumer or mortgage interest deductibility.[9] Looking at other elements in the tax system, Canada's much greater reliance on sales and excise taxes reinforced the consumption tax aspect of its overall system. The greater use of social security payroll taxes in the U.S., and lack of integration of CIT with PIT means that other elements of at least the federal tax structure in the U.S. could be viewed as augmenting the income tax approach. Without exaggerating too much, one could claim that Canada was largely pursuing a consumption tax strategy, and the U.S. more of an income tax approach in the preform period.[10]

9. Under the now-standard consumption tax approach, set out, for example, by Bradford in *Blueprints* (1984), taxpayers would have access to saving in both "qualified" and "nonqualified" forms. Qualified accounts correspond with IRAs and Keoghs in the U.S. and with RPPs and RRSPs in Canada, and provide essentially expenditure tax treatment. The income on nonqualified assets would not be taxed, providing, like any exemption for capital income, essentially wage tax treatment. Perhaps the most important breakthrough of *Blueprints* was to show how these two forms of treatment could, working side-by-side, create a workable personal consumption tax system. Nontaxation of nonqualified assets implies nondeductibility of interest, so that the Canadian approach to consumer and mortgage interest deductibility represents appropriate consumption tax treatment. See Davies and St-Hilaire (1987).

10. This assessment does not deny that the U.S. had been moving *in the consumption tax direction,* via erosion of the CIT and the buildup of payroll taxes, which in ideal form are equivalent to consumption taxes for life-cycle savers operating in a perfect capital market.

Tax reform in Canada has been more drawn out than that in the U.S. and has seen significant changes since its announcement in the June 1987 White Paper. The reform was scheduled to take place in two stages. Stage I, beginning with the 1988 tax year, would see the phasing in of PIT and CIT reforms over a two- or three-year period. Stage II, federal sales tax reform, was scheduled to take effect in January 1991. The White Paper indicated that Stage II would see the replacement of the federal manufacturers' sales tax (MST) by a broad-based "multistage sales tax," and the attendant elimination of PIT and CIT surtaxes and reduction in the middle PIT rate from 26% to 25%. The Stage II package was intended to be roughly revenue-neutral, so that it would see a shift in tax mix away from PIT and CIT toward sales tax. Three alternative forms of the new sales tax were suggested in the White Paper, one involving integration with existing provincial sales taxes. In April 1989 it was announced that the government would "go it alone" with a federal-only Goods and Services Tax (GST), is a destination-basis consumption-type credit invoice method value-added tax, levied at a rate of 9%. Public opposition led to a revised plan, announced in December 1989, with a GST rate of 7% and no accompanying PIT or CIT reductions. Thus, the originally anticipated shift in tax mix towards the sales tax seems to have been abandoned.

The most important features of the 1986 U.S. tax reform were: (1) revenue shift away from PIT towards CIT; (2) base broadening under CIT, including elimination of the investment tax credit; (3) base broadening under PIT, including, for example, elimination of the former 60% exclusion of capital gains, repeal of rapid acceleration of real estate depreciation, and limitation on passive activity losses; (4) increases in personal exemptions and standard deduction, removing six million individuals from the tax·rolls; and (5) replacement of fourteen PIT tax brackets with marginal tax rates of 11–50% by (nominally) two brackets with rates of 15% and 28%, and reduction of the top CIT rate from 46% to 34%.

The key features of the Canadian reform, including both Stage I, implemented in the 1988 tax year, and the modified Stage II, are: (1) replacement of MST with GST; (2) base broadening under CIT, including decelerated depreciation allowances (general investment tax credit was already eliminated prior to reform); (3) base broadening under PIT, including an increase in the capital gains inclusion rate from 50% to 75%, capping of the lifetime capital gains exemption at $100,000, and reduction in the dividend tax credit rate from 33 1/3% to 25%; (4) conversion of personal exemptions and most deductions to (non-refundable) tax credits, and enhancement of refundable tax credits (child tax credit and sales tax credits); and (5) replacement of ten tax brackets with marginal tax rates of 6–34% by three brackets with rates of 17%, 26%, and 29%, and reduction in the CIT rate from 36% to 28%.

There is considerable similarity in the basic thrust of U.S. and Canadian tax reform. In line with the global trend, both countries have "broadened the base and reduced the rates" under both personal and corporate income taxes. However, although both countries have moved toward the income tax end of the consumption tax–income tax spectrum, the gap between them on this scale has probably not altered very much. The conversion of exemptions to credits in Canada, and the enhancement of refundable tax credits (child tax credit and sales tax credits), is a notable difference in the Canadian rate reform. However, it is perhaps more important to note the *similarity* between the two countries in the desire to offset the redistributive consequences for low-income families of moving to a flatter rate structure by enhancing protection for low incomes.

4.5.1   Canadian versus U.S. Rate Structure

Table 4.10 explores the postreform comparison between direct federal taxes on persons in the U.S. and Canada. It shows average effective 1988 tax rates for single-earner married couples with two children receiving all income from wages and salaries. Most of the income levels represent particular percentile points in the respective countries' income distributions. In one case, the 95th percentile, an income figure was not available for Canada, so the U.S. income at this percentile was simply converted to Canadian dollars (at an exchange rate of .81 U.S. dollars to one Canadian dollar, the average 1988 noon exchange rate). In addition, incomes of $10,000 and $200,000 (U.S.) were selected to give some feel for the treatment of incomes at the extremes.

Table 4.10 indicates, first, that both the PIT and overall direct federal tax burdens were quite similar at the very high income level of $200,000 (U.S.). However, as one moves lower in the distribution, the overall Canadian rate becomes quite a bit lower than the U.S. rate. There is a floor under the overall U.S. rate, set by the 15.02% combined employer and employee OASDI contribution rate in 1988. On the other hand, Canadian federal PIT rates are quite a bit higher than U.S. rates at most positions in the income distribution. The difference is greatest at the top of the 60th percentile (top of the third quintile), where the Canadian rate was 20.6%, versus a U.S. average rate of just 14.6%.

If the taxes reflected in table 4.10 were the only taxes at the federal level in each country, one might be tempted to conclude that the official Canadian federal rate structure is now clearly more progressive than the U.S. structure. However, both countries have federal CIT and excise taxes, the U.S. has federal gift and estate taxes, and Canada has a federal sales tax. (In addition, Table 4.10 does not tell us what pattern would emerge if we included other family types and nonlabor income.) By far the most important item in this omitted category is Canada's federal sales and excise taxes. In 1988 they provided $17,197,000 in revenue, which was equal to 3.4% of personal income. Given the sharp regressivity typically displayed in calculations of sales and excise tax incidence using annual data, if appropriate allowance were made for this additional source of federal revenue in table 4.10 it is quite possible that the difference in progressivity between federal taxes in Canada and the U.S. would be wholly eliminated.

Table 4.10   **Average Federal Tax Rates for Single-Earner Married Couple with Two Children (1988)**

Percentile	Income in U.S. $	Income in Cdn $	PIT	Social Security	Unemployment Insurance	Total
United States						
n.a.	$10,000	$12,346	0.0%	15.0%	2.1%	17.1%
20	15,102	18,644	0.8	15.0	1.4	17.2
40	26,182	32,323	7.6	15.0	0.8	23.4
60	38,500	47,531	9.9	15.0	0.5	25.5
80	55,906	69,020	14.6	12.1	0.4	27.1
95	92,001	113,581	20.2	7.3	0.2	27.8
n.a.	200,000	246,914	27.1	3.4	0.1	30.6
Canada						
n.a.	10,000	12,346	n.a.	3.2	5.6	n.a.
20	17,825	22,006	2.4	3.5	5.6	11.6
40	28,426	35,094	11.5	2.7	4.7	19.0
60	38,792	47,891	17.0	2.0	3.5	22.5
80	52,546	64,871	20.6	1.5	2.6	24.6
n.a.	92,001	113,581	24.8	0.8	1.5	27.1
n.a.	200,000	246,914	27.9	0.4	0.7	29.0

Notes: **U.S. and Canada:** All income is assumed to be from wages and salaries. **U.S.:** The couple qualifies for $13,000 total in standard deduction ($5,000) and personal exemptions ($2,000 × 4). Marginal tax rates according to taxable income are: <$29,750, 15%; $29,750–71,900, 28%; $71,900–194,050, 33%; >$194,050, 28%. The lowest two income levels benefit from the earned-income tax credit, which equals 14% of wage and salary income up to $5,714, and is taxed back at a 10% rate on income between $9,000 and $17,000. The OASDI contribution rate (employer and employee) is 15.02% on the first $45,000. An unemployment insurance contribution rate of 3% on the first $7,000 is assumed. **Canada:** The couple qualifies for nonrefundable credits equal to 17% of $12,276 ($6,000 for taxpayer, $5,500 for spouse, and $776 for two children) plus CPP/QPP and UI contributions. There is also a refundable child tax credit of $559 per child, taxed back at a rate of 5% on family income above $24,000, as well as a refundable sales tax credit totaling $210 ($70 per adult and $35 for each child), taxed back at a rate of 5% on family income over $16,000. Marginal tax rates (including surtaxes) according to taxable income are: <$27,500, 17.51%; $27,501–55,000, 26.78%; >$55,000, 29.87%. Contributions at the combined employer and employee rate are 4% of income between $2,600 and $26,500 for CPP, and 5.64% of income up to $29,380 for UI.

4.5.2   Changes in Tax Bases

Tax brackets and rates of course only tell part of the story about the incidence of any tax. We also need to take into account the base. There are interesting differences in the base-broadening exercises carried out in the U.S. and Canadian tax reforms. These partly reflect the differing composition of prereform tax expenditures in the two countries. Canada went into reform with RRSP contribution limits more generous than those on IRAs in the U.S., the $1,000 investment income deduction, and a generous dividend tax credit, for example. The U.S., on the other hand, had unrestricted consumer and mortgage interest deductibility and serious problems with the use of passive activity losses to offset other income. Canada eliminated its investment income deduction, cut back the dividend tax credit, and slowed down the scheduled phase-in of higher RRSP/RPP contribution limits. The U.S., on the other hand, restricted consumer and mortgage interest deductibility. It also separated income into three categories: ordinary (earned) income, investment income, and passive income. Losses in one category cannot be used to offset income in another.

Other differences in tax reform in the two countries cannot simply be explained in terms of the differences in preexisting loopholes. Both countries tightened up the treatment of capital gains, but the U.S. went much further, to full inclusion of realized capital gains in income. A further unexpected divergence in reform is in the treatment of interest deductibility for investors. In contrast to its rectitude on interest deductibility for consumers, Canada has always had wide-open deductibility on loans for investors. This feature was undisturbed in Canadian tax reform. The U.S. reform, in contrast, limited the interest deduction to the amount of investment income received (a reform frequently advocated in Canada). This implies a major continuing loophole in the Canadian PIT, relative to the U.S.[11]

4.5.3   Changes in Tax Mix

While there are broad similarities between Canadian and U.S. tax reform, there are also important differences. In addition to the differences noted above, the murky nature of the change in tax mix caused by tax reform in Canada contrasts sharply with the clearcut shifts in tax mix in the U.S. The shift toward increased CIT revenue in the U.S. showed up clearly in the 1987 and 1988 tax years (see table 4.8). Together with the continued rise in Social Security payroll taxes, it is in line with a long-run shift away from PIT. In contrast, what is happening to the federal tax mix in Canada is very confused.

The June 1987 tax reform White Paper in Canada projected that by 1991–92, with Stage I of tax reform fully phased in, PIT revenues would decline by $2.5 billion, CIT revenues would increase by $1.5 billion, and sales tax revenues would rise by $1.3 billion. In Stage II of tax reform, it was intended that PIT and CIT surtaxes would be removed, the PIT middle rate would be reduced from 26% to 25%, a much enhanced sales tax credit would be introduced, and the revenue losses from these measures would be made good by levying a sufficiently high new sales tax. Clearly, a tax mix shift away from PIT toward sales tax (and to a lesser extent CIT) was contemplated.

What is left out of this story is that in the immediate prereform period the series of measures taken to close PIT loopholes, and partial de-indexation,

---

11. Unlimited interest deductibility, unconstrained even by the alternative minimum tax, is one of the features of the Canadian tax system of greatest benefit to high-income taxpayers. It has always been objectionable, in that if the income generated by investments financed with the loans in question was in the form of capital gains, it would be taxed at an effective rate far below the subsidy rate on interest expense. The problem became more serious with the advent of the $500,000 lifetime capital gains exemption in 1985, although the implied hemorrhage has been reduced by the reduction in the lifetime exemption to $100,000 and the increase in the capital gains inclusion rate from 50% to 75%.

had resulted in a shift in tax mix toward PIT. Whatever the original intention, the relative importance of PIT revenues continued to increase in 1988 and 1989, as Stage I was being implemented. It is possible that the originally projected reform would have produced a shift in mix away from PIT with the implementation of Stage II in 1991 and 1992. However, the reduction in the planned GST rate from 9% to 7%, and the abandonment of plans to reduce PIT and CIT surtaxes and the PIT middle rate mean that this shift will not occur.

What is sometimes neglected in discussions of the tax mix changes under Canadian PIT is the fact that partial de-indexation, which began in 1985, creates a long-run tendency for a relative rise in PIT revenues and decline in PIT progressivity. The extraordinary public resistance to the GST, and international competitive pressures to keep CIT rates down, suggest that it may be difficult for governments to offset this tendency in the future via GST or CIT rate increases. A return to full indexation is unlikely in the forseeable future, since partial de-indexation is one of the strongest weapons the Canadian minister of finance has in his anti-deficit armory. Thus, at least for the present, Canada is set on a course, after 1991 or 1992, for an increasing shift away from CIT and sales tax revenues and toward PIT.

4.5.4 Estimates of Overall Incidence Effects of Reform

The United States

Initial assessments of the overall redistributive impact of the Tax Reform Act of 1986 (TRA86), by the Joint Committee on Taxation, for example, suggested that it would make the federal income tax slightly more progressive. Pechman (1987) has made a stronger statement, indicating that "the distributional effect of the act is distinctly progressive, especially if the increases in corporate income tax liabilities are taken into account." Assuming that CIT is a tax on capital in general, the top 1% of U.S. families would see an average 5% increase in federal taxes, whereas the bottom 10% would experience a 44% drop. Similar to Pechman, Ballentine (1986) and Feldstein (1988) have both argued in favor of calculations in which the CIT burden is not shifted onto consumers or workers.

Clearly, views on the redistributive impact of TRA86 must depend quite a bit on who one believes bears the burden of the corporate income tax. In addition, Koppelman (1988) has argued that the increase in progressivity would be less if behavioral responses and general equilibrium effects were taken into account. Galper, Lucke, and Toder (1988) find that GE effects do, in fact, erode the increase in progressivity. Finally, there has been some controversy about whether continuing increases in Social Security taxes after 1986 should be considered part of the tax reform package.

The numbers presented by Kasten and Sammartino (1987) and reported here in table 4.11, indicate the picture that emerges if some of these points are

Table 4.11   Effective Combined U.S. Federal Tax Rates, with Constant 1988
                    Incomes (Estimates of Kasten and Sammartino)

| | Income-Indexed 1984 Tax Law: CIT Allocated to | | Actual 1988 Tax Law: CIT Allocated to | |
| | Capital | Labor | Capital | Labor |
Decile	Income	Income	Income	Income
1	10.6%	10.5%	9.7%	9.6%
2	9.1	8.8	8.6	8.3
3	13.6	13.5	13.3	13.3
4	16.2	16.5	16.5	16.8
5	18.0	18.6	18.5	19.2
6	19.4	20.0	20.2	20.9
7	20.4	21.3	21.4	22.3
8	21.6	22.6	22.3	23.6
9	22.4	23.4	23.4	24.7
10	24.7	23.7	26.6	25.0
Total	21.5	21.6	22.7	22.7

Source: Kasten and Sammartino (1987), table 4, p. 159.

taken into consideration. They show that if an income-indexed version of all 1984 U.S. tax law had continued to apply in 1988, the overall federal tax system would have been quite a bit less progressive, irrespective of whether capital or labor bore the CIT burden. This comparison takes into account changes in Social Security taxes, as well as PIT and CIT. Thus, the impact of the full set of changes in federal taxes in the U.S. between 1984 and 1988 was very likely a considerable increase in progressivity.

Canada: Stage I

The main estimates of the incidence effects of Canadian tax reform are those produced by the federal government itself. On the government's assessment, the Stage I PIT changes would reduce by 1.5% the share of federal tax payable by the 76% of tax filers with income below $30,000, and increase it for groups above this level. Even those with incomes over $100,000 would experience an increased share of federal PIT, although a greater increase was projected for taxpayers in the $50,000–$100,000 range. As indicated in table 4.12, all income groups were projected to gain between 0.6 and 1.4% of income, with the percentage gains not moving up or down systematically as one goes up the income scale.

An alternative to the June 1987 White Paper calculations was provided by Maslove (1989), which, as described earlier, made use of the new SPSD database produced by Statistics Canada. For the most part his estimates were in reasonable agreement with the government's. However, he estimated a 2.1% gain for the top 1% of families, significantly higher than the government's figure for the top group, which gives the impression of marked regressivity at

Table 4.12   **Department of Finance Forecasts of Distributional Impacts of**
                    Canadian Tax Reform: Estimated Changes in Total Tax Burden

Stage I Reform: PIT and CIT			Stage II Reform: GST[a]	
Income Group (thousands of 1988 $)	% of Households	Change as % of Income	Income (1991 $)	Change as % of Income
< 15	26.7%	−0.8%	15,000	−0.6%
15–30	30.9	−1.4	20,000	−0.9
30–50	24.0	−0.8	25,000	−1.6
50–100	16.2	−0.6	30,000	−0.8
> 100	2.2	−1.0	35,000	0.1
			40,000	0.4
			45,000	0.4
			50,000	0.4
			60,000	0.5
			75,000	0.8
			100,000	0.8

Sources: Stage I—Government of Canada, Department of Finance, *Tax Reform 1987, Income Tax Reform,* June 18, 1987, table 4.2, p. 33; Stage II—Government of Canada, Department of Finance, *Goods and Services Tax,* December 19, 1989, table 2, p. 34.

[a]The Stage II reform figures given here are for a single-earner couple with two children.

very high incomes. Part of the reason that Maslove obtained a larger gain for his top group than did the government is simply that his top group was cut off at a higher income level. As indicated in table 4.12, the government's top group included 2.2% of households, in contrast to Maslove's 1%. The government's own figures indicate rising benefits at the highest income levels, so that an income gain in excess of 1.0% for the top group would likely have been obtained for the top percentile, using the government's own procedures. The rest of the difference is apparently due to differences in how base changes were modeled.

Canada: Stage II

The rate of tax innovation in Canada has not slowed down much since the 1987 Stage I reform. In January 1991, under the Stage II reform, the MST will be replaced by the more broadly based GST, which will be levied at a rate of 7%. GST zero-rating for basic groceries and rent, the exemption of most services of financial intermediaries, and rebates intended to ensure that the tax burden on new houses does not rise, imply that the major change in federal sales tax coverage under GST is the extension of tax to nonfinancial services. There is very little implied change in the progressivity of the federal sales tax.[12] What is more important in redistributive terms is the enhancement of

12. According to the Department of Finance (1989) figures, for the most part the increase in sales tax liabilities is approximately proportional to income, breaking down only at very low income levels, where the increased burden is disproportionately large. This largely accounts for

the (refundable) sales tax credits. In 1990 the credits stand at $140 per adult and $70 per child, with a "phaseout threshold" of $18,000. The credit is taxed back at a 5% rate above this threshold. In 1991, the new GST credits will provide $190 per adult and $100 per child, or $580 for a family of four, versus $420 in 1990. In addition, the threshold will be raised to about $24,000.

The estimated net effect of replacing the MST by GST and increasing sales tax credits is shown here in table 4.12 for a single-earner married couple with two children. (Four other illustrative cases are detailed in the original Department of Finance document.) For the most part the impact appears to be progressive. Families with income below $30,000 gain between 0.6% and 0.8% of income, while there are increasing losses for higher-income groups. Note, however, that at the very lowest incomes gains are increasing relative to income, so that Stage II could be characterized as slightly regressive at the lowest income levels. (As argued in the next section, however, this may not be much of a concern when one takes a longer-term viewpoint than the annual.) And, once again, the impact at the highest income levels is obscured by not going very far into the upper tail. It is likely that losses as a percentage of income decline past the $100,000 family income level.

While the GST represents the official Stage II of tax reform, important income tax changes were introduced in the April 1989 budget, which modify the status of both the PIT and CIT. Continued concerns over the deficit led to an increase in the personal income surtax on all individuals from 3% to 5%, and the introduction of a high-income surtax at a rate of 3% on incomes over about $70,000. In addition, PIT phaseouts for family allowances and old age security pensions, which would see these payments taxed away at a rate of 5% for income in excess of $50,000, were introduced. The combined result of these measures is a considerable increase in marginal tax rates over the affected income range in Canada, and a pattern of declining marginal tax rates at high incomes for taxpayers with children or receiving OAS. These changes clearly go some way to reducing the divergence in treatment for high-income groups identified above in the official PIT reforms enacted in the two countries. They were supplemented by the introduction of a new Large Corporations Tax to be levied on corporate capital employed in Canada in excess of $10 million, at a rate of 0.175%.

4.6   Annual versus Lifetime Tax Incidence

As pointed out earlier in this paper, there is increasing impatience with the *annual* frame of most existing work on overall tax incidence. This finds

---

the fact that the percentage benefits indicated in table 4.12 (which include the impact of the enhanced sales tax credits) are lower for a family with an income of $15,000 than for a family with an income of $25,000.

expression in the work of Pechman (1985) and Browning and Johnson (1979), as discussed earlier and in the Appendix. There have been other notable examples of attempts to move toward something like a lifetime view of tax incidence. As argued earlier (e.g., with respect to indirect taxes), if lifetime views of the incidence of particular types of taxes differ from annual views, then the overall progressivity of Canada and the United States in tax mix may be quite different, depending on whether one takes an annual or lifetime viewpoint. It is therefore worth taking a closer look at how lifetime calculations differ from annual.

The tax rates we have been discussing each represent a ratio of a tax burden to some measure of income. It is therefore clear that lifetime tax rates can differ from annual because of nonproportionality of either lifetime tax payments or income with annual taxes or income. A complete move to a lifetime basis for incidence calculations requires estimates both of lifetime tax burdens and lifetime incomes. Pechman's "competitive" approach to property taxes and Browning and Johnson's approach to sales and excise taxes both correct the apparent tax burdens from annual data, essentially turning them into estimates of lifetime burdens. However, there is no attempt to adjust the denominator, and other tax payments continue to be annual rather than lifetime.

Other attempts to go part of the way toward lifetime incidence calculations include the approach to the estimation of sales and excise tax incidence pioneered by Davies (1959) and recently revived by Poterba (1989). The idea is to use consumption as a proxy for permanent income. This provides a reasonable correction in the case of sales and excise tax burdens, since if consumption is smoothed over the life cycle then the sales and excise tax payments in a particular year are also proportional to lifetime payments. Thus both the numerator (the tax burden) and the denominator (income) have been adjusted to a lifetime basis—if the permanent income model of consumption behavior is correct.

Both Davies and Poterba found that sales and excise taxes are much less regressive in their approach than in the usual procedure, embodied, for example, in the work of Pechman. Regressivity does not decline as much as in the work of Browning and Johnson, however, since the argument that there is a sources side effect between transfer and factor income is not taken into account.

While the Davies-Poterba technique works for sales and excise taxes, it would not work for taxes whose burdens fluctuate with changes in income from year to year or vary over the lifetime. Unfortunately, this category essentially includes most other taxes. Thus, in order to go any further it is necessary to make explicit estimates of lifetime tax burdens and lifetime income. Since we do not have longitudinal data covering entire lifetimes, and since if we did it would be of mostly historical interest, *simulation* of lifetime tax burdens and lifetime incomes is inevitably involved. Davies, St-Hilaire, and Whalley (1984) illustrated how such simulation could be carried out using only cross-section data, under the assumption that cross-section data provides a snapshot of a society in balanced growth equilibrium.[13] Alternative approaches making some use of longitudinal data could of course be devised.

While the balanced growth assumption can be relaxed, and the simulation of lifetime income and tax stories can be made quite sophisticated, full estimates of lifetime tax incidence will inevitably remain somewhat less firmly grounded in actual observation than in annual estimates. Thus both approaches have a role to play, and one should expect to see both thrive in the future. It is not clear, however, that there is any benefit to "mixing and matching." As the following summary of the Davies, St-Hilaire, and Whalley ("DSW") results makes clear, a halfway house between annual and lifetime calculations may be worse than the pure form of either.

The DSW calculations used 1970 Canadian data and were based on the microsimulation model of earnings, saving, and inheritance reported in Davies (1982). They considered the pattern of hypothetical lifetime tax burdens for a cohort exposed to the 1970 tax system throughout their lives. Two main conclusions were emphasized. One was that, since the lifetime distributive series (e.g., consumption as a fraction of income) were much flatter than the annual, lifetime incidence calculations were much more robust to changes in shifting hypotheses than annual calculations. The other was that, somewhat surprisingly, overall lifetime incidence was about the same as annual. In both variants considered, both annual and lifetime incidence were mildly progressive.

The reason DSW did not find a sharp difference between annual and lifetime incidence lies in the fact that there are conflicting changes in the progressivity of different taxes when one moves to the lifetime. Both the personal income tax and taxes allocated to capital income become less progressive over the lifetime, but social security payroll taxes and taxes borne by consumers become less regressive. This is why it is dangerous to adopt lifetime incidence ideas piecemeal in conventional incidence analysis based on annual data. As we saw earlier, both Pechman, in his most redistributive variant, and Browning and Johnson denied the uses side effects of particular taxes, despite their effects on relative consumer prices, on the grounds that these uses side effects would disappear in the long run. What they did not realize, or at least did not take into account, is that other components of the tax system, such as PIT and CIT, would become less progressive over the lifetime.

There are other findings of DSW that become quite relevant in the current context. For example, the decline in PIT progressivity in going from the an-

---

13. If the cross-section represents a snapshot of a society in balanced growth, the incomes and tax burdens of successive age groups can be "blown up" to get estimates of the incomes and taxes of a *cohort* born in a particular year, as it moves through its lifetime. Alternative assumptions can be made about how individuals or families move around in the intracohort income distribution over time. These processes can be parameterized by reference to the considerable body of results now available on patterns of earnings and income mobility from longitudinal surveys.

nual to lifetime results featured a much larger change in effective tax rates at the bottom than at the top. Evidently earnings and income mobility at the bottom of the distribution ensures that the representative person with low lifetime income has moved around between the bottom several deciles of the annual income distribution, so that his lifetime tax rate is, roughly speaking, an average of the rates for the bottom several deciles. One implication is that the fact that, in both stages of Canadian tax reform the very lowest income groups benefit less, proportionally, than the slightly higher groups, may largely "wash out" in lifetime data. While the regressive incidence of the benefits in annual data is naturally of *some* concern, the lifetime viewpoint indicates that that concern should not be exaggerated.

Finally, table 4.13 summarizes the progressivity rankings of alternative taxes in annual and lifetime data, in alternative shifting variants. Table 4.13 shows, first, that in all variants and in both annual and lifetime data, personal income tax is always the most progressive element in the tax system. Thus, the recent increasing relative importance of PIT in Canadian tax mixes likely makes for a more progressive tax system, overall. But the table also indicates a remarkable contrast between annual and lifetime stories. Again, the lifetime results are much more robust, indicating a unique ranking of the alternative

Table 4.13   **Annual versus Lifetime Progressivity Rankings of Alternative Taxes (Canadian Data)**

	Incidence Variant		
Tax	Competitive	Noncompetitive	Browning & Johnson
1. *Whalley (1984): Annual*			
PIT	1	1	1
CIT	2	2	3
Indirect	5	5	2
Property	3	4	3
Social Insurance	4	3	5
2. *Davies, St-Hilaire, and Whalley (1984): Lifetime*			
PIT	1	1	1
CIT	2	2	2
Indirect	4	4	4
Property	2	2	2
Social Insurance	5	5	5

Sources: Part 1—Whalley (1984), table 3, p. 662. Part 2—Davies, St-Hilaire, and Whalley (1984), tables 2, 3, pp. 643, 644.

Notes: Part 1 estimates are based on 1972 Canadian data; Part 2 estimates are based on 1970 Canadian data. The "competitive" and "noncompetitive" cases in part 1 are, respectively, the Pechman and Okner most progressive and least progressive variants; in part 2, they are, respectively, the central and noncompetitive cases in Davies, St-Hilaire, and Whalley (1984). Progressivity is measured here by taking the ratio of the effective tax rate of the top income group to that of the bottom group; in part 1, the top group has 8.6% and the bottom group has 16.6% of the population; in part 2 the top and bottom groups are deciles.

taxes according to progressivity, whereas in the annual data the progressivity ranking depends very much on the incidence variant considered.

In the annual data the corporate income tax ranks next to the PIT in terms of progressivity, and indirect taxes (sales and excise) are the worst, except under the Browning and Johnson assumption, in which the apparent progressivity of sales and excise taxes becomes so great that they nudge aside CIT for the second most progressive position. The relative ranking of property taxes and social insurance contributions also varies between the shifting variants.

In the lifetime data, the taxes always rank as follows, in order of descending progressivity: PIT; CIT and property taxes; sales and excise taxes; social insurance contributions. For comparing overall U.S. and Canadian tax incidence, this ranking may be highly significant. By far the most important global difference in the U.S. and Canadian tax systems is that, in terms of revenue, sales and excise taxes occupy approximately the position in Canada that social insurance contributions have in the U.S. On the basis of the annual results, it would appear that the Canadian tax system is therefore less progressive, unless one adopts the Browning and Johnson viewpoint. However, the lifetime results tell a different story: sales and excise taxes are more progressive than social insurance contributions under each of the competitive, "noncompetitive," and Browning and Johnson shifting scenarios. This agreement suggests that if we try to evaluate the difference in incidence between Canada and the U.S. from something like a lifetime viewpoint, the replacement of social insurance contributions by greater sales and excise taxes in Canada, relative to the U.S., tends to make the overall Canadian tax system more progressive than the U.S. tax system.

4.7   Conclusion

This paper has studied the role of tax systems in Canada and the U.S. in helping to determine the distribution of real income and the overall degree of economic inequality. We have found that there are important similarities between the two countries. Transfer payments equalize the distributions of income to about the same extent, and individual taxes appear to have similar impacts on the shape of the income distribution. However, there are also some significant differences between the countries.

One important difference between Canada and the U.S. is that Canada now relies more heavily on the most progressive tax source, personal income tax. This is partly the result of recent PIT increases, but also reflects the fact that PIT is a relatively more important revenue source for Canadian provinces than for U.S. states. This difference in tax mix tends to reduce the overall progressivity of the U.S. tax structure relative to the Canadian.

Another important difference in tax mix between the two countries reflects the contrasting roles of sales and excise taxes and social insurance contributions. Sales and excise taxes are relatively more important in Canada, which has a federal sales tax; social insurance contributions are more important in the U.S., which funds its old age pensions entirely from such contributions. In studies of overall tax incidence using annual data, this difference has ambiguous consequences. However, Davies, St-Hilaire, and Whalley (1984) found that sales and excise taxes are approximately proportional from a lifetime viewpoint, whereas social insurance contributions are markedly regressive. This conclusion is robust to alternative shifting hypotheses. Thus, the difference in tax mix also suggests that, overall, the Canadian tax structure is more progressive than the U.S.

The conclusion that the U.S. tax system is less equalizing than the Canadian is especially interesting in view of the fact that the distribution of income *before* transfers and taxes is now significantly more unequal in the U.S. than in Canada. As argued in section 4.2, there is therefore some truth in the perception that Canada is "more equal" than the U.S., and the differences in taxation act to widen the gap.

We have also examined how the overall impact of taxes on income distribution has changed in Canada and the U.S. over the last two decades. It is useful to consider the last two decades as a whole, and then to turn to the last five or six years separately. The early 1970s saw similar progressivity in estimates of overall U.S. and Canadian tax incidence. Since then, overall progressivity in the two countries has been affected by changes in tax bases, rate structures, and tax mix.

The trend in income tax bases over the last two decades initially was toward additional tax expenditures, but has recently been toward their removal, turning us in the direction of the early 1970s starting point. The absence of bracket and exemption indexation through most of the period reduced progressivity of the U.S. federal income tax sharply. Canada, in contrast, had indexation throughout the subperiod with highest inflation, and introduced measures like child and sales tax credits, which reduced tax burdens on low-income families significantly. Finally, the shift in tax mix in the U.S. has been toward rising social insurance contributions, whereas in Canada it has been toward increasing PIT. Hence, the U.S. has seen a buildup of one of the least progressive tax sources, while Canada, in contrast, has seen an increase in the importance of the most progressive form of taxation. The conclusion seems to be that, over the last two decades as a whole, the overall Canadian tax system has likely become more progressive than the U.S. tax system.

Turning to the last five or six years, underlying inequality in pretax income has continued to rise in the U.S., but U.S. tax reform has unambiguously increased overall progressivity. Since U.S. progressivity has not returned to its 1970 level, however, the much-increased underlying income inequality means that the U.S. after-tax distribution of income is now much less equal than it was in 1970. In Canada, PIT changes in the immediate prereform period (1985–87) produced a redistribution of relative income away from the middle toward both extremes. Families at the bottom gained disposable income, whereas those at the top saw small losses. Stage I of tax reform was projected to reduce PIT burdens at all levels, but the introduction of federal surtaxes calls into question whether this has actually occurred. There is some evidence that the reduction in the top marginal tax rate was not sufficiently offset by base broadening to prevent the reform from reducing progressivity at very high income levels. Stage II is projected to be more definitely progressive, so that the overall reform may turn out to have been mildly progressive, overall.

Thus, although over the last two decades overall Canadian tax progressivity has likely increased relative to that in the U.S., and after-tax income inequality has increased markedly in the U.S. relative to Canada, in the last five or six years progressivity changes in Canada have been mixed, whereas in the U.S. they have clearly been in the direction of increased progressivity.

What is the outlook for the future? The most significant factor is that the Canada-U.S. contrast on bracket indexation has now switched. In the 1970s and early 1980s, Canadian taxpayers benefited from full bracket indexation, while taxpayers in the U.S. suffered every year from strong "bracket creep." Now the shoe is on the other foot. Canadian taxpayers will suffer regular 3% bracket creep, as long as the inflation rate remains in excess of 3%. The outlook is therefore for a continued shift in the tax mix toward PIT, and an increasingly less progressive PIT. Taking into account other factors, such as the absence of estate and gift taxes in Canada, indicates that the trend of the 1970s and early 1980s toward increased progressivity in Canada compared with the U.S. may be reversed. As far as taxes are concerned, it may become steadily less true that Canada is "more equal" than the U.S., even if greater inequality of pretax income in the U.S. and more generous Canadian health and welfare policies continue to make Canada less unequal overall.

Appendix
Methods of Assessing Tax Incidence in Annual Data

The goal of tax incidence studies, in a famous phrase, is to estimate "who pays the taxes." A fundamental difficulty is that the true incidence of a tax generally departs from its statutory incidence. Increased excise taxes on tobacco, for example, may hurt not only smokers (who bear the statutory incidence), but also tobacco farmers and the owners of the large tobacco companies and their workers. The corporate income tax may be borne partly by owners of capital other than corporate equity, workers, consumers, or even foreigners. Property taxes are shared in some fashion by landlords and tenants. And so we could go down the list. Clearly the task of estimating (in truth, guessing) the ultimate incidence of all these taxes is extremely demanding.

Despite the conceptual and computational burdens of estimating overall tax incidence, such estimates have been painstakingly put together for both the United States and Canada, as well as for many other countries. There have been two main approaches. These are often labeled the *partial* and *general* equilibrium approaches, although this terminology is somewhat misleading. The general equilibrium approach specifies, and solves, a complete general equilibrium model of the economy with taxes. The partial equilibrium approach, on the other hand, is more of an accounting exercise. On the basis of often only implicit theorizing, its proponents propose a "shifting hypothesis" for each tax. With a consistent database, including all the relevant "distributive series," it is possible to compute the hypothetical incidence of each tax and to aggregate to get overall incidence. The difficulty with this approach is that one cannot be sure that the shifting hypotheses are mutually consistent, or could be generated by a fully specified model of an economy with taxes. There is nothing to stop the implicit theorizing from being general, rather than partial equilibrium in nature, however, or from being made explicit.

In order to understand the alternative shifting hypotheses that are typically employed in the partial equilibrium approach, note that taxes can have their incidence effects either on the *sources* or *uses* side of household budgets. If a proportional tax on labor, for example, reduces labor income relative to other factor incomes, there is a "sources side effect," which can be captured by distributing the relevant tax payments across households in one's dataset, in proportion to their labor income. In principle, the same tax could also have uses side effects, since it might alter the relative price of different goods. (This will not necessarily occur. If the stock of labor is fixed, in a competitive economy a tax on labor will be borne entirely by labor, and there will be no changes in relative prices of goods.) In practice, such a uses side effect would likely be ignored in partial equilibrium tax incidence calculations, on the grounds that it is too difficult to trace through the likely relative price changes and their effects. An excise tax on a particular commodity (e.g., alcohol or tobacco) may have its principal effect on relative prices of consumer goods, the impact on relative factor rewards being negligible. It then has its effect on the uses side, and the burden of the tax would be allocated in proportion to expenditures on the taxed commodity across different households. Finally, some taxes, like a flat comprehensive income tax, might be regarded as having *neither* sources nor uses side effects, if they did not disturb either relative factor rewards or relative consumer prices.

Partial equilibrium incidence calculations by Pechman have figured importantly in this paper, both in tracing changes over time in the impact of taxes on income distribution in the U.S., and in performing Canada-U.S. comparisons. Pechman's "most progressive variant" is based on an implicit competitive model of the economy, with fixed stocks of all factors of production and free factor mobility (Pechman 1985, pp. 35–36). In such a model, given the fixed factor supplies, broad-based taxes on factor income, such as PIT and social security payroll taxes, are not shifted. The burden of a sector-specific factor tax, however, will affect factor owners outside the taxed sector equally with those in the taxed sector (since factor rewards are the same in all sectors due to free mobility), and may, in principle, be shifted onto consumers or workers. Harberger (1962) suggested that the corporate income tax could be modeled as a tax on capital used in the corporate sector, and computed the incidence of such a tax using U.S. data for the 1950s in a simple two-sector general equilibrium model. He found that capital appeared to bear about 100% of the burden of CIT. Pechman's most progressive variant is very much in this spirit, except that it allocates only one-half of the CIT burden to capital in general. The other one-half is allocated to holders of corporate equity (dividend recipients), presumably on the argument that in the real world there is some departure from perfect long-run sharing of CIT burdens among all capital owners.

Pechman's "most progressive" treatment of the property tax is based on reasoning that reflects the degree of sophistication in current discussions of tax incidence, as well as the increasing importance being placed on taking something more like a lifetime, rather than merely an annual, viewpoint.

For structures and improvements, Pechman's analysis of the property tax parallels that of the corporate income tax. A tax on a particular *type* of capital is analytically similar to a tax on capital in a particular sector, and so the competitive model would suggest that the component of the tax on structures and improvements borne by capital is shared equally by *all* capital. However, an interesting contrast with CIT is that it is not difficult to discern uses side effects in annual data. In equilibrium the tax on structures and improvements raises the price of housing relative to other goods, so that part of the burden should be allocated according to housing expenditures. Since housing is a fairly strong necessity in annual data, this part of the exercise would make the property tax appear regressive. Interestingly, Pechman (1985) decides to ignore such uses side effects in his competitive variants, on the grounds that the elasticity of housing expenditure with respect to *permanent* income is close to unity. In other words, he would ideally like to use a much longer time frame than a single year, and is prepared to ignore spurious annual incidence effects even if he is constrained to use annual data by the exigencies of available data. This kind of reasoning was extended further, by Browning and Johnson (1979) in their treatment of sales and excise taxes. Such accommodations to the lifetime viewpoint turn out to have major effects on perceptions of tax incidence, although it is questionable whether they should be performed on an ad hoc or piecemeal basis.

Turning to the other component of property taxes, the traditional assumption, embodied here in the "least progressive" variant, has been that a tax on unimproved land is borne by landowners. Pechman (1985, p. 34) reports some recent interest in an alternative view that the tax on land may have no effect on landowners if it is part of a general tax on capital. The general tax reduces the after-tax rate of return, and therefore the discount rate applied to after-tax rents in computing the value of a piece of land. The result is that the value of the land does not change, and landowners do not suffer relative to owners of other capital. The tax on land is therefore borne by owners of capital in general, it is argued.

Finally, in Pechman's most redistributive variant, sales and excise taxes are assumed to have their effects solely on the uses side. While sources side effects of selective sales taxes are a possibility, as pointed out above, tracing them through is too daunting without an explicit general equilibrium model.

Pechman's "least redistributive variant" is based on various concessions to the view that, given conditions like imperfections of competition or immobility of some factors in the real world, things may not work as nicely as portrayed in the most progressive variant. It is still assumed that PIT and social security payroll taxes are not shifted, and that sales and excise taxes continue to be borne by consumers. The half of the corporate income tax attributed to dividends, however, is now allocated to consumers; the property tax on land is allocated to landowners, following the traditional view; and the property tax on improvements is allocated to shelter and consumption. The tendency to view more of the tax burden as shifted forward onto consumers results in reduced apparent progressivity of the overall tax system, since consumption declines fairly sharply as a fraction of income as we go up the income scale, in contrast to dividends or capital income.

References

Ballentine, J. Gregory. 1986. The Short-Run Distributional Effect of Tax Reform. *Tax Notes* 31 (June 9):1035.

Bradford, David, and U.S. Treasury Tax Policy Staff. 1984. *Blueprints for Basic Tax Reform*. 2d ed., rev. Arlington, VA: Tax Analysts.

Browning, Edgar K. 1978. The Burden of Taxation. *Journal of Political Economy* 86 (4):649–71.

Browning, Edgar K., and William R. Johnson. 1979. *The Distribution of the Tax Burden*. Washington: American Enterprise Institute.

Colm, G., and H. Tarasov. 1940. Who Pays the Taxes? Washington: Temporary National Economic Committee.

Davies, David G. 1959. An Empirical Test of Sales-Tax Regressivity. *Journal of Political Economy* 67 (February):72–78.

Davies, James B. 1982. The Relative Impact of Inheritance and Other Factors on Economic Inequality. *Quarterly Journal of Economics* 97 (August):471–98.

Davies, James B., and France St-Hilaire. 1987. *Reforming Capital Income Taxation in Canada: Efficiency and Distributional Effects of Alternative Options*. Ottawa: Economic Council of Canada.

Davies, James B., France St-Hilaire, and John Whalley. 1984. Some Calculations of Lifetime Tax Incidence. *American Economic Review* 74 (4):633–49.

Feldstein, Martin, 1988. Imputing Corporate Tax Liabilities to Individual Taxpayers. *National Tax Journal* 41 (1):37–60.

Galper, Harvey, Robert Lucke, and Eric Toder. 1988. A General Equilibrium Analysis of Tax Reform. In *Uneasy Compromise,* ed. Henry J. Aaron, Harvey Galper, and Joseph Pechman. Washington: Brookings Institution.

Gillespie, W. Irwin. 1976. On the Redistribution of Income in Canada. *Canadian Tax Journal* 24:419–50.

———. 1980. *The Redistribution of Income in Canada.* Ottawa: Gage.

Government of Canada, Department of Finance. 1989. *Goods and Services Tax.* Dec. 19.

Harberger, Arnold C. 1962. The Incidence of the Corporation Income Tax. *Journal of Political Economy* 70 (3):215–40.

Kasten, Richard A., and Frank J. Sammartino. 1987. The Changing Distribution of Federal Taxes. In *Proceedings of the 80th Annual Conference,* National Tax Association - Tax Institute of America. Pittsburgh, November.

Koppelman, Stanley A. 1988. Progressivity Effects of the Tax Reform Act of 1986. *National Tax Journal* 41 (3):285–90.

Maslove, Allan M. 1989. *Tax Reform in Canada: The Process and Impact.* Ottawa: Institute for Research on Public Policy.

Meng, Ronald, and W. Irwin Gillespie. 1986. The Regressivity of Property Taxes in Canada: Another Look. *Canadian Tax Journal* 34 (6):1417–30.

Musgrave, Richard A., J. J. Carroll, L. D. Cook, and L. Frane. 1951. Distribution of Tax Payments by Income Groups: A Case Study for 1948. *National Tax Journal* 4 (1):1–53.

Musgrave, Richard A., K. E. Case, and H. Leonard. 1974. The Distribution of Fiscal Burdens and Benefits. *Public Finance Quarterly* (2):259–311.

Pechman, Joseph A. 1985. *Who Paid the Taxes, 1966–1985?* Washington: Brookings Institution.

———. 1987. Tax Reform: Theory and Practice. *Journal of Economic Perspectives* 1(1):11–28.

Pechman, Joseph A., and Benjamin A. Okner. 1974. *Who Bears the Tax Burden?* Washington: Brookings Institution.

Poterba, James M. 1989. Lifetime Incidence and the Distributional Burden of Excise Taxes. *American Economic Review* 79 (2):325–30.

Rogers, Diane Lim. 1988. A Computable General Equilibrium Model of Lifetime Tax Incidence. University of Virginia. Manuscript (November).

Slovak, Julianne. 1989. The Billionaires Ranked by Net Worth. *Fortune,* Sept. 11, 73–129.

Vaillancourt, François, and Marie-France Poulaert. 1985. The Incidence of Provincial Sales Taxes in Canada, 1978 and 1982. *Canadian Tax Journal* 33, (3):490–510.

Whalley, John. 1984. Regression or Progression: The Taxing Question of Incidence Analysis. *Canadian Journal of Economics* 17:654–82.

5 Tax Effects on the Cost of Capital

Kenneth J. McKenzie and Jack M. Mintz

5.1 Introduction

Given the important economic linkages and the mobility of capital between the United States and Canada, it is important to understand and compare how the tax systems may distort the investment decisions of firms in the two countries. Although considerable work on the distortions caused by taxes has been undertaken separately in each country, less has been done in the way of a systematic comparison of the United States and Canada, especially on a historical basis.[1]

A tax comparison of this sort is particularly important for two reasons. The first concerns the impact of the recent free-trade agreement on capital flows between the two countries. Differences in capital taxes that affect the relative cost of production may lead to an outflow of capital from one country to the other once tariffs are removed. The second concerns the recent tax reforms in both countries. The claim has been made in the popular press in Canada that the tax reform measures had to reduce differences in the taxation of income from capital so that a flight of capital to the United States would not take place. In other words, the corporate tax systems needed to be made more "harmonious."

Given the scope and complexity of the tax regimes in the two countries, the

Kenneth J. McKenzie is assistant professor of economics at the University of Toronto and the University of Calgary. Jack M. Mintz is the Arthur Andersen Professor of Taxation in the Faculty of Management at the University of Toronto.

The authors are indebted to Alan Auerbach, Vijay Jog, and James Poterba, and to the Department of Finance, Canada, which provided data for this project.

1. In the United States, cost-of-capital and effective-tax-rate studies have been undertaken by Auerbach (1983), King and Fullerton (1984), and Gordon (1985). Similar Canadian studies include Boadway, Bruce, and Mintz (1984), Daly and Jung (1987), and Jog and Mintz (1989). For a survey on effective tax rates and an explanation of the differences in methodologies, see Boadway (1987).

existence of distorting effects of taxation on the decision to invest in capital is not self-evident.[2] A framework that lends itself to comparative analysis is thus required. Toward this end, we focus on the impact of taxation on the *user cost of capital* (Jorgenson 1963), which is the economic cost of acquiring and holding the last, or marginal, unit of capital. We use the user cost of capital to compute a summary measure of the distorting effects of taxation on capital accumulation, conventionally referred to as the *marginal effective tax rate* (hereafter referred to simply as the effective tax rate [ETR], as in Auerbach 1983, King and Fullerton 1984, and Boadway, Bruce, and Mintz 1984). The ETR assesses the effect that taxation has on the incentive to hold capital, by determining the amount of taxes paid as a proportion of the operating income generated by the last, or marginal, unit of capital of a particular type held by the firm. The last unit of capital just "breaks even," earning only enough income to cover the economic cost of holding it. A positive ETR on a certain type of capital means that the tax system increases the cost of a marginal unit of that capital relative to the income it generates, which means that it must earn more income in order to break even; this discourages investment. A negative ETR means that the tax system actually subsidizes investment, lowering the user cost and providing an incentive for firms to hold that type of capital.

The tax system distorts the allocation of investment in the economy by affecting the investment decisions of firms, both among different types of capital and among industries. These distortions impose real costs on the economy, as capital is inefficiently allocated. When capital is internationally mobile, there is an additional concern that tax systems may provide incentives for firms to invest in one country rather than another. ETR differentials between industries and capital types in two countries imply *scope* for the tax-induced movement of resources from highly taxed capital in one country to tax-favored capital in the other. Whether this movement actually takes place depends upon a number of factors, such as the mobility and substitutibility of capital between countries, sectors, and uses; differences in economic conditions; the institutional and regulatory environment; and labor, material, and transportation costs. Differences in ETRs between Canada and the United States may not, therefore, actually precipitate a flight of capital. We do not explicitly examine this issue, nor do we attempt to estimate how differences in the tax systems in the United States and Canada may have contributed to actual capital movements between the two countries. These require an extensive empirical investigation, which is beyond the scope of this paper. Rather, we seek merely to identify the distortions in the cost of capital caused by the tax systems in the two countries, and by comparing them arrive at some con-

---

2. We survey these differences for the current corporate tax regimes in an earlier version of this paper, McKenzie and Mintz (1991).

clusions regarding the degree of "harmony" in the corporate tax regimes and the potential for tax-motivated capital movements.[3]

We calculate ETRs for various types of capital in different industry groups in both countries for large and medium-sized businesses, for the years 1975, 1980, 1985, and 1990. Small companies taxed at lower statutory rates are ignored, since cross-country mobility of capital does not seem to be as important an issue for them. Due to the lack of available data, we do not include property taxes, sales taxes on capital inputs, Canadian provincial capital taxes, the Canadian tax on large businesses, or the corporate minimum tax in the United States. We thus compute ETRs only for capital income taxes, which are important contributors to differences in the costs of capital across the two countries.

We arrive at some rather interesting, and we think important, conclusions. Although we compute ETRs under a number of alternative assumptions (which will be discussed at length in subsequent sections), we conclude generally that in 1975 and 1980, ETRs were significantly higher in Canada than in the United States, for fully taxpaying companies. Although the extent of the distortions vary significantly by industry and by type of capital, overall ETRs in these years tended to be significantly higher in Canada. This means that the Canadian capital income tax system tended to discourage capital accumulation to a greater extent over this period than the U.S. regime did. To the extent that firms were able to choose freely between Canada and the United States when making their investment decisions, the capital income tax system in the United States may have attracted investments that otherwise would have been made in Canada.

In 1985, just prior to major tax reforms in both countries, the difference in the overall ETR moderated somewhat. However, ETRs in 1985 were highly variable in both countries between industry groups and types of capital. Capital in some industries faced very high ETRs, while capital in other industries faced very low (even negative) ETRs. The tax systems served to distort investment decisions *between* the two countries, but also *within* each country, between industry groups and different types of capital.

The recent tax reforms in the United States (1986) and Canada (1986–87) changed matters somewhat. Overall ETRs for Canada in 1990 are still higher than for the United States, but to a lesser extent than was the case in the prereform period. Differences in ETRs between the United States and Canada

---

3. Whether a comparison of ETRs is the appropriate way to assess the "harmony" of the two tax regimes may be open to question; it clearly depends upon the issues one is addressing. In our case, when we are comparing the pressure that the tax systems may place upon the type and location of capital firms choose to employ, assessing differences and/or similarities in ETRs between the two countries appears to be an appropriate way of measuring the extent to which the tax regimes are "harmonized." Other measures or definitions of "harmonization" may be more appropriate in other circumstances.

for specific industries or types of capital have also been reduced. Thus, insofar as ETRs on capital in the two countries have converged somewhat, the tax systems appear to have become *more harmonious,* at least for fully taxpaying companies. An important reason for the higher overall postreform ETR in Canada is the treatment of inventories, which are taxed at a much lower rate in the United States. Our estimates indicate that the ETRs on buildings, machinery and equipment, and land are quite close between the two countries in 1990. This narrowing of ETRs between the two countries appears particularly important in light of the free-trade agreement, as the removal of trade distortions may make any tax distortions that continue to exist all the more important. On the basis of our estimates, we conclude that the overall ETR differentials currently existing between Canada and the United States for fully taxpaying firms do not appear to give rise to a significant incentive for capital to flow one way or the other, at least relative to the past. Nevertheless, some significant differences across sectors remain: ETRs are much higher in Canada than in the United States in the Construction, Transportation and Storage, and Wholesale Trade sectors, while U.S. rates are much higher in Communications. There may be scope for some tax-motivated capital movements in these industries.

All of the above results apply to fully taxpaying companies. As is well documented (Mintz 1988; Altshuler and Auerbach 1990), Canada has a much higher proportion of companies not paying taxes in a given year. For a company that has accumulated tax losses over time, the effective rate of taxation may be significantly different from that faced by a fully taxpaying firm. We examine this issue for 1990 and find that Canadian tax-loss companies face a far lower ETR than their U.S. counterparts. Important reasons for this are the discretion allowed Canadian companies in claiming tax depreciation deductions, which may be postponed until the company becomes taxpaying, and the longer period of nontaxability we estimate for Canadian tax-loss firms. In addition, there is a much greater proportion of capital assets held by nontaxpaying companies in Canada compared to the United States. When this is taken into account, we find that the overall ETR on capital in Canada, aggregating over taxpaying and tax-loss firms, is almost identical to that of the United States. However, two factors suggest that the aggregate ETR estimates for Canada may be understated. First, the recent tax reform measures should reduce the number of companies in a loss position over time, so that the aggregate ETR will increase. Second, in theory the existence of tax losses could raise, rather than reduce, the ETR on capital for start-up and risky companies, compared to fully taxpaying companies. If we were to include these types of companies in our calculations, aggregate Canadian ETRs would likely be somewhat higher (but then so would U.S. ETRs). Nevertheless, on the basis of our estimates for tax-loss companies, we conclude that the ETR differentials between the two countries are somewhat lower than suggested by the fully taxpaying case, and therefore that the scope for tax-induced capital flows is lower.

Competitiveness of tax systems is particularly important for cross-border flows of direct investment by multinational corporations. This issue is important, since multinational companies are taxed on their foreign-source income earned by branches and subsidiaries operating abroad. We compare the ETRs on taxpaying U.S. multinationals with subsidiaries operating in Canada and on taxpaying Canadian multinationals with subsidiaries operating in the United States, with their counterparts operating at home. We find that there exists a tax disincentive for U.S. multinationals to operate in Canada rather than at home, and a tax incentive for Canadian multinationals to operate in the United States.

The divergent results for fully taxpaying firms, tax-loss companies, and multinational corporations emphasize an important message of this study—that there is no single ETR measure that easily captures the rich institutional features of the economies and tax systems of the two countries. ETR estimates must thus be interpreted with caution and with an eye to the assumptions which underlie the estimates.

5.2 Methodology

In this section we discuss the method used to determine the effects of taxes on the user cost of capital. The theory has been presented extensively elsewhere (e.g., Boadway 1987), so the discussion will focus on the areas important for an understanding of the ETR estimates that follow in subsequent sections.

The manner in which the tax system impinges upon the investment decisions of firms may be seen by considering the following simple idea. Firms invest in all projects that yield a rate of return in excess of some "hurdle" rate required by the market. This hurdle rate is the real (inflation-adjusted) market cost of the funds invested in the project, net of depreciation, and is equal to the weighted average of the real interest rate on debt and the real rate of return required by equity holders prior to the payment of personal taxes.[4] For example, if the nominal interest rate on debt is denoted i, the required return to equity is ρ, the expected rate of inflation is π, and the proportion of the investment financed by debt is β, the hurdle rate of return is $R = \beta i + (1 - \beta) \rho - \pi$. If we assume for analytical purposes that investment prospects are continuously divisible, firms accumulate capital until the last increment earns just enough operating income, net of taxes paid by the corporation, so that its

---

4. A risk premium may be included as well. In the discussion that immediately follows we ignore risk. Risk considerations will be dealt with in more depth later in this section. See also Shoven and Topper (ch. 6 in this volume).

rate of return is just equal to the hurdle rate.[5] This last increment of capital, therefore, just "breaks even" in an economic sense, and is referred to as the *marginal* unit of capital. To evaluate the impact of taxation on the capital accumulation decision, we determine how taxes affect the difference between the rate of return to capital, gross of taxes, and the hurdle rate of return.

To develop the methodology, we first consider a closed economy, where all funds are supplied by domestic savers. Capital investment in a closed economy is affected by both corporate taxes and personal taxes levied on the interest, dividends, and capital gains income received by the corporation's owners. Owners of capital are concerned with the rate of return on their investments net of the payment of both corporate and personal income taxes. We initially show how the hurdle rate of return may be adjusted to reflect the payment of personal income taxes.

If the expected rate of inflation is π, the personal tax rate on nominal interest income is m, and the tax rate on equity (perhaps a weighted average of the effective capital-gains and dividend tax rate) is c, then the net-of-tax real hurdle rate of return is $R^n = \beta i (1 - m) + (1 - \beta) \rho (1 - c) - \pi$. To be viable, all investments must earn at least this net-of-tax rate of return, and the marginal project will earn it exactly. If household arbitrage holds, equilibrium in the capital market requires that the real after-tax rate of return on debt equals the real after-tax rate of return on equity, or $i (1 - m) - \pi = \rho (1 - c) - \pi$.[6] Since we can observe i directly, but not ρ, we may use this equilibrium condition to determine that $\rho = i (1 - m)/(1 - c)$, in which case $R^n = i (1 - m) - \pi$ is the net-of-personal tax rate of return required on a marginal investment. Note that $i = \rho$ only if $m = c$.

The imposition of corporate taxes on business income affects the cost of capital in the following way. As indicated above, the firms will accumulate capital until the rate of return earned by the last unit just equals the rate of return required by the market. To yield R^n after personal taxes, a marginal investment must earn $R = \beta i + (1 - \beta) \rho - \pi$ after corporate taxes. Let R^g denote the gross-of-corporate-tax, net-of-depreciation, rate of return on a unit of capital required to yield R after corporate taxes. This gross-of-corporate-tax rate of return will reflect various tax provisions, such as debt interest deductibility, investment tax credits, and depreciation allowances. It appears intuitively that corporate income taxes affect the cost of capital in the following way. The deductibility of nominal interest expenses from corporate income means that the nominal cost of debt finance to the firm is $i (1 - u)$, where u is the statutory corporate tax rate. A company that is given an investment tax credit (ITC) at the rate ϕ and annual depreciation allowances that yield tax savings of uA in present value terms on the original cost of the asset faces an

---

5. Operating income is equal to revenues net of salaries, expenditures on materials, depreciation of capital, interest, and inventory costs.
6. This is an assumption discussed in more detail below.

effective purchase price of capital that is lowered by the amount $uA(1 - k) + \phi$ per dollar, where the base for computing depreciation allowances is reduced by the ITC at rate k ($k = \phi$ means that the tax depreciation base is fully reduced by the ITC; $k = 0$ means that the ITC does not lower the base). Corporate income taxes levied at the rate u on income also reduce the rate of return, gross of depreciation, δ, by $(1 - u)$. It is then possible to show that in equilibrium the before-corporate-tax-rate of return on a marginal unit of capital, R^g, must equal:

$$(1) \qquad R^g = \frac{(R^f + \delta)}{(1 - u)}(1 - \phi - uA(1 - k)) - \delta$$

where,

$$(2) \qquad R^f = i(1 - u)\beta + \rho(1 - \beta) - \pi.^{[7]}$$

R^f is the real weighted average net-of-corporate-tax cost of funds to the firm, where β is the debt/asset ratio of the company, which we assume to be determined independently of the capital-stock decision.[8] The present value of depreciation allowances on one dollar of capital, A, is calculated by discounting the annual tax saving of depreciation costs by $R^f + \pi$, which reflects the fact that depreciation allowances are not indexed for inflation.[9] The parameter k is equal to ϕ in Canada, and 0 (prior to 1981) or $\phi/2$ (after 1981) in the United States. This is because the depreciation base is fully reduced by the ITC in Canada and, after 1981, only by one-half in the United States. The economic rate of depreciation, δ, includes changes in the real price of capital goods and physical depreciation. The right-hand side of equation (1) plus δ is the conventional user cost of capital expression in the presence of taxes. The firm accumulates capital until the gross return to capital, the left-hand side of equation (1), is just equal to the user cost.

The ETR is the hypothetical rate of tax τ, which if applied to the gross-of-tax rate of return on the marginal unit of capital R^g, would just yield the net-of-personal-tax rate of return R^n. Thus the ETR solves $(1 - \tau)R^g = R^n$; therefore:

$$(3) \qquad \tau = \frac{R^g - R^n}{R^g}.$$

An ETR may be computed using the expressions for R^g and R^n given above for various types of capital in different industries in each country. The above expressions were developed for depreciable capital. They may be easily mod-

---

7. See Boadway (1987).

8. For models in which this is appropriate, see Bartholdy, Fisher, and Mintz (1987).

9. For example, under a declining balance approach, annual tax savings given at the end of each period is $u\alpha(1 - \alpha)^t$, where α is the declining-balance tax depreciation rate and t is the time since the asset was purchased. If this annual amount is divided by the factor $(1 + R^f + \pi)^{t+1}$, the present value of the infinite stream of tax depreciation allowances is $A = \alpha/(\alpha + R^f + \pi)$.

ified to determine an ETR for nondepreciable capital, such as land, by setting $\delta = 0$ and $A = 0$. A similar expression may also be developed for inventory capital, although it is not reported here (see Boadway, Bruce, and Mintz 1982).

An important consideration in the computation of ETRs is what has come to be known as the *arbitrage assumption*. The issue arises because the corporate and personal tax systems treat various sources of finance differently, which means that some agents may face different rates of return on assets financed in different ways. The arbitrage assumption specifies who bears the tax differential on these assets (firms, savers, or both). For example, in the above determination of the ETR for a closed economy, we assumed that rates of return are such that savers receive the same after-corporate-and-personal-tax rate of return on a marginal unit of capital, regardless of the form of the investment—debt or equity. The arbitrage assumption in this case is known as "closed economy household arbitrage," because the after-tax return to domestic households is assumed to be the appropriate arbitrage margin. But if households earn the same after-tax return on debt and equity, then the firm must face different after-tax costs for debt and equity. This can be easily seen be noting that the firm pays $i(1 - u)$ for a unit of debt finance, and $\rho = i(1 - m)/(1 - c)$ for equity. Under household arbitrage the firm bears the entire tax differential unless it just so happens that $u + c(1 - u) = m$, in which case the firm is indifferent between its sources of finance.[10] Miller (1977) has suggested that this condition will in fact hold in equilibrium, if there are different classes of investors facing different personal tax rates. Miller's model is not entirely applicable for our analysis, because it assumes that there is a single corporate tax rate in the economy. But statutory corporate tax rates in fact differ both between and within Canada and the United States. Miller's model would suggest that companies facing low statutory tax rates would be entirely equity-financed, while high-tax-rate companies would be entirely debt-financed (see Bartholdy, Fisher, and Mintz 1987). This is clearly not the case in practice.

Various arbitrage assumptions are possible, and ETR estimates are sensitive to the assumption used. In the calculations presented in the following sections, we compare two alternative assumptions. The first is the closed economy household arbitrage case discussed above. Although this assumption has been used to undertake international ETR comparisons in the past, it does not appear to be entirely appropriate when it is presumed that capital is internationally mobile.[11] In this case, a more appropriate assumption is one of "open economy arbitrage", which was initially formulated by Boadway, Bruce, and

10. Of course, this is strictly true only if there are no agency, bankruptcy, or other costs associated with debt or equity.
11. The closed economy assumption was used by King and Fullerton (1984) in their comparison of effective tax rates across countries.

Mintz (1984).[12] Under the assumption of open economy arbitrage, the firm must earn a net-of-corporate-tax rate of return on capital at least as great as that required by international financial markets. For example, suppose that an investor can earn i on each dollar invested in Canadian bond assets or i^* on each dollar invested U.S. bond assets. Let m' be the tax rate on interest income and x' the tax rate on foreign currency gains (g) earned by the marginal investor holding Canadian dollar assets. In equilibrium the investor is indifferent between the two assets only if:

$$(4) \qquad i(1 - m') + g(1 - x') = i^*(1 - m').$$

If foreign currency gains reflect purchasing power parity, then $g = \pi^* - \pi$, which is the difference between anticipated rates of inflation in the two countries. The relationship between Canadian and U.S. interest rates under international arbitrage is then $i = i^* + (\pi - \pi^*)(1 - x')/(1 - m')$. This implies that real rates of interest, net of personal taxes, are equal, but real rates of return gross of personal taxes are not, unless $m' = x'$. An equation similar to (4) must also hold for equity assets yielding net-of-tax nominal returns of ρ $(1 - c')$ and $\rho^*(1 - c')$ in each country.

Interest rates are determined by international arbitrage, where the marginal investor holding a country's corporate securities may be some foreign investor rather than a domestic investor. Thus, personal taxes on domestic investors are irrelevant in the calculation of R^n, as they determine only the supply of domestic savings and therefore whether the country is a net capital importer or exporter. Instead, we must determine the net-of-tax rate of return required by the international marginal investor for both bond and equity assets. This is not possible without making an assumption about where the marginal investor resides. Since the marginal investor's tax rate is assumed to be the same for both Canada and the United States, there is no serious difficulty in measuring the cost of capital as long as gross-of-personal-tax rates of interest are observable, allowing us to ignore personal tax rates. However, to determine the relationship between ρ and i in each country, we must know c', x', and m'. To abstract from this problem, we assume for our calculations that $m' = x' = c'$, implying that $i - \pi = \rho - \pi = i^* - \pi^* = \rho^* - \pi^*$ and $R^n = R$ in the above equations.[13] An alternative case in which m', x', and c' are not equal

12. Gordon (1986) models an international equilibrium using a model similar to that of Miller (1977) and derives a capital market equilibrium similar to that discussed in Boadway, Bruce, and Mintz (1984). In Gordon's model, the identity of the investor who is indifferent between holding an asset of a particular country or that of another depends on each country's inflation rate and the difference between taxes on interest income and capital gains. Investors facing high personal tax rates on interest tend to hold unindexed bond assets originating in countries with high inflation rates.

13. One case in which this obviously holds is when there are no taxes levied on interest or equity income earned by the marginal investor. This is the case if the marginal investor is a tax-exempt institution or an individual residing in a country with no capital income taxes (which may well be a reasonable assumption).

was also considered. In this case, real net-of-tax interest rates are not the same across countries, and therefore hurdle rates of return differ across countries. Calculations for this case are not reported, as they do not substantially change our conclusions.

As we assume that the marginal investor is the same for both countries, the ETR estimates for the open economy arbitrage case reflect only differences in corporate tax provisions, rather than differences in personal tax rates. With equal rates of personal tax on equity and debt, the open economy arbitrage assumption restricts real interest rates to be the same in the two countries, although nominal interest rates and rates of inflation may differ. It is our belief that the case of open economy arbitrage, with $m' = x' = c'$, provides the most meaningful basis for comparison between the United States and Canada; we thus treat this as our "base case" against which the alternative assumption of closed economy household arbitrage is measured.

Aside from the arbitrage assumption, a number of other assumptions must be made in the computation of ETRs. Two particularly important ones involve the treatment of risk and loss offsetting. We deal with each in turn.

Following Gordon (1985), Bulow and Summers (1984), Gordon and Wilson (1989), and McKenzie (1989), a distinction is made between two types of risk that are important in the calculation of ETRs. *Income risk* refers to uncertainty regarding future net revenues, arising from the stochastic movement of output prices or demand faced by the firm. *Capital risk* refers to uncertainty regarding the economic rate of depreciation, due either to an unknown future supply price of capital or a stochastic physical rate of depreciation.

If the tax system grants full loss offsets, so that companies receive a full refund for taxable losses when they are incurred, as was assumed in the preceding discussion, then an income risk premium, h', may be added to both R^n and R^g in the above equations. However, if we then express the rate of return on capital net of risk, and subtract the income risk premium from the net and gross rates of return, it is evident that the ETR expression for income-risky investments is identical to the expression for equivalent riskless investments. The reason for this is intuitive. With full loss offsetting, the tax liability of the firm fluctuates perfectly with its income. The government therefore shares equally in both the profits and losses of the company. In other words, the government shares in $100u\%$ of the profits and absorbs $100u\%$ of the risk. The cost of bearing income risk (h') is thus implicitly fully deducted in a full loss offset tax system, and no additional distortions are introduced for income-risky investments vis-à-vis comparable riskless investments.

The matter is somewhat different for capital-risky investments. In both the United States and Canada, tax depreciation allowances are based on the original cost of the asset, and there is no accrual valuation of capital gains and losses on the assets. This means that tax depreciation allowances and accrued capital gains income do not fluctuate with unanticipated changes in the replacement value of the capital. The implication is that the tax system does not deduct the full cost of bearing capital risk. The imputed cost of bearing capital risk can be thought of as an upward adjustment in the economic rate of depreciation that is not compensated for by an equivalent increase in the tax depreciation rate. With the capital risk premium denoted by h^c, the ETR for capital-risky investments may be determined by replacing δ with $\delta + h^c$ in the expression for R^g in equation (1).

One of the problems in measuring ETRs on risky capital is that it is difficult to measure the risk premium associated with capital risk. We follow Bulow and Summers (1984), who argue that the market value of a firm is equal to its asset value, so that fluctuations in market values reflect changes in the value of the firm's underlying assets. This implies that capital-asset-pricing-model (CAPM) estimates would be appropriate to use for the capital risk premium. However, as Gordon and Wilson (1989) point out, it is the correlation between the economic cost of depreciation and consumption that is really relevant, and this correlation could well be negative. If that were the case, we would err considerably in our use of CAPM estimates for risk premiums.[14]

The analysis to this point has assumed that the tax system allows for the full refundability of tax losses, or equivalently, that all companies are fully taxpaying. Although the resulting ETR estimates are informative, only about 50% of investment in Canada and 80% in the United States is conducted by firms that are fully taxpaying at a particular point of time. For firms that are experiencing tax losses, the assumption of full loss offsetting is not appropriate. A firm may be in a nontaxable position, for example, due to large banks of past tax losses. In this case, the income (write-offs) generated by the marginal investment may not be taxed (deducted) until some later time. Alternatively, a young firm may be making its initial investment, which will earn income only at some later, uncertain time. In that case, tax credits and deductions cannot be written off against income generated from past investments and must be postponed.

Loss offsetting is imperfect in Canada and the United States. In both countries, tax losses may be carried back for three years. In the United States, operating losses may be carried forward for fifteen years, but without interest. In Canada the carry-forward period (also without interest) is only seven years;

---

14. See the paper by Shoven and Topper (ch. 6 in this volume), for a more in-depth discussion of the effects of risk. Although our approach is similar, it differs in some important respects. First, Shoven and Topper consider the cost of capital under a continuum of risk premiums, while our calculations are based upon specific risk-premium estimates taken from Jog and Mintz (1988), which differ by industry. Second, Shoven and Topper use price-earnings ratios to determine the market-risk premium, while we again use an estimate based on the CAPM from Jog and Mintz (1988). Third, our ETRs are disaggregated by industry and asset type; Shoven and Topper consider illustrative investments in a manufacturing plant and automobiles. Finally, our treatment of income risk differs slightly; see Boadway, McKenzie, and Mintz (1989) for a formal derivation of the type of cost-of-capital expression for risky assets we use in this paper.

however, depreciation and other important capital cost deductions may effectively be carried forward indefinitely, due to their discretionary nature.[15] Moreover, consolidated tax accounting is allowed in the United States, but not in Canada. This means that the losses of U.S. firms can be offset against the profits of associated companies. Given the different treatment of operating losses, it is important to determine how the ETRs for loss corporations may differ between the two countries. To compute ETRs for loss corporations, we assume that the firm is risk-neutral and in an initial tax-loss position, expecting to become taxable T years from the current period t. Given the paucity of data, we only undertake calculations for 1990, when there was no investment tax credit. We estimate a "tax loss refundability parameter," $\xi = (1 + \rho + \pi)^{-(T-n)}$, which is the present value of the proportion of the last dollar of tax losses used by the corporation.[16] As shown in Mintz (1990), the marginal rate of return, gross of taxes, for a company in a tax-loss position depends on its history and whether capital is depreciated during the loss period. The marginal rate of return is equal to the following:

$$(5) \qquad R^g = \frac{(\delta + R^f)}{(1 - v)} [1 - v_t A_t] + \frac{(1 - R^f)}{(1 - v_t)} [v_t A_t - v_{t-1} A_{t-1}] - \delta,$$

where $A_t = 1 - (1 - \alpha)^{T-t} + A(1 - \alpha)^{T-t}$, if capital is depreciated for tax purposes during the loss period (as in the United States), and $A_t = A$, if capital is not depreciated during the loss period (as in Canada). The term v is the effective statutory tax rate for the loss company, equal to ξu. As before, R^f is the real cost of finance, $\beta i(1 - v) + (1 - \beta) \rho - \pi$. Note that A is the present value of tax depreciation allowances that would be normally calculated for a taxpaying firm, and A_{t-1} is the value of tax depreciation allowances calculated in the previous period. To compute ETRs for tax loss companies we use the R^g given in equation (5).

The final modification that we make to the base case analysis is the determination of ETRs for multinational corporations. One of the important questions raised in debates regarding capital mobility is whether companies of a given country may find it advantageous to locate production facilities in another country. For multinational companies resident in a capital-exporting country, an additional level of taxation must be considered. This is the tax on foreign-source earnings that may be imposed by the home country. In Canada an exemption approach is used, and multinationals are allowed to repatriate

15. Capital deductions are mandatory in the U.S. and discretionary in Canada. Thus, although the carry-forward period in longer in the U.S., firms must continue to write off assets during the loss period. In Canada, deductions can be postponed until the firm becomes taxable. See McKenzie and Mintz (1991) for a more in-depth discussion of the carryover provisions in the two countries.

16. This is the procedure for "currently nontaxpaying" firms used in Mintz (1988). We use the Mintz figures for ξ in Canada. For the U.S., we use calculations provided in Altshuler and Auerbach (1990) for companies in a loss position for two consecutive years.

dividends tax-free from foreign affiliates operating in the United States (a foreign affiliate's equity must be owned at least 10% by the parent). In the United States, a deferral approach is used, where the remitted foreign-source earnings received by the parent from its subsidiary are taxed, but a foreign-tax credit for the corporate and withholding taxes attributed to those earnings is granted. If there are excess credits associated with a particular source of earnings, such as dividends (i.e., foreign-tax credits are more than U.S. tax liabilities on dividends received from Canada), the company may use the credits against U.S. tax liabilities on other foreign sources of income that are in the same "basket." If not all credits are fully used, the company is in an excess foreign-tax-credit position. If the credits are fully used, the company is in an overall deficient foreign-tax-credit-position.

Under the deferral method, the cost of capital for the multinational depends on the functional currency used by the home country to convert subsidiary income into home country tax liabilities. In the case of U.S. companies operating in Canada, two functional currencies may be used, depending on the ownership of the subsidiary and the type of business. A qualifying U.S. multinational company may use the U.S. dollar as the functional currency. In this case, foreign-source income is measured by converting Canadian dollars into U.S. dollars as the income is earned. The alternative is to use the Canadian dollar as the functional currency. In that case, foreign-source income is measured in U.S. dollars only when the income is remitted. The difference between these two approaches leads to two different costs of capital. If the first approach is used, the tax depreciation allowances granted by the United States for foreign investments are calculated by converting the cost of the asset into U.S. dollars and then depreciating that amount. If the second approach is used, there is no conversion of asset values into U.S. dollars; instead, the U.S. determination of tax-depreciation allowances is based on the Canadian dollar, and depreciation claims are converted into U.S. dollars when the income is remitted.

Leechor and Mintz (1990, 1991) provide the costs of capital for U.S. multinational companies operating in Canada and for Canadian multinationals operating in the United States.[17] In the case of deferral taxation, the cost of capital depends upon the "tax-adjusted" dividend-payout ratio of the multinational, the "repatriation tax" rate of U.S. tax on remitted dividends (which could be positive or negative), and the capital-cost provisions of the home and host countries. We use the before-tax rate of return on equity and the steady-state conditions for the capital stock to derive the repatriation tax rate on remitted dividends. The accounting dividend-payout ratio is used as a proxy for the tax-adjusted payout ratio, based on the U.S. definition of subsidiary income earned in Canada.

---

17. Leechor and Mintz (1990, 1991) ignore rules regarding the attribution of interest that have recently been adopted in the United States.

5.3   Comparative Analysis: The Base Case

In this section we compare the ETR estimates for Canada and the United States for our "base case," which employs the following assumptions: (i) the tax systems grant full loss offsets, or all firms are fully taxpaying; (ii) the investments are riskless; (iii) there is open economy arbitrage with debt and equity income taxed at the same personal tax rate; and (iv) none of the investments involve cross-border direct investment by multinationals. Some of these assumptions will be modified in subsequent sections.

ETRs were estimated for four years—1975, 1980, 1985, and 1990. These "snapshots" represent important periods in each country, when economic conditions and the tax regimes varied substantially. For example, 1975 and 1980 were both periods of relatively high inflation with moderate real interest rates in both countries, while in 1985 and 1990, inflation rates were lower but real interest rates were higher. As we shall see, the interaction between the tax system and inflation and interest rates has important effects on ETR estimates. Moreover, the tax systems in both countries underwent important changes over the period considered. Two major regime changes occurred in the United States: the Economic Recovery Tax Act of 1981 increased write-off rates and enhanced the ITC, while the Tax Reform Act of 1986 lowered depreciation rates, eliminated the ITC, and reduced the statutory tax rate. In Canada, in late 1977 the ITC (originally introduced in 1975) was enhanced, and a 3 percent inventory allowance was introduced to offset the taxation of inflationary gains on inventories due to the use of FIFO accounting. In 1986 the first stage of tax reform eliminated the inventory allowance, lowered ITC rates, and reduced the statutory corporate tax rate slightly. In 1987 the process was continued, as the ITC was virtually eliminated (except for a few regional credits), depreciation rates were lowered, and the tax rate was further reduced.

We begin with a discussion of the changes in ETRs over time for each country and follow with a comparative discussion. The ETRs are listed in table 5.1.

5.3.1   Canada

In 1975, the weighted average ETR for the four types of capital across the nine industries was a very high 40.3% in Canada. The implication is that on average, in 1975 the Canadian tax system acted as a significant deterrent to investment. When we examine individual assets and industries, we see that this figure does not tell the whole story. Investments in inventory capital were highly taxed in most sectors, with the exception of Agriculture, where inventories are expensed under cash accounting. The high rate of tax on inventory investment was due to the relatively high inflation rate in 1975, coupled with the use of FIFO (first in, first out) accounting, which results in the taxation of inflationary gains on inventories. Provisions to offset this (the inventory al-

Table 5.1   **Effective Tax Rates; Base Case**

Industry or Asset[a]	1975		1980		1985		1990	
	Canada	United States	Canada	United States	Canada	United States	Canada	United States
AFF	30.2	21.6	22.1	16.5	31.9	31.7	27.6	26.2
MAN	43.2	33.0	28.0	30.7	21.3	28.8	31.1	27.0
CON	63.1	40.0	62.3	35.8	45.7	34.4	43.4	24.0
T&S	25.0	(40.3)	10.7	(67.8)	25.5	(12.0)	21.7	8.3
COM	7.2	36.6	(5.4)	34.5	26.2	23.7	17.5	25.2
PUT	11.8	(5.9)	1.0	(25.3)	22.8	2.7	19.8	12.5
WST	53.8	24.3	41.9	20.0	31.5	31.4	34.9	24.8
RET	47.4	13.5	35.0	5.3	28.4	26.0	30.5	21.3
SER	28.3	(16.1)	19.0	(34.7)	26.2	13.8	22.9	16.1
BLD	17.6	14.9	5.4	(0.2)	24.7	12.8	21.1	17.6
EQP	28.7	6.0	14.2	10.0	16.2	1.6	25.6	18.9
INV	67.7	35.1	59.0	31.9	37.1	38.4	43.2	28.0
LND	(26.3)	(23.4)	(36.0)	(49.9)	29.3	27.7	20.2	19.0
Total	40.3	14.7	27.7	7.5	26.0	18.9	28.9	20.4

Note: Brackets indicate negative numbers.
[a]AFF = Agriculture, Forestry, Fishing; MAN = Manufacturing; CON = Construction; T&S = Transportation and Storage; COM = Communications; PUT = Public Utilities; WST = Wholesale Trade; RET = Retail Trade; SER = Services. BLD = buildings and structures; EQP = machinery and equipment; INV = inventories; LND = land.

lowance) were not put in place until 1977. As a result, industries that devote a large proportion of their investments to inventories, such as Construction, Wholesale Trade, and Retail Trade, tended to be highly taxed on average. By way of contrast, the high inflation rates and low real interest rates combined to provide a tax subsidy to investments in land, as evidenced by the negative ETR. This was due to the deductibility of nominal rather than real debt interest payments. As such, the tax subsidy was particularly large in highly leveraged sectors such as Transportation and Storage and Services.

In 1980, ETRs declined rather significantly in Canada, averaging 27.7% overall. The decline was due to a number of factors. First, there was a modest reduction in the corporate tax rate from 1975 (1 percentage point). Second, the higher inflation rate in 1980 tended to reduce the ETR on some assets while increasing it for others. With nominal debt interest deductibility and low real interest rates, for example, there was a substantial increase in the tax subsidy for investments in land (-36% in 1980 versus -26% in 1975). If it had not been for the introduction of the inventory allowance in 1977, the high inflation rate would have also increased the ETR on inventories relative to 1975. As it turned out, the inventory allowance actually resulted in a decline in the ETR on inventories, from about 68% in 1975 to 59% in 1980. Finally, investment tax credits were somewhat richer in 1980, with a basic rate of 7% versus 5% in 1975. This was particularly important for equipment, where the effective ITC rate was higher and asset lives shorter. Thus, the ETR on equipment declined from 28.5% in 1975 to 14.2% in 1980. The Manufacturing sector was a particular beneficiary of the enhanced ITC. The ETR on buildings also declined significantly, to only 5.4%, due to relatively low real interest rates and a high rate of inflation.

In 1985, while the overall average ETR did not change very much (26% versus 28% in 1980), the configuration of ETRs changed considerably. This was the result almost entirely of changes in inflation and real interest rates, as the tax system was largely unchanged from 1980. In particular, a large reduction in the rate of inflation from 1980 to 1985 eliminated the tax subsidy on land, which now faced a positive ETR of 29% on average. The ETR on inventories declined substantially, from 59% in 1980 to 37% in 1985, also due to the reduction in inflation. The increase in real interest rates and reduction in inflation also caused the ETR on buildings to increase quite significantly, to 24.7%.[18]

In 1986 and 1987, a tax reform was instituted in Canada. From the 1990 ETR estimates, we see that the net result of this reform was actually a slight increase in the aggregate ETR, from 26% to almost 29%. However, inflation rates were somewhat higher and real interest rates were somewhat lower in 1990 than in 1985. While these changes exacerbated the impact of the elimination of the inventory allowance, they were offset somewhat by the reduction in the statutory tax rate. The net result was only a slight increase in the ETR on inventories, from 37% to 43%. The decline in the ETR on land was due largely to the reduction in the corporate tax rate. The ETR on buildings also declined slightly in 1990 from 1985. The elimination of the ITC did not have much of an impact on buildings, and the reduction in write-off rates was relatively minor for structures; the tax rate reduction thus offset these effects and lowered the ETR on buildings. The ETR on equipment was substantially higher in 1989, particularly in the Manufacturing sector, because of the elimination of the ITC and the reduction in write-off rates, including the elimination of the accelerated write-off for manufacturing and processing assets. As a result, Manufacturing moved from a position with a lower-than-average ETR in 1985 (21%) to a higher-than-average ETR in 1989 (31%). Overall, the tax reforms tended to smooth ETRs across sectors and between assets. Investments in buildings, equipment, and land all bear an ETR of around 22%, while inventories are more highly taxed at 43%, due to the use of FIFO accounting.

18. These results generally correspond to the "prereform" estimates made by Jog and Mintz (1989). Their effective tax rates on large companies were lower primarily due to the use of a lower discount rate for equity finance, where they assumed $m > c$, so that ρ is lower than i. We take the case that $m = c$, so $\rho = i$.

5.3.2   The United States

In the United States, the overall ETR for the nine industries and four assets was 14.73% in 1975.[19] Investment in land was largely subsidized due to the relatively high rate of inflation and the deductibility of nominal borrowing costs, which proved beneficial for highly leveraged industries such as Transportation and Storage. The high inflation rate also led to a relatively high ETR on inventories. Although firms in the United States have the option of using LIFO (last in, first out) accounting, which eliminates the taxation of inflationary gains on inventories, about one-quarter of businesses opt to use FIFO in any event, and the ETR estimates reflect this. The low ETR on equipment was due largely to a relatively rich ITC, which actually created a tax subsidy for investments in equipment in many industries.

In 1980, the aggregate ETR was about half the 1975 rate, at 7.5%. This change occurred for a number of reasons, including a slight reduction in the corporate tax rate from 1975 (about 1 percentage point); enhanced ITCs (particularly for some structures, such as those used in the Transportation and Storage and the Public Utilities industries); and a higher inflation rate coupled with a lower real rate of interest, which increased the tax subsidy on investments in land, again due to the use of nominal debt interest deductions.

The Economic Recovery Tax Act of 1981 sought to increase corporate investment in the United States by increasing write-off rates and enriching the ITC. Despite these measures, our estimates show that the average ETR actually increased from 1980 to 1985, to almost 19%. The reason for this was the substantial increase in real interest rates, which led to an elimination of the tax subsidy on land. Land had a positive ETR of almost 28% on average. The increase in real interest rates also led to an increase in the ETR on inventories and buildings. Despite the increase in real interest rates, the enhanced write-offs and ITCs led to a significant decline in the ETR on machinery and equipment, which benefited the most from the tax changes. In 1985, investments in equipment were virtually distortion-free, with an average ETR of approximately 2%. The Communications, Manufacturing, and Construction industries all had lower ETRs in 1985 relative to 1980, despite the higher real interest rates.

The Tax Reform Act of 1986 sought to eliminate many of the tax breaks introduced in 1981 and earlier. The result was an increase in the average ETR to over 20%. The elimination of the ITC and the reduction in tax depreciation rates were particularly important for investments in equipment. On average,

---

19. Results reported here and below roughly correspond to those reported by Auerbach (1983), who provided us with U.S. data on depreciation and asset classes. The main difference in our results and his is that we use a weighted average discount rate based on estimates of the debt/asset ratios by industry and the observed interest rates for the U.S., while Auerbach used a constant 4% real discount rate.

investments in equipment moved from a position of virtual neutrality in 1985 to a positive average ETR of almost 19% in 1990. The ETR on buildings also increased slightly, due to longer write-off periods. The elimination of the ITC and lengthening of write-off periods for depreciable assets were offset by a tax rate reduction of over 10 percentage points. As a result of this rate reduction, the ETRs on investments in both land and inventories decreased significantly from their 1985 levels. Overall, the tax reforms in 1986 served to smooth out the ETRs among assets and across sectors. In fact, buildings, equipment, and land all had an ETR of around 18.5%, while inventories were taxed at a higher rate of 28% (because of the elective use of FIFO accounting by some businesses). Moreover, the large tax subsidies that had existed for some industries, particularly Transportation and Storage and Public Utilities, were eliminated. All sectors had a positive ETR in 1990.

5.3.3 Comparing Effective Tax Rates

We now turn to a more direct comparison of ETRs between the two countries. There are a number of similarities, particularly in the pattern of changes in ETRs over time. In both countries, the 1970s and early 1980s were typified by a wide divergence of ETRs across assets and industries, with investments in some assets and industries highly subsidized while others were highly taxed. In 1990, following the tax reforms in both countries, ETRs were "smoothed" substantially across assets and among industries. In both countries, overall ETRs declined rather significantly from 1975 to 1980, then increased slightly in 1985 and again in 1990. This pattern in large part resulted from similar movements in inflation and interest rates in the two countries. However, parallel tax-regime changes also contributed. For example, in the late 1970s and early 1980s both countries modestly reduced corporate tax rates and enhanced ITCs, and in the mid-1980s both implemented tax reforms of a similar nature, eliminating ITCs, lowering depreciation rates, and reducing statutory tax rates.

Although there are similarities, the differences in ETRs between the two countries are perhaps more striking. Most obvious is the fact that overall ETRs in Canada have tended to be higher than those in the United States, particularly in 1975 and 1980. This difference was due to number of factors, three of which appear to be particularly important. The first was the investment tax credit. Prior to the elimination of the credit in both countries, the ITC in the United States was richer than in Canada. The basic ITC rate was higher,[20] the credit was available for a broader range of assets (structures in particular), and, depreciation deductions were not reduced by ITC claims in the United States (unlike Canada) until after 1980, and then only partially.

---

20. This is not strictly true, as historically ITC rates vary by region in Canada, with very high rates available in regions considered economically depressed. However, investment in these high-ITC regions has typically been low relative to the rest of the country; their presence has very little impact on the weighted-average ITC calculations.

The more generous ITC in the United States was particularly advantageous for investments in equipment. A second reason for the higher ETRs in Canada was the optional use of LIFO accounting for inventories in the United States and the mandatory use of FIFO in Canada. As discussed above, the use of FIFO leads to the taxation of inflationary gains in the cost of inventories, which significantly increases the ETR on inventories during high inflation periods, such as 1975 and 1980. Although some firms in the United States use FIFO in any event, and the inventory allowance moderated the impact of inflation in Canada somewhat in 1980 and 1985, the ETR on inventories in the United States has tended to be lower than in Canada. For example, in 1990 the overall ETR on investments in inventories was 15.2% higher in Canada. The third factor contributing to higher ETRs in Canada was the slightly higher rates of inflation. The open economy arbitrage model used for the base case restricts real interest rates to be the same in both countries. However, inflation rates, and therefore nominal interest rates, have been higher in Canada than in the United States over the period examined. This has been an important factor in the higher ETRs in Canada for assets like inventories, structures, and certain forms of equipment.

Despite the historical differences, ETRs in the two countries have moved closer together recently. Similar tax changes no doubt contributed to this. Tax reforms contributed to the decline in the overall aggregate ETR differential between the two countries, from 25.6% in 1975 to only 8.5% in 1990. By examining each industry and asset class individually, we see that differences between Canadian and U.S. ETRs declined virtually across the board from 1975 to 1990. Insofar as ETRs in the two countries have moved closer together, the corporate tax regimes seem to have become more "harmonious." Indeed, ETRs on buildings, equipment, and land were quite similar in 1990 (the fourth asset, inventories, is highly taxed in Canada). The overall ETRs in key sectors such as Manufacturing, which accounts for more than 30% of nonresource investment in both the United States and Canada, were also very close. Yet even though it appears that overall the Canadian and U.S. tax systems have become more harmonious over time, considerable differences remain in specific sectors. For example, in 1990 Canadian ETRs exceeded United States ETRs by 19.5% in Construction, 13.4% in Transportation and Storage, and 10.1% in Wholesale Trade.

Given the apparent convergence in overall ETRs over time, it might be argued that the governments deliberately attempted to harmonize the corporate tax systems. At times, specific provisions such as the DISC program in the United States and accelerated depreciation for manufacturing in Canada were implemented in response to international trends. But there is little direct evidence of an intent by Canada and the United States to harmonize their corporate tax systems in the late 1980s. Canada's corporate income tax reform, which actually began prior to U.S. reform, was mainly concerned with problems arising from the instability of the corporate tax base due to the substantial amount of tax-loss carry-forwards and with a desire to make the tax system less distortive. U.S. tax reform was largely motivated by a desire to improve upon the efficiency of the tax system and upon the mix between corporate and personal tax revenues (with a shift toward collecting more revenue from the corporate sector). Although the countries ended up adopting similar reforms (as have other countries around the world), we would argue that this result may have occurred more by accident than by design.[21]

Another important point to note is that the absence of indexing for inflation in both tax systems may well lead to a greater divergence in ETRs in the future, even if no other tax changes are made. As indicated above, ETRs in both Canada and the United States are highly sensitive to interest and inflation rates. If the inflation rate in either country changes significantly relative to the other, ETRs will diverge.

5.4   Changes in the Underlying Assumptions

A number of assumptions underlie the base case estimates discussed above. In our view, there is no single or unique method to measure ETRs that captures all of the institutional details of the tax systems and economies of the two countries, in part because there is no consensus regarding the appropriate assumptions that should underlie the model. In this section, we examine the implications of modifying some of the assumptions. In particular, we examine: a different treatment of risk; an alternative view of financial arbitrage; the presence of nontaxpaying companies; and multinational companies.

5.4.1   Capital Risk

In the base case, it was assumed that investments were riskless. As discussed in section 5.2, ETRs on riskless and income-risky investments are identical if the tax system grants full loss offsets. This is not the case for capital risk. Since tax depreciation allowances are determined ex ante, based upon the original or historic cost of the asset, these allowances do not fluctuate with unforeseen changes in the replacement values of assets. As such, the economic cost of bearing capital risk is not fully deducted, even with full loss offsetting. Unless an upward adjustment is made in the tax-depreciation rate to account for capital risk (something done by neither country explicitly), we would expect the distortions caused by the tax systems to be higher for capital-risky investments in both the United States and Canada.

This expectation is confirmed in table 5.2, where we see that the presence of capital risk leads to a significant increase in ETRs. In 1990, the aggregate Canadian ETR on capital-risky assets was almost 48%, versus 29% for comparable riskless or income-risky investments; for the United States, the figures

---

21. John Whalley discusses this issue in more detail in the introduction to this volume.

Table 5.2   **Effective Tax Rates, 1990**

Industry or Asset[a]	Base Case		Capital Risk		Closed Economy	
	Canada	United States	Canada	United States	Canada	United States
AFF	27.6	26.2	55.6	52.5	44.6	42.4
MAN	31.1	27.0	47.9	43.9	49.3	44.3
CON	43.4	29.0	60.0	47.9	58.6	45.1
T&S	21.7	8.3	45.0	24.0	43.9	33.3
COM	17.5	25.2	28.1	29.5	39.9	41.4
PUT	19.8	12.5	39.0	25.9	40.7	34.4
WST	34.9	24.8	51.1	43.6	52.8	43.5
RET	30.5	21.3	47.6	40.4	49.6	41.1
SER	22.9	16.1	46.5	38.7	44.1	37.6
BLD	21.1	17.6	42.3	33.8	41.5	37.9
EQP	25.6	18.9	43.7	26.5	45.7	39.7
INV	43.2	28.0	56.7	49.0	59.5	45.3
LND	20.2	19.0	49.0	46.4	38.1	37.7
Total	28.9	20.4	47.6	37.6	48.0	40.0

[a]As defined in table 5.1.

were 38% and 20%, respectively. Both systems thus act to significantly deter investments characterized by capital risk, to a much greater extent than comparable riskless or income-risky investments.

The presence of capital risk does not alter our general conclusion that the current tax system in the United States is less distortive than the Canadian system. Indeed, if anything the ETR in favor of the United States appears to be even greater than it was with riskless investments. For example, the aggregate ETR for riskless investments was 8.5% higher in Canada than in the United States; for capital-risky investments the Canadian aggregate ETR exceeded the American by 10%. One reason for this is the higher statutory tax rate in Canada, which penalizes capital risk. For Manufacturing, where the statutory tax rates of the two countries are much closer, the ETRs were almost the same.

5.4.2   Closed Economy Arbitrage

As discussed in section 5.2, there are other financial arbitrage assumptions that may be used to assess the impact of taxes on capital-investment decisions. One possibility is closed economy household arbitrage, in which both personal and corporate taxes in the home country affect the user cost of capital faced by domestic firms. In table 5.2 we report ETRs under the closed economy assumption, in which households in each country must earn the same net-of-personal-tax rate of return on equity and bond assets. Allowing personal taxes on interest and equity income to differ according to estimates of effective personal tax rates in Canada and the United States (in both cases

$m > c$), we compute the combined corporate and personal tax rate on capital.[22] These numbers are not strictly comparable to those in the base case, since the base case provides only an effective corporate tax rate (domestic personal taxes do not affect the level of investment under our open economy arbitrage assumption).

Given that the closed economy case includes domestic personal taxes on capital income, it is not surprising to find that ETRs are about 20 percentage points higher than the base case. What might be surprising is that the differences in ETRs between the two countries are similar to those in the open economy base case. The reason is that our calculations of the effective personal tax rate on nominal interest income for the United States and Canada are very close, at about 25%; similarly, the ETR on nominal equity income is about 8% in both countries (assuming that the capital-gains tax rate, rather than dividend tax rate, is the most important factor influencing the cost of equity finance). On the basis of these calculations, we conclude that the effective personal tax rates are more harmonized in Canada and the United States than the corporate tax rates! This might be considered anomalous, as one might expect countries to be more concerned about the harmonization of corporate income tax systems than personal tax systems; the latter depend on the residence of households, which are far less mobile.

5.4.3   Tax-Loss Firms and Imperfect Loss Offsetting

Another important consideration for a United States–Canada comparison is the presence of nontaxpaying companies. As also discussed in section 5.2, we consider only one particular case of tax losses, in which a firm is assumed to be in a tax-loss position currently and expects to remain so for some specified amount of time. As a result, our estimates of ETRs are lower for loss firms than for fully taxpaying companies. However, our calculations may tend to understate the ETR on companies with tax losses since, under alternative approaches, tax losses could increase rather than reduce ETRs. For example, Mintz (1988) and Jog and Mintz (1989) show that in some cases, loss firms may face very high ETRs relative to fully taxpaying firms.

We compute the cost of capital for tax-loss companies in the United States and Canada, taking into account the flexibility allowed in Canada in claiming tax-depreciation allowances; see equation (5) above. Aside from full loss offsetting, we use the base case assumptions and assume risk neutrality. Using calculations from Altshuler and Auerbach (1990), we estimate that in the United States only 20% of investment was undertaken by tax-loss companies in 1990, which expect, on average, to be nontaxpaying for about eight years.[23]

---

22. Canadian calculations are based on Glenday (1989) and Boadway, Bruce, and Mintz (1987). U.S. numbers are based on data given to us by James Poterba and Alan Auerbach.

23. Altshuler and Auerbach (1990) calculate that another large portion of companies were constrained in claiming investment tax credits in 1981. We assume that all these companies would be taxpaying in 1990.

Using 1977–85 data from the Department of Finance, compiled by Glenday and Mintz 1991, we estimate that approximately 50% of investment was undertaken by tax-loss companies in Canada, and that Canadian tax-loss companies take an average of eleven years to become taxpaying. We suspect that one of the reasons for the shorter tax-loss period in the United States is the use for tax purposes of consolidated accounting, which allows associated companies to aggregate profits and losses. Consolidation is not allowed in Canada.

Table 5.3 provides ETR estimates for taxpaying and illustrative tax-loss firms in Canada and the United States. It is immediately apparent that the ETR on loss companies was far lower in Canada. The lower ETR on loss companies in Canada arises for two reasons: the longer estimated time for Canadian companies to become taxpaying, and the ability of Canadian companies to postpone depreciation deductions until they become taxpaying.

It is interesting to consider the ETRs aggregated over taxpaying and non-taxpaying companies. As shown in the last column of table 5.3, the overall aggregate Canadian ETR was virtually identical to the U.S. ETR (18.7%, compared to 19.2%). In fact, Canadian ETRs were lower for the Agriculture, Forestry, and Fishing, Manufacturing, and Communications industries. There was also a reversal of ETRs on buildings, machinery, and land, with Canadian ETRs now lower than U.S. ETRs.

These calculations emphasize that conclusions regarding the impact of taxes on capital can be reversed if certain institutional details, such as tax losses, are taken into account. Although, as emphasized above, the ETRs re-

Table 5.3   **Effective Tax Rates, 1990**

Industry or Asset[a]	Taxpaying Firms[b]		Loss Firms		Aggregate	
	Canada	United States	Canada	United States	Canada	United States
AFF	27.6	26.2	8.6	17.0	17.8	24.3
MAN	31.1	27.0	1.9	11.0	20.5	24.6
CON	43.4	29.0	6.3	15.7	31.4	27.0
T&S	21.7	8.3	6.6	18.0	14.8	10.4
COM	17.5	25.2	6.9	23.1	12.5	24.8
PUT	19.8	12.5	6.6	17.6	13.6	13.5
WST	34.9	24.8	2.6	8.8	24.8	22.7
RET	30.5	21.3	2.9	8.7	21.4	19.5
SER	22.9	16.1	4.0	9.3	14.9	14.9
BLD	21.1	17.6	4.2	14.8	13.8	17.1
EQP	25.6	18.9	5.7	20.1	17.2	19.1
INV	43.2	28.0	1.1	6.4	28.6	24.8
LND	20.2	19.0	1.8	4.5	12.3	16.6
Total	28.9	20.4	3.8	13.7	18.7	19.2

[a]As defined in table 5.1
[b]Base case.

ported for loss companies may be understated, they suggest that we may not know as much as we would like to about how taxes influence the cost of capital in either Canada or the United States.

5.4.4 Multinationals

A comparison of the ETRs on direct investments undertaken by multinational corporations may well be the most relevant of all, as cross-border direct investment flows are likely to be quite sensitive to differences in tax regimes. As discussed in section 5.2, when evaluating the ETRs imposed on resident multinationals, one must take account of the tax treatment of foreign-source income.

In table 5.4, we present 1990 effective corporate tax rate estimates for U.S. multinationals investing in Canada through a subsidiary, and for Canadian-based multinationals investing in the United States through a subsidiary. For the U.S. multinational, three cases are considered: overall deficient credit position with the use of the U.S. dollar as the functional currency; overall deficient tax-credit position with the use of the Canadian dollar as the functional currency; and overall excess credit position. It has been argued by U.S. Treasury officials that most U.S. multinationals would be in an excess tax-credit

Table 5.4   **Effective Tax Rates, 1990**

| | U.S. Multinational | | | | | United |
| | Deficient Credit | | Excess | Canada | Canada | States |
Industry[a]	United States $[b]	Canada $[c]	Credit[d]	Multinational[e]	Domestic[f]	Domestic[f]
AFF	n.a.	n.a.	n.a.	n.a.	27.6	26.2
MAN	28.8	33.0	33.2	26.9	31.1	27.0
CON	38.6	42.0	42.8	33.9	43.4	29.0
T&S	20.0	14.0	24.7	5.7	21.7	8.3
COM	17.0	18.4	21.4	5.8	17.5	25.2
PUT	18.7	19.7	21.8	9.8	19.8	12.5
WST	25.5	26.4	28.6	22.1	34.9	24.8
RET	21.9	23.3	27.8	20.2	30.5	21.3
SER	31.4	36.3	41.5	35.5	22.9	16.1
Total	25.8	28.1	30.5	21.8	28.9	20.4

[a]As defined in table 5.1.
[b]U.S. multinational operating in Canada in a deficient foreign-tax-credit position; functional currency denominated in U.S. dollars.
[c]U.S. multinational operating in Canada in a deficient foreign-tax-credit position; functional currency denominated in Canadian dollars.
[d]U.S. multinational oeprating in Canada in an excess foreign-tax-credit position.
[e]Canadian multinational operating in the U.S.
[f]Base case.

position after the 1987 tax reform. However, many U.S. companies are changing the ownership and financial structure of their subsidiaries so as to fully utilize excess credits. This means that the deficient credit case may be the most relevant in the future. Moreover, as will be confirmed below by our estimates, there can be an incentive for companies to be in deficient credit position. As Leechor and Mintz (1991) discuss, one important strategy is for the subsidiary to increase its leverage so that excess credits can be fully used.

For a Canadian multinational investing in the United States, remitted dividends from foreign affiliates operating in the United States are essentially exempt from the Canadian corporate tax. This case is similar to that of a U.S. multinational being in an excess credit position.

We first deal with U.S. multinationals operating in Canada and determine whether a U.S. multinational would prefer investing in a Canadian subsidiary rather than at home. The ETRs for U.S. multinationals operating in Canada are reported in the first three columns of table 5.4, while the last column contains estimates for U.S. domestic investments. A comparison of these figures shows that overall the ETR for U.S. companies operating domestically is slightly lower than for all three cases of U.S. subsidiaries operating in Canada. The aggregate ETR, for example, is 20.4% for domestic investment and ranges from 25.8% to 30.5% for investments in Canada. The implication is that the tax systems tend to discourage U.S.-based firms from investing in Canadian subsidiaries. An important reason for this is that U.S.-based firms must use a less generous tax depreciation schedule for capital employed in other countries; straight-line depreciation based upon ADR (asset depreciation range) midpoint lives must be used for foreign investments, while MACRS (modified accelerated cost recovery system) may be used for investments at home.

For Canadian companies operating in the United States, the opposite situation arises, as the ETR on investments by Canadian firms in the United States is slightly less than the ETR on domestic investments. Canadian-based multinationals thus have a small incentive to invest in U.S. subsidiaries rather than at home. This is not surprising, given the exemption approach followed in Canada, and it reflects the same factors that lower ETRs on U.S. domestic investments relative to Canadian domestic investments.

The ETRs on investments made by Canadian companies in the United States tend to be slightly higher than for U.S.-owned domestic investments. This is due to our assumption that Canadian companies issue some debt in Canada to finance investments by subsidiaries in the United States. Whether it is cheaper to issue debt in the United States rather than in Canada depends upon differences in statutory tax and inflation rates. Debt is more likely to be issued in the country with the higher corporate tax rate and higher inflation rate. If we had assumed that the debt was raised in the United States, the ETRs would have been identical for Canadian multinational and U.S. domestic investments. The same applies for U.S. companies in the excess credit position and Canadian domestic investments, where it is assumed that U.S. companies issue some debt in the United States. The fact that the ETRs are not significantly different suggests that there is not a large incentive for companies to issue more debt in Canada or the United States. This absence of incentive is the result of the similarity in statutory corporate tax rates and the rates of inflation.

5.5 Summary and Conclusions

We conclude that for fully taxpaying companies investing domestically, ETRs in Canada are somewhat higher than those in the United States. This is due in large part to the significantly higher ETR on inventories in Canada. Similarly, Canadian multinationals face lower ETRs on direct investments in the United States than on domestic investments, while for U.S. multinationals the ETR on domestic investments is lower. ETRs for nontaxpaying companies in Canada are significantly lower than for their U.S. counterparts, due partly to the flexibility granted to Canadian loss companies when claiming depreciation deductions. Aggregated over fully taxpaying and tax-loss firms, overall ETRs are very similar in the two countries.

As there appears to have been a convergence in aggregate ETRs across the two countries in recent years, we find that the corporate tax systems in the United States and Canada have become more "harmonious." Although we believe that this convergence may have occurred more by accident than design, tax reform in both countries has no doubt contributed to it. Nevertheless, significant differences in ETRs remain and may become greater in the future, if large differences in inflation and interest rates between the two countries emerge.

Throughout our discussion, we have argued that there is no single ETR estimate that easily captures the institutional features of the economies and tax systems of the two countries. We have tried to address some of the issues involved by computing ETRs under a number of alternative assumptions regarding the treatment of risk, financial arbitrage, tax losses, and multinational investments. We do not believe, however, that we have addressed all of the interesting problems that arise in the measurement of ETRs on capital. Remaining problems include the treatment of minimum taxes, financial and inflation risk, resource firms, real estate, regulated and finance companies, adjustment costs, and international tax planning. Moreover, the paucity of data has not allowed us to incorporate other taxes that may be relevant to capital decision making, such as property taxes, sales taxes on capital inputs, the corporate minimum tax, and provincial capital taxes. Despite these limitations, we suspect that our general conclusions regarding the level of corporate taxation in Canada relative to the United States are at least qualitatively accurate.

References

Altshuler, Rosanne, and Alan J. Auerbach. 1990. The Significance of Tax Law Asymmetries. An Empirical Investigation. *Quarterly Journal of Economics* 105:61–86.

Auerbach, Alan J. 1983. Corporate Taxation in the United States. *Brookings Papers on Economic Activity* 2:451–505. Washington, D.C.

Bartholdy, Jan, Gordon Fisher, and Jack M. Mintz. 1987. Taxation and the Financial Policy of Firms: Theory and Empirical Applications to Canada. Economic Council of Canada Discussion Paper no. 324.

Boadway, Robin W. 1987. The Theory and Measurement of Effective Tax Rates. In *The Impact of Taxation on Business Activity,* ed. Jack M. Mintz and Douglas D. Purvis. Kingston, Ont: John Deutsch Institute.

Boadway, Robin W., Neil Bruce, and Jack M. Mintz. 1982. Corporate Taxation and the Cost of Holding Inventories. *Canadian Journal of Economics* 15:278–93.

———. 1984. Taxation, Inflation and the Effective Marginal Tax Rate on Capital in Canada. *Canadian Journal of Economics* 17:62–79.

———. 1987. *Taxes on Capital Income in Canada: Analysis and Policy.* Toronto: Canadian Tax Foundation.

Boadway, Robin W., Ken J. McKenzie, and Jack M. Mintz. 1989. *Federal and Provincial Taxation of the Canadian Mining Industry: Impact and Implications for Reform.* Kingston, Ont.: Centre for Resource Studies.

Bulow, J., and L. H. Summers. 1984. The Taxation of Risky Assets. *Journal of Political Economy* 92:20–39.

Daly, Michael, and Jack Jung. 1987. The Taxation of Corporate Investment Income in Canada: An Analysis of Marginal Effective Tax Rates. *Canadian Journal of Economics* 20:555–87.

Glenday, Graham. 1989. Personal Savings and Portfolio Composition: Changing Tax Incentives. In *Economic Impacts of Tax Reform,* ed. Jack M. Mintz and John Whalley. Toronto: Canadian Tax Foundation.

Glenday, Graham, and Jack M. Mintz. 1991. The Nature and Magnitude of Tax Losses of Canadian Corporations. In *Policy Options for the Treatment of Tax Losses in Canada.* Toronto: Clarkson Gordon Foundation.

Gordon, Roger H. 1985. Taxation of Corporate Capital Income: Tax Revenues versus Tax Distortions. *Quarterly Journal of Economics* 100:1–28.

———. 1986. Taxation of Investment and Savings in a World Economy. *American Economic Review* 76:1086–1102.

Gordon, Roger H., and John D. Wilson. 1989. Measuring the Efficiency Cost of Taxing Risky Capital Income. *American Economic Review* 79:427–39.

Jog, Vijay M., and Jack M. Mintz. 1989. Corporate Tax Reform and its Economic Impact: An Evaluation of the Phase I Proposals. In *Economic Impacts of Tax Reform,* ed. Jack M. Mintz and John Whalley, 83–124. Toronto: Canadian Tax Foundation.

Jorgenson, Dale. 1963. Capital Theory and Investment Behavior. *American Economic Review* 53:247–59.

King, M. A., and D. Fullerton. 1984. *The Taxation of Income from Capital: A Comparative Study of the United States, United Kingdom, Sweden and West Germany.* Chicago: University of Chicago Press.

Leechor, Chad, and Jack M. Mintz. 1990. On the Taxation of Multinational Corporate Investment when the Deferral Method is Used by the Capital Exporting Country. University of Toronto Working Paper no. 9013. Toronto.

———. 1991. Taxation of International Income by a Capital-Importing Country: The Perspective of Thailand. In *Tax Policy in Developing Countries,* ed. Javad Khalizadeh-Shirazi and Anwar Shah. Washington, D.C.: World Bank.

McKenzie, Kenneth J. 1989. The Neutrality of Business Taxation in the Presence of Adjustment Costs and Risk. Queen's University Discussion Paper no. 759. Kingston, Ont.

McKenzie, Kenneth J., and Jack M. Mintz. 1991. Tax Effects on the Costs of Capital: A Canada-United States Comparison. University of Toronto. Manuscript.

Miller, M. 1977. Debt and Taxes. *Journal of Finance* 32:261–76.

Mintz, Jack M. 1988. An Empirical Estimate of Corporate Tax Refundability and Effective Tax Rates. *Quarterly Journal of Economics* 103:225–31.

———. 1990. Corporate Tax Holidays and Investment. *World Bank Economic Review* 4(1):81–102.

6 The Cost of Capital in Canada, the United States, and Japan

John B. Shoven and Michael Topper

6.1 Introduction

The cost of capital in a country is a key variable determining that country's ability to compete for internationally mobile capital. It sets the level of investment in the economy and is thus a central factor in the determination of real wages and economic growth. In the United States, at least, the allegedly high cost of capital is often blamed for the slow rate of growth of productivity and the perceived loss of international competitiveness. The same concerns are expressed in Canada, along with a host of additional factors. Among them are that tax changes in the U.S., if not matched by changes in Canada, can have adverse impacts on the Canadian economy. For instance, when the U.S. lowered its basic federal corporate tax rate from 46 to 34 percent in 1986, concern was expressed that this might lead to large amounts of new debt financing by Canadian affiliates of U.S. corporations, and thereby erode the tax base of the Canadian corporate income tax.

It is probably accurate to portray the U.S. and Canada as sharing a common capital or financial market. Because the U.S. economy is so large, it is likely that policies to encourage saving in the U.S. have significant impact on interest rates and other terms in world capital markets, whereas the effects of Canadian saving policies on capital market terms are probably much less pronounced. It is probably reasonable to model Canada as a small open economy facing an exogenous rate of return on financial capital. Whether that capital market is best characterized as a world capital market or one for North America is open to question.

A comparison of the cost of capital in the two countries is interesting for

John B. Shoven is professor of economics at Stanford University and a research associate of the National Bureau of Economic Research. Michael Topper is assistant professor of economics at the College of William and Mary.

both policy makers and economists. One aspect of the question is whether the recent Canadian tax reforms have effectively alleviated the problem of erosion of the corporate tax base because of international financial shuffling.

Both Canada and the U.S. are concerned not only with their relative costs of capital, but also with their collective competitiveness with respect to the rest of the world. To gauge this relative position, we include in the paper some previous calculations from Bernheim and Shoven (1989) on the cost of capital in Japan. Japan is of interest because it is the world's largest capital market participant (aggregate investment and savings in Japan exceed the corresponding aggregates for the U.S.) and an important trading partner for both Canada and the U.S.

The methodology of this paper and the Bernheim-Shoven paper is fairly traditional and comparable in many respects to the detailed analyses of Boadway, Bruce, and Mintz (1987) of taxes on capital income in Canada. Their work, in turn, is related to the King-Fullerton (1984) study. Relative to this earlier work, however, the methodology of this paper emphasizes the role of risk premia in determining the cost of capital and the interaction of risk and tax considerations. The cost-of-capital concept computed in this paper is exactly the same one that business people refer to as the "hurdle rate" for new investments. That is, it is the expected net rate of return before corporate taxes that is required in order for an incremental real investment to be in the interest of the owners of the firm. Unlike the procedure in most previous studies, the cost of capital is not presented as a single number, but rather as a schedule of figures for projects involving different amounts of risk.

The plan of this paper is to discuss the cost-of-capital concept in section 6.2. Section 6.3 deals with empirical difficulties in measuring the cost of capital and describes the measurement approach taken in this paper. Section 6.4 lays out the analytics for determining the cost of capital, given the terms in financial markets. That is, given the real interest rate and the expected return and riskiness of equity portfolios, the cost of capital is derived for debt- and equity-financed projects. Section 6.5 briefly contrasts the tax systems of Canada, Japan, and the U.S., and includes a table of parameter values for capital market terms and tax regimes used in the cost of capital calculations. Section 6.6 presents and interprets the results.

6.2   Defining the Cost of Capital

Although the cost of capital is a central concept in determining investment and economic growth, relatively little empirical work has been done in actually calculating its cost. Further, the work that has been done often uses inconsistent and misleading definitions of the cost of capital. Three common measures that appear in the literature are the real interest rate, the Hall-Jorgenson (1967) tax-adjusted real interest rate, and the weighted-average cost of capital (see for example, Copeland and Weston 1979, pp. 272–298). All three have major flaws as measures of the cost of capital. The real interest rate ignores all tax and risk factors and is thus only appropriate as a hurdle rate for safe investments taxed exactly like Treasury bills. The Hall-Jorgenson approach adds detailed (corporate and personal) tax factors, but it still ignores all risk considerations.

The weighted-average cost of capital is the before-tax return necessary to offer competitive rates of return on all of the claims out against a firm, and is the correct cost-of-capital measure for the firm's existing assets. However, it is inappropriate to use this measure as the hurdle rate for new investments, unless the new investments have exactly the same risk and return characteristics as the firm's existing assets. For instance, General Motors can undertake a relatively risky project to develop improved solar cells and finance the undertaking with quite safe debt. To act in the interest of the shareholders, the appropriate hurdle rate should be tied to the riskiness of the incremental real investment, rather than to the relative safety of the debt.

Corporate investment decisions should take into account the opportunity cost of the money. The fact that the corporation is making decisions about real investments (plant expansion, a truck, or a new computer network, for example) is immaterial. In order to be in a stockholder's interest, risky real investments at the corporate level have to be competitive with equally risky financial investments available in retail financial markets.

Since observed risk premia in retail financial markets are quite large, the appropriate hurdle rate for risky real investments is much higher than for safe investments. The simplest illustration of the risk premia is a comparison of long-run average real rates of return on a diversified portfolio of common stocks with the average real returns on safe, short-term investments such as Treasury bills. In the U.S., the arithmetic-average real rate of return on the Standard and Poor's 500 between 1926 and 1989 was 8.8%, whereas the average real return on U.S. Treasury bills was 0.5% (Ibbotson Associates 1990). In Canada, there was a similar gap between average equity and Treasury bill yields. Between 1950 and 1987, the average real rate of return of the Toronto Stock Exchange composite 300 was 7.5%, whereas the average real yield on Canadian Treasury bills was 1.2% (Hatch and White 1988).

In this paper, we define the cost of capital as the expected rate of return (or hurdle rate) necessary to satisfy both financiers and tax authorities. This measure includes an interest factor, a risk premium, and a number of tax factors.

The first component in this calculation is the capital market line of the familiar capital-asset pricing model (CAPM), which summarizes the financial market's required expected returns on securities of different riskiness (see, e.g., Sharpe 1970). In figure 6.1, the intercept, R_T, represents the real return on completely safe assets, whereas the point m represents the expected return and riskiness of a market portfolio or a standardized diversified portfolio of securities, such as the S&P 500. The riskiness of other investments is determined as the systematic or nondiversifiable risk of the asset with respect to the

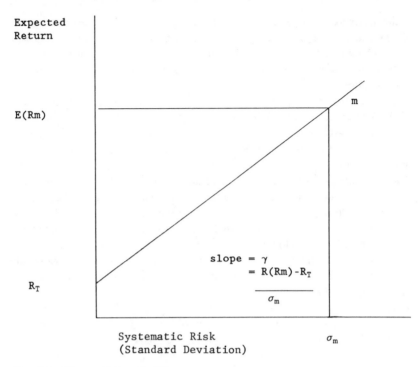

Fig. 6.1   **The capital market line**

market portfolio. Under the conventional assumptions of the CAPM model (perfect securities markets, no restrictions on short selling or borrowing, etc.), all investments must offer returns on the capital market line in order to be viable in the market.

The second step is to calculate the necessary expected rate of return on real investments before corporate and personal taxes. The relationship between the cost-of-capital line, capital market line, and the post-tax return the investor ultimately realizes after the payment of all corporate and personal taxes is illustrated in figure 6.2.[1]

6.3   Measuring the Capital Market Line

In principle the capital market line can be simply constructed by observing two points on the line: the return on a zero-risk safe asset and the return on a market portfolio of given riskiness. In practice, this is no easy task. For short-term safe assets it is reasonable to assume that the expected return is the con-tractual return (e.g., Treasury bills). Of course, the capital market line is ex-

---

1. For readers familiar with the King-Fullerton framework (which did not include risk), these three schedules correspond to their variables p, s, and r.

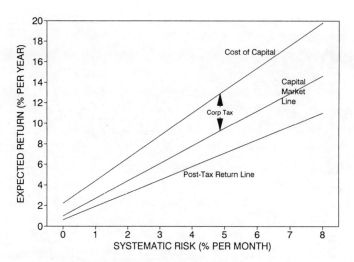

Fig. 6.2   Relationships between risk and return

pressed in real terms rather than in the nominal terms of the contracts. Also, Treasury bill yields are not perfectly safe in real terms. We follow the usual procedure of ignoring this and assume that Treasury bill yields are safe and that the expected real return is equal to the contractual rate less the average rate of inflation over the past six or twelve months.

The major problem is determining the expected return and standard deviation of the market portfolio, since there are no contracts to refer to and the expected return is unobservable. If the monthly or annual real total (dividends plus real capital gains) rates of return on the market were independently drawn from an identical distribution, then the average of a large number of realizations would give an accurate measure of the expected future returns. Similarly, the standard deviation of realizations would give an accurate guide to the standard deviation of the constant underlying real-rate-of-return distribution. Real returns in U.S. and Canadian equity markets do not seem to conform to the independent draws from an identical distribution model, however. The long-term average realization is very sensitive to the precise period covered. An example of this instability of average returns is shown in figure 6.3; while the ten-year average of annual real returns on the Toronto Stock Exchange was 8.33% between 1963 and 1972, it was only 0.10% between 1965 and 1974. This instability makes the past-realization approach unfeasible. The problem with using averages of past realizations as proxies for expected future rates of return on the market portfolio is that nonrecurring events (e.g., the formation of OPEC) may greatly affect past realizations.

The earnings-price ratio serves as a second possible proxy for the expected return on the market portfolio. Earnings are meant to reflect the amount of money a firm has left over after setting aside enough income to keep its capital

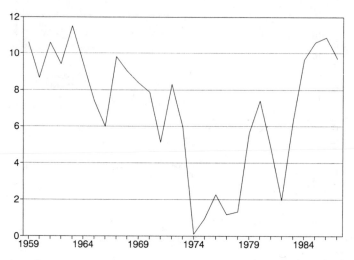

Fig. 6.3   Ten-year average real rate of return on the market portfolio in Canada

intact. If earnings were paid out to shareholders, then the shareholders would maintain a claim on a constant amount of capital. The only way that their total return could differ from the amount of earnings would be if the relative value of that constant amount of capital were to change. If one expects the relative prices of the firm's constant stock of assets to remain unchanged, then the expected total return would equal earnings, and the expected rate of return would be the earnings-price ratio. Although several accounting problems arise in measuring earnings, we adopt the annual average of monthly earnings-price ratios as our proxy for the expected return on the market portfolio. Boadway, Bruce, and Mintz use a similar procedure with an additional adjustment for inflation. In our base year of 1988, capital market lines based on E-P ratios are almost identical in the U.S. and Canada.

The 1988 E-P figure for Canada is 8.33%, while for the U.S. it is 8.55%. The 1988 real Treasury bill rate for Canada is 4.02%; it is 3.91% for the U.S. The riskiness of the market portfolio (measured as the standard deviation in monthly returns) is 4.77% for the U.S. and 5.44% for Canada. These figures are the realized standard deviation in returns for the ten-year period 1979–88.

Japanese equity markets featured very high rates of return in the 1980s and sharply increasing price-earnings ratios. Price-earnings ratios in Japan were lower than in the U.S. and Canada in 1970, but were almost 55 (or four times the levels in North America) by 1988. Even after adjusting Japanese earnings for U.S. accounting practices and Japanese cross-ownership to make them comparable, the P-E ratio in Japan exceeded 30 in 1988,[2] with a correspond-

2. See French and Poterba (1989) for details.

ing E-P ratio of 3.1%. According to the E-P approach, the Japanese capital market line is much lower than the Canadian or the U.S. capital market line, with higher equity prices effectively lowering the Japanese cost of capital. Thus, the 1988 figures suggest an integrated North American financial market segmented from the Japanese market.

6.4 An Analytical Calculation of the Cost of Capital

In this section we derive the before-tax cost of capital faced by the firm as a function of the interest rate, the risk aversion shown in the capital market line, and the design of the tax system. Consider a hypothetical investment project costing one dollar. Initially, consider a simple world without uncertainty or taxes. If $f'(k)$ is the cash flow generated by the investment and $\check{S}$ is the depreciation rate, then the project should be undertaken when the net-of-depreciation cash flow exceeds the real interest rate $i - Ð$, where i is the nominal interest rate on Treasury bills and $Ð$ is the inflation rate. The cost of capital, P, is the net cash flow that just satisfies this hurdle rate:

$$(1) \qquad P \equiv f'(k) - \delta = i - \pi.$$

In this certain world without taxes, the relevant opportunity cost is the real rate of return on a safe financial asset.

Now consider a world with uncertainty about both the cash flow generated by the project (income risk) and the depreciation of the investment (capital risk). The net-of-depreciation cash flow for a single period is then:

$$(2) \qquad f'(k) (1 + \varepsilon_f) - k(\delta - \varepsilon_\delta),$$

where $\ddot{Y}_f$ and $\ddot{Y}_S$ are random variables capturing the uncertainty in income and capital risk, respectively. When $\ddot{Y}_S$ is high, depreciation is low, so that net income is high. Thus, positive values of $\ddot{Y}_f$ and $\ddot{Y}_S$ both correspond to favorable returns for investors.

Without loss of generality, assume that $E(\ddot{Y}_j) = 0$ for $j = f,\check{S}$. For simplicity, suppose that the $\ddot{Y}_j$ are distributed independently across periods. Since investors are risk-averse, a claim on $\ddot{Y}_j$ has negative value. Let $V(x)$ denote the certainty-equivalent value of the random variable x. Then

$$(3) \qquad V(\varepsilon_j) = -\lambda_j,$$

for $j = f,\check{S}$. One can also think of λ_j as the risk premium that one must pay to an investor in order to induce him to hold the claim $\ddot{Y}_j$. In practice, the value of λ_j will depend upon investors' risk aversion, and upon the level of nondiversifiable risk subsumed in $\ddot{Y}_j$. In certainty-equivalent terms, the total single period return is:

$$(4) \qquad f'(k) (1 - \lambda_f) - (\delta + \lambda_\delta).$$

Now the proper hurdle rate is to accept all projects whose certainty-equivalent yield exceeds the real interest rate. If one equates the above equation to $i - \bar{D}$ and solves for the cost of capital, the result is

$$(5) \qquad P = f'(k) - \delta = (1 - \lambda_f)^{-1}(i - \pi + \delta + \lambda_\delta) - \delta,$$

with both types of risk premia (λ_f and λ_s) increasing the cost of capital.

The next step is to add tax considerations to this framework. Since equity and debt finance are taxed differently, the cost of capital will vary with the source of finance. In this section, we outline the derivation of the cost of capital for equity-financed investment.[3]

The role of taxes will depend on just which stockholders the investment-decision maker takes into account. Are they domestic owners or foreign owners? What tax brackets are domestic owners in? What taxes do foreigners pay on dividends, interest, and capital gains? This will be discussed again in the next two sections. For now, the results will be derived for a relatively high-income domestic stockholder's tax situation.

The new notation that needs to be introduced is:

τ the corporate tax rate;

m the average marginal rate of taxation for personal income in the form of interest;

d the average marginal rate of taxation for personal income in the form of dividends;

z the average rate of taxation for personal income induced (either through future realized capital gains or future dividends) by real retained earnings;

z_n the average rate of taxation for personal income induced by nominal capital gains on the stock of corporate capital (see below for further discussion);

A the present discounted tax value of depreciation allowances and tax credits associated with a unit of capital;

$\acute{A}$ the marginal propensity to pay dividends out of permanent changes in the level of earnings;

$\acute{A}_\dot{y}$ the marginal propensity to pay dividends out of transitory changes in the level of earnings; and

q marginal Tobin's q (the ratio of the marginal value of installed capital to the replacement cost of capital).

It will simplify the equations to follow if we let

$$(6) \qquad\qquad T = 1 - \alpha d - (1 - \alpha) z$$

---

3. A more detailed analysis of the equity-finance case, as well as the corresponding analytics for debt finance, can be found in Bernheim and Shoven (1989).

and

(7) $$T_\varepsilon = 1 - \alpha_\varepsilon d - (1 - \alpha_\varepsilon) z.$$

T and $T_{\ddot{y}}$ represent the fractions of one dollar of permanent and transitory earnings, respectively, that are available for consumption by shareholders.

Note that the government effectively pays A for a unit of investment, while the net cost to the investor is $1 - A$. The total random return on one dollar invested by a shareholder is

(8) $$(1 - A)^{-1} \{T[f'(k)(1 - \tau) - \delta(1 - A)] - z_n \pi q$$
$$+ T_\varepsilon[\varepsilon_f f'(k)(1 - \tau) + \varepsilon_\delta(1 - A)]\},$$

where $\ddot{Y}_f$ and $\ddot{Y}_\delta$ are realized randomly in each year.

The above equation includes the term $-z_n Ð_q$. When the corporation installs an additional unit of capital and finances this acquisition through equity, its value rises by \$$q$. If it subsequently maintains higher capital stock by undertaking all necessary replacement investment, then in each period investors will accrue a nominal capital gain (in real dollars) of $Ð_q$. It seems likely that most corporations would not raise dividends in a subsequent period after accruing nominal gains on installed capital. In contrast, they might well subsequently raise dividends in response to an increase in real retained earnings. Likewise, investors may have different patterns of realization for nominal and real gains. Accordingly, we have allowed for the possibility that z_n (the average marginal rate of taxation on personal income induced by nominal gains on corporate capital) may differ from z (the average marginal rate of taxation on personal income induced by real retained corporate earnings).

The three appearances of $(1 - A)$ in the equation may also require explanation. The first simply reflects the fact that one dollar buys $(1 - A)^{-1}$ units of incremental capital. The remaining two appearances reflect the effect of depreciation by replacement capital costing $(1 - A)$ per unit.

If the corporation chooses the level of equity-financed investment to maximize its value, then it must be indifferent about raising an additional dollar of capital. If an investor contributes an additional dollar to the firm, its value rises by $(1 - A)^{-1}q$. Indifference therefore implies that $(1 - A)^{-1}q = 1$, or $q = (1 - A)$. Making this substitution into the above equation and converting to certainty equivalents, by applying the function $V(\cdot)$, one obtains

(9) $$(1 - A)^{-1} \{T[f'(k)(1 - \tau) - \delta(1 - A)] - T_\varepsilon[\lambda_f f'(k)(1 - \tau) +$$
$$\lambda_\delta(1 - A)]\} - z_n \pi.$$

As in the case without taxes, the certainty equivalent of net income in any year must equal the real riskless after-tax rate of return. Since personal income taxes are levied on nominal interest payments, this return is $i(1 - m) - Ð$. Setting these quantities equal and solving for $f'(k) - \check{S}$, one obtains

(10)
$$p^e = \left(1 - \frac{T_\varepsilon}{T}\lambda_f\right)^{-1}\left(\frac{1 - A}{1 - \tau}\right)\left(i\left(\frac{1 - m}{T}\right)\right.$$

$$\left. - \pi\left(\frac{1 - z_n}{T}\right) + \delta + \left(\frac{T_\varepsilon}{T}\right)\lambda_\delta\right) - \delta,$$

where p^e is the cost of equity-financed capital.

The above equation is the basic formula for the cost of equity-financed capital. Note that the corporate tax enters the cost of capital only in the single term

(11)
$$\frac{1 - A}{1 - \tau}$$

which multiplies both the real interest terms and the risk premia. If A were equal to τ, as with expensing (where investors are allowed to deduct immediately the full cost of their investments, presuming that they have taxable income to offset), then the corporate tax would not affect the cost of equity-financed capital at all. In that case, the government would effectively pay a fraction of the cost of the investment (τ) and would receive the same fraction of the cash generated by the project. Effectively, the government would be a proportional partner in the cost, return, and riskiness of the investment. With expensing, any investment undertaken in the absence of the corporate tax would still be undertaken with the corporate tax. The same is true if the present value of the sum of the tax savings from depreciation deductions and investment tax credits equals τ. For some investments (particularly equipment), this was the case after the U.S. 1981 tax reform.

Since A is expressed in present-value terms that depend on the nominal rate of interest, which in turn depends on the inflation rate, the effect of the corporate tax on the cost of capital and investment depends crucially on this rate of interest. This helps to reconcile the various contradictory claims about the Japanese tax system. On the one hand, a number of studies have found Japan to have one of the world's highest corporate tax rates. On the other hand, despite Japan's having depreciation schedules similar to those of the U.S. and Canada, other studies have found the Japanese corporate tax system to be relatively nondistortionary. The explanation is that the tax system is less distortionary because of the low Japanese nominal interest rates. One can see this most clearly by noting that at $i = 0$, $A = \tau$, and the corporate tax is nondistortionary regardless of the tax rate and the depreciation schedule.

The λ_f and λ_δ risk premia terms in the main formula are determined from the observed equity premium on the capital market line. In order to identify them with the available data, one has to assume that the fractions of the total premium are attributable to income and depreciation risk. Following Bulow and Summers (1984), we assume that 90 percent of the total risk is due to depreciation risk.

The cost-of-capital formula for debt finance corresponding to the formula for equity finance is:

$$(12) \quad p^d = \left(1 - \frac{T_\varepsilon}{T}\lambda_f\right)^{-1} \left(\frac{1 - A}{1 - \tau}\right) \left((1 - \tau) i - \pi + \delta + \frac{T_\varepsilon}{T}\lambda_\delta\right) - \delta.$$

Note that the only difference between the equity and debt cases are in the terms multiplying i and $Đ$. These differences arise because corporate interest payments are deductible against the corporate income tax, whereas equity earnings are obviously not. Further, corporate interest income is taxed like Treasury bill interest at the personal level, while equity earnings are treated differently.

6.5 Corporate and Personal Income Taxes in Canada, the U.S., and Japan

Corporate tax systems in Canada, the U.S., and Japan share many features (Shoven 1989; Whalley 1990). Representative tax and market parameters for 1988 are shown in table 6.1.[4] Although the tax code in each country contains special provisions for different industries, regions, and activities, these parameters capture the main features of each tax code in stylized form.

Comprehensive tax reforms in Canada and the U.S. during the 1980s were motivated in part by the perception that uneven tax treatment of different assets and industries was leading to costly misallocations of capital. In both countries, there was movement towards "leveling the playing field" by eliminating the investment tax credit, decelerating depreciation deductions, and bringing depreciation schedules into closer alignment with economic depreciation.[5] In 1988 the Canadian and U.S. systems had very similar tax rates and depreciation schedules, reflecting concern with the mobility of capital and tax liabilities across the countries.

The countries differ much more in their personal tax systems. Unlike the U.S., Canada attempts to offset double taxation of dividends partially by providing a dividend tax credit against "grossed up" dividends at the personal level. This effectively reduces the total taxation faced by dividend payments. The Japanese have a somewhat similar dividend tax credit that allows dividends and interest to be taxed separately from other income, generally at lower rates.

With respect to capital gains, the U.S. has moved to full taxation at the time of realization. Canada has a lifetime capital gains exclusion of $100,000 Canadian dollars (on nonhousing capital gains; housing is treated separately). After using up the exclusion, three-quarters (two-thirds in 1988 and 1989) of realized capital gains are taxed at ordinary rates. Until the recent reform, cap-

---

4. Tax figures include state/provincial taxes as well as federal taxes.
5. In addition, Canada reduced special tax advantages for the Atlantic provinces.

Table 6.1   **Parameter Values Used in the Calculation of the Cost of Capital in 1988**

	United States	Canada	Japan
Corporate Tax Rate (τ)	.380	.400	.499
Average Marginal Personal Tax Rate on Interest (m)	.300	.450	.200
Average Marginal Personal Tax Rate on Dividends (d)	.300	.312	.250
Effective Average Marginal Personal Tax Rate on Retained Earnings (z)	.21	.169	.08
Effective Average Marginal Tax Rate on Purely Nominal Capital Gains (z_n)	.13	.10	.02
Fraction of Long-term Earnings Paid as Dividends (α)	.5	.5	.33
Fraction of Transitory Earnings Paid as Dividends (α_e)	.02	.02	.02
Fraction of Total Risk Attributable to Capital Risk (η)	.9	.9	.9
Short-term Nominal Interest Rate (i)	.0809	.0817	.04092
Expected Rate of Inflation (π)	.0418	.0415	.011904
Exponential Rate of Depreciation for Autos & Plants (δ)	1/7, 1/31.5	1/7, 1/31.5	1/7, 1/31.5
Tax Depreciation Lifetimes for Autos & Plants (L)	5/31.5	(3.33/25)[a]	4/26
Present Value of Tax Value of Depreciation Deductions & Tax Credits for Autos & Plants (A)	.3325 .1418	.325 .129	.473 .344
Expected Real Rate of Return on Market Portfolio from Adjusted Earnings-Price Ratio (r_2^e)	.0855	.0832	.0312

[a]Actual Canadian depreciation is exponential at rates 30% for cars and 4% for buildings.

ital gains on securities were not taxed at all in Japan. Even now, taxpayers are given the option of paying a tax equal to 1 percent of the value of the stock transaction or paying a separate tax on the actual gain, at a rate of 20 percent. The 1-percent option would be chosen for all significant gain situations. Its availability means that capital gains remain extremely lightly taxed in Japan.

A further difference is that Canadian interest is taxed more heavily than dividends (unlike interest in the U.S.), and the effective rate of tax on capital gains is lower in Canada. The latter fact is due to the three-quarters inclusion rate (in contrast to full inclusion in the U.S.). We have assumed that the representative Canadian stockholder exhausts the $100,000 lifetime exclusion.

6.6   Cross-Country Cost-of-Capital Comparisons

Cost-of-capital schedules for plants and cars in Canada, the U.S., and Japan are shown in figures 6.4a–d and 6.5a, b. In all cases, the cost-of-capital lines are steeper than the capital market lines, reflecting a greater price of risk at the corporate level than at the investor level. Each of the tax systems discriminates against riskier investments, primarily because the present value of the tax benefits of the depreciation deduction, A, fall short of the corporate tax rate. This bias is strongest in Canada and weakest in Japan and is more severe for the relatively long-lived plant.

In all cases, the cost of capital with debt finance is less than with equity finance, reflecting the deductibility of interest payments from the corporate income tax. This difference is much smaller in Canada than in the U.S. because of the dividend tax credit system, lower effective capital gains rates, and higher personal taxes on interest income in Canada. In Canada, the advantage of debt at the corporate level is almost completely offset by its disadvantage at the personal level. Despite these differences between the Canadian and U.S. schedules, the cost of capital is close enough in the two countries that differences in hurdle rates are unlikely to be a key factor in investment location decisions.

In both countries, however, risk premia are large and the cost of capital for even moderately risky undertakings can be substantial compared to real interest rates. In Canada, the cost of capital for an investment with a standardized riskiness of 5 percent per month is about 13 percent for plant and 11 percent for autos for both debt and equity financing. The U.S. numbers are slightly higher than the Canadian ones for equity-financed capital and somewhat lower for debt-financed investments.

The cost of capital in Japan is substantially lower than in North America, primarily because of cheaper equity finance. The tax system plays a relatively minor direct role in determining the low cost of capital in Japan. The cost of capital for investments of the riskiness discussed above is roughly 5 percent in Japan. The evidence points to an integrated U.S.-Canada capital market, with a segmented one in Japan offering far better terms for new investments.

The results reported above are based on the decisions of managers acting on behalf of relatively high-income domestic owners. If, on the other hand, the ownership of a company is internationally diversified, a manager may conclude that the interests of the owners are best served by making sure all investments offer certainty-equivalent yields at least as great as Treasury bills, taking only corporate taxes into account. The representative owner, in effect, is treated as tax-free. The cost of capital for Canada and the U.S. under these assumptions is shown in figure 6.6a–d. The gap between the cost of equity- and debt-financed capital widens considerably in Canada because the relative tax preference for equity income for Canadian stockholders is no longer rele-

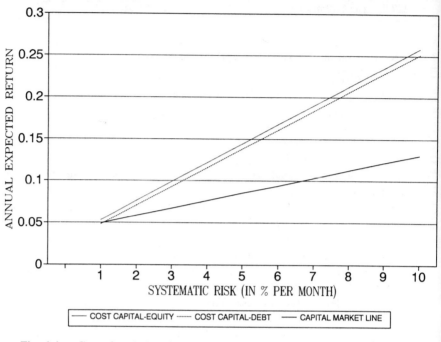

Fig. 6.4a   Cost of capital in Canada in 1988 for equity- and debt-financed plant

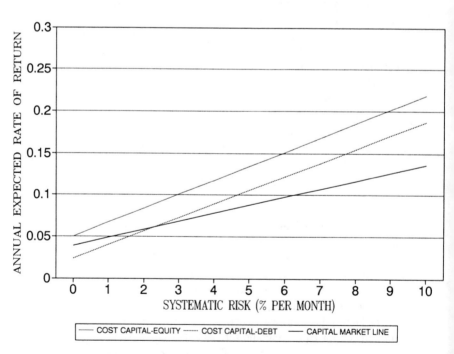

Fig. 6.4b   Cost of capital in U.S. in 1988 for equity- and debt-financed plant

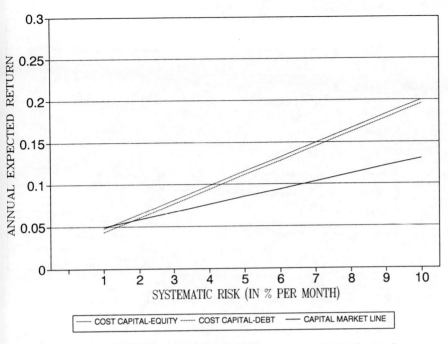

Fig. 6.4c   Cost of capital in Canada in 1988 for equity- and debt-financed cars

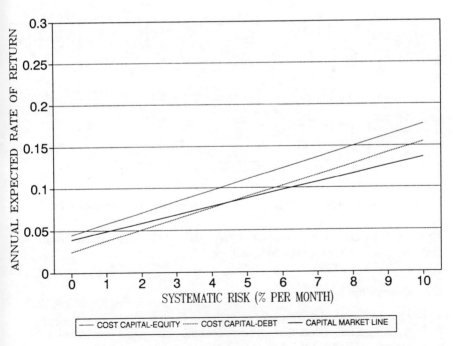

Fig. 6.4d   Cost of capital in U.S. in 1988 for equity- and debt-financed cars

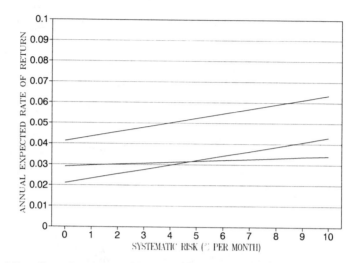

Fig. 6.5a   Cost of capital in Japan in 1988 for equity- and debt-financed plant

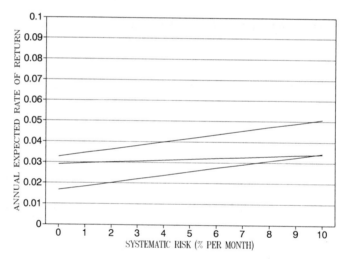

Fig. 6.5b   Cost of capital in Japan in 1988 for equity- and debt-financed cars

vant. The basic conclusion, however, remains that the Canadian and American cost-of-capital figures are very comparable.

6.7   Concluding Remarks

This paper has calculated the cost of capital in Canada, the U.S., and Japan in 1988, using a framework that accounts for both risk and tax considerations and financial market and tax data from each country. Several findings are of

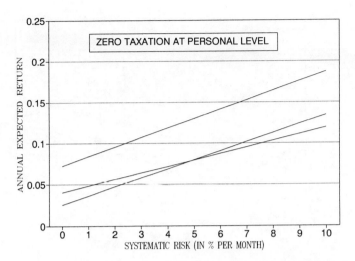

Fig. 6.6*a*   **Cost of capital in Canada in 1988 for equity- and debt-financed plant**

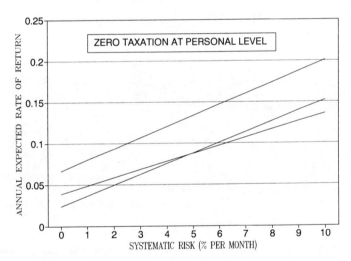

Fig. 6.6*b*   **Cost of capital in U.S. in 1988 for equity- and debt-financed plant**

interest in the policy debate about recent Canadian and U.S. tax reforms and the international competitiveness of North American firms.

First, risk premia are extremely important components of the cost of capital. In all three countries, the corporate and personal tax systems magnify risk premia; that is, the extra return required of risky real investments at the corporate level exceeds the premium apparent in financial markets.

Second, Canada and the U.S. have a common financial market and have

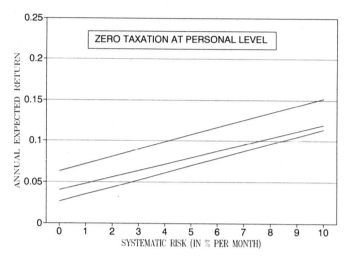

Fig. 6.6c   **Cost of capital in Canada in 1988 for equity- and debt-financed cars**

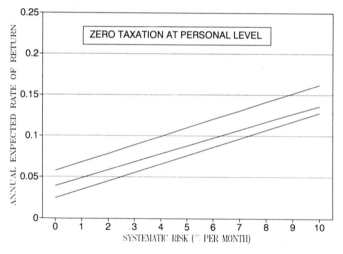

Fig. 6.6d   **Cost of capital in U.S. in 1988 for equity- and debt-financed cars**

adopted tax systems that give similar treatment to risky investments. The result is that for a particular investment the cost of capital is similar in Canada and the U.S. This suggests that investment location decisions will be driven by productivity factors, and not distorted by tax and financial market concerns.

Finally, the Japanese have a large cost-of-capital advantage relative to both Canada and the U.S. This differential stems from high Japanese equity prices and the correspondingly low cost of risk capital, with tax factors playing a relatively minor role. Thus, the evidence suggests that Japanese and North American financial markets are currently segmented, although the increased globalization of financial markets will tend to equalize this differential over time.

References

Bernheim, B. Douglas, and John Shoven. 1989. Comparison of the Cost of Capital in the U.S. and Japan: The Roles of Risk and Taxes. Center for Economic Policy Research Working Paper no. 179.

Boadway, Robin W., Neil Bruce, and Jack M. Mintz. 1987. Taxes on Capital Income in Canada: Analysis and Policy. Canadian Tax Paper no. 80. Toronto: Canadian Tax Foundation.

Bulow, Jeremy I., and Lawrence H. Summers. 1984. The Taxation of Risky Assets. *Journal of Political Economy* 92(1):20–39.

Copeland, Thomas E., and J. Fred Weston. 1979. *Financial Theory and Corporate Policy.* Reading MA: Addison-Wesley Publishing Company.

French, Kenneth R., and James N. Poterba. 1989. Are Japanese Stock Prices Too High? Paper presented at seminar, Analysis of Security Prices. Center for Research in Security Prices, Chicago, May 4.

Hall, Robert E., and Dale W. Jorgenson. 1967. Tax Policy and Investment Behavior. *American Economic Review* 57(3):391–414.

Hatch, James E., and Robert W. White. 1988. *Canadian Stocks, Bonds, Bills, and Inflation: 1950–1987.* Charlottesville VA: Research Foundation of the Institute of Chartered Financial Analysts.

Ibbotson Associates. 1990. *Stocks, Bonds, Bills, and Inflation: 1990 Yearbook.* Chicago.

King, Mervyn A., and Don Fullerton, eds. 1984. *The Taxation of Income from Capital.* Chicago: University of Chicago Press.

Sharpe, William F. 1970. *Portfolio Theory and Capital Markets.* New York: McGraw-Hill.

Shoven, John B. 1989. The Japanese Tax Reform and the Effective Rate of Tax on Japanese Corporate Investments. In *Tax Policy and The Economy,* ed. Lawrence H. Summers. Cambridge: MIT Press.

Whalley, John. 1990. Recent Tax Reform in Canada: Policy Responses to Global and Domestic Pressures. In *World Tax Reform,* ed. Michael J. Boskin and Charles E. McLure, Jr. San Francisco: ICS Press.

7   The Impact of U.S. Tax Reform on Canadian Stock Prices

Joel Slemrod

The international spillover effects of taxation have been widely reflected upon but sparsely documented.[1] Tax reform in one country, particularly a large country like the United States, potentially can affect economic activity in other countries, through macroeconomic channels such as the level of interest rates and through effects on the relative attractiveness of locales for production, incorporation, and the reporting of taxable income. Because of the high degree of integration between the U.S. and Canadian economies, these countries are a natural place to look for empirical evidence of spillover effects.

The goal of this paper is to begin a quantitative assessment of how tax reform in the United States has affected Canadian business. The proposed methodology is an event study of the impact of the Tax Reform Act of 1986 on the abnormal stock market returns to publicly traded Canadian corporations. It is based on the presumption that changes in the prospects for Canadian enterprises induced by the tax reform were reflected in the stock market valuation of the firms' shares.

Section 7.1 of the paper briefly discusses some other recent research on the stock price impact of U.S. tax reform. In section 7.2, I outline some potential avenues of influence of U.S. tax reform on Canadian business, and in section 7.3 introduce a model in which these effects are present. Section 7.4 discusses the methodology employed to assess empirically how important these potential effects actually were for the Tax Reform Act of 1986. In section 7.5, I

Joel Slemrod is professor of economics, professor of business economics and public policy, and director of the Office of Tax Policy Research at the University of Michigan. He is a research associate of the National Bureau of Economic Research.

The author is grateful to Aileen Thompson for able and resourceful research assistance, as well as valuable advice. Drew Lyon and conference participants provided helpful comments on an earlier draft.

1. A notable exception is McLure (1990), which documents several examples of international spillovers.

present and discuss the results of these investigations. I find that during tax reform events there was an extraordinary inverse relationship across industries between the returns on U.S. and Canadian stocks. This relationship is consistent with a story that Canadian firms are helped by whatever hurts their U.S. competitors. However, I am unable to relate the strength of this inverse relationship to industry characteristics that proxy for the likely cross-industry impact of tax reform.

7.1 Previous Research

Previous event studies of the effect of the Tax Reform Act of 1986 on U.S. stock prices have not been particularly successful in documenting a quantitatively significant response. Cutler (1988), in a study of the effect of TRA86 on U.S. stock prices, found only a very small aggregate market reaction and concluded that tax reform news is indistinguishable from normal market noise. Among his negative findings was that the correlation of returns across positive tax reform events was only 0.036, with a t-statistic of 0.057. Cutler offers two potential explanations for the small reaction to tax reform news: that the events may have been largely anticipated, or that any tax reform enacted was perceived to be temporary and therefore not important in a present-value sense.

A few other studies have investigated the effect on U.S. stock prices of other recent changes in U.S. tax laws. Downs and Tehranian (1988) found "moderate support" for a valuation model in predicting the effect of the Economic Recovery Tax Act of 1981 on three industry groups. Lyon (1989b) found substantial evidence that previous increases in the investment tax credit positively affected stock value for firms that had relatively high expected investment, but little evidence that existing assets fell in value. Lyon (1989a), studying the stock price impact of the introduction of the accelerated cost recovery system, also failed to support any wealth effect on existing assets, but found less strong evidence that firms that are expected to invest in capital goods favored by the depreciation provisions increase in value relative to other firms.

There is no existing study that I am aware of that attempts to measure the cross-border effects of tax changes in the way proposed here. Because of the potential importance of the international spillover effects of taxation, I believe it is worthwhile to begin an assessment of this issue.

7.2 Three Stories About the Impact of U.S. Tax Reform on Canadian Business

The Tax Reform Act of 1986 had a significant impact on the overall (average and marginal) rate of taxation applied to U.S. corporations and on the relative burden of taxation on corporations. TRA86 lowered the statutory rate of corporation tax applying to most income from 46% to 34%, eliminated the investment tax credit, and accelerated depreciation for equipment but decelerated it for structures. On balance, the change in a corporation's average tax rate depended inversely on its capital intensity and on its debt-capital ratio. Note that these tax changes applied equally to U.S. corporations that are subsidiaries of foreign-incorporated parent companies.

How would these major changes in U.S. taxation of corporations be expected to affect Canadian corporations? In what follows, I develop three avenues of impact. Then, in section 7.3, I present a formal model of U.S.-Canadian competition in which these avenues are made explicit.

7.2.1 "My enemy's enemy is my friend"

An increased tax burden on U.S. firms, by raising their costs, reduces the ability of the U.S. firms to compete with Canadian firms. Thus, if tax reform affects U.S. firms adversely it will be a boon to Canadian firms in competition with U.S. firms, and vice versa. For example, if tax reform increases the tax burden of U.S. beverage firms, it will help Canadian beverage firms.

There are a number of provisos that must be attached to this scenario. First, if a U.S. industry is hurt by tax reform because its customers are likely to be adversely affected, Canadian firms in the same industry will be hurt to the extent they have U.S.-based customers. Second, it may be important to distinguish the effect of tax reform on the valuation of "old" capital and on the present value of "new" capital. It is well known that a tax change such as eliminating the investment tax credit may tend to increase the former at the same time it decreases the latter. But only the latter will affect the tilt of the playing field between U.S. and Canadian firms. The former represents a windfall to the owners of existing capital that must compete with the now more expensive new capital. This effect would tend to increase the stock value of both U.S. and Canadian firms.

7.2.2 "As the U.S. goes, so goes Canada"

The Canadian government was contemplating fundamental reform of its corporate tax system even before the U.S. tax reform debate began in earnest. Nevertheless, the U.S. tax reform movement arguably increased the likelihood in Canada of a rate-reducing, base-broadening reform designed to reduce interindustry and interasset divergences in taxation. This argument relies principally on economic pressures for the two countries' tax systems to be harmonized.[2] A lower statutory corporate tax rate in the U.S. would probably cost the Canadian Treasury revenues, and a lower U.S. effective tax on new investment would induce real investment to locate in the U.S., costing Canada

---

2. The U.S. tax reform movement may have provided an intellectual impetus to Canadian tax reform, as well as strengthened the political case for fundamental tax restructuring. See Whalley (1990) for an assessment of the relative importance for Canadian reform of the economic pressures for harmonization and intellectual cross-fertilization.

jobs and tax revenues, at least in the short run. Thus, any change in the U.S. corporate tax law causes pressure on Canada to enact similar changes in its tax law. This argument suggests that any competitive advantage or disadvantage to U.S. firms caused by U.S. tax reform is bound to be short-lived, and therefore the present value of the gain or loss will be much less than if the first scenario were the only consideration.

7.2.3 "But I'm half American"

Income earned in the U.S. by U.S. subsidiaries of Canadian multinationals is essentially exempt from Canadian taxation. For this income, it is the U.S. tax law that applies. Thus, to the extent that a Canadian parent has income from U.S. subsidiaries, it should react to U.S. tax reform more like a U.S. firm than a Canadian firm. This argument suggests that the effect of tax reform on abnormal returns will look similar for U.S. firms and Canadian firms with significant operations in the U.S.

The three stories have strikingly different implications for the effect of U.S. tax reform on Canadian business. According to the first, there should have been an inverse relationship between what kind of U.S. firms gained and what kind of Canadian firms gained. The second story suggests that the relative competitive position of the two countries' firms is not important, and that U.S. tax reform affects Canadian firms in much the same way as Canadian tax reform, but with less punch due to the lag in the enactment of imitative Canadian tax reform. The final story also suggests that Canadian firms will be affected much like U.S. firms, but only to the extent that they are multinationals with U.S.-source income.

These three stories do not exhaust the possible avenues of impact of U.S. tax reform upon Canadian business. For example, I do not pursue how changes in the individual income tax, such as the increased tax on realized long-term capital gains and the decreased tax on dividends and interest, would affect the market for Canadian and U.S. shares. These are potentially confounding factors, which deserve attention in future research on this topic.

7.3 A Simple Model of How U.S. Tax Reform Affects a Canadian Firm

In what follows I present a simple model in which all three transmission mechanisms discussed above are present. The model builds on the one presented in Dixit (1983).

Consider a homogeneous product oligopoly featuring firms from two countries. Firms do not incur any transport costs in supplying either market, but third-party arbitragers are unable to take advantage of any price differential. The demand curves in the two markets are independent. Each firm assumes that the quantities supplied by all other firms are fixed (the Cournot equilibrium concept). Each firm has a fixed cost of production and a constant marginal cost.

I follow Dixit's notation, where f is the fixed cost and c is the constant marginal cost of each firm. The variable y represents sales of each firm in its domestic market, and x is export sales. The corresponding variables in the foreign country are denoted by corresponding upper-case letters. Thus, total sales in the home country's market are $q = ny + NX$, where n and N represent the (assumed to be constant) number of firms in the home and foreign market, respectively. The inverse demand functions are $p = p(q)$ in the home country and $P = P(Q)$ in the foreign country.

Rather than introducing capital income taxes explicitly, I investigate the effect on firms' profits of a production tax at rate T imposed in the foreign country. The home country production tax is denoted t. (Recall that by assumption each firm produces only in its home country.) The maximands of the typical home firm and foreign country firm are then

(1a) $$\pi = py + Px - [c(y + x) + t(y + x) + f]$$

(1b) $$\Pi = PY + pX - [C(Y + X) + T(Y + X) + F]$$

and the first-order conditions are

(2a) $$y: p + yp' = c + t$$

and

(3a) $$x: P + xP' = c + t$$

for the home firm and

(2b) $$Y: P + YP' = C + T$$

and

(3b) $$X: p + Xp' = C + T$$

for the foreign firm.

In order to determine the impact of a change in T on firms' profits, a necessary first step is to calculate its impact on the market equilibrium. I totally differentiate the home market equations (2a) and (3b) and assume linear demand curves to obtain

(4) $$\begin{bmatrix} (n + 1)p' & Np' \\ np' & (N + 1)p' \end{bmatrix} \begin{bmatrix} dy \\ dX \end{bmatrix} = \begin{bmatrix} 1 & 0 \\ 0 & 1 \end{bmatrix} \begin{bmatrix} dt \\ dT \end{bmatrix}$$

with the solution

(5) $$\begin{bmatrix} dy \\ dX \end{bmatrix} = \frac{-1}{(n + N + 1)p'} \begin{bmatrix} -(N + 1) & N \\ n & -(n + 1) \end{bmatrix} \begin{bmatrix} dt \\ dT \end{bmatrix}.$$

From the foreign market equations (3a) and (2b) one can obtain similarly

(6) $$\begin{bmatrix} dY \\ dx \end{bmatrix} = \frac{-1}{(n + N + 1)P'} \begin{bmatrix} -(n + 1) & n \\ N & -(N + 1) \end{bmatrix} \begin{bmatrix} dT \\ dt \end{bmatrix}.$$

Note that the assumption of constant marginal costs allows the home market and foreign market analysis to be segmented, so that taxes that apply to one market do not affect the equilibrium in the other.

Using (5) and (6), one can express the equilibrium change in prices as a function of tax changes, as follows:

(7a) $$dp = (1/(n + N + 1)) (ndt + NdT)$$

and

(7b) $$dP = (1/(n + N + 1)) (ndt + NdT).$$

After-tax profits of a typical firm are given by expressions (1a) and (1b) which, in differential form, are

(4a) $$d\pi = \begin{array}{l} ydp + xdP + (p - c - t)dy \\ + (P - c - t)dx - (y + x)dt \end{array}$$

and

(4b) $$d\Pi = \begin{array}{l} YdP + Xdp + (P - C - T)dY \\ + (p - C - T)dX - (Y + X)dT. \end{array}$$

Substituting for dp and dP using (7a) and (7b), and for dy, dY, dx, and dX using (5) and (6), yields

(8a) $$d\pi = \frac{2}{n + N + 1} \left[N(y + x)dT - (N + 1) (y + x)dt \right]$$

(8b) $$d\Pi = \frac{2}{n + N + 1} \left[n(Y + X)dt - (n + 1) (Y + X)dT \right].$$

Using (8a) and (8b), we can now calculate how a change in the foreign country's tax rate will affect profits of the typical firm in the home country and foreign country:

(9a) $$\frac{d\pi}{dT} = \frac{2N(y + x)}{n + N + 1} - \left(\frac{2(N + 1) (y + x)}{n + N + 1} \right) \left(\frac{dt}{dT} \right)$$

(9b) $$\frac{d\Pi}{dT} = -\frac{2(n + 1)(Y + X)}{n + N + 1}.$$

Expression (9a) allows for the possibility that the home country tax rate will react to a change in the tax policy of the foreign country. Whether the typical home country firm's profits will rise or fall when T increases depends on the value of $\frac{dt}{dT}$, the responsiveness of the home country's tax rate. If there is no response at all $\left(\frac{dt}{dT} = 0 \right)$, then home country profits rise. This is the pure version of the "my enemy's enemy is my friend" scenario. If the home country tax rate rises in step with the foreign country's tax rate $\left(\dfrac{dt}{dT} = 1\right)$, then $\dfrac{d\pi}{dT}$ reduces to $-2(y + x)/(n + N + 1)$, which is always negative. In this case the "as U.S. goes, so goes Canada" scenario dominates. In general, the typical home country firm's profits increase when T increases as long as $\dfrac{dt}{dT}$ is less than $N/(N + 1)$.

The ratio of the change in profits of the two countries' firms is, using $q = x + y$ and $Q = X + Y$,

$$(10) \qquad \frac{\dfrac{d\pi}{dT}}{\dfrac{d\Pi}{dT}} = \frac{q\left(N - (N + 1)\dfrac{dt}{dT}\right)}{Q(n + 1)}.$$

7.3.1 Extending the Model to Include Multinational Production

The model analyzed above assumes that all production is carried out in the home country. In fact, there is substantial production by Canadian firms in the U.S., and by U.S. firms in Canada. The rationale for multinational production, and how the location of production responds to taxation, is a complicated matter and one that has not been well integrated into analytical models of taxation. A simple way to take account of multinational production is to assume that each firm produces a fixed fraction of its exports in the foreign country. Letting that fraction be a for the domestic firm and A for the foreign firm, after-tax profits become

$$(11a) \qquad \pi = py + Px - [c(y + x) + t(y + (1 - a)x)$$
$$+ (T + b(t - T))ax + f]$$

$$(11b) \qquad \Pi = PY + pX - [C(Y + X) + T(Y + (1 - A)X)$$
$$+ (t + B(T - t))AX + F].$$

This formulation reflects the fact that, for the home firm, home production of $y + (1 - a)x$ is taxed at the home country rate of t. Production in the foreign country of ax is taxed first at the home country rate of T, and then may face a residual tax of $b(t - T)$ assessed by the home country. In fact, by treaty Canada effectively imposes no residual tax on the income earned in the U.S. by its multinationals, so that b is zero. The U.S., on the other hand, may impose some residual tax, so that B is positive but less than one.

The analysis of section 7.3 can then be repeated, yielding the following expressions for the response of profits to tax policy:

$$(12) \qquad \frac{d\pi}{dT} = \frac{2}{n + N + 1}\left[\frac{N(1 - A - AB)y - (N + 1)}{a(1 - b)x + Nx}\right]$$

$$-\frac{2}{n + N + 1}\left[\begin{array}{l}(N + 1)y - NA(1 - B)y \\ + (N + 1)(1 - a + ab)x\end{array}\right]\frac{dt}{dT}$$

(13) $\quad\dfrac{d\Pi}{dT} = -\dfrac{2}{n + N + 1}\left[\begin{array}{l}(n + 1)Y - na(1 - b)Y \\ + (n + 1)(1 - A + AB)X\end{array}\right]$

(14) $\quad\dfrac{\dfrac{d\pi}{dT}}{\dfrac{d\Pi}{dT}} = \dfrac{\left[\begin{array}{l}N(1 - A - AB)y - (N + 1) \\ a(1 - b)x + Nx\end{array}\right] - \left[\begin{array}{l}(N + 1)y - NA(1 - B)y \\ + (N + 1)(1 - a + ab)x\end{array}\right]\dfrac{dt}{dT}}{\left[\begin{array}{l}(n + 1)Y - na(1 - b)Y \\ + (n + 1)(1 - A + AB)X\end{array}\right]}.$

Unsurprisingly, the greater is a (the fraction of each home firm's exports produced and taxed abroad), the more likely is there to be a direct negative impact of the foreign country's tax system on home country profits. Or, using the terminology of section 7.2, the strength of the "but I'm half American" effect depends on the extent of the home firm's production in the foreign country.

The objective of what follows is to assess whether the response of Canadian stock prices to news about the U.S. tax reform followed the patterns suggested by equations (12) and (14). Equation (12) implies that the stock price response depends in a nonlinear way on the relative number of firms from each country, each country's system of taxing foreign-source income, the extent of each country's foreign production, and the expected response of the Canadian tax system to U.S. reform. Keep in mind also that equation (12) is derived from a very simple model of the economic environment, which ignores such factors as firms from third countries, product differentiation, and the endogeneity of foreign direct investment. Thus, equation (12) is useful primarily as a guide to understanding the response of Canadian stock prices to news about U.S. tax reform. It does support the plausibility of each of the three avenues of impact discussed in section 7.2 in particular that

(i) $\quad\dfrac{d\left|\dfrac{d\pi}{dT}\right|}{dN}\Bigg|_{\frac{dt}{dT} = 0} > 0$

(ii) $\quad\dfrac{d\left(\dfrac{d\pi}{dT}\right)}{d\left(\dfrac{dt}{dT}\right)} < 0$

(iii) $\quad\dfrac{d\left|\dfrac{d\pi}{dT}\right|}{da}\Bigg|_{\frac{dt}{dT} = 0} < 0.$

Equation (14) characterizes the relationship between how a typical home firm's profits react to a change in the foreign tax rate and how a typical foreign country's profits react. This ratio is different from the one that would apply if the source of profit changes were some other kind of shock to the economic environment. Thus, it would be interesting to assess not only whether the response of Canadian firms' profits to news about U.S. tax reform followed the patterns described above, but also whether the *relationship* of Canadian firms' abnormal profits to U.S. firms' abnormal profits during tax reform events was different than at other times.

7.4 Methodology and Data

In order to measure the change in stock prices caused by news about tax law changes, a model of the stock returns in the absence of news is required. I will assume, as is standard in event studies, that equity is priced to yield a normal expected return that is adjusted for its risk characteristics. In particular, I first estimate models of the following form:

$$(15) \qquad r_{cit} = \alpha_i + \beta_i r_{mt} + \lambda_i r_{uit} + \delta_{ie} D_{et} + \varepsilon_{it},$$

where r_{cit} = the return on Canadian industry i at time t; r_{mt} = the return on the U.S. market portfolio at time t; r_{uit} = the return on U.S. industry i at time t; D_{et} = a dummy variable equal to 1 on days in "event-window" e (when news about tax reform is revealed) and equal to 0 otherwise; and ε_{it} = a serially uncorrelated random-error term. The estimated coefficient of the event dummy, δ_{ie}, measures the effect of news on the return of industry i during dummy event-window e and is referred to as an "abnormal" return. This equation is estimated over a three-year period that precedes and includes the event windows.

The value of δ_{ie} for a given industry is presumed to depend on certain industry characteristics that influence how tax reform affects the value of Canadian firms. The model in section 7.3 suggests that the abnormal return will depend on, inter alia, the following three factors: the degree of penetration of U.S. firms in the Canadian firms' market (USPEN), the likely consequences for the Canadian firm of induced Canadian tax reform (CATAX), and the fraction of the Canadian industry's income that is earned in the U.S. (CAUSI). In terms of a regression line, each of these factors could affect both the intercept term and the slope of the relationship between the countries' returns. Prior expectations of the signs of these terms are listed in figure 7.1.

In the next step of the analysis, I estimate over fifteen manufacturing sectors the following equation:[3]

$$(16) \quad \delta_{ie} = a_{e0} + a_{e1} \text{ USPEN}_i + a_{e2} \text{ CATAX}_i + a_{e3} \text{ CAUSI}_i$$

$$+ r_{uit} \cdot (b_{e0} + b_{e1} \text{ USPEN}_i + b_{e2} \text{ CATAX}_i + b_{e3} \text{ CAUSI}_i) + u_{ie}.$$

3. The sectors are chemicals, electrical equipment, fabricated metal, food, furniture, lumber, machinery, nonmetallic mineral products, paper primary metals, printing, rubber, textiles, tobacco, and transportation products. Industry portfolios are formed by weighting each firm by its stock market value at the beginning of the estimation period.

Variable	Intercept	Slope
1. Degree of penetration of U.S. firms in Canadian market (USPEN)	0	–
2. Likely impact of Canadian tax reform (CATAX)	+	0
3. Extent of Canadian industry's income earned in U.S. (CAUSI)	0	+

Fig. 7.1. Expected signs on industry characteristics variables

These analyses are done separately for each event, and also for all events together, assuming $a_{11} = a_{21} = a_{31} = a_{41}$, etc.[4]

Stock return data for U.S. and Canadian firms are drawn from the daily return files compiled by the Center for Research on Security Prices (CRSP) and the Toronto Stock Exchange/University of Western Ontario, respectively.[5]

I study four separate events associated with TRA86. The first event is the release of the Treasury Department's initial proposal for tax reform in November 1984. The second event is the May 1985 release of the president's own tax reform proposal. The third and fourth events correspond to critical moments in the legislative history, when the probability that tax reform would be passed dramatically increased. They are the passage of a tax reform bill by the House of Representatives at 11 P.M. on 17 December 1985, and the passage of a bill by the Senate Finance Committee at 12:30 A.M. on 7 May 1986. Neither of these events was widely anticipated, and each arguably increased the probability of tax reform in a discrete way.

Note that in the nearly two years between the Treasury's initial proposal and the president's signing the law on 22 October 1986, the details of the proposal being considered changed substantially. Thus, even if each of the four events discretely increased the probability of tax reform, they increased the probability of *different* tax reforms happening. For example, while the Treasury's pro-

---

4. One alternative to the empirical model outlined here was pursued. In it, the value of r_{uit} in equation (16) was taken to be the abnormal return of the U.S. industry, estimated using equation (15). This change did not affect the principal qualitative results discussed in the text, although the details are altered. Further information about the alternative specification is available upon request from the author.

5. The sample of firms is defined as those firms that were traded during the entire three-year sample period. A few firms were deleted from the sample due to a large number of missing observations. To create industry portfolios, firms are classified according to the two-digit Standard Industrial Classification (SIC) code assigned to them by Dunn and Bradstreet's *Canadian Key Business Directory*. Firms not listed in this directory are classified according to their annual reports or the "nature of business" assigned to them by the Toronto Stock Exchange. Value-weighted portfolios are then created based on the price data and the number of shares outstanding found in the *Toronto Stock Exchange Review* at the beginning of the sample period. (For a few firms the necessary data was not available for this time period. For these firms, weights were computed based on deflated values at later dates.) U.S. industry value-weighted portfolios are created according to the two-digit SIC code listed for each security on the CRSP tape. There were days in which one exchange was open and the other was closed due to different holidays in the U.S. and Canada. These observations, as well as the observations following the holidays, are excluded from the sample.

posal treated the oil and gas industry fairly harshly, the president's proposal was relatively generous toward that sector. Thus, it is possible that a given industry's response was not entirely consistent across events. This possibility could explain Cutler's (1988) finding of a near-zero correlation of sectoral abnormal returns across tax reform events.

In the empirical research, two versions of the length of the four event windows are examined: "short windows," which consist of the trading day of the announcement, or, for the nighttime legislative breakthroughs, the trading day immediately following; and "long windows," which, for the first two events, include a week before and a week after the public unveiling of the proposal, and for the third and fourth events, a week after the legislative breakthrough. The long windows allow for the effect of the leaking of parts of the proposal (for the first two windows only) and for the gradual assimilation of the impact of complicated tax packages subsequent to their announcement.

7.5 Results

7.5.1 Country Aggregates

Before proceeding to the analysis that is disaggregated by industry, it is worthwhile to inspect the behavior of the overall U.S. and Canadian stock markets during the U.S. tax reform event windows. This information is presented in table 7.1.[6]

For both the short- and long-window event definitions, the return on U.S. stocks was generally negative, except for a positive return for the first event using the short window and for the second event using the long window. The pattern of Canadian returns was somewhat different. The short-window return for all events was negative, but the long-window return was positive for the second and fourth events. On balance, then, the Canadian stock market performed worse than usual during the U.S. tax reform events.

Was the relationship between the U.S. and Canadian returns during the tax reform windows unusual, or did it follow the usual pattern? To investigate that issue, I estimated a regression model explaining the Canadian daily rate of return as a linear function of the U.S. daily return over the period 1981–84. The estimated regression line is plotted in figure 7.2. Also plotted in figure 7.2 are the eight pairs of aggregate returns for the eight event windows, where an S after the event number denotes the short window and an L denotes the long window. Figure 7.2 shows that, in six of eight cases, the actual return to the Canadian stock portfolio was lower than what was predicted by the regression equation. Also of interest is whether the relationship between the U.S. and Canadian returns during the tax reform windows looks any different than

---

6. The overall return for the U.S. and Canadian stock markets is the value-weighted return of all the securities included in the CRSP and TSE/Western databases, respectively.

Table 7.1   **Returns to Overall U.S. and Canadian Stock Portfolios and Abnormal Canadian Returns**

	Overall Returns (%)		Abnormal Return (%)
	U.S.	Canada	Canada
Event 1			
One-Day Window	0.478	−0.203	−0.474
			(0.358)
Two-Week Window	−0.132	−0.184	−0.134
			(0.120)
Event 2			
One-Day Window	−0.064	−0.137	−0.122
			(0.358)
Two-Week Window	0.113	−0.056	−0.135
			(0.114)
Event 3			
One-Day Window	−0.418	−0.268	−0.065
			(0.359)
One-Week Window	−0.294	−0.020	0.116
			(0.161)
Event 4			
One-Day Window	−0.426	−0.440	−0.233
			(0.359)
One-Week Window	−0.012	0.071	0.058
			(0.161)

Notes: Figures for long windows refer to average daily returns over the period. Abnormal return is calculated as the residual of the equation $r_c = 0.019 + 0.529 \cdot r_u$. The figures in parentheses refer to the forecast error of the estimating equation.

usual. This is impossible to pin down, given only four independent observations, but my own eyeballing of figure 7.1 suggests that the slope of a line that fits the event-window points is not different from the regression line that fits the pre–tax reform period.

7.5.2 Industry Analysis

In this section, I take advantage of information that is disaggregated by industry to further investigate the impact of U.S. tax reform on Canadian stock prices. In all its versions, tax reform had a differential impact by industry. Broadly speaking, a reduced rate on corporate income combined with elimination of the investment tax credit and scaled-back depreciation allowances would hurt relatively those industries that benefited relatively from the ITC and accelerated depreciation. Industries also differ in the likely cross-border impact of U.S. tax reform, depending on the factors discussed in sections 7.2 and 7.3. Note, though, that the tax reform package under active consideration changed considerably between the time of the release of the Treasury proposal in 1984 and Congressional passage of tax reform in 1986.

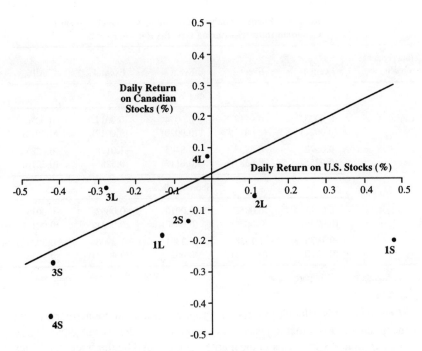

Fig. 7.2   Relationship between overall Canadian and U.S. stock market returns during tax reform events

For this reason, one should not assume that the relative impact on industry of tax reform news would be uniform across the four events being studied here.

Before proceeding to the multivariate analysis of cross-industry abnormal returns, I begin with a simple test of whether stock prices displayed any unusual behavior during the event windows. I regress the Canadian abnormal returns against a constant and the U.S. industry return. This is equivalent to estimating equation (16) assuming that a_{e1}, a_{e2}, a_{e3}, b_{e1}, b_{e2}, and b_{e3} are all zero. Table 7.2 shows that, for the short-window event definitions, the relationship between the Canadian and U.S. returns is consistently more negative during tax reform events than at other times. This effect is statistically significantly different from zero for events 2 and 4 and for all events combined. The extraordinary negative relationship is also partly evident using the long-window event definitions for events 2 and 4, as well as for all events combined. These results suggest that there may have been an unusual inverse relationship between the U.S. and Canadian counterpart industry returns during the tax reform events. This pattern is consistent with the predominance of the "my enemy's enemy is my friend" scenario, which implies that whatever hurts the U.S. industry will help the competing Canadian industry. In what follows, I pursue this finding to see if it can be related to the characteristics of the industries.

Table 7.2   **Results of Further Analyses Explaining Abnormal Returns of Canadian Industries during U.S. Tax Reform Events**

Independent Variable	Event 1	Event 2	Event 3	Event 4	All
			Long Windows		
Constant	0.0023	0.0017	0.0074	0.0017	0.0026
	(0.0021)	(0.0017)	(0.0020)	(0.0017)	(0.0013)
r_{uit}	0.0672	−0.5738	0.8405	−1.0128	−0.4285
	(0.9755)	(0.6587)	(0.6112)	(0.5286)	(0.3016)
			Short Windows		
Constant	0.0027	0.0057	−0.0010	−0.0062	0.0015
	(0.0035)	(0.0024)	(0.0040)	(0.0031)	(0.0013)
r_{uit}	−0.1976	−1.1938	−0.3381	−1.2906	−0.3926
	(0.3910)	(0.3991)	(0.6021)	(0.4693)	(0.1856)

Note: Standard errors in parentheses.

As always, it is difficult to obtain appropriate empirical counterparts to the conceptual variables that appear in the theoretical model. USPEN$_i$, the degree of penetration of U.S. firms in the market, is measured by the fraction of sales in Canada for industry i accounted for by U.S. imports. CATAX$_i$, the likely direction of an imitative Canadian tax reform, is measured by the difference between industry i's average tax rate in 1984–85 and the mean of the fifteen average tax rates.[7] The motivation underlying this measure is that, because the spirit of the U.S. corporate tax reform was a leveling of the playing field, an imitative Canadian tax reform would penalize those sectors with a relatively low average tax rate and help those sectors with a relatively high average tax rate. CAUSI$_i$, the extent of Canadian firms' income earned in the U.S., is measured by the value-weighted proportion of Canadian firms in industry i that has U.S. subsidiaries.

The results of these regression analyses using the short-window event-window definitions are presented in table 7.3, and table 7.4 shows the results

7. The average tax rate is measured as the ratio of taxes paid to book income adjusted for capital gains and intercorporate dividends, for profitable corporations only. These data were graciously provided by Statistics Canada.

Because reform of the Canadian tax system was proceeding during the period of the four events studied here, it is especially problematic to capture with a single variable the likely industry impact of Canadian tax reform induced by the U.S. reform. The Canadian budget of May 23, 1985, released a discussion paper that offered an "illustrative proposal [that] would broaden the corporate tax base and lower corporate rates" within a revenue-neutral framework. The budget of February 26, 1986, proposed to reduce the basic federal corporate tax rate from 36% to 33% in 1989 (by 1% per year), reduce the rate on manufacturing profits from 30% to 26% in 1989, phase out the general investment tax credit and eliminate the 3% inventory allowance. Further corporate income tax reform was promised for the future.

Table 7.3   **Results of "Short-Window" Regression Analyses Explaining Abnormal Returns of Canadian Industries during U.S. Tax Reform Events**

Independent Variable	Event 1	Event 2	Event 3	Event 4	All
Constant	.0082	.013	.0029	−.0094	.0026
	(.0145)	(.0154)	(.0117)	(.0157)	(.0032)
USPEN$_i$	−.0018	−.0138	.0026	.0174	.0055
	(.0514)	(.0173)	(.029)	(.0197)	(.0071)
CATAX$_i$	−.236	.0707	.0217	.0016	−.056
	(.2193)	(.276)	(.1745)	(.3187)	(.0443)
CAUSI$_i$	−.013	−.0102	−.0067	−.0027	−.004
	(.0159)	(.019)	(.0149)	(.0214)	(.004)
r_{uit}	−.1745	−2.0935	.1953	−1.5198	−.4982
	(1.3517)	(1.0544)	(2.9087)	(1.72)	(.4301)
USPEN$_i \cdot r_{uit}$	−.8116	3.5307	−.2783	−.2671	−.0729
	(4.892)	(2.5948)	(4.8803)	(2.7948)	(.9519)
CATAX$_i \cdot r_{uit}$	21.5798	.2043	18.5144	−9.854	3.8028
	(24.0374)	(32.2833)	(25.8221)	(48.5951)	(6.1892)
CAUSI$_i \cdot r_{uit}$	1.4504	−.4762	−.3381	−.4165	.4889
	(1.5165)	(2.0096)	(3.2603)	(2.1545)	(.5181)

Note: Standard errors in parentheses.

Table 7.4   **Results of "Long-Window" Regression Analyses Explaining Abnormal Returns of Canadian Industries during U.S. Tax Reform Events**

Independent Variable	Event 1	Event 2	Event 3	Event 4	All
Constant	−.0118	.0105	.0093	.0024	.0044
	(.0165)	(.0049)	(.0054)	(.0091)	(.0022)
USPEN$_i$	.0121	−.0026	−.0138	−.0378	.0001
	(.0402)	(.0124)	(.0162)	(.0497)	(.0056)
CATAX$_i$	−.1267	−.0639	−.0159	.1118	−.0639
	(.1598)	(.0671)	(.0863)	(.1263)	(.0324)
CAUSI$_i$	−.0183	−.0126	.0002	.0065	−.0024
	(.0208)	(.0061)	(.0063)	(.0084)	(.0028)
r_{uit}	−8.8823	−.0202	−.7253	−1.8705	−.4815
	(10.283)	(1.8843)	(2.4497)	(2.9535)	(.7159)
USPEN$_i \cdot r_{uit}$	7.9331	.1781	−.2815	−7.1965	1.16
	(19.3755)	(3.4399)	(4.0798)	(13.2475)	(1.6071)
CATAX$_i \cdot r_{uit}$	−36.8866	−50.7429	31.2024	−21.7592	−11.9968
	(98.2421)	(41.8461)	(37.9002)	(43.7236)	(10.8054)
CAUSI$_i \cdot r_{uit}$	10.472	−.3173	2.3138	−2.9507	.2965
	(12.1859)	(2.6349)	(3.1052)	(3.2517)	(.9642)

Note: Standard errors in parentheses.

using the long-window event-window definitions. In neither case are the results particularly supportive of the hypotheses offered in this paper and summarized in figure 7.1. The prereform average tax rate of the Canadian industry is not positively related to its abnormal return in a consistent way. The relationship between the Canadian industry abnormal return and the U.S. industry return is not related in a consistent way to either the extent of U.S. import penetration or the extent of U.S. activity by the Canadian firms.

That a consistent pattern of abnormal returns fails to appear may be the result of any of a number of factors. It may be simply because the impact of U.S. tax reform on the prospects of Canadian firms was too small to be distinguished from the normal daily fluctuations of Canadian stock prices. It may be that the indicators of industry characteristics are too flawed to pick up the differences in the response of Canadian stock prices. It may be that the probability that tax reform would happen did not change during the event windows in a quantitatively significant way. My own guess is that each of these explanations is partly behind the failure of a significant pattern of response to appear. Recall that prior work has failed to establish clear patterns of response of U.S. stock prices to U.S. tax reform, so it is perhaps not too surprising that the identification of cross-border effects, which are bound to be of smaller magnitude than domestic effects, is not easy.

7.6   Conclusions

Events that changed the probability of fundamental U.S. tax reform had little noticeable impact on the U.S. stock market, either in terms of its aggregate movement or in the cross-industry pattern of stock price movements. Given this, it is perhaps too much to ask that analysis uncover systematic cross-border stock price effects of tax policy. Yet some weak evidence of systematic response is present. The cross-industry correlation of abnormal Canadian and U.S. returns is negative during some of the event periods, suggesting that because Canadian firms compete with U.S. firms, what is good for the latter is bad for the former, and vice versa. There is no evidence, though, that this "my enemy's enemy is my friend" effect is stronger in industries that have a high degree of U.S. firms' sales in the Canadian market (a rough indicator of the competitiveness of U.S. and Canadian firms).

This paper does not definitively establish the presence of cross-border spillover effects of tax policy. More research is needed. If the finding of negative cross-industry correlations of abnormal returns stands up to future testing, it suggests that the profitability of industry A in country B can be affected (inversely) by how favorable the tax treatment of industry A is in country C. This finding does not, however, necessarily imply that country C should respond by matching the policy of country B. The normative question of how one country's policy ought to react to another's depends on such things as the nature of the strategic interaction among firms. Theoretical research on this question is in an early stage of development,[8] and should be accompanied by empirical work of the kind begun in this paper.

References

Cutler, David M. 1988. Tax Reform and the Stock Market: An Asset Price Approach. *American Economic Review* 78(December): 1107–17.
Dixit, Avinash. 1983. International Trade Policy for Oligopolistic Industries. *Economic Journal* 94(supp.): 1–16.
Downs, Thomas W., and Hassan Tehranian. 1988. Predicting Stock Price Responses to Tax Policy Changes. *American Economic Review* 78(December): 1118–30.
Levinsohn, James, and Joel Slemrod. 1990. Taxes, Tariffs and the Global Corporation. NBER Working Paper no. 3500. Cambridge MA: National Bureau of Economic Research.
Lyon, Andrew B. 1989a. Did ACRS Really Cause Stock Prices to Fall? NBER Working Paper no. 2990 (May). Cambridge MA: National Bureau of Economic Research.
Lyon, Andrew B. 1989b. The Effect of the Investment Tax Credit on the Value of the Firm. *Journal of Public Economics* 38(2): 227–47.
McLure, Charles E., Jr. 1990. International Aspects of Tax Policy for the 21st Century. In *International Tax Policy: Agenda for the Nineties* (Proceedings of Conference, American College of Tax Counsel, ALI-ABA Committee on Continuing Professional Education, and National Tax Association. Washington, D.C., April 20–21).
Thompson, Aileen. 1990. Trade Liberalization, Comparative Advantage, and Stock Prices: An Event Study Analysis of the U.S.-Canadian Free Trade Agreement. University of Michigan.
Whalley, John. 1990. Foreign Responses to U.S. Tax Reform. In *Do Taxes Matter? The Impact of the Tax Reform Act of 1986*, ed. J. Slemrod. Cambridge MA: MIT Press.

8. For an example, see Levinsohn and Slemrod (1990).

8 Tax Aspects of Policy toward Aging Populations

Alan J. Auerbach and Laurence J. Kotlikoff

8.1 Introduction

Recent political and economic events, such as the U.S.-Canada free-trade agreement and the generally increasing integration of world capital markets, have strengthened the already close ties between the economies of the United States and Canada. These close ties, along with the two countries' shared cultural and economic characteristics, have provided researchers with good justification for using the experience of one country to draw inferences about the effects of potential policy changes in the other (e.g., Carroll and Summers 1987).

In this paper, however, we are concerned less with the lessons of policy differences than with their potential spillover effects. In particular, we consider how demographics and fiscal structure are likely to interact over the next several decades in influencing each country's rate of capital accumulation, and the implications of differences in projected saving with respect to patterns of trade and capital flows between the two countries.

A U.S.-Canada comparison on this issue promises to be particularly interesting because the countries' future demographic characteristics are projected to be quite different, and their fiscal systems for providing public expenditures for the elderly are also quite different. Moreover, the great difference in size between two countries should lead to very different macroeconomic effects of changes in national saving. Whereas increases in U.S. saving might significantly spur U.S. domestic investment through reduction in interest rates, the

Alan J. Auerbach is professor of economics at the University of Pennsylvania and a research associate of the National Bureau of Economic Research. Laurence J. Kotlikoff is professor of economics at Boston University and a research associate of the National Bureau of Economic Research.

The authors are grateful to several of the conference participants and to participants in the NBER Summer Institute, for comments on an earlier draft.

relatively small size and the openness of the Canadian economy suggest that increases in Canadian national saving may have a smaller impact on domestic investment, but perhaps a greater relative impact on capital flows and the current account.

Changes in population structure and fiscal policy are related in a very complex manner, and an accurate perspective on this relationship requires that one account for the general equilibrium effects of significant policy changes. For example, demographic changes leading to a higher dependency ratio of nonworking to working population may also induce saving and labor supply responses which, in turn, may affect capital-labor ratios and real wages, softening the increase in tax burden required to finance public old-age support programs. To provide such general equilibrium analysis, we utilize the model presented in Auerbach and Kotlikoff (1987) and extended in Auerbach et al. (1989).

In the next section, we review the model and how it will be applied to the current problem. Section 8.3 presents the data for the United States and Canada that are used to calibrate the model for the experiments we wish to consider, and section 8.4 presents the simulations of the model for the two countries.

8.2   Modeling a Demographic Transition

The model used in this paper is a numerical, general equilibrium simulation model of a single country, which we calibrate separately to study each country. This is a modified version of the model used by Auerbach et al. (1989) in a related comparison study of the demographic transitions in four OECD countries—Japan, Sweden, the United States, and West Germany. It contains three sectors: a household sector, a production sector, and a government sector. The optimal behavior of each sector gives rise to nonlinear equations, which are combined to solve numerically for a perfect foresight transition path for the economy as a whole that is consistent with the behavior of individual agents.

Among the features that distinguish this model from other general equilibrium models are its fully dynamic character, its specification of life-cycle household behavior, augmented to include bequests, and its explicit treatment of family structure and demographics. As we have described the model in some detail in our earlier work, we present only a brief review here, concentrating on the features of the model that are particularly relevant and the changes that have been made for the current investigation.

8.2.1   Household Behavior

At each date, the household sector comprises seventy-five overlapping generations, corresponding to children aged 1 to 20 and adults aged 21 to 75. Each year all the 75-year-olds die (there being no uncertainty in the model), and new children are born. At age 21, each individual changes status from child to adult and at the same time becomes the parent of a number of children determined exogenously by the model (but allowed to vary over different generations). Each generation between ages 21 and 75 has a representative household that consists of an adult and (for adults aged 21 to 41) that adult's minor children.

Each household maximizes an identical utility function of its lifetime consumption, labor supply, and bequests that is assumed to take the form:

$$(1) \qquad U_t = \sum_{j=21}^{75} (1 + \delta)^{-(j-21)} u_{pjt} +$$

$$N_t \sum_{j=21}^{40} (1 + \delta)^{-(j-21)} u_{kjt} + N_t (1 + \delta)^{-54} u_{bt}$$

where δ is a pure rate of time preference, N_t is the number of children per parent, and u_{pjt}, u_{kjt}, and u_{bjt} are the instantaneous period utilities generated by parent's consumption, children's consumption, and the parent's bequest per child, at age 75. The annual utility components, u_{pjt} and u_{kjt}, are functions of contemporaneous consumption and leisure assumed to have the constant elasticity-of-substitution form:

$$(2) \qquad u_{ijt} = \omega_{ij} \left(c_{ijt}^{1-\frac{1}{\rho}} + \alpha \ell_{ijt}^{1-\frac{1}{\rho}} \right)^{\frac{1-\frac{1}{\gamma}}{1-\frac{1}{\rho}}} \quad i = p, k$$

where c_{ijt} and ℓ_{ijt} are, respectively, consumption and leisure of the generation t parent and this adult's child at the parent's age j. The term α is a leisure share parameter, while ρ and γ are, respectively, the intratemporal and intertemporal elasticities of substitution. In the model, retirement occurs endogenously when an individual chooses to consume his entire labor endowment as leisure. The term ω_{ij} is a weighting parameter, meant to account for the smaller consumption needs of children. It is set equal to 1 for adults and grows linearly from .25 to .50 for children between the ages of 1 and 20.

The utility of bequests term is assumed to take the form:

$$(3) \qquad u_{bt} = \beta b_t^{1-\frac{1}{\gamma}}$$

where b_t is the bequest made to each child by adults in generation t and β is a preference parameter indicating the intensity of preferences for bequests. When $\beta = 0$, no bequests are left.

Households maximize the utility function (1) subject to a budget constraint that the present value of the labor endowment of the adult (from age 21 to 75) and the child (from age 1 to 20), plus the adult's inheritance (received at age 55 from a dying parent), equal the consumption and leisure of the adult and child and the bequest left by the adult. Each individual's wage rate (adjusted for productivity growth) grows from childhood through late adulthood and then falls, reflecting observed empirical patterns.

The presence of government policy alters this budget constraint in several ways. The model includes proportional taxes on labor income, capital income, and consumption, which affect the after-tax wage, interest rate, and price of consumption goods, respectively. These taxes are assumed to finance general expenditures that do not directly influence the private decisions of households.

In addition, there is an autonomous social security system that finances public old-age pensions through a payroll tax. If each individual's pension were actuarially based on his own contributions, it would be appropriate to view payroll taxes as forced saving, which (in our model without liquidity constraints) would not be perceived as "taxes" at all and would have no effect on the individual's choices. However, in both the United States and Canada, public pensions are only imperfectly related to individual payroll taxes. Hence, we assume that households consider a fraction λ of all payroll taxes as if they were ordinary taxes on labor income, treating the remaining payroll taxes and all benefits as if they were simply lump-sum taxes and transfers, respectively.

8.2.2   Firm Behavior

The model has a single production sector that is assumed to behave competitively, using capital and labor subject to a constant-returns-to-scale Cobb-Douglas production function with capital's share of production (net of depreciation) equal to .25. Capital and labor are each homogeneous and assumed to be perfectly mobile within each country.[1] We assume that the economy experiences an exogenous, constant rate of technological change, set equal to 1.5 percent in all our simulations.[2]

8.2.3   Government

As already mentioned, we divide the government into two sectors: a public pension system financed by payroll taxes, and a general sector financed by proportional taxes on labor income, capital income, and consumption. The model's social security benefits are determined as a fraction of the average of wage-indexed labor earnings from age 21 through the social security age of

1. In the simulations for Canada, we also assume that capital can enter and leave the country freely.

2. Introducing technological progress into a model with variable labor supply requires some care. The simplest approach of assuming constant tastes and rising wage levels would lead to successive generations working more and more or less and less, depending on the value of the intratemporal elasticity ρ. To avoid this problem, we allow each generation to experience the steeper wage profile implied by technological progress, but interpret the rise in the overall wage profile experienced by each generation as if it were time-augmenting, and hence neutral with respect to the choice between market and nonmarket uses of labor. See Auerbach et al. (1989) for further discussion.

retirement (which may differ from the age of true retirement). The wage-indexation procedure involves multiplying earnings in years prior to the social security retirement age by the ratio of the standardized wage at retirement, adjusted for the 1.5 percent rate of technological change, to the standardized wage in the past year in which earnings were received.

Within the general government sector, we distinguish four categories of spending. One category, meant to encompass items such as national defense, is assumed to be independent of the age structure of the population, growing at a rate equal to the sum of the population's growth rate and the rate of technological change. The other expenditure categories are those targeted at three age groups: 1 to 24, 25 to 64, and over 65. In our baseline simulations, we calculate the shares of total spending accounted for by each type of targeted spending in 1985, and assume that thereafter the growth rates of each of these categories of expenditure equals the rate of technological progress plus the growth rate of the relevant age group. Hence, overall government spending will grow more quickly as the population shifts to a category that receives more age-specific expenditures per capita.

In addition to raising taxes and spending, the government is assumed to utilize public debt in financing its operations. The patterns of spending and revenues for both the general and social security sectors of the government are required to satisfy an intertemporal budget constraint specifying that initial debt plus the present value of expenditures equal the present value of taxes. We assume that debt per capita is constant (normalized for productivity growth) and use the level of debt as an initial condition in calibrating the model.

8.2.4   Solution for Equilibrium

Each country's economy is assumed to be in a steady-state equilibrium in 1960, at which time a demographic transition begins.[3] We study changes in government policy and population structure that take place over the period 1960–2050, after which time we impose the assumption that no further policy changes occur and birth rates are consistent with zero population growth. The economy is then allowed to converge to a new steady state, for which we allow an additional 160 years. Although the behavior of the economy during these later years is not of particular interest or relevance, such future conditions must be incorporated into the model to accommodate our assumption that individuals during the first 90 years have perfect foresight with respect to the economy for the remainder of their own lifetimes, which may extend well beyond the year 2050.

Since our model can only be solved for one country at a time, we approxi-

3. While we are primarily interested in studying the behavior of the economies from the present onward, beginning the simulations in 1960 permits us to analyze economies that are already undergoing a demographic transition.

mate a full, two-country general equilibrium solution in the following way. We solve first for the equilibrium path of the United States, treating it as a closed economy by imposing the constraint that national saving equals national investment. We then take the implied U.S. interest rate for each year and assume that Canada is a small country that takes these (and hence the wage rate as well) as given.[4]

This solution technique means that, in the model, current account imbalances do arise in the solution for Canada, but not for the United States. Another consequence is that additional saving may raise domestic investment and raise real wages in the United States, but not in Canada. While this treatment is, of course, oversimplified, it does bring out some of the important consequences of the differences in size and openness of the two economies.

8.3   Calibrating the Model

For every simulation, projections begin in 1960 in order to produce conditions in the 1980s that actually prevailed, including the non-steady-state structure of the population. For both countries, the model's parameters are adjusted so that simulated household behavior patterns are realistic and aggregate variables match those actually observed during the period 1960–85. The targeted variables are the rate of national saving, the social security contribution rate, the share of government spending in national income, and the tax rates on consumption, labor income, and capital income.

8.3.1   Demographics

While, in reality, demographic structure may change as the result of many factors (such as life expectancy, immigration, and age of child-bearing), all changes in the model's population age structure result from changes in birth rates. We choose the birth rates N_t for the years 1961–2050 in order to approximate, as closely as possible, values by decade of the age distribution of the population, based on OECD data. Table 8.1 provides historical age distributions for 1960–1980 and projected age distributions for 1990–2050 for the United States and Canada.[5] The table also presents the age distributions generated by the birth rates used in our model simulations.

The actual data show that Canada had a younger population in 1960, with 33.7 percent of the population below age 15 and 7.6 percent above age 65, compared to 31.0 percent and 9.2 percent, respectively, for the United States. However, by 1990, the population age structures had become more similar, with Canada still having a slightly smaller fraction above age 65, but the United States having a larger fraction under age 15. Both populations have

---

4. In assuming that Canadians face the U.S. interest rate, before tax, we are essentially assuming that U.S. capital income taxes on Canadian investments are fully creditable against Canadian taxes, if Canadians are the marginal investors in the two countries.

5. The figures for 1990 are "projected" in the sense that they were calculated in the late 1980s.

Table 8.1   **Population Age Distributions (percentage of population)**

Year	Age Group				
	0–14	15–34	35–54	55–64	65+
1. *United States*					
1960					
Actual	31.0	26.3	24.8	8.6	9.2
Model	30.0	31.7	22.2	8.4	7.7
1970					
Actual	31.0	26.3	24.8	8.6	9.2
Model	27.3	32.9	23.0	8.8	8.0
1980					
Actual	22.5	35.3	21.3	9.6	11.3
Model	23.1	34.0	24.9	9.5	8.6
1990					
Actual	21.8	31.9	25.4	8.6	12.3
Model	23.4	30.3	26.6	10.2	9.3
2000					
Actual	21.1	27.4	30.5	8.8	12.2
Model	21.0	28.9	28.4	11.3	10.3
2010					
Actual	19.3	27.0	28.5	12.6	12.6
Model	20.2	28.5	26.7	12.8	11.7
2020					
Actual	19.0	26.0	25.2	13.7	16.2
Model	18.3	27.7	26.6	13.7	13.6
2030					
Actual	18.5	24.9	25.4	11.5	19.6
Model	19.1	26.5	27.4	12.2	14.8
2040					
Actual	18.2	25.0	25.4	11.4	20.0
Model	18.2	26.5	27.5	14.1	13.7
2050					
Actual	18.3	24.9	24.8	12.2	19.7
Model	19.0	26.1	26.4	13.4	15.1
2. *Canada*					
1960					
Actual	33.7	28.2	23.4	7.1	7.6
Model	34.1	32.1	21.4	7.9	7.0
1970					
Actual	30.3	31.3	22.5	7.9	8.0
Model	30.7	33.3	22.3	8.2	7.3
1980					
Actual	23.0	36.5	22.3	8.8	9.5
Model	24.3	35.7	24.5	9.0	8.0
1990					
Actual	20.8	32.4	26.3	9.0	11.4
Model	21.5	32.9	27.7	10.2	9.0
2000					
Actual	19.5	27.5	30.7	9.5	12.9
Model	19.3	28.2	31.3	11.9	10.5

(continued)

Table 8.1   (continued)

Year	Age Group				
	0–14	15–34	35–54	55–64	65+
2010					
Actual	17.2	26.4	29.0	12.9	14.6
Model	17.3	26.3	30.6	14.2	12.6
2020					
Actual	16.9	24.8	25.6	14.0	18.7
Model	16.6	24.8	27.7	16.5	15.5
2030					
Actual	17.2	23.1	25.3	11.9	22.5
Model	17.2	23.6	27.1	14.7	18.5
2040					
Actual	17.6	23.6	24.6	11.6	22.6
Model	17.8	24.3	27.1	14.7	17.3
2050					
Actual	18.2	24.4	23.5	12.1	21.8
Model	18.7	25.1	26.0	14.7	16.8

aged considerably since 1960, with the fraction below age 15 dropping from about one-third to about one-fifth.

Beyond 1990, the projections indicate a much more gradual demographic transition for the United States than for Canada. By the year 2000, Canada is predicted to have a larger fraction of its population in the over-65 category, as well as a smaller fraction younger than 15. The gap continues to widen for several more decades, until the age structures finally begin to converge again near the year 2050.

As can be seen by comparing the model's age distributions to these actual population figures, the model's assumed fertility patterns provide a reasonably good approximation of the projected demographic transitions in both countries, at least if the age groups 55–64 and 65+ are combined.[6]

8.3.2   Preference Parameters

Several parameters must be set in specifying household behavior: γ, the intertemporal elasticity of substitution; ρ, the intratemporal elasticity of substitution; α, the leisure intensity parameter; δ, the pure rate of discount; and β, the bequest intensity parameter. Following our past modeling work (Auerbach et al. 1989), we set $\alpha = 1.5$, $\rho = .8$, and $\gamma = .35$. Because we are unaware of any evidence about the relative importance of bequests in the two countries, we use the same value of β for each country, 15,000,000.[7] Finally,

---

6. The tendency to understate the fraction of the population over 65 is due primarily to the model's assumption that all individuals live exactly until age 75. In future work, we hope to relax this assumption.

7. This value is consistent with the simultaneous achievement of realistic rates of national saving and realistic household consumption profiles.

we choose δ to ensure that the 1960 national saving rates match actual national saving rates in each country. The resulting values are $\delta = 0$ for the United States and $\delta = 0.006$ for Canada.[8] This and fertility are the only differences between Canadian and U.S. households in our model, although government policies also contribute to differences in simulated household behavior.

8.3.3   Fiscal Parameters

In 1960, tax rates for each country on capital and labor income are set at historical values of the average rates of tax on these types of income, according to the *OECD Revenue Statistics*.[9] We do the same for consumption taxes, and choose the initial level of government debt to produce the 1960 share of government in GDP for each country.[10] The values chosen cause national debt to equal 46 percent of total private assets in Canada and 31 percent in the United States. After 1960, the level of public debt per capita is kept constant.

Between 1960 and 1985, income tax rates are kept at their historical levels, while we adjust the growth rate of government spending (measured net of the rate of growth of population plus total factor productivity) to ensure that the remaining general fiscal instrument, the consumption tax rate, also follows the appropriate trend between 1960 and 1985. After 1985, income tax rates are kept constant at their 1985 values, and the consumption tax rate serves as the marginal sources of funds, being adjusted to maintain balance between government spending and interest service and other tax revenues.[11]

Although the normal age of initial public pension receipt is 65 in both countries, the systems and their funding differ considerably. In the United States, the primary function of the Social Security system historically has been the provision of old-age and survivors' pension insurance (OASI). It also provides disability insurance (DI) and a growing health insurance (HI) component, Medicare. At the same time, the primary source of revenue for the OASDHI system, and the sole source of revenue for the pension component, has been the payroll tax.

In Canada, however, the association of the payroll tax and the old-age public pension scheme has been much weaker. The payroll tax has traditionally

8. The slightly higher rate of discount for Canada arises because Canada's lower rate of government absorption of GDP and its greater emphasis on consumption taxes would otherwise lead (in our model) to a higher rate of national saving, while the rates in 1960 for the two countries were actually quite similar.

9. OECD revenue statistics for Canada begin only in 1965, so we extrapolate values for 1960. The use of average tax rates is consistent with the model's specification of proportional tax rates, which does not allow us to incorporate tax progressivity and the more complicated elements of capital income taxation in the two countries. In particular, we do not incorporate the incentive effects of sheltered savings plans such as IRAs in the United States and RRSPs in Canada.

10. Since the interest rate exceeds the growth rate in our simulations, a higher level of debt per capita leads to a lower level of government spending, given taxes.

11. We use the consumption tax as the marginal source of funds in each country for the sake of comparison. Knowing how the tax structure would actually respond to changes in revenue needs would depend on a variety of factors, including the types of expenditures being increased and the level of government (e.g., federal vs. state or provincial) making the expenditures and raising the revenue.

funded a wider range of social insurance spending, such as unemployment compensation (funded by employer payments in the United States), while most funding of public old-age pensions has been through general revenues. The Canada and Quebec Pension Plans (CPP/QPP), like the OASI system in the United States, are financed by payroll taxes, with benefits loosely and indirectly related to past contributions. Older Canadians also receive demogrants, called Old Age Security (OAS) payments, and many also receive Guaranteed Income Supplements; both systems are financed by general revenues. According to Musgrave et al. (1987), OAS payments were nearly twice as large, in the aggregate, as CPP/QPP payments in 1984.

We accommodate these important institutional differences by making two adjustments to each country's data so that they conform more closely to the structure of our model. The social security system we simulate is funded exclusively by payroll taxes and provides only old-age pension benefits. One data adjustment, discussed more fully below, is to include in general spending (rather than pension spending) the part of public pension spending that is funded by general revenues. Also, since all nonpension spending is excluded from our model's social security system and included instead in general spending, we reduce the measured payroll tax in each country to account for the nonpension spending financed by payroll taxes, increasing labor income taxes over their historical values by the same amount as we reduce payroll taxes.[12] The resulting adjusted values of labor income taxes and payroll taxes are shown (for 1960 and 1985) in table 8.2 along with the values of capital income taxes and consumption taxes calculated from the OECD revenue data.

General (nonpension) government spending is divided into four categories: age-specific spending on the young (f_k), middle-aged (f_m) and old (f_o), and non-age-specific spending (f_n), with $\Sigma f_i = 1$. To determine these shares, we follow the following procedure. Using unpublished OECD data for 1985 on the levels of government expenditure on education, family benefits, health, and unemployment compensation directed to each age group in each country, we form an estimate of the fraction of nonpension, age-specific expenditures going to each age group.[13] We then use published data on all nonpension government spending (net of interest payments) for the same year to derive the fraction of all spending that is in these age-specific categories, and multiply this fraction by the fractions of age-specific spending on the young, middle-aged, and old, to arrive at the fractions f_i. Finally, we adjust the calculation by adding to age-specific spending on the old those public pension benefits that are funded by general revenues, rather than by the payroll tax.

---

12. For the United States, we use the adjustment made by Auerbach et al. (1989) using unpublished OECD data. For Canada, we use an estimate that one-third of all payroll taxes were CPP/QPP contributions from 1966–85, based on the number cited in Musgrave et al. (1987). From 1960–65, before the advent of these plans, we assume all payroll taxes were for nonpension expenditures.

13. We used 1980 as a base year for the United States in Auerbach et al. (1989), and use these calculations of U.S. government expenditures here, rather than redoing all the calculations for 1985. The differences between the two years should be minimal.

Table 8.2   Tax Rates for 1960 and 1985

	United States		Canada	
Tax	1960	1985	1960	1985
Wage	19.2	18.7	11.3	21.4
Capital Income	16.2	15.7	10.0	16.6
Consumption	9.8	9.7	21.0	22.2
Social Security	7.1	7.6	0.0	2.4

Thus, our social security system for each country accounts only for that part of old-age pensions financed by payroll taxes; all nonpension social insurance spending and all payroll taxes financing nonpension spending are consistently accounted for in the general government budget calculations.

Based on our calculations, the government spending shares f_i for the United States are .291 (young), .060 (middle-aged), .071 (old) and .578 (non-age-specific). The corresponding shares for Canada are .306, .172, .141, and .381. Since the age distributions in the two countries were fairly similar in the 1980s, one can attribute the differences between the two countries primarily to differences in underlying policy. In Canada, relative to the United States, a much greater share of government spending (excluding payroll-tax-financed pension benefits) is targeted toward the middle-aged and the elderly. The larger old-age component in Canada is primarily attributable to the large fraction of pension benefits financed by general revenues. The larger middle-aged component is due to the higher levels of spending per capita on health benefits (for non-aged adults) and unemployment compensation.

Because the public pension scheme that remains is fully financed by payroll taxes, its characteristics are similar for the two countries. We set the parameter λ, corresponding to the fraction of payroll taxes actually perceived to be taxes rather than contributions, to .5 for both countries.

8.4 Simulation Results

Our simulations for the United States are quite similar to those presented in Auerbach et al. (1989).[14] For both countries, we begin by calibrating the initial steady states to match the 1960 shares of national saving and government spending in national income (GDP less depreciation), using as tools the pure rate of time preference δ and the level of initial public debt. This procedure produces realistic values for both countries: national saving rates of approxi-

---

14. They differ primarily in two ways. First, we have introduced the term λ, representing the fraction of Social Security pension contributions viewed as taxes. Previously, we implicitly set this term equal to zero. Second, we have chosen to calibrate government spending so that government's share of output corresponds to the value actually observed in 1960. This leads to an increase in private saving (via a lower assumed pure rate of time preference) and a reduction in public saving (via a higher assumed level of national debt per capita).

mately 10 percent for both the United States and Canada, and government shares of 20.4 percent of national income in the United States and 17.5 percent in Canada. For each country, all simulations presented share the same initial steady state.

8.4.1 Baseline Simulations

After fixing the initial 1960 steady states, we then run trial transition simulations to choose a base case rate of growth of per-capita government spending that, given the assumed tax rates on labor and capital income (in table 8.2) and the level of per-capita government debt established in the initial steady state, provides a consumption tax in 1985 that is consistent with the actual observed value.[15] The results for the base case simulations for the United States and Canada are given in table 8.3. For each country, we present simulated values of several variables for the years 1960 (the initial steady state), 1985, 1990, 2010, 2030, 2050, and the "long run" (the final steady state with zero population growth).

The consumption and social security taxes for 1960 and 1985 may be compared to the actual values given in table 8.2, which are closely approximated by the simulations. Table 8.3 also presents for each year the national saving rate (national income less private and public spending as a share of national income), the real, detrended after-tax wage rate,[16] and the current account (relative to national income), which is constrained to be zero in the closed economy simulations for the United States.

As we already have discussed, the simulations are constrained to conform to fiscal measures in both 1960 and 1985, and to the aggregate national income shares of saving and government in 1960. After 1960, there is nothing to guarantee that simulated saving rates will conform closely to historical levels, and indeed the simulated patterns for both countries diverge from actual experience.

The model predicts a decline in saving for Canada and an increase in the United States between 1960 and 1990, a pattern that is precisely opposite to that which actually occurred. The actual Canadian saving rate was 12.3 percent in 1985, and just 3.6 percent in the United States.[17] These divergent trends in saving behavior over the past few decades have provoked some at-

---

15. This requires a U.S. government growth rate of 0.5% per capita, and a Canadian one of 2.6%. Although government's share of income did grow more quickly in Canada, these growth rates understate the actual rate of growth in the United States and overstate the actual rate of growth in Canada. The differences are due to the fact that our model does not account for all components of the government budget.

16. The formula for this variable is $[w_t \cdot (1 - \tau_t - \lambda \cdot \theta_t) / (1 + \phi_t)] / 1.015^t$, where w_t is the wage rate at date t, τ_t, θ_t, and ϕ_t are the wage tax rate, the social security tax rate, and the consumption tax rate, respectively, and λ is the fraction of the social security tax perceived to be a tax, equal to .5 in all the simulations presented here.

17. Although since 1985 the U.S. saving rate has risen somewhat and the Canadian rate has fallen, a gap remains between the two.

Table 8.3   **Base Case Simulations**

Year	United States	Canada
	Consumption Tax Rate	
1960	9.8	21.0
1985	8.3	21.8
1990	8.6	19.5
2010	5.7	14.3
2030	5.8	17.5
2050	5.5	17.6
Long Run	5.3	17.1
	Social Security Tax Rate	
1960	7.1	0.0
1985	7.6	2.4
1990	8.0	2.5
2010	10.2	3.6
2030	12.8	5.3
2050	12.8	4.7
Long Run	12.3	4.1
	National Saving Rate[a]	
1960	10.1	9.8
1985	12.2	8.1
1990	11.7	8.9
2010	9.5	9.1
2030	6.5	3.3
2050	5.8	2.1
Long Run	6.3	5.0
	Real After-Tax Wage[b]	
1960	.70	.73
1985	.74	.65
1990	.74	.67
2010	.78	.78
2030	.78	.72
2050	.79	.72
Long Run	.79	.67
	Current Account[a]	
1960	0	−1.5
1985	0	−5.0
1990	0	−4.1
2010	0	1.6
2030	0	0.9
2050	0	−3.3
Long Run	0	−1.3

[a]Saving rate and current account expressed as fractions of national income.
[b]Real wage is detrended and is net of wage tax, consumption tax, and half of social security tax.

tempts at explanation (e.g., Carroll and Summers 1987). In our own empirical analysis of the United States, based on microeconomic consumption data (Auerbach and Kotlikoff 1990), we confirmed that demographic factors should have led U.S. saving to increase between 1960 and 1985; we encountered considerable difficulty identifying other factors (including fiscal policy) that could explain the observed decline.

While we could induce the model to track actual saving behavior in each country more closely, for example by changing taste parameters over time, we believe that to do this is unwarranted, in light of the scant evidence on the subject. Instead, we present the simulations based on constant preferences and emphasize the changes in rates of saving over time associated with demographic factors, rather than the saving rate levels themselves.

Certain patterns associated with the shift to an older population are observable in both countries' baseline simulations. Both countries experience a decline in needed consumption taxes after 1985, although the rate rises again in Canada. These patterns result from the interaction of several factors. First, in each country, as the population ages, consumption per capita rises, reducing the required consumption tax rate. This is particularly significant in Canada, which depends more on consumption taxes than the United States does. On the other hand, the old receive more government spending per capita, so the amount of revenue required is increased, particularly in Canada. Finally, the timing of the demographic transition differs across the two countries. Canada's shift occurs earlier and more sharply; it leads to an earlier decline in consumption taxes, but also to a stronger reversal of the initial effect.

This difference in timing is also apparent in the predicted pattern of social security tax rates. These tax rates rise in both countries as the ratio of retired population to working population increases. However, the U.S. tax rate is roughly constant at its peak level of 12.8 percent over the period 2030–50, not declining until later. In contrast, the Canadian tax rate peaks in 2030 and has already begun declining to its long-run value by 2050, when the ratio of retired to working population has already begun to decline from its peak value associated with the retirement of the baby boom generation.

The relatively larger and more rapid Canadian demographic transition also influences the predicted pattern of national saving over the next 60 years. The simulations predict that the U.S. saving rate will decline steadily through the year 2050, with the most significant drop during the period 1990–2030. In Canada, however, the saving rate is projected to rise slightly until 2010, but then drop much more sharply than in the United States. This difference is easily understood in terms of the changing fractions of the population of young, old, and middle-aged in each country.

One may simplify things a bit by thinking of the young and old as dissavers and the middle-aged as savers. A demographic shift toward an older population has offsetting effects, then, as the population share of the young declines but that of the old rises. In Canada, beginning with a much younger population than the United States, the first effect dominates initially. However, Canada's sharper birth-rate change ultimately leads to a larger increase in the share of the elderly in the population, causing a sharper decline in the saving rate.

Many who have considered the coming demographic transition have emphasized the potential fiscal burden associated with the increasing dependency ratio. We have found here that social security tax rates will rise in each country. However, there are other factors that act to counterbalance this burden. First, as we have already discussed, general expenditures per capita will rise, but so may tax bases. Second, as the population ages, one may expect an increase in capital-labor ratios and hence a rise in real wages. In the simulations presented, the real U.S. wage rate (normalized for trend growth) rises by over 8 percent between 1985 and 2050. By assumption, the same growth in real wages is experienced in Canada.

One way of combining these factors is in terms of the real, after-tax wage rate (relative to trend), which, beginning in 1985, rises in both countries through the year 2010. It then levels off in the United States, but falls in Canada, as the consumption tax rises once again. However, even in Canada, the real after-tax wage rate in 2050 is predicted to be higher than it was in 1985.

The last set of numbers given in table 8.3 is for the current account in Canada, which we have assumed in these simulations to be a small open economy that takes its factor returns from the United States. One must recognize that this polar open economy assumption, with no adjustment costs to trade or capital flows and assets being perfect substitutes across national borders, can give rise to large and volatile annual measures of the current account surplus or deficit. Taking this into account, the predicted current account balances in the table provide an interesting picture of the influence of the demographic transition on trade and capital flows.

The model predicts a Canadian current account deficit of 1.5 percent of national income in 1960, higher than the actual deficit of about .4 percent. It then swings away from reality, predicting an increase to a 5.0 percent deficit in 1985, when there was actually a surplus of 2.7 percent. The error is clearly associated with the model's significant underprediction of the 1985 Canadian national saving rate; once again, future patterns are more useful in predicting changes than levels. The model predicts that the Canadian current account will swing strongly toward surplus from the present until around 2010, after which, with the saving rate declining, Canada will move again toward a deficit position.

8.4.2 Alternative Simulations

In this section, we consider the effects of alternative dynamic fiscal policies on the transition paths for the United States and Canada. Table 8.4 presents the alternative U.S. simulations, while those for Canada appear in table 8.5. For convenience, the first column of each table repeats the baseline simulation

Table 8.4   **Alternative Simulations: United States**

Year	Base Case	No Spending Rise	Increase in Retirement Age
Consumption Tax Rate			
1985	8.3	8.3	8.2
1990	8.6	8.6	8.4
2010	5.7	5.5	5.2
2030	5.8	5.2	4.9
2050	5.5	4.8	4.5
Long Run	5.3	4.6	4.1
Social Security Tax Rate			
1985	7.6	7.6	7.5
1990	8.0	7.9	7.9
2010	10.2	10.2	8.0
2030	12.8	12.8	10.2
2050	12.8	12.8	10.1
Long Run	12.3	12.3	9.9
National Saving Rate			
1985	12.2	12.2	12.4
1990	11.7	11.7	12.0
2010	9.5	9.4	10.1
2030	6.5	6.6	7.2
2050	5.8	5.9	6.3
Long Run	6.3	6.3	6.6

from table 8.3. Since all simulations are the same in 1960, we do not report the results for that year. Likewise, we focus our attention on three of the variables reported in table 8.3, the consumption tax rate, the social security tax rate, and the national saving rate.

The first set of alternative simulations, given in the second columns of tables 8.4 and 8.5, imposes a different assumption about the response of general government spending to a change in the age structure of the population. Previously, we assumed that age-specific spending stayed constant (except for trend productivity growth) per member of the relevant age group. As the populations shift toward those groups to which more spending is targeted (the young and the elderly), this leads to an overall rise in government spending relative to the population as a whole. As we have defined it, to include public pension payments financed by general revenues, the Canadian general public sector has a considerably larger fraction of its spending targeted toward the elderly. This helps explain the rise in the required consumption tax rate in Canada after 2010 in the baseline simulation.

In the alternative simulations labeled "No Spending Rise," we assume in-

Table 8.5   **Alternative Simulations: Canada**

Year	Base Case	No Spending Rise	Increase in Retirement Age	Initial Rise in Benefits
		Consumption Tax Rate		
1985	21.8	21.9	21.8	22.0
1190	19.5	19.5	19.5	19.9
2010	14.3	12.5	14.2	15.2
2030	17.5	12.1	17.2	18.7
2050	17.6	13.1	17.4	18.8
Long Run	17.1	13.6	16.9	18.2
		Social Security Tax Rate		
1985	2.4	2.4	2.4	2.4
1990	2.5	2.5	2.5	3.1
2010	3.6	3.6	2.8	6.1
2030	5.3	5.3	4.4	9.1
2050	4.7	4.7	3.8	7.9
Long Run	4.1	4.1	3.3	7.0
		National Saving Rate		
1985	8.1	7.8	8.2	7.4
1990	8.9	8.5	9.0	8.1
2010	9.1	8.8	9.4	8.0
2030	3.3	4.1	3.6	2.0
2050	2.1	2.5	2.4	1.3
Long Run	5.0	5.1	5.1	4.2

stead that all general government spending remains constant per member of the overall population, *not* per member of the affected age group. Implicitly, this assumes that age-specific spending per capita is reduced as benefit-intensive age groups become more important components of the population. The results of these simulations confirm that this alternative fiscal-policy assumption leads to lower spending and hence to lower required consumption tax rates. Also as expected, the effect is considerably larger for Canada. While the U.S. consumption tax is reduced by as much as .7 percentage points (in 2050 and the long run), the Canadian consumption tax is reduced by 5.4 percentage points in 2030 and 3.5 percentage points in the long run. This reduction in Canada, unlike the much smaller one simulated for the United States, is important enough to influence the national saving rate, which is .8 percentage points higher in 2030.[18]

The next set of simulations, presented in the third columns of tables 8.4 and

18. It is lower in earlier years, such as 1990 and 2010, because individuals feel wealthier and hence spend more, knowing that government taxes will be lower in the future.

8.5, considers the impact of a gradual, announced increase in the retirement age, modeled after the one currently in process in the United States. The simulations assume that the retirement age rises from 65 to 66 in the year 2000 and from 66 to 67 in the year 2010, remaining constant thereafter. These experiments have an obvious impact on the social security tax rates in each country. In the United States, the tax rate peaks at 10.2 percent in 2030, rather than 12.8 percent. In Canada, the tax rate peaks at 4.4 percent rather than 5.3 percent, also in 2030. In both countries, this leads to a higher rate of saving. Given the nature of pay-as-you-go social security systems and our life-cycle model, such an increase is to be expected; individuals must save more for their own retirement. In the United States, the saving rate rises by as much as .7 percentage points (in 2030), and .3 percentage points in the long run. The respective numbers for Canada are .3 (also in 2030) and .1, smaller because of the smaller size of the payroll-tax-financed portion of public pensions.

Our final simulation, which we present for Canada, is motivated by the recent relative trends in payroll tax rates and benefit levels. Unlike the U.S. system, the Canadian public pension system is relatively young. Immature pension schemes operating on a pay-as-you-go basis initially run surpluses, as few individuals are eligible to receive benefits in the early years of operation. Once the pension plan has been in place for enough years for the retired population to be eligible for full benefits, one gets a truer picture of whether promised benefit levels can be sustained by payroll taxes.

In Canada, expenditures on benefits were less than the pension contribution component of payroll taxes until about 1985. By the year 2000, benefit expenditures are projected to rise to a level about 70 percent higher than pension contributions, suggesting that the payroll tax rate will have to rise in the near future (Musgrave et al. 1987, p. 668). Our model sets the payroll tax rate at the level needed to pay for current benefits and maintain system budget balance on a cash-flow basis. Therefore, we simulate this projected rise in the payroll tax by letting the social security replacement rate, which was held constant in the previous simulations, rise gradually by 70 percent over the period 1985–2000, remaining constant thereafter.

The results of this simulation are given in the last column of table 8.5. The payroll tax rate rises to a peak of 9.1 percent in 2030, instead of 5.3 percent, making the level of the Canadian tax rate much closer to that of the United States. Note that this tax increase is slightly higher than 70 percent, since the increased tax rate does reduce labor supply somewhat. For the same reason, the levels of consumption taxation must be higher than in the baseline simulation, by about 1.2 percentage points in 2030 and thereafter.

The higher level of benefits in this simulation leads to a lower level of national saving as well. Since benefits as currently scheduled appear to require a considerable increase in payroll taxes, the benefit levels in our baseline simulations are much lower than those currently planned. Hence, the alternative simulation amounts to an increase in benefit levels relative to the baseline assumptions.

The simulated effect of this increase on national saving is considerable, depressing the saving rate by as much as 1.3 percentage points in 2030 and .8 percentage points in the long run. This effect is several times larger in magnitude than the increase in saving that we project for a gradual increase in the retirement age.

8.5 Conclusions

Our analysis indicates that demographic transitions are likely to have significant effects on rates of saving and taxation in both the United States and Canada. These two countries and their fiscal systems differ in several ways, which we have tried to incorporate into our analysis.

Canada's economy differs from that of the United States in being much smaller, relying more heavily on consumption taxes to finance public spending, and financing much of its public old-age pensions out of general revenues. Moreover, the relative immaturity of the pay-as-you-go part of Canada's pension scheme suggests that, even without a demographic transition, a considerable rise in payroll taxes may be required. Combined with the sharper demographic transition that is projected for Canada, these fiscal differences lead us to predict a later and more severe drop in the national saving rate in Canada, with potentially a much greater increase in the payroll tax as well.

As our real wage calculations indicate, one should not necessarily infer that lower national saving reduces welfare. Tax increases may be more than offset by rising real wages. Ultimate judgments about changes in welfare really require a fuller treatment of why these demographic transitions are occurring, in these two countries and in most other highly developed countries as well.

References

Auerbach, Alan J., and Laurence Kotlikoff. 1987. *Dynamic Fiscal Policy.* Cambridge: Cambridge University Press.

———. 1990. Demographics, Fiscal Policy, and U.S. Saving in the 1980s and Beyond. In *Tax Policy and the Economy,* ed. Lawrence H. Summers, vol. 4, 73–101. Cambridge: MIT Press.

Auerbach, Alan J., Laurence Kotlikoff, Robert P. Hagemann, and Giuseppe Nicoletti. 1989. The Economic Dynamics of an Aging Population: The Case of Four OECD Countries. *OECD Economic Studies* 12 (Spring):97–130.

Carroll, Christopher, and Lawrence Summers. 1987. Why Have Private Savings Rates in the United States and Canada Diverged? *Journal of Monetary Economics* 20 (September):249–79.

Musgrave, Richard, Peggy Musgrave, and Richard Bird. 1987. *Public Finance in Theory and Practice.* Canadian ed. Toronto: McGraw-Hill.

OECD. Various issues. *Revenue Statistics of OECD Members.*

9 Taxation and Housing Markets

James M. Poterba

The tax treatment of housing is a central issue of income tax design. The United States tax code, which allows homeowners to deduct mortgage interest and property taxes but does not tax their imputed rental income, provides a substantial subsidy to owner-occupied housing relative to other consumption goods. The Canadian tax code resembles the U.S. code in not taxing imputed income, but Canadian taxpayers cannot deduct mortgage interest or property tax payments. Both tax systems provide important tax relief on housing capital gains. Canadian households are not taxed on capital gains on owner-occupied housing, while U.S. households are eligible for a one-time $125,000 tax exemption.

This paper presents a framework for analyzing how the tax and economic changes of the last decade have affected households' marginal incentives to consume owner-occupied housing. Tax rules toward housing interact with other tax provisions such as the level of marginal tax rates, as well as with macroeconomic conditions such as inflation, to determine the net cost of owner occupation. Two aspects of the tax system are important in this regard. The first is the relative tax burden on housing in comparison with other portfolio assets. A high burden on housing capital will reduce housing consumption. The second is the relative tax burden on housing services and other consumption goods. High excise taxes on other goods will induce households to consume housing services.

The paper is divided into four sections. The first describes the basic tax

James M. Poterba is professor of economics at the Massachusetts Institute of Technology and a research associate of the National Bureau of Economic Research.

The author thanks Gary Engelhardt for exceptional research assistance, Frank Clayton, Jack Mintz, John Whalley, and Thomas Wilson for very helpful comments, and the National Science Foundation, the John M. Olin Foundation, and the Alfred P. Sloan Foundation for research support.

rules that affect owner-occupied housing investment in Canada and the United States. In Canada, the tax system has no direct effect on the user cost of home ownership for many households. Rather, its effects operate through the burdens placed on other assets and other goods. The second section presents background data on the housing markets in the two nations. Broad comparisons of the home ownership rate and the size of the housing capital stock are useful, because they shed light on the potential effects of the different tax rules. While there is some evidence that the United States is more housing-capital-intensive than Canada, the home ownership rates in the two nations are similar. The third section outlines a simple asset-market model of housing investment and consumption, and discusses recent evidence on the applicability of this model to the housing market. The fourth section calibrates this model using time series data for each country, and contrasts the resulting parameters with those from earlier studies of the United States. The fifth section uses this model to estimate how housing prices and the demand for owner-occupied housing would respond to the tax and interest rate changes of the last decade, assuming all other factors were held constant. The concluding section notes several important limitations of the simple asset-price model and suggests extensions that could address these problems.

9.1   The Tax Treatment of Housing: Canada and the United States

This section begins with a brief summary of the user-cost approach to measuring housing costs, and then describes the principal tax provisions in both nations that affect user costs. It concludes by noting other features of the policy environment, principally financial policies, that affect the cost of housing.

9.1.1   The User Cost of Home Ownership: Canada

The user cost of home ownership measures the marginal cost of an incremental unit of owner-occupied housing. It reflects both cash outlays within the year and the foregone return on the owner's equity. The most convenient assumption for computing the user cost is that property taxes (τ_p), physical decay (δ), and the cost of home maintenance (m) are all constant fractions of house value. In addition, all households are assumed to borrow and lend at a pretax interest rate i, to expect house price appreciation at rate π_e, and to require a risk premium of α to invest in housing. The real purchase price per unit of owner-occupied housing is set equal to P_o.

A central issue in modeling the user cost for Canadian households involves the tax treatment of returns on alternative assets. These assets determine the opportunity cost of investing funds in housing capital. Given the widespread availability of Registered Retirement Saving Plans (RRSPs) and other tax-deferred saving vehicles, the benchmark assumption is that returns on other assets are untaxed. Investors' after-tax returns equal their before-tax returns.

The user cost of owner-occupied housing for a Canadian household is therefore

$$(1) \qquad c_{o,Can} = [i + \tau_p + \delta + \alpha + m - \pi_e]P_o.$$

By subtracting expected house price inflation from the nominal interest cost, this expression recognizes that housing capital gains are untaxed.

Households with constraints on other tax-deferred saving face a different user cost. During 1974–85, they also derived additional housing incentives from a subsidized saving plan, the Registered Homeownership Saving Program (RHSP), that effectively reduced the price of home purchase for first-time home buyers. This program enabled first-time buyers to contribute $1000 per year, up to a maximum of $10,000, to an account for use in financing home purchase. For households with unused capacity to contribute to other tax-deferred saving accounts, the RHSP program did not affect the user cost of housing. For households facing constraints on other tax-deferred contributions, however, the RHSP did lower the cost of housing. This program transformed one dollar of after-tax income into more than one dollar, provided the funds were used for house purchase.

To evaluate the subsidy, consider a two-person household planning to purchase a home in k years, that contributed $2,000 ($1,000 per household member) to the RHSP each year. The total value of the household's RHSP account k periods hence would be

$$(2) \qquad V_{RHSP} = 2000*[(1 + i)^k + (1 + i)^{k-1} + \ldots + 1].$$

By comparison, if these funds had been invested in taxable instruments, their value in k periods would have been

$$(3) \qquad V_{TAX} = 2000*(1 - \theta)*[(1 + i(1 - \theta))^k + (1 + i(1 - \theta))^{k-1} + \ldots + 1].$$

Table 9.1 illustrates the magnitude of V_{RHSP} and V_{TAX} for several values of the marginal tax rate, θ, and the number of years until planned house purchase. For constrained households, the subsidy is worth several thousand dollars, largely because RHSP contributions are made with before-tax dollars.

The entries in the third row of each panel in table 9.1 suggest that for taxpayers facing constraints on their tax-deferred saving contributions, the RHSP changes the effective user cost by several percentage points for first-time buyers, especially late in the subsidy program when buyers could have accumulated for as long as ten years.[1] For a household participating in the program and purchasing a median-priced house in 1980, the subsidy would have amounted to 7–9 percent of the house value.

1. The RHSP program, while created to encourage home ownership, could have caused some households to *defer* first-time buying, in order to take greater advantage of the RHSP subsidy. Engelhardt (1990) presents a more complete discussion of RHSPs and their effects.

Table 9.1   Incremental Buying Power of Canadian RHSP Accounts

	Number of Years until House Purchase			
	3	5	7	9
$i = 10\%$				
V_{RHSP}[a]	9.3	15.4	22.9	31.9
$\Delta = V_{RHSP} - V_{TAX}$[a]	3.1	5.5	8.7	12.8
Δ/Median House Price	4.8%	8.4%	13.4%	19.6%
$i = 7\%$				
V_{RHSP}[a]	8.9	14.3	20.5	27.6
$\Delta = V_{RHSP} - V_{TAX}$[a]	2.9	4.9	7.3	10.3
Δ/Median House Price	4.5%	7.5%	11.2%	15.8%

[a]Thousands of dollars.

Note: Calculations assume a nominal interest rate of 10% (upper panel) or 7% (lower panel), a marginal federal tax rate of 21% (corresponding to the 1981 rate for a couple with no children, earning the average taxable income, $16,254), and a provincial tax rate of 44%, for a total marginal tax rate of 30.7%. The household is assumed to be constrained in making further contributions to other tax-deferred saving vehicles; otherwise the RHSP is worthless.

For a first-time buyer participating in the RHSP, for whom this program has value, the effective price of a house of size H (costing P_o^*H) is $\mu = [P_o^*H - (V_{RHSP} - V_{TAX})]/P_o^*H$. Since households for whom RHSPs are valuable have also exhausted their tax-exempt investment options, they face an opportunity cost of $(1 - \theta)i$ on the equity invested in a home. For these households, the user cost is:

$$(4) \quad c_{o,Can} = [i\{(1 - \beta)(1 - \theta) + \beta\} + \tau_p + \delta + \alpha + m - \pi_e]P_o\mu,$$

where β is the loan-to-value ratio for the house. Note that the after-tax cost of mortgage borrowing is still i.

9.1.2   The User Cost of Home Ownership: United States

The key distinction between the U.S. and Canadian tax rules is that U.S. homeowners *who itemize their deductions* can deduct property taxes and mortgage interest from their taxable income. For an itemizing homeowner, the user cost is therefore

$$(5) \quad c_{o,US} = [(1 - \theta)(i + \tau_p) + \delta + \alpha + m - \pi_e]P_o.$$

The loan-to-value ratio is irrelevant, because the household can deduct interest payments, and would be taxable on interest or dividend receipts.

The average cost of home ownership can differ significantly from the marginal cost for some households who forego the standard deduction that they would receive if they did not itemize. For taxpayers who would not have itemized without the property tax and mortgage interest deduction, but do itemize because of these deductions, the tax saving from home ownership is $\theta * (\tau_p +$

Table 9.2   **Itemization Status of U.S. Homeowners, 1985**

	Millions
Number of Homeowners	56.2
Number of Homeowners with Mortgages	32.2 (57.3%)
Number of Tax Returns with Mortgage Deducation	28.1 (50.0%)
Number of Tax Returns with Real Estate Tax Deduction	32.1 (57.1%)

Sources: Homeowner information is from Bureau of the Census, *Housing in America, 1985–86,*
Current Housing Report H-121, no. 19. Tax information is drawn from *1985 Statistics of Income:*
Individual Income Tax Returns.

$i*\beta)*P_o*H - S$, where H is the quantity of housing and S is the household's
standard deduction. For homeowners who do not itemize even with their
housing-related deductions, the marginal user cost is

$$(6) \quad c_{o,US}' = [\{(1 - \beta)(1 - \theta) + \beta\} i + \tau_p + \delta + \alpha + m - \pi_e]P_o.$$

This expression is the same as the user cost for Canadian households with
constraints on tax-exempt saving, but it does not include the RHSP term.

Table 9.2 presents evidence on the tax status of U.S. homeowners in 1985,
prior to the Tax Reform Act, which reduced the probability that homeowners
would choose to itemize. The number of tax returns with itemized property
tax deductions was only 57% of the total number of owner-occupied properties. More than 40% of the homeowning population therefore faced the non-
itemizer user cost for housing. In part, the surprisingly small share of homeowners who itemized reflects the fact that only 57.3% of homeowners in 1985
had mortgages. There is a very high rate of home ownership among elderly
households, many of whom have paid off their mortgages.

9.1.3   User Cost Comparisons, 1980–1989

Table 9.3 reports user costs of home ownership for U.S. and Canadian
households at several points in the income distribution, in 1980, 1985, and
1989. The calculations consider families with adjusted gross incomes of
$25,000, $50,000, and $250,000, and are based on actual interest rates and
inflationary expectations (calculated as an average of actual inflation values
for the five prior years). There are differences in the observed long-term interest rates in the two nations, and these are partly reflected in the user-cost
calculations. The user costs assume the same values of depreciation and maintenance costs and the same risk premium for housing investment in Canada
and the United States. Marginal tax rates in each case combine federal and
state or provincial marginal tax rates.[2] The reported user costs are *percentages
of price;* that is, they are the user costs in earlier equations divided by P_o.

---

2. The Canadian calculations assume that each household faces Ontario provincial taxes, as
well as federal income tax. The U.S. calculations assume a 6% state income tax on the same base
as the federal tax.

Table 9.3   **Homeowner User Costs, United States and Canada, 1980–1989**

	1980		1985		1989	
	Canada	U.S.	Canada	U.S.	Canada	U.S.
AGI = $25,000[a]	.147	.103	.133	.131	.167	.140
AGI = $50,000	.147	.076	.133	.116	.167	.125
AGI = $250,000[b]	.147/.094	.039	.133/.098	.088	.167/.134	.119
Background Parameters						
Marginal Tax Rates						
AGI = $25,000	30	23	28	21	26	20
AGI = $50,000	47	41	37	32	40	32
AGI = $250,000	62	6	50	53	44	37
Mortgage Rate	14.3	12.7	11.7	11.6	12.2	10.1
Expected Inflation	8.7	8.9	7.5	5.5	4.6	3.6

Note: AGIs are in 1989 U.S. dollars.
[a]For a U.S. homeowner in the AGI = $25,000 category who does not itemize, the user costs are .119, .145, and .152 in 1980, 1985, and 1989 respectively. All other U.S. entries assume that the homeowner itemizes and therefore claims the mortgage interest and property tax deductions.
[b]The two entries for Canada correspond to a taxpayer who is not, and who is, taxed on marginal portfolio investments. The calculations assume no RHSP value to the household.

The calculations in table 9.3 reflect the various important changes in the U.S. and Canadian tax environment during the last decade.[3] In the United States, the Economic Recovery Tax Act of 1981 and the Tax Reform Act of 1986 lowered personal income tax rates. With a constant pretax interest rate at which households borrow and lend, a lowered personal income tax rate *raises* the after-tax cost of home ownership. In 1980, the weighted-average marginal federal tax rate on mortgage interest deductions was 32%. By 1984, when the rate reductions of 1981 had taken full effect, this average tax rate was 28%. Although data on the post-1986 average are not yet available, it will surely be lower than that for previous years.

The 1986 reform also reduced the fraction of the nonhomeowning population that would itemize. For a joint filer, the standard deduction's rise from $3,670 to $5,000 exerted a negative effect on the incentive to own for households in lower and middle income brackets.

3. None of the reported calculations depend on the household's loan-to-value ratio. For some households, however, this can be a central parameter in the user cost, because there are different after-tax costs to borrowing and lending. Some high-income Canadian households face this situation. For the United States, the average loan-to-value ratio for owner-occupied real estate has varied between 36% (1978) and 50% (1989). Surveys by Chicago Title Insurance Company suggest an average down payment as a fraction of sales price of 24% in 1988, with smaller down payments (15%) by first-time buyers. Analogous data on loan-to-value ratios are not available for Canada. Data from the Canadian Bankers' Association indicate that 61% of all new mortgages by major Canadian chartered banks involve down payments of 25% or more. The debt-to-value ratio is higher (the median is more than 90%) for loans under the National Housing Act.

The largest effects of the 1986 reform were at high tax rates. For a household with income of $250,000 and the average deductions for this group, the tax reform lowered the federal marginal tax rate from 50% to 33%, raising the user cost (at 1985 interest rates) by 2.3 percentage points when the nominal mortgage rate is 11.7% and the property tax rate is 2%. The reform would have had to reduce interest rates by nearly three hundred basis points to offset this change in the value of the tax deduction. The effect of rate reductions on home ownership incentives for those in lower income brackets is much smaller, since the decline in tax rates in the 1986 reform was less pronounced. For the household with AGI of $25,000 in 1989, the tax reform lowered the federal marginal tax rate from 16% to 15% and raised the user cost (in the benchmark case) slightly. Some middle-income households actually experienced increases in marginal tax rates as a result of the 1986 reform (see Hausman and Poterba 1987). For those households, the user cost may even have declined.

Table 9.3 shows that the changes in marginal tax rates in Canada during the last decade are less pronounced than those in the United States. A household with an adjusted gross income of $50,000, for example, experienced a marginal tax rate decline from 47% to 40% during the 1980s. The substantial rise in real interest rates during the decade, however, is the principal factor influencing user costs in Canada.[4] Real interest rate movements alter the user cost by more in Canada than in the United States, because there is no tax wedge to blunt their effects. For most households, user costs at the end of the decade are estimated to be between two and three hundred basis points above their level at the beginning of the decade.

One implication of the calculations in table 9.3 is that there is less cross-sectional variation in housing user costs in Canada than in the United States. This is because marginal tax rates play a role in determining the user cost in the United States. In addition, most of the Canadian entries in table 9.3 do not reflect the sort of variation that results from itemization status in the United States. In 1980, for example, an itemizing homeowner faced a marginal user cost of .103, while a first-time buyer with AGI of $25,000 who did not itemize faced a marginal user cost of .119. This is more than three times the level of the user cost facing high-tax-rate itemizing households.

An important limitation of the calculations in table 9.3 is their partial-equilibrium nature. The 1981 and 1986 tax reforms in the United States changed the tax treatment of housing, as well as of many other assets. In particular, the 1986 reform raised the tax burden on corporate assets while bringing tax burdens on equipment, structures, and other assets into closer alignment. If tax rates on housing and all other assets rise and capital is incompletely mobile internationally, so that changes in the U.S. system affect after-tax returns to U.S. investors, then a tax change of this type should reduce

---

4. For some households, the changes in marginal rates could have influenced user costs, but this is not the benchmark case we consider.

real after-tax interest rates. The amount of such a decline is crucial for calibrating the actual changes in housing user costs. In the case of the United States and Canada, differences in the tax treatment of *nonhousing* assets (e.g., the more generous treatment of capital gains in Canada) may be a central factor in determining the tax system's net subsidy to housing. For the benchmark households my analysis focuses on, virtually all of the effects of the Canadian tax code must enter through the required return on housing assets.

General-equilibrium simulations of the type performed by Hendershott (1987) or Berkovec and Fullerton (1989) are needed to aggregate the different tax changes on various assets into the single summary measure—the change in the interest rate—through which other aspects of tax reform affect the housing market. Such models can provide insight into the importance of differences in the taxation of nonhousing assets to the net tax subsidy to housing. They are also the only practical way to handle changes in the indirect tax burdens on nonhousing goods, such as the Canadian Goods and Services Tax, which took effect in early 1991.

9.1.4   Rental User Costs and Tenure Choice

For a homeowner with a particular pattern of income and deductions and facing a given tax rate, it is straightforward to compute the user cost of owning a home. A similar statement applies to the user cost of a rental property. In the rental context, the disparities across potential landlords are more controversial, however, because the law of one price implies that the rental housing market must clear at some real rent, and it is not clear which landlord is the marginal supplier of rental property. This conceptual difficulty confounds studies of how tax reforms affect the tenure-choice incentives of different households, as well as tests of how such reforms affect real rent levels. Gravelle (1987) and Poterba (1990) discuss these issues in more detail.

A complete model of taxation and housing markets, incorporating the tax treatment of rental housing and with endogenous tenure choice, is beyond the current modeling exercise. The central role of the tax treatment of rental housing has been noted by Clayton (1974) for Canada and by Titman (1982) for the United States. Fallis and Smith (1989) discuss the effects of the recent Canadian changes with respect to rental markets and owner-occupants; Poterba (1990) provides a similar treatment for the United States.

9.2   Housing in Perspective: U.S.-Canadian Comparisons

In standard models of housing demand, the differences in the tax treatment of owner-occupied housing in the United States and Canada should lead to different patterns of housing wealth, home ownership, and housing investment. This section presents simple summary statistics on each of these issues.

Table 9.4 shows the share of owner-occupied capital in the net national capital stock, and as a fraction of gross domestic product, for both the United

Table 9.4   **Residential Capital Intensity, Canada and the United States, 1960–1989**

Year	Canada	U.S.
	Owner-Occupied Capital/Total Capital[a]	
1961	.178	.264
1970	.204	.245
1980	.228	.263
1989	.271	.270
	Owner-Occupied Capital/GDP	
1961	.550	.598
1970	.573	.547
1980	.686	.708
1989	.733	.632
	Owner-Occupied Capital/Residential Capital	
1961	.820	.719
1970	.808	.715
1980	.827	.710
1989	.830	.723

Sources: Board of Governors of the Federal Reserve System, *Balance Sheets for the U.S. Economy, 1945–89;* Statistics Canada, Flow of Funds Division, *Canadian National Balance Sheets, 1961–84, 1964–89.*

[a]The total capital stock is the sum of plants and equipment, residential capital, consumer durables, and inventories.

States and Canada. The data suggest that the United States has traditionally been a more residential-capital-intensive nation than Canada. In the early 1960s, more than one-quarter of the U.S. capital stock was owner-occupied housing, while the analogous fraction for Canada was less than one-fifth. There has been little change, however, in the residential share of the U.S. capital stock during the last three decades, while the Canadian residential capital stock has expanded significantly relative to other components of capital. At the end of 1989, the Canadian share was 27.1%, essentially the same as the U.S. value.

The center panel of table 9.4 shows owner-occupied residential capital as a share of current GDP. Again, the data suggest a higher ratio for the United States than for Canada in the 1960s, but with relatively rapid convergence. The Canadian owner-occupied capital/GDP ratio was .733 in 1989, above the U.S. value of .632. For the United States, this ratio declined from over 70% at the beginning of the 1980s, as real house prices fell.

The bottom panel of table 9.4 shows the share of total residential capital accounted for by owner-occupied housing. In the United States, this fraction is slightly greater than 70%, while in Canada, it exceeds 80%. While these figures are not necessarily inconsistent with the differential tax treatment of owners in the two nations, since rental housing also receives somewhat different treatment, it is not prima facie support for the view that the more generous tax treatment of homeowners in the U.S. has expanded the stock of owner-occupied housing.

To evaluate the influence of tax policy on home ownership, table 9.5 reports the rates of home ownership, both in aggregate and for particular age groups, in the United States and Canada during the last two decades. The standard claim that the U.S. tax code encourages home ownership receives some support in these data, since the U.S. home ownership rate exceeds that of Canada in each year. At young ages, however, the pattern reverses in the 1980s. At the beginning of the 1970s, the home ownership rate for persons under age 35 was 6 percentage points higher in the United States than in Canada. The combination of high house prices and interest rates in the United States, and the RHSP program in Canada, reversed this pattern by 1980. In that year, the home ownership rate for persons under age 35 was 9 percentage points higher in Canada than in the United States. The difference has narrowed since then, but the home ownership rate for young households is still higher in Canada than in the United States. For older households, the higher home ownership rate persists in the United States throughout the time period.

These data are somewhat difficult to reconcile with more standard analyses of the housing subsidy. If the U.S. tax system encourages home ownership as much (relatively) as the user costs suggest, then one would expect higher home ownership rates in the United States than in Canada. The failure of the data to confirm this prediction suggests an important need for further modeling of the housing markets in both countries.

Figures 9.1 through 9.3 present data on the time-series pattern of three macroeconomic features of the housing market in each nation. Figure 9.1 shows

Table 9.5   **Age-Specific Home Ownership Rates, Canada and the United States, 1973–1988**

Age Group	1970		1980		1986	
	Canada	U.S.	Canada	U.S.	Canada	U.S.[a]
<35	35.9%	41.6%	56.3%	47.5%	42.0%	39.2%
35–64	70.6	71.8	73.7	78.4	72.7	73.5
>65	67.7	68.1	63.0	74.1	64.0	75.1
Total	60.3	63.3	62.1	68.0	62.1	64.0

Sources: U.S.: 1970 Census, 1980 and 1987 Annual Housing Survey. Canada: Unpublished data provided by Statistics Canada.

[a]1986 U.S. entries correspond to March 1987.

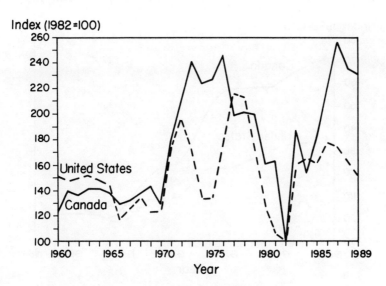

Fig. 9.1   Indices of single-unit housing starts, 1960–89

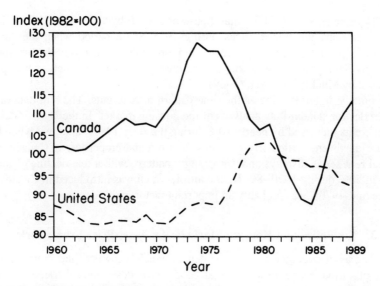

Fig. 9.2   Indices of real house prices, 1960–89

the time path of single-family housing starts in the United States and Canada. The relatively weak performance of the U.S. market during the late 1980s is not matched by a slump in Canadian building.

Figure 9.2 plots data on real single-family house prices and suggests that tax factors may have affected house prices in the United States. Canadian house prices did not increase during the late 1970s. While U.S. prices rose by

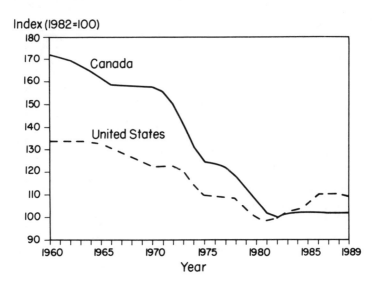

Fig. 9.3   Indices of real rents, 1960–89

18% during 1975–80, Canadian house prices *fell* by 14%. The 35% decline in real Canadian house prices during 1975–85, a period when the "baby boom" generation was entering its home-buying years, raises doubts about purely demographic explanations for house price changes, such as that proposed by Mankiw and Weil (1989).

Finally, figure 9.3 shows the time pattern of real rents. The rent data raise puzzles for standard tax analyses of the housing market. In the United States, real rents increased by nearly 10% during the early 1980s, at a time when tax subsidies were particularly generous toward rental properties. In Canada, the real rent series displays an even stranger pattern, with a real decline of more than 50% during 1970–89. Rent control, which was introduced in Canada in the mid-1970s, was probably an important factor in this decline.

9.3   Tax Policy and Housing Markets: An Asset-Price Framework

The asset-price approach to incidence, which recognizes the short-run fixity of various categories of capital goods, provides a natural framework for analyzing how taxation affects the owner-occupied housing market. This approach, applied by Summers (1981) and Poterba (1984) among others, recognizes that both the market for housing services and the market for the flow of new construction must simultaneously clear.

If $H(t)$ denotes the total stock of housing at time t, and the service flow of housing services is proportional to the stock of existing units, then there is a market-clearing rental rate $R(H(t))$, $R' < 0$, at which all rental units will be held. In equilibrium, this rental rate must equal the user cost of owner-occupied housing services:

$$(7) \qquad\qquad R(H(t)) = c_o(t).$$

For given values of the interest rate, tax parameters, depreciation, and maintenance, this equation can be satisfied either through variation in the real price of houses or through movements in expected rates of price appreciation. In the Canadian context, for example, this equation can be solved to find the expected real appreciation rate as a function of the current housing stock and current house price:

$$
\begin{aligned}
(8) \qquad E[P_o(t + 1) - P_o(t)] = &[(1 - \theta) i + \delta + m + \alpha \\
&+ \tau_p - \pi_e]P_o(t) - R(H(t)).
\end{aligned}
$$

One implication of this equation is that, assuming households have rational expectations, the value of real house prices at t can be written as a discounted integral of future housing service flows, net of depreciation and maintenance costs. The discount rate is the after-tax borrowing rate plus the risk premium, α:

$$(9) \qquad P_o(t) = \int_o^\infty R(H(t + s)) \, e^{-[(1 - \theta)i + \alpha + \delta + \tau p + m - \pi]s} ds.$$

The flow of new construction is determined by the relative price of houses; builders compare this price with the cost of new construction and choose the level of building to undertake. This can be represented as an investment supply curve,

$$(10) \qquad\qquad I(t) = \dot{H}(t) + \delta H(t) = \xi(P_o(t)),$$

where $H(t)$ denotes net investment in owner-occupied housing. A steady state obtains when net investment is zero.[5]

This framework can be used, as in Poterba (1984), to study how various tax reforms should affect house prices and the level of housing investment. For example, consider a decline in the marginal tax rate for the housing consumer. In this case housing demand falls, and the steady-state housing stock contracts. There is a short-run decline in house prices followed by a period of gradual return to the steady state. Given the model's saddle-point stability property, there is a *unique* house price at the time of the shock that will lead to the new steady state. The adjustment dynamics following such a policy shock are shown in Figure 9.4. Finding this price decrease is the objective of section 9.5. Before considering such experiments, however, the next section

---

5. In a growing economy, with population growth at rate n and productivity at rate g, the real housing capital stock will experience steady-state growth at rate $n + \Delta g$, where Δ is the income elasticity of housing demand.

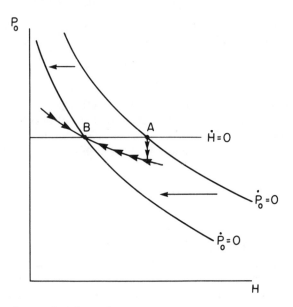

Fig. 9.4   Housing market dynamics

reports estimates of the investment-supply functions for the United States and Canada.

9.4   Calibrating the Housing Investment Function

To evaluate the housing market effects of various policies using the foregoing asset-price framework, it is necessary to calibrate the stock-demand equation for housing services, as well as the flow-supply equation for new construction. There are many estimates, based on household-level data, of housing demand; most use U.S. data, but there is some confirmatory evidence for Canada as well. Previous research provides less guidance on the investment-supply equation. After summarizing prior work on housing demand, this section reports new estimates of housing supply equations for Canada and the United States.

9.4.1   Housing Demand Elasticities

The voluminous literature on the demand for owner-occupied housing, based largely on household data for the United States and summarized in Rosen (1985) and Olsen (1987), suggests price elasticities with respect to the user cost of approximately −1.0. Similar estimates do not appear to be available for Canada; therefore, a value of −1.0 has been assumed for Canada as well.

In calibrating the asset-price model, I assume a price elasticity of −1.0 and specify a constant-elasticity housing demand function:

(11) $H(t) = c_o(t)^\gamma.$

9.4.2 The Flow Supply of New Construction

The second component of the housing market model sketched above is a flow supply of new construction. This relates the level of new construction activity to the relative price of single-family houses. The relative house price is the summary statistic for all of the demand-side factors that affect the housing market.

To facilitate comparisons of the United States and Canada, a very simple investment-supply equation is used for both nations:

(12) $(I_t/GNP_t) = \beta_o + \beta_1 * (P_{o,t}/P_{gnp,t}) + \varepsilon_t.$

I_t is the level of new single-family housing investment in each nation, and the dependent variable is this investment as a share of GNP, to reflect the allocation of resources between house building and other activities. The independent variable is the price of owner-occupied houses, in each case excluding the value of land, relative to the GNP deflator. The latter is a proxy for the costs of construction. Because builders may be choosing between constructing new houses and other types of building, in some cases this specification is augmented with a variable for the real price of nonresidential structures. This specification ignores many factors (e.g., the presence of credit constraints) that have typically been included in models of single-family housing investment. It reflects the strict interpretation of the asset-price model. Earlier work (Poterba 1984) included additional variables for the United States, and there should be future work to apply the same approach to Canadian data.

Data on house prices are available beginning with 1969 for both Canada and the United States. Prior to 1976, the Canadian index is based on a simple average of new-house prices (excluding land)in six cities. After 1976, the data series is more comprehensive. In the United States, the data series on house prices is the result of a hedonic procedure for correcting quality change; the series reports the price of a constant-quality house, of the type constructed in 1982, in each quarter since 1969. For the price of nonresidential structures, we used the GNP deflator for these structures.

The results of estimating these equations are reported in Table 9.6.[6] The first column for each nation presents ordinary least squares estimates of equation (12). For both nations, there is a positive relationship between the level of real house prices and the construction of single-family houses. The link appears statistically and substantively more significant in Canada than in the United States. The last two columns for each nation report alternative specifications of the investment function. Inclusion of the alternative price variable,

---

6. Treating the national housing market as one, in which builders choose to supply new structures based on a single price, neglects the very important regional variation in housing markets. In principle, an investment-supply equation like the one I estimate for the nation could also be estimated for specific regions.

Table 9.6   Housing Investment Supply Equations, United States and Canada

Estimation Method	United States			Canada		
	OLS	OLS	IV	OLS	OLS	IV
Constant	1.73	6.40	7.13	−1.06	5.92	6.06
	(1.20)	(1.92)	(2.06)	(0.90)	(1.92)	(2.52)
Real house price	0.53	2.00	1.13	2.38	3.54	3.15
	(1.22)	(1.26)	(2.52)	(0.78)	(0.65)	(0.82)
Real price of		−6.42	−6.28		−8.44	−8.16
nonresidential		(2.13)	(2.58)		(2.21)	(2.40)
structures						
Autoregressive	.95	.95	.94	.84	.75	.77
parameter	(.04)	(.04)	(.05)	(.06)	(.08)	(.09)
R^2	.90	.91	.91	.88	.90	.90

Note: Equations for both countries are estimated for the 1969:1–1989:4 sample period. Standard errors are shown in parentheses. See text for further data description. The instrumental variables estimates (column 3) treat the contemporaneous real house price as endogenous and use lagged values of the house price as instruments.

the nonresidential structures deflator, strengthens the positive effect of real house prices in both nations. The last column in each set of estimates recognizes the potential endogeneity of real house prices in the investment model. Since shocks to the investment function affect the growth of the housing stock, they affect the future trajectory of real rents and hence current house prices. Positive innovations in the supply function reduce real house prices, and vice versa. To address this possibility, the last column in each case uses lagged values of the real house price as instruments for the actual house price, following Fair's (1970) procedure. This does not significantly affect the estimated coefficients for either country.

The results are broadly supportive of a positive link between investment and real house prices. In the United States, a 10% increase in real house prices would raise housing investment by between .1% and .2% of GNP, or approximately seven billion 1989 dollars. For Canada, the elasticity is even larger; a similar-sized relative house price move would lead to an increase of .3% of GNP in single-family housing investment, or nearly a two-billion-dollar increase (in 1989 Canadian dollars).

The investment supply equations reported here are not fully articulated investment equations for either nation. Nevertheless, they provide a foundation for calibrating the asset-price model of the last section and for estimating how changes in tax policy might affect house prices.

9.5   Policy Experiments in the Asset-Price Framework

The estimated investment-supply equations can be linked with demand elasticities from the literature to assess how various tax and macroeconomic changes during the last decade would affect the housing market in the simple asset-price framework. To impose the condition that the steady-state house price is constant in the simulations, the investment equations are respecified in the form

(13) $$I/H = \beta_0 + \beta_1 * P_o,$$

by multiplying through by the average value of GNP/H, approximately 1.6 in both the United States and Canada. In steady state, a real house price of 1 must call forth the level of replacement investment plus the level needed to accommodate economic growth. Housing demand growth of 2% per year is assumed, implying that $I/H = .014 + .02 = .034$ (where .014 is the depreciation rate) in steady state. This requirement, along with the modified value of β_1 from the foregoing equations, is used to find the respecified investment functions:

(14a) $$(I/H)_{Can} = -.014 + .048 * P_o \quad (I/H)_{US}$$

(14b) $$= .010 + .024 * P_o.$$

The investment equations suggest that housing investment responds more quickly to a given price change in Canada than in the United States. Smaller price increases are thus implied in response to favorable policy shocks in Canada.

Table 9.7 reports simulation results for housing market responses to three sets of policy shocks: a shift in the United States from 1980 or 1985 tax rates to 1989 values, holding constant all macroeconomic factors; a shift in the United States from 1980 or 1985 inflation rates to 1989 values, holding the real interest rate and tax parameters constant; and an increase in the Canadian retail sales tax by 5 percentage points on all nonhousing goods. The results focus on the user-cost effects for a homeowner with an AGI of $50,000; different calculations would obtain for the other example households considered above.

Although each of the first two reforms has a substantial effect on the U.S. housing market, neither affects the Canadian market because neither marginal tax rates nor the inflation rate enter the benchmark user cost calculation. The first panel of table 9.7 shows the effects of the tax rate changes in the United States. The long-run reduction in housing demand from falling marginal tax rates is calculated at 17.1% since 1980. This figure reflects the large change in marginal rates in the United States and the important interaction between marginal rates and housing user costs because interest payments are tax-deductible.

The second panel of table 9.7 considers the effects of inflation shocks. The U.S. user cost of home ownership is sensitive to the inflation rate, while the Canadian user cost is not, at least for households that are not taxed on marginal portfolio investments. Assuming that expected inflation in the United

Table 9.7   Housing Market Reactions to Tax and Economic Changes

	1980	1985
Shift to 1989 Tax Rates (U.S.)		
Base Case Tax Rate	41	32
Hypothetical Tax Rate	32	32
Base Case User Cost	.076	.116
Hypothetical User Cost	.089	.116
Long-run Housing Demand	−.171	0
Short-run House Price Change	−.128	0
Shift to 1989 Inflation Rate (U.S.)		
Base Case Inflation Rate	.089	.055
Hypothetical Inflation Rate	.036	.036
Base Case User Cost	.076	.116
Hypothetical User Cost	.099	.122
Long-run Housing Demand	−.303	−.050
Short-run House Price Change	−.237	−.038
Shift to Higher Retail Sales Tax (Canada)		
Base Case User Cost	.147	.133
Hypothetical User Cost	.140	.126
Long-run Housing Demand	+.050	+.050
Short-run House Price Change	+.032	+.032

Note: Estimates are based on change in user costs for households with 1989 AGI of $50,000; the underlying user costs are reported in table 9.3. The simulation algorithm employs the investment-supply models in equation (14) and finds the perfect-foresight price change associated with each policy.

States declined by more than 5% between 1980 and 1989, and holding other factors fixed, the asset-price model suggests that the demand for owner-occupied housing by the stylized person in table 9.7 should have been reduced by nearly 30 percent.

The final policy experiment, shown in the bottom panel of table 9.7, is confined to Canada. This is an increase of 5 percentage points in the retail sales tax on all goods except housing services. Assume that the revenue effects of the tax are offset with lump-sum transfers. This policy raises the demand for housing by 5% in the long run, and in the short run it increases the demand for housing by 3.2%. By comparison, a similar-sized shock to long-run housing demand would raise U.S. house prices by 3.8%, because of the lower elasticity of housing supply.

9.6 Conclusions

This paper has only begun to exploit the rich research opportunities for tax economists presented by the U.S. and Canadian housing markets. Although the nations are similar in many ways, the tax treatment of both housing and nonhousing assets varies substantially, and the timing of tax changes toward rental and owner-occupied housing differs between nations. A set of natural experiments is thus provided for assessing whether housing demand is sensitive to tax parameters, how user costs affect tenure choice, and how macroeconomic factors operate through disparate tax codes to affect the housing market.

Future research could focus on how the RHSP program has affected the housing market in Canada, how the differential tax subsidies to rental properties have affected rents, and how the divergent patterns of real price and real rent movements in the two countries are related to tax considerations. The findings should provide substantial input for calibrating more complete general-equilibrium models that endogenize tenure choice, as well as the quantity of housing consumed (see Goulder and Summers 1989).

Another research priority should be the modeling of housing markets at a more disaggregate level. My analysis focuses on the aggregate level of housing investment, neglecting the important variation across metropolitan housing markets. One possible topic for case-study analysis is: How does the housing market in a pair of similar U.S. and Canadian cities compare? Regional variation in income growth, tax rates, and other factors should also prove useful in studying more general questions of housing market dynamics.

References

Berkovec, James, and Don Fullerton. 1989. The General Equilibrium Effects of Inflation on Housing Consumption and Investment. *American Economic Review* 79: 277–82.

Clayton, Frank A. 1974. Income Taxes and Subsidies to Owners and Renters: A Comparison of U.S. and Canadian Experience. *Canadian Tax Journal* 22 (May/June): 295–305.

Engelhardt, Gary. 1990. House Prices and the Saving Behavior of Young Renters: Evidence from the RHOSP Program. MIT. Manuscript.

Fair, Ray C. 1970. The Estimation of Simultaneous Equation Models with Lagged Endogenous Variables and First Order Serially Correlated Errors. *Econometrica* 38:507–46.

Fallis, George, and Lawrence Smith. 1989. Tax Reform and Residential Real Estate. In *The Economic Impacts of Tax Reform,* ed. Jack Mintz and John Whalley. Toronto: Canadian Tax Foundation.

Goulder, Lawrence H., and Lawrence H. Summers. 1989. Tax Policy, Asset Prices, and Growth: A General Equilibrium Analysis. *Journal of Public Economics* 38:265–96.

Gravelle, Jane G. 1987. U.S. Tax Policy and Rental Housing: An Economic Analysis. Congressional Research Service Report no. 85–208E. Washington, D.C.

Hausman, Jerry A., and James M. Poterba. 1987. Household Behavior and the Tax Reform Act of 1986. *Journal of Economic Perspectives* 1: 101–19.

Hendershott, Patric H. 1987. Tax Changes and Capital Allocation in the 1980s. In *The Effects of Taxation on Capital Formation,* ed. M. Feldstein. Chicago: University of Chicago Press.

Mankiw, N. Gregory, and David Weil. 1989. The Baby Boom, the Baby Bust, and the Housing Market. *Regional Science and Urban Economics* 19:235–58.

Olsen, Edgar O. 1987. The Demand and Supply of Housing Service: A Critical Survey of the Empirical Literature. In *Handbook of Regional and Urban Economics* ed. Edwin S. Mills, vol. 2. Amsterdam: North Holland.

Poterba, James M. 1984. Tax Subsidies to Owner Occupied Housing: An Asset Price Approach. *Quarterly Journal of Economics* 99: 729–52.

———. 1990. Taxation and Housing Markets: Preliminary Evidence on the Effects of the Tax Reform Act of 1986. In *The Effects of the Tax Reform Act of 1986,* ed. Joel Slemrod. Cambridge: MIT Press.

Rosen, Harvey S. 1985. Housing Subsidies: Effects on Housing Decisions, Efficiency, and Equity. In *Handbook of Public Economics,* ed. M. Feldstein and A. Auerbach, vol. 1, 375–420. Amsterdam: North Holland.

Summers, Lawrence. 1981. Taxes and Corporate Investment: A Q-Theory Approach. *Brookings Papers on Economic Activity* 1:67–127. Washington, D.C.

Titman, Sheridan. 1982. The Effects of Anticipated Inflation on Housing Market Equilibrium. *Journal of Finance* 37:827–42.

10   What Can the United States Learn from the Canadian Sales Tax Debate?

Charles E. McLure, Jr.

10.1 Introduction

The United States has considered introducing a value-added tax (VAT) since at least 1966, most recently for the purpose of reducing the federal budget deficit. Since the United States currently has no federal sales tax, a VAT would be a net addition to the fiscal arsenal of the federal government.

Canada, by comparison, has had a manufacturers' level sales tax (MST) since 1924, and is scheduled to replace that notoriously defective levy with a VAT on January 1, 1991, provided the Senate approves the legislation passed by the House.[1] However, there is such widespread disapproval of the VAT that the Senate may block the legislation—an action it rarely takes. The proposed Canadian VAT is flawed, so badly that some observers feel perhaps the VAT should not be approved, despite the well-known problems with the existing sales tax and the benefits of a well-designed VAT (See Whalley 1989).

The Canadian debate on sales tax reform—like sales tax debates in other countries—has important lessons for the United States. In some respects the Canadian experience merely confirms that of other countries. Some of the lessons are more novel, reflecting the differences in the Canadian context. The purpose of this paper is to discuss the most important of these lessons. While the focus is on the recent debate about what kind of tax should replace the existing Canadian tax, the defects of the manufacturers' tax are also dis-

Charles E. McLure, Jr., is a senior fellow at the Hoover Institution at Stanford University and a research associate of the National Bureau of Economic Research. From 1983 to 1985 he was deputy assistant secretary of the U.S. Treasury Department.

1. On December 14, 1990, the Senate approved the legislation, and Canada joined the ranks of VAT countries, as scheduled. In order to convey the sense of uncertainty that prevailed until then, I have not revised the text to reflect this action. The government employed extraordinary constitutional powers to appoint an additional eight members of the Senate to overcome opposition to the VAT.

cussed, since they are relevant for the U.S. debate. At various points lessons will be drawn from the VAT experience—including implementation—of Europe, Japan, and New Zealand, which has perhaps the world's best VAT. I do not discuss alternatives for the United States, such as increases in income taxes or introduction of a (non–Social Security) payroll tax, since to do so would take me too far afield. Not surprisingly, I draw some conclusions for Canada from the debates in Canada and elsewhere.

The traditional U.S. discussion of introducing a VAT has also considered the pros and cons of introducing a federal retail sales tax (RST) instead of a credit-method VAT of the type found in the European Community.[2] More recently a third horse has been added to the race, a subtraction-method VAT, which has commonly been called a business transfer tax (BTT). Interest in the BTT can only be increased by Japan's recent adoption of a 3 percent subtraction-based VAT. It is sometimes suggested that the BTT should extend only through the wholesale level, to avoid trespassing on the fiscal turf of the states. The BTT was also seriously considered in Canada before being abandoned in favor of a traditional credit-method VAT. Section 10.2 briefly describes the basic mechanics of the three retail-level sales taxes (VAT, RST, and BTT) and the two preretail taxes mentioned above (MST and wholesale-level BTT), practical differences in the actual operation of the three retail-level taxes, and the problems with sales taxes such as the Canadian MST or a wholesale level BTT, which stop short of the retail level.[3] The U.S. and Canadian debates are briefly summarized in section 10.3; the remainder of the paper elaborates on key issues in the debates. The Canadian debate focuses largely on defects identified in section 10.2.

One of the most important issues in both the U.S. and Canadian debates is how to introduce a federal sales tax into a federal system in which lower-level governments (states and provinces) already rely on retail sales taxes and resist the idea of federal intrusion into their fiscal preserve. This question, which has been almost totally absent from the discussion in Europe and New Zealand, helps explain the interest in the BTT in both countries. It is the subject of section 10.4.

Liberals in the United States have generally opposed introduction of the VAT, arguing that it would impose a heavy burden on low-income households and be regressive across income classes. These concerns could be lessened by exempting certain products and levying lower rates on "necessities," or by increasing transfer payments to the poor. An expansion of the refundable earned-income tax credit would be the obvious tool to use in implementing the latter policy in the United States. In Canada the zero-rating of basic gro-

---

2. The mechanics of these taxes are described in section 10.2, which also provides references to further literature.

3. One could include discussions of a single-stage wholesale tax and a credit-method VAT that stops short of the retail level. Nothing much would be gained from doing so, as fortunately no one has suggested such ill-advised levies.

ceries has been proposed, even though a program of refundable income tax credits has been in place since 1986. See section 10.5.

The VAT—and to a lesser extent any broad-based sales tax—has the potential of raising a large amount of money in a way that does not seriously distort economic decision making. If, however, the tax base is shot through with exemptions and differential rates, neutrality will be lost, and complexity will be increased. Canada appears to be headed down a path that will produce a sales tax far inferior to what it could have achieved. Some of the most important problem areas are discussed in section 10.6.

The preparations required for implementation of a sales tax are discussed in section 10.7, and the coordination of Canadian, Mexican, and U.S. sales taxes in the context of a North American free-trade area is discussed in section 10.8. The lessons from the Canadian debate are summarized in section 10.9.

10.2   Alternative Forms of Sales Tax

10.2.1   Retail-Level Sales Taxes

The Basic Mechanics

To see the difference in the three forms of sales tax that extend through the retail level, consider the following simple example. Suppose that a manufacturer produces a product and sells it to a wholesaler for $300. The wholesaler sells the product for $700 to a retailer, who then sells it to the public for $1,000. Value added—the difference between purchases and sales—is $300 in the manufacturing stage, $400 in wholesaling, and $300 in retailing. These transactions and the calculation of value added are described in the top part of table 10.1; the three sales taxes that extend through the retail level, each levied at a (tax-exclusive) rate of 10 percent, are described in the middle part of the table.[4] (In this simple example, it is assumed that the production-distribution process is linear; thus, neither the manufacturer nor the wholesaler makes sales to consumers and no stage sells to earlier stages. Violation of this simplifying assumption creates important differences in the effects of the three types of sales taxes; these are considered later in this section.)

Both the retail sales tax and the credit-method VAT are levied on individual transactions at the time of sale. The RST applies only to the $1,000 of sales to consumers; thus, in the example, $100 is collected from retailers and none from manufacturers and wholesalers, as shown in lines 4–5 in table 10.1. Value added is not actually calculated under the credit-method VAT; rather, tax is levied on sales, but credit is allowed for tax paid on purchases. Thus, for example, the wholesaler has a tentative liability of $70 (10 percent of sales of $700) and credit of $30, leaving a net liability of $40. Adding to this the

---

4. The part of this example dealing with retail-level taxes is taken from McLure (1989); such examples are developed in greater detail in McLure (1987).

Table 10.1   **Alternative Forms of Sales Taxes**

	Manufacturer	Wholesaler	Retailer	Total
Basic Transactions (3 Stages)				
1. Sales	$300	$700	$1,000	$2,000
2. Purchases	-0-	300	700	1,000
3. Value Added	300	400	300	1,000
Taxes Extending through the Retail Level				
10-Percent RST				
4. Retail Sales	-0-	-0-	1,000	1,000
5. Retail Sales Tax	-0-	-0-	100	100
10-Percent Credit/Invoice VAT				
6. Tax on Sales	30	70	100	200
7. Tax on Purchases	0	30	70	100
8. VAT Liability	30	40	30	100
10-Percent Subtraction-Method BTT				
9. Sales	300	700	1,000	2,000
10. Purchases	-0-	300	700	1,000
11. Value Added	300	400	300	1,000
12. Business Transfer Tax	30	40	30	100
Pre-Retail Level Sales Taxes				
33⅓-Percent MST				
13. Manufacturers' Sales	300	-0-	-0-	300
14. Manufacturers' Sales Tax	100	-0-	-0-	100
14.3-Percent Wholesale-Level BTT				
15. Sales	300	700	n.r.[a]	1,000
16. Purchases	-0-	300	n.r.	300
17. Value Added	300	400	n.r.	700
18. Business Transfer Tax	42.9	57.1	n.r.	100

[a]Not relevant

$30 collected from the manufacturer and the $30 collected from the retailer gives a total of $100, as under the RST; see lines 6–8 of table 10.1. Because credit can be taken only for tax shown on invoices, this tax is sometimes also called an invoice-based VAT.

The subtraction-method BTT achieves the same result in a different manner, by applying the tax rate to value added calculated at each stage in the production-distribution process; see lines 9–12 of table 10.1. This tax is not, however, levied on individual transactions; rather, it is based on the accounting records of firms.

Treatment of International Trade

It is important to consider what happens if the retailer in the example exports, rather than sells to domestic consumers. Under virtually all extant VATs, a zero rate is applied to exports; that is, exports are "zero-rated." This means that no tax is collected on exports and the tax collected by the wholesaler is rebated to the retailer; thus, exports enter world trade unencumbered by VAT.

If imports occur at any stage in the production-distribution process, they are taxed, and, except in the case of imports by households, credit is allowed for the tax collected on import at the time of the first domestic sale. Thus, imports are taxed in the same way as domestic production. Exact "border tax adjustments" (BTAs) are also possible under a BTT with uniform rates applied to all value added, but not under one with rates that do not apply uniformly (see also the discussion below).

In principle the same result is achieved automatically under the RST simply by exempting export sales and including imported goods in the base of the sales tax. In fact, this is not likely to be achieved completely since, as noted below, it is generally impossible to eliminate all tax on capital and intermediate goods.

Some Important Complications

While the simple example presented above is useful in understanding the basic mechanics of the three types of sales taxes, it conceals important differences in the way the taxes actually operate. The remainder of this section examines several differences that are especially important for the discussion that follows.

Problems of RST. Not all retail sales are made to households. To the extent taxable sales are made to businesses, there can be an element of "cascading," as taxes collected by retailers are built into the price charged for business inputs. Instead of being neutral, RSTs impose differential burdens on various products, depending on the nature and extent of cascading. Moreover, it is generally impossible to free exports from RST or to burden imports with the same RST as domestic goods.

Various means have been devised to avoid cascading, notably the exemption of certain products and the registration of businesses, who are then allowed to buy tax-free. No system of exemption can eliminate RST from all business inputs. In principle, registration for tax-free purchases can do so, but only by creating administrative complications and opportunities for abuse.

Under the RST the tax authorities get "one bite at the apple"; that is, any tax not collected at the time of retail sale is lost. By comparison, under the VAT tax is collected in increments as products move through the production-distribution process. For this reason it is often thought that the VAT can be levied at higher rates than the RST. In addition, under the credit method, invoices used to verify eligibility for credits provide a mechanism for cross-checking that the RST lacks. These invoices create a paper trail that facilitates audit of the income tax, as well as the VAT. These administrative advantages should not be overemphasized, because of the possibility of claiming credit for tax supported by bogus invoices and the difficulty of actually making the requisite cross-checks.[5] No tax is truly self-enforcing. But the invoices do help.

For reasons such as these, Canada opted for the multistage VAT, instead of the RST (see Wilson 1987, pp. 25–27).

Exemptions and Zero-Rating under the VAT. In this simple example, in which it is assumed that all value added is subject to the same uniform tax rate, the ultimate results are the same under the BTT as under the conventional credit-method VAT and the (idealized) RST. In a more realistic setting in which there may be exemptions and differential rates, equivalence quickly evaporates. This is most easily seen by considering what happens under the two types of VAT when there is exemption or zero-rating of the one stage in the above example.

Under certain circumstances either exemption or zero-rating can create potentially severe administrative problems. The easiest case is exemption of the entire activity of a business; the exempt business is simply "out of the system," and thus pays no tax on sales and receives no credit for tax paid on purchases. The situation is significantly more complicated for a business that makes both taxable and exempt sales (and thus is in the system). It is necessary to distinguish between purchases related to taxable and to exempt sales, since credit is allowed only for tax paid on the former; in some cases it is necessary to use formulas to apportion taxes on purchases between taxable and exempt activities. A business making zero-rated sales is "in the system," and must bear the same administrative burden as a fully taxable business. But there is no need to distinguish between purchases related to taxable and zero-rated sales, since credit is allowed for taxes on both.

Exemption of retail sales under the credit-method VAT eliminates the tax on the value added at the retail level, but not that collected at earlier stages. By comparison, zero-rating retail sales eliminates the entire tax on such sales. It is equivalent to exemption under the (ideal) RST.

If the wholesale stage is exempt, aggregate VAT liability actually rises, to $130 in the example. Because the wholesaler is not a taxpayer, no credit is allowed for the $30 tax on purchases; on the other hand, the retailer collects $100 and has paid no tax on purchases for which to take credit. Because of this break in the chain of credits, pre-retail exemptions are not popular under the credit-method VAT.

Zero-rating (or another preferential rate) applied to pre-retail sales, on the other hand, has no effect on ultimate tax liability, since only the rate applied

5. It has been suggested that small-business opposition to the credit-method VAT helps explain why the government of Japan decided *not* to impose such a tax, opting instead for a subtraction-method VAT operating without invoices. Homma (1992) and Noguchi (1992) suggest this interpretation.

at retail actually matters under a credit-method VAT. If pre-retail taxes are lower, credits are lower as well.

Problems of BTT. The results are very different under the BTT.[6] Since tax is levied on "slices" of value added, the exemption or preferential taxation of a given stage reduces aggregate tax liability (but cannot eliminate it unless all stages are exempt) and distorts resource allocation. This produces incentives to lobby for preferential treatment, which in turn means that a subtraction-method VAT is not likely to be neutral. It is also generally impossible to provide accurate BTAs under the BTT if the base is not comprehensive and the rate is not uniform. (Suppose that one slice of value added incorporated into production for exports or competition with imports is taxed at 10 percent, one is exempt, and another is taxed at 4 percent. How is the exporter to calculate the export rebate? What rate should be applied to competing imports? What if the slices differ in size for different production-distribution channels?) Finally, there are important administrative questions of defining just which activities benefit from the exemption or preferential rates.

Some have suggested that the inability of the BTT to accommodate multiple rates and exemptions is one of its advantages—that this form of taxation forces politicians to apply a single rate to all economic activity. Experience, most notably the Canadian elimination of the option patterned after the BTT, which was acknowledged to be workable only with a single rate and a broad base, seems to support my view that one cannot be so optimistic—that politicians will not easily be dissuaded from doing what they want to do simply because it is technically impossible. It will be interesting to see whether Japan can maintain the relative purity and uniformity of its new subtraction-based tax, especially if the rate rises above its present low level of 3 percent. (See Homma 1992, where it is explicitly recognized that virtually all value added must be taxed at one rate under the Japanese tax.)

There remains another area of uncertainty: the treatment of the BTT under article 3 of the General Agreement on Tariffs and Trade, which deals with "national treatment." This provision allows BTAs for indirect taxes, but not for direct taxes. A BTT resembles an indirect tax in some respects; under certain circumstances it is exactly equivalent to a credit-method VAT or an RST, taxes for which BTAs are allowed. But the BTT also has characteristics of a direct tax; in particular, the tax base is calculated as the difference between receipts and purchases. Moreover, the effects of differential rates are felt by taxpayers, rather than washing out, as under the credit method (see Carlson and McLure 1984; McLure 1989). It is not clear how the GATT would react to a BTT, but the new Japanese subtraction-based tax may shed some light on the issue, especially if there is a shift to nonuniform rates.

6. This discussion is necessarily incomplete. See McLure (1987, ch. 6) for a more complete indictment of the BTT.

Both the credit-method VAT and the RST have a further advantage not shared by the BTT. Whereas the VAT is almost inherently visible, because of the need for separate quotation on invoices, and the RST is commonly quoted separately, the account-based BTT is invisible. Thus, consumers are much less likely to know the tax content of goods and services subject to BTT than that of goods and services subject to RST or VAT.

10.2.2   Pre-retail Sales Taxes

The Mechanics

The Canadian MST is applied to sales by manufacturers. In the example in table 10.1, a rate of 33 1/3/ percent would be required to produce the same revenue as the 10 percent rate applied to retail sales (see table 10.1, lines 13–14).

A BTT limited to the wholesale level would be a truncated version of the BTT illustrated in the top part of table 10.1; thus, it would apply only to value added at the manufacturing and wholesale stages (see lines 15–18). To raise the same revenue as the 10 percent retail-level tax, a rate of 14.3 percent would be required.

Problems

Any tax that does not extend to the retail level inevitably raises difficult definitional problems: What is manufacturing, or wholesaling, and what is not? In addition, pre-retail taxes discriminate against those activities in which the value is added early in the production-distribution process; discrimination in favor of services is especially severe. Pre-retail taxes encourage the artificial shifting of functions from the taxable (manufacturing or wholesale) stage to nontaxable stages. In the case of vertically integrated activities extending beyond the last taxable point, transfer prices must be employed to determine tax liability, absorbing resources and opening the way for evasion. Since there is no way for businesses beyond the last taxable point to recover tax paid on business inputs, cascading occurs. This distorts resource allocation and prevents accurate BTAs, causing discrimination against domestic manufacturers in international markets. Efforts to prevent cascading produce the same problems as are produced under the RST. Moreover, whereas the rate applied to business imports under the credit-method VAT makes no ultimate difference, this is not true under pre-retail taxes. It is for reasons such as these that the U.S. Treasury Department (1984, vol. 3, p. 217), concluded: "The retail sales tax and a value-added tax extending through the retail level are the only types of sales tax that should be considered. . . . The United States should categorically reject: a single stage tax levied before the retail level, such as a manufacturers or wholesale tax; a value-added tax that does not include the retail stage. . . ."

10.3 Some History

10.3.1 United States

In 1966 a conservative business group, the Committee for Economic Development, proposed that the United States replace its corporate income tax with a value-added tax (see Committee for Economic Development 1966; see also McLure 1973 and 1987, ch. 1). Much of the impetus for the proposal was the belief that such a substitution would improve the U.S. balance of payments. To some extent this belief was a misunderstanding of the purpose and effect of the BTAs allowed for the newly enacted European VATs; BTAs were seen by some as export subsidies and import tariffs. In any event there was interest in replacing a tax for which BTAs are not allowed under the GATT (the corporate tax) with one for which BTAs are allowed (the VAT).[7]

Nothing much came of this idea, and the idea of a U.S. VAT lay dormant until 1972. It was revived when President Richard Nixon suggested that a federal VAT be used to replace revenues from local property taxes, which were under judicial attack. Although a blue-ribbon committee appointed by the president issued a report on the topic, the report was largely ignored as the president and the public became preoccupied with Watergate.

The idea of a U.S. VAT surfaced again in 1979, when Al Ullman, then Chairman of the House Ways and Means Committee, proposed the Revenue Act of 1979. Since Ullman's electoral defeat in 1980, members of Congress have been chary about supporting a VAT. Nonetheless, in 1986 Senator Roth (R-Delaware) proposed the introduction of a Business Transfer Tax.

During the 1980s the BTT has been advocated especially by the American Council for Capital Formation, as a means of reducing the federal budget deficit and thus increasing total (private plus public) saving. The wholesale-level BTT was chosen over the conventional credit-method VAT in large part to avoid appearing to step on the fiscal toes of state and local governments. The accounts-based BTT is also said to be simpler to implement than the credit-method VAT.

Neither the U.S. Treasury Department nor the Internal Revenue Service participated in the debate, even though the latter would presumably be responsible for implementation of any federal sales tax.[8] To remedy this, examination of a value-added tax was included in the Treasury Department's tax reform project that eventually led to the Tax Reform Act of 1986.[9] Nothing

---

7. The discussion at the conference revealed a new twist to this old issue. Some in the Canadian government fear that the United States might use a VAT or another form of sales tax to reduce its corporate tax rates. Capital and tax base might then be attracted from Canada, in the absence of matching rate reductions by Canada. See also the papers by Gordon and by Boadway and Bruce (chs. 2 and 1 in this volume).

8. Carlson (1980) was written while its author was an employee of the Treasury Department, but it was not an official departmental study.

9. See U.S. Department of the Treasury (1984 especially vol. 3).

came of this effort, since President Reagan had decreed that tax reform would be revenue-neutral, and no one would have seriously—or at least credibly—suggested that a VAT be introduced except as part of an effort to reduce the deficit.

10.3.2   Canada

Canada's manufacturers' sales tax has long been widely recognized as one of the worst sales taxes levied by any advanced country.[10] After an effort to eliminate the tax was rendered ineffective by the revenue needs of the Great Depression, the tax was gradually accepted as a permanent part of the Canadian fiscal landscape. The defects of the tax have been documented and changes have been suggested by several high-level commissions: the Rowell-Sirois Commission on Dominion-Provincial Relations in 1940, the Royal Commission on Taxation (the Carter Commission) in 1966, and the Federal Sales Tax Review Committee (the Goodman Committee) in 1983.[11]

In June 1987, Finance Minister Michael Wilson proposed replacing the existing sales tax, which he described as "seriously flawed," with a value-added tax. Wilson's indictment of the MST was similar to the criticisms I presented in the last part of section 10.2. He argued that switching to a VAT would help Canadian industry compete in foreign and domestic markets and improve the balance of revenue sources (Wilson 1987, p. 1).[12]

The base of the manufacturers' tax is extremely limited; only about one-third of consumption is directly affected by the tax, and five items (tobacco, alcoholic beverages, automobiles, automobile parts, and motor fuels) account for 40 percent of revenues.[13] "Complexity arises because the tax is not applied to all products and because the distinction between taxable and exempt items is often difficult to define and to sustain," according to Wilson (1987, p. 19).[14]

10. For example, Due (1959), a textbook I used as an undergraduate student almost thirty years ago, catalogs the defects of the tax, as well as efforts made through 1955 to replace it with a more rational alternative.

11. Gillis (1985) and Whalley (1989) provide modern surveys of the defects of the existing MST, which have led Gillis to quip that "Canada is a civilized country, except for its sales tax". It might be noted that the defects of the MST have assumed even greater importance in recent years, as the rate has risen to 13.5 percent from 9 percent as recently as 1984. I appreciate Jon Kesselman's pointing this out to me.

12. Wilson (1989a, p. 5) stated, with only slight exaggeration, "The existing tax is the only consumption tax in the industrialized world known to favor imports over domestically produced goods."

13. Perhaps it should be noted that no VAT reaches all consumption spending; because of exemptions and zero rates a figure of one-half to three-fourths of consumption would be more typical.

14. Wilson cites the following examples of line-drawing: athletic headbands are exempt as clothing, while athletic wrist bands are taxable as sporting equipment; the ripening of green bananas and the blasting of rock into rubble are both classified as manufacturing (to the benefit of taxpayers). He also mentions the following questions raised by court cases: If heating fuels are exempt, should candles be exempt because they produce heat? If electricity is not taxed, should batteries be exempt as boxed electricity? Should facial tissues be taxed as a cosmetic or exempt as a health good?

Because the tax is levied at the manufacturing level, almost half of it falls on business inputs in the first instance. The tax is hidden from the consumers who ultimately pay it, but cascades into highly differentiated taxation of various products and even the same product made by different manufacturers in the same industry. As Wilson noted, the existing system "taxes goods capriciously, scattering and compounding its impact through the distribution chain in a frequently unpredictable manner" (Wilson 1989a, p. 4). There are estimates that these distortions cause a loss of efficiency of $9 billion annually, the equivalent of the value added by Canada's manufacturers of steel, aluminum, and other primary metals.

The tax also distorts choices of distribution channels. In the effort to prevent distortions of trading patterns, "notional values" (or transfer prices) are used to approximate values at the manufacturing level, creating further complexity. One measure of the complexity of the system is the fact that 22,000 special provisions and administrative interpretations have been issued for a system with only 75,000 taxpayers (Wilson 1987, pp. 10–11, 23).

Wilson proposed replacing the manufacturers' sales tax with a value-added tax, rather than with a retail sales tax, citing the difficulty of removing all tax on business inputs under the RST and the greater susceptibility to noncompliance (Wilson 1987, pp. 25–27; Wilson 1989a, p. 14). (Though not mentioned explicitly by Wilson, the potential for strong opposition from the provinces, which levy retail sales taxes, almost certainly also motivated the decision to recommend a VAT.) He offered three alternatives for further debate: a credit-method VAT that would absorb provincial sales taxes, a uniform-rate comprehensive federal tax that would closely resemble a BTT and operate without invoices, and a conventional credit-method federal VAT. (These are described in greater detail in the next section.)

By April 1989, the menu had been pared down to only one alternative, the credit-method VAT, which is now being called the Goods and Services Tax (GST). Interestingly enough, deficit reduction was added to the listed virtues of the VAT. This addition has caused some (e.g., Whalley 1989) to wonder whether the true reason for the proposed VAT substitution for the MST is long-run revenue enhancement, rather than simply structural improvement. Though the initial proposal was for a rate of 9 percent, it has since been reduced to 7 percent.

It is worth noting that simply eliminating the MST and replacing its revenue with revenue from the individual and corporate income taxes seems to have been ruled out because of the implied change in the "tax mix" from indirect taxation to direct taxation.[15]

15. This point is noted in Whalley (1989) and in Dodge and Sargent (1988, p. 53). See Kesselman (1986) for this "tax mix" argument in the Australian context.

10.4   Intergovernmental Issues

10.4.1   The U.S. Issues

The states have long been uneasy about the prospect of a federal value-added tax.[16] Concerns about "federal preemption" may often have been poorly articulated; they have to do with the amount of room that exists for two jurisdictions to tax the same base. In fact, it appears that there is something very real behind these concerns.

First, and most obviously, if federal and state rates were added together, the total rate applied to any one sale might be so high that evasion would become extremely attractive and thus very difficult to control. At the very least, it might be necessary to rely on the techniques of the VAT, which leaves more of a paper trail for auditors than the RST. This might be disconcerting to states, who have an RST tradition.

Second, it is clearly more trouble for businesses to comply with two sales taxes than with one. Difficulties would be maximized, all else equal, if the states and the federal government chose different forms of transactions-based sales tax (e.g., state RST and federal VAT). Difficulties would be compounded if the taxes levied by the two levels of government involved different patterns of exemptions and rate differentiation. Sales personnel would have to know the rules for both taxes.[17] In order to avoid maddening complexity for business, a high degree of intergovernmental cooperation and uniformity would be needed. In the extreme case, states would be allowed to choose no more than rates, the base having been chosen by the federal government. But this solution involves a loss of state fiscal sovereignty.

By comparison, if the federal government employed the accounts-based BTT, intergovernmental problems would be minimized. Salespersons would need to be concerned only with the rules for the state RST, leaving the complexity of the BTT to the accountants to worry about. There is also much less need for uniformity and cooperation, and thus less concern about loss of state fiscal sovereignty. The fly in this ointment is, of course, the basic difficulties posed by a BTT that is not levied at a single rate on all value added. There is little reason to believe that the Congress would resist the temptation to levy multiple rates.

10.4.2   The Canadian Debate

The concerns identified above also existed in Canada, though perhaps to a lesser degree. As a result, the April 1987 proposal (Wilson 1987) contained

16. This discussion is based on McLure (1987, ch. 9) and McLure (1988). See U.S. General Accounting Office (1990) for the results of a survey of views of state policy makers and tax administrators.

17. Modern technology (bar codes and holography) reduces the importance of this problem, but does not eliminate it, especially for small business.

not one but three alternatives for consideration. The first of these was called a "national sales tax"; it was a credit-method value-added tax administered by the federal government with rates that could vary by province. It would, at the option of the individual provinces, replace both the federal and provincial sales taxes (see Wilson 1987, pp. 54).

Taxes on interprovincial trade would be handled through a central collection agency acting as a clearing house. Each invoice issued for sales to businesses would show the province of origin and the province of destination of the sale; tax would be charged at the rate prevailing in the province of destination (plus the federal rate). The central agency would then credit provincial accounts for tax at destination and debit them for tax at origin of business sales.[18] The federal and provincial tax bases would need to be identical for this scheme to work.

An approach such as this has been considered by the European Community as part of its "1992 scheme" to "complete the internal market." There has, however, been a reluctance to adopt such a scheme, which would require mutual honesty and trust, as well as considerable sacrifice of national fiscal sovereignty. It appears that there is reluctance to trust either the taxpayers or the fiscal authorities of other member nations (see Tait 1988, pp. 158–61; Culp 1989).

The second alternative was essentially a federal BTT, "which would be levied at a single rate on virtually all goods and services in Canada, with minimal exceptions."[19] It was anticipated that "this system could operate without invoices." (The mechanics were those of the credit method. But credit was calculated as the product of the tax rate and taxable inputs. Of course, it could operate without invoices only if, indeed, virtually all sales were subject to tax.) For reasons indicated above, such a tax could operate in parallel with existing provincial RSTs (see Wilson 1987, pp. 54–57).

The third alternative was a federal credit-method VAT similar to those found in Europe. This tax would have the advantage of allowing exemptions (and differential rates, something not mentioned by Wilson), but the disadvantage of posing greater administrative burdens on retailers. It was recognized that some retailers would find it necessary to replace their cash registers with newer, more sophisticated ones capable of recording sales in four categories.[20]

18. This is based on Poddar (1990) and Cnossen (1983, 1990). It is summarized in Whalley and Fretz (1990, p. 83). Note that this technique avoids the need to employ the "restricted origin principle" of the Neumark Committee, in which all provinces would be required to levy VAT at a uniform rate (see Cnossen 1983, 1990).

19. This option was called the Goods and Services Tax, or GST. Since this name was later given to the credit-method VAT proposed in 1989, it is not used in this paper, in order to avoid confusion.

20. See Wilson (1987, pp. 57–58). It is worth noting that on August 8, 1989, in conjunction with release of the Technical Paper on the GST, Wilson proposed immediate write-off for equipment for scanning electronic bar codes and for cash registers capable of calculating and recording sales taxes imposed by more than one jurisdiction. See "Changes to Capital Cost Allowance Rate Announced For Electronic Point-of-Sale Equipment" (1989).

The government ultimately settled on the federal credit-method VAT, which it is now calling the Goods and Services Tax (GST). It is worth commenting briefly on two alternatives that did not appear on this list. First, there was no federal RST, presumably because of the expectation of severe opposition from the provinces, as well as the problems identified above. Second, there was no proposal for a joint federal-provincial BTT. Given existing differences in provincial sales tax rates, there would seem to be little hope for a uniform rate, without which the BTT cannot operate (see Whalley and Fretz 1990, p. 83).

At the end of August 1990, after the presentation and penultimate revision of this paper, another important development occurred. The governments of Canada and Quebec signed an agreement for the joint collection of federal and provincial sales taxes. While appearing on the surface to be a promising development, this action left some important questions unanswered.[21]

First, it is far from obvious what the Memorandum of Understanding means when it speaks of Quebec making "a change from a retail sales tax to a tax harmonized with the GST." In particular, there is no indication how interprovincial trade will be treated. Second, it is anomalous—if understandable in the unique Canadian situation involving relations with Quebec—that the provincial government is given responsibility for administration of the federal tax. One would ordinarily prefer federal administration of provincial taxes in order to assure uniformity and prevent provincial favoritism to local business.

10.5 Low-Income Relief

10.5.1 The U.S. Debate

The discussion of the VAT prepared by the U.S. Treasury Department in 1984 considered three ways of dealing with the distributional problem posed by sales tax burdens on low-income households and regressivity.[22] It noted that exemptions of food and other necessities are extremely blunt and inefficient instruments to use for this purpose. First, most food is not consumed by the poor, and tax rates must be substantially higher to make up for the loss in tax base. Second, exempting food distorts consumer choices. Third, exemptions pose troublesome administrative problems. It concluded that other ways should be found to deal with the problem.

To the extent that transfer payments are indexed for inflation or are made in kind, recipients of transfers would not be harmed by the introduction of a federal VAT. But not all the poor receive transfers. Thus, it was concluded

21. This discussion is based on "Wilson Announces Sales Tax Reform Agreement with Quebec" (1990), a news release that also includes the Memorandum of Understanding, exchange of letters, Wilson's statement on the Memorandum of Understanding, and background information.
22. For an analysis extending that found in U.S. Department of the Treasury (1984), see Brashares et al. (1988).

that it would be necessary to accompany introduction of a VAT with a comprehensive program of direct transfers, such as a negative income tax, if the poor were to be insulated from the effects of the VAT. Expansion of the existing earned-income tax credit under the individual income tax would be one way to implement such a program.

10.5.2 The Canadian Resolution

The report of a conference held at the Brookings Institution in 1980 concluded that:

> The central technical lesson of the European experience is that multiple rates can be used to eliminate the regressivity of the value-added tax, but that the penalties in administrative complexity, increased compliance costs, and distortions in consumption decisions have been high and probably unjustified. Most conference participants agreed . . . that it would be preferable to use other taxes and transfer payments to alleviate the undesirable distributional consequences generated by a value added tax imposed at uniform rates. (Aaron 1981, p. 16)

Yet the conference participants did not hold out much hope that the United States would resist the temptation to impose preferential rates on such necessities as food, housing, and medicine.

Canadian experience certainly does not provide reason for optimism on this score. The 1989 Canadian proposal would zero-rate basic groceries, even though there exists a refundable sales tax credit for the poor, first enacted in 1986 and subsequently made much more generous.[23] This approach, said to be necessary to gain provincial acceptance of the federal tax base, promises to create the problems identified above, which were explicitly recognized by Wilson (1989a, p. 21).

The zero-rating of groceries doomed any prospect of using the BTT approach. Moreover, as European experience with zero-rating, multiple rates, and exemptions makes clear, it creates substantial difficulties of compliance and administration. This is especially sad, since the existence of the refundable credit mechanism should have made the zero-rating of groceries unnecessary. This problem is discussed further in the next section.

---

23. At the time of the initial Wilson proposal in 1987, refundable credits of $50 per adult and $25 per child were allowed families with incomes below $15,000, with the credit being reduced by 5 percent of the excess of income over $15,000. Under the initial 1987 proposal, the credit would be increased by $20 for adults and $10 for children and the ceiling increased to $16,000. See Wilson (1987, p. 7). The figures for 1990 were increased to $140 for adults and $70 for children, with a ceiling of $18,000. In the August 1989 proposal, the figures were $275 for adults and $100 for children, with a ceiling of about $25,000. See Wilson (1989b, pp. 3, 15–16).

During the conference it was noted that the New Zealand GST, which applies to food, was introduced by a socialist government. Whereas it might be possible for a Democratic administration in the United States to propose such a tax successfully, it would be much more difficult for a Republican administration to do so.

10.6 Neutrality

The proposed Canadian VAT falls far short of neutrality. In addition to zero-rating basic groceries, prescription drugs, and medical devices, it would exempt residential rents, most health and dental services, day care services, legal aid services, and most educational services. In addition, public sector institutions (hospitals, local governments, libraries, colleges, and universities) would receive rebates for a percentage of the taxes paid on their purchases, in order to avoid an increase in the sales taxes they pay. Sales by farmers and fishermen would be zero-rated in order to facilitate zero-rating of groceries. Financial institutions would be tax-exempt, except on specific services. Finally, businesses with turnover below $30,000 per year would have the option of being exempt. This section examines several of these key issues in greater detail.

10.6.1 Food

Under the proposed legislation, basic groceries will be zero-rated throughout the production-distribution process. Rather than defining basic groceries, the law specifies that the following categories of food will be taxable: candy and confectioneries, snack food, soft drinks, prepared food sold in a grocery store, and all food sold in eating establishments, except those not suitable for immediate consumption (e.g., coffee beans). This list is essentially the same as the list of goods that are taxable under the existing MST. In addition, meals offered by schools, universities, charities, nursing homes, and other such institutions will be exempt. Two streamlined methods of accounting are provided to facilitate small-business compliance with the law.

The approach chosen in Canada has little to recommend it. As noted above, there is little reason to exempt groceries, given the existence of the system of refundable credits; doing so creates unnecessary complexity. Even the Consumers Association of Canada favored taxing food, with a compensating reduction in rates (noted in Whalley and Fretz 1990, p. 70).

Beyond that, if a food exemption is to be provided, it makes little sense to limit the exemption to basic groceries; it is hard to see what this achieves, and it creates serious problems of compliance and administration.[24] Certainly Wilson's statement does not offer adequate justification: "Consistent with their treatment under the existing federal sales tax, soft drinks , candies and confections, and snack foods will continue to be taxable" (Wilson 1989b, p. 11). It would have been much simpler to exempt all food, and the implied loss of revenue probably would not have been great.

10.6.2 Housing

The 1987 proposals called for a tax on new residential construction and on the sale or rental of real estate for commercial use; residential rentals and the

---

24. Wilson (1990, p. 12) acknowledges, "There are some food products that are not easily placed in one or the other broad categories of basic groceries and prepared foods."

resale of residential real estate would be exempt (Wilson 1987, p. 113). The 1989 legislation is similar to the 1987 proposal, but contains rebates intended to soften the blow to low-income home buyers from the increase in taxation of housing caused by the switch from the MST to the GST. It provides a rebate of 36 percent of GST (just over 2.5 percent of the purchase price), up to a maximum of $8,750, on a new house with a price of up to $350,000. The rebate is phased out on a proportionate basis over the range of housing prices to $450,000.[25]

This proposal raises several questions for the United States. First, the approach proposed for Canada would create capital gains for owners of existing residential real estate, to the extent the GST on housing exceeds the tax included in the value of housing under the MST. An alternative that would avoid these windfall gains would include in the tax base the first sale of any home. Such an approach would also substantially increase the tax base and allow lower rates. It is not without problems, however. It would be necessary for homeowners to keep track of the cost of improvements incurred after the introduction of the VAT—and to distinguish them from nondeductible maintenance—in order to avoid double taxation (Whalley and Fretz 1990, pp. 79–82). And, of course, it would be politically unpopular with homeowners. Second, the inclusion of land in the value of new houses subject to GST creates some distortions or inequities. Tax would be saved by buying an existing house, demolishing it, and contracting for the construction of a new house.

The rebate scheme proposed for Canada is also problematic. It would impose an effective marginal tax rate of 15.75 percent (7 percent GST, plus the phaseout rate of 8.75 percent) on new housing with purchase prices falling in the phaseout range of $350,000–450,000.[26] Rates of this magnitude, besides creating obvious distortions of economic decisions, would almost certainly give rise to evasion.[27] The preferential rate on housing included in Ullman's 1979 proposal might be preferable, if relief must be offered.

10.6.3 Financial Services

The financial sector poses difficult problems under any credit-method VAT.[28] Value added in this sector is measured by the sum of the spread between interest received and interest paid and charges for nonfinancial services,

---

25. The 1989 proposals called for a rebate of 4.5 percent of the purchase price up to $310,000, phased out on homes valued between $350,000 and $400,000; see Wilson (1989b, pp. 17–20).

26. Under the 1987 proposal, the implicit tax would have been a staggering 36.9 percent (9 percent GST, plus the phaseout rate of 27.9 percent).

27. One would expect, for example, that the purchaser of a home valued in the phaseout range would conspire with the seller to pay only $350,000 for the home and pay the rest of the true purchase price for something else in order to maximize the rebate. One commentator thought this type of gimmick would not work, because land prices and building costs are well established in Canada.

28. For an excellent discussion of various approaches to the taxation of financial services and their problems, see Hoffman, Poddar, and Whalley (1987). Similar problems are encountered in the case of insurance. They are not discussed here, for lack of space. See, however, Barham, Poddar, and Whalley (1987).

less costs of providing both financial and nonfinancial services. Both types of services are provided to both businesses and households. It will be convenient in what follows to focus primarily on value added in intermediation, ignoring for the most part nonfinancial services and their costs. It is recognized fully that we are setting aside important administrative problems: that explicit charges may not be made for such services, and that there are problems of allocating costs between types of service. Such problems are especially important, for example, for integrated financial institutions, such as banks, and for realtors.

The objective of policy in the purely financial sphere is ideally to tax intermediation services, allow businesses a credit for the tax on such services, and allow financial institutions a credit for taxes on purchased inputs. The problem is that interest payments involve both a pure interest charge, which should not be taxed under a consumption-based VAT, and a charge for financial intermediation, which should be.[29] It is difficult to determine what part of interest charges should be subject to VAT (see Hoffman, Poddar, and Whalley 1987, pp. 547–48).

Zero-rating would be an ideal solution if all financial services were offered to businesses. But to the extent financial services are offered to consumers, zero-rating loses revenue and may be seen as undesirable discrimination favoring the financial sector. This could be handled with a separate tax on financial transactions with households, but only at the cost of considerable complexity, including the need to segregate business and nonbusiness transactions.

The common European practice in dealing with this problem is to exempt financial institutions, but to zero-rate foreign transactions for competitive reasons. That is, interest is treated as it is in other sectors (not taxed and thus carrying no credit), and (except for expenses of foreign lending) no credit is allowed for purchases. This treatment of domestic lending discriminates against financial services offered to business, since, as noted above, exemption of pre-retail activities creates a burden, rather than a benefit; this may be especially onerous and undesirable, given the competitive pressure from foreign financial institutions. Moreover, it is necessary to distinguish between taxable nonfinancial services and exempt financial services, and some favoritism for consumer services would remain.

It is sometimes proposed that the addition or subtraction methods be employed to impose what is, in effect, a separate tax on the financial sector.[30] This does not solve the problem of allowing credits for purchasers of financial services. In addition, under either of these approaches it would be necessary

---

29. It is not universally agreed that household costs of intermediation should be subject to tax. This issue was hotly debated within the Finance Ministry of Canada.

30. The addition method of implementing a VAT involves adding together the various components of value added. As noted in McLure (1987, p. 102, n. 40), the addition and subtraction methods are closely related.

to construct border tax adjustments to avoid competitive disadvantage for domestic financial institutions.

The only conceptually attractive and administratively feasible approach seems to be one based on cash flow to and from financial institutions. Unfortunately, it suffers from perception problems that are probably fatal.

Canada has wrestled at length with this problem; indeed, one of the most perceptive analyses of the problem (Hoffman, Poddar, and Whalley 1987) was prepared in the Ministry of Finance. The initial 1987 White Paper proposed to utilize the subtraction method for financial institutions, that is, to levy the tax on revenues from implicit charges represented by the margin on financial intermediation (Wilson 1987, pp. 130–31). Customers of financial institutions would be allowed no credit for such taxes, since they are not computed on a transactions basis. Services provided to nonresidents would be zero-rated (see also Clarkson Gordon 1989).

Apparently because of insurmountable technical difficulties, the 1989 proposals retreated to the conventional treatment of the financial sector—exemption of services rendered to residents and zero-rating of services to nonresidents (Wilson 1989a, p. 14; see also Clarkson Gordon 1989, Ernst and Young 1990).

It is difficult to know what lesson to draw from the Canadian experience in this area, except that the taxation of financial institutions is, indeed, difficult. Perhaps we can do no better than agree with Yolanda Henderson's (1988) conclusion:

> If policymakers are concerned mostly with totally avoiding a tax on saving and with simplifying the VAT rules, then deciding to exempt financial intermediaries is a reasonable compromise. If they are instead concerned with creating parity of treatment between financial intermediation and other goods and services, then they should consider using the subtraction-method VAT for intermediaries and formulating rules that provide credits to business users of these services.

10.6.4 Nonprofit Activities

Many nonprofit organizations engage in commercial activities (e.g., bookstores, cafeterias), as well as in the activities that give rise to their tax-exempt status under the income tax (e.g., health care, education). While the commercial activities should be taxable, it is commonly felt that the noncommercial activities should not be taxed. Nontaxation can take the form of either exemption or zero-rating. In the former case, tax is paid on purchases, for which no credit is allowed.

Canada has chosen to deal with this problem in a particularly complicated manner. Commercial activities will be taxed, with credit for input taxes. Other activities will be exempt, but to prevent the switch from the MST to the GST from either increasing or decreasing the tax burden on such activities, partial rebates of input taxes will be provided to certain organizations (e.g., registered charities, certain government-subsidized organizations). The standard rebate rate will be 50 percent, but special rebate rates are to be determined for each of the following four sectors providing exempt services: municipalities, universities, schools, and hospitals (the so-called MUSH sector). Allowing only partial credit means that research and education functions in the MUSH sector will taxed more heavily than in the private sector and more heavily than private investment in physical capital. There has been support for a less complex and more neutral approach, such as zero-rating. But this would result in a net transfer from the federal to subnational governments.

10.6.5   Small-Business Exemption

Several studies have indicated that small businesses find compliance with the VAT to be particularly burdensome, especially relative to large firms (see Sandford et al. 1981; Sandford and Godwin 1990). The 1984 Treasury Department study (1984, vol. 3, p. 61), concluded, however, that no small-business exemption would be needed in the United States.

The 1987 Canadian proposal for a federal GST called for making a small-business exemption available to firms with annual turnover of no more than $5,000 (Wilson 1987, p. 97).[31] The turnover figure was raised to $30,000 in the 1989 proposals. Firms with turnover below this level would be allowed to apply for registration, in order to avoid breaks in the chain of credits. Simplified accounting techniques (under which liability would be based on purchases, rather than on sales) would be available to small businesses, and those with sales below $50,000 would only be required to file annual reports (with quarterly payment of tax).[32] In addition, it was suggested that small businesses would be able to base tax liability on purchases and be paid an administration fee to help defray their costs of compliance; this practice is common in some states and provinces (Wilson 1989b, p. 22–23). In December 1990, the last feature was scaled back to a one-time credit of no more than $1,000, in order to help pay for the reduction of the rate to 7 percent (Ernst and Young 1990; Whalley and Fretz 1990).

10.6.6   Agriculture

Due in part to the zero-rating of basic groceries, the tax treatment of agriculture and fishing is relatively complex. Most output of these sectors would be zero-rated, as would much of the major equipment they use.

31. Such firms could register, in order to take advantage of input credits. The proposal indicated that the exemption level could be higher under the National Sales Tax (The quasi-BTT) and the federal VAT. I have argued elsewhere that high exemptions under the BTT create extraordinary latitude for evasion of tax through fragmentation of firms; see McLure (1987, pp. 117–23). That was in response to the proposal by Senator Roth for a BTT exemption of $10 million.

32. Japan exempts firms with annual sales of less than ¥ 300,000 and assumes for firms with sales of less than ¥ 500 million (roughly US$3.4 million or C$3 million) that purchases equal 80 percent of sales (90 percent for wholesalers). This creates a form of turnover tax, levied at an equivalent rate of 0.6 percent (0.3 percent for wholesalers) on sales of these firms.

If groceries were taxable, the tax treatment of these sectors would be somewhat less obvious. There seems, however, to be no reason that they could not be subject to tax in the United States.

10.7 Preparation

10.7.1 The U.S. Discussion

One of the most notable findings of the U.S. Treasury Department's 1984 VAT exercise was an estimate by the IRS that introduction of a VAT would require an additional 20,000 IRS employees and an additional annual expenditure of $700 million (at 1984 levels). In addition, it was estimated that eighteen months lead time would be required to get ready to implement the tax; this time would be needed for the recruitment of agents, public education, and other preparation.[33] Although these estimates have been questioned (e.g., by Tait 1988, ch. 12), it is clear that a VAT cannot be introduced without adequate preparation.

10.7.2 The Canadian Situation

In August 1989, Wilson stated that draft legislation would be released in early fall, in order to form the basis of technical discussions with business and to provide a starting point for planning and developing the systems needed to comply with the new tax to be introduced in January 1991. In addition, he said, "Well in advance of the start-up of the tax on January 1, 1991, Revenue Canada will be working closely with businesses to assist them in preparing for the new system. And most important, the government will act to ensure that the Canadian public is well-informed in advance about the GST" (Wilson 1989b, p. 35).

Despite growing skepticism in the private sector, Wilson has stated that preparation to implement the tax has been adequate, even though the legislation was only tabled on January 24, 1990, and has not yet (as of August 1990) passed the Senate.[34] Public discussion of the VAT has already stretched over three years. Registration forms were mailed to taxpayers in May 1990, and taxpayer information bulletins have been distributed. Drafts of tax returns have been prepared but not circulated.

The Canadian Ministry of Finance estimates that, whereas administration of the existing MST requires 1,500 person-years, administration of the GST

33.U.S. Treasury Department (1984, vol. 3, pp. 113, 124, 128). U.S. Internal Revenue Service (1986) estimates that a BTT extending through the retail level would require more than 16,000 additional staff members and cost almost $700 million per year. Note that these estimates are not fully comparable, for reasons stated there.

34. As indicated in note 1, the Senate passed the VAT legislation on December 14, 1990, and the tax became effective on January 1, 1991. Since business expected the tax to be implemented, new price lists and catalogs reflected the VAT. It might have been more inconvenient not to introduce the tax than to do so.

will require an additional 3,400–3,900 person years. The administrative cost of the mature system is estimated at $380 million. The estimates are based on the assumption of a ratio of 300 taxpayers to each member of the tax administration staff; this figure is rather high by European standards.[35] The additional personnel are being hired, and regional taxpayer assistance offices are being set up. It appears that implementation will occur on schedule, unless the legislation fails to pass the Senate, or is passed only with substantial amendment.

10.8   Sales Taxes in a North American Free-Trade Area

The United States and Canada have recently entered into a free-trade agreement, and there is talk of eventually including Mexico to form a North American free-trade area. This prospect raises the important question of whether coordination of sales taxation in the three countries would be necessary or desirable, and how it might be achieved.[36] Though a comprehensive discussion of these issues is beyond the scope of this paper, some preliminary thoughts are offered, concentrating on U.S.-Canadian relations.

At a formal and superficial level one can conclude, if somewhat tautologically, that tax harmonization is not necessary for the creation of a free-trade area, since a free-trade area involves only the elimination of import duties within the area. Nor is tax harmonization required for the creation of a customs union, which involves common external tariffs. But if economic integration is to go further, as it has in Europe, tax harmonization will be appropriate. The next stage in economic integration, a tax union, clearly requires harmonization. Such harmonization involves the tax bases and perhaps tax rates. Harmonization in the EC began with the VAT, and still does not encompass income taxation.

The problem is even more complicated in North America than in the European context, because of the existence of separate state and provincial sales taxes in the United States and Canada. It would clearly be easier to contemplate coordination of three unified systems than of one unified system (Mexico's) and two nonunified ones. It is conceivable that the federal government of the United States will adopt a VAT or a RST and that the state sales taxes might be merged into it, either through piggybacking or a clearinghouse mechanism. Moreover, such a result may yet occur in Canada. But this is far from a safe bet; the continued existence of parallel systems in one or both countries seems more likely. For the foreseeable future, that parallel system in the United States will take the form of no federal tax and uncoordinated state

35. This information was provided in correspondence with the author.

36. The term "coordination" is used in the generic sense of meshing tax systems to avoid undesirable economic effects or administrative burdens. "Unified" is used below to denote a sales tax system in which national and subnational taxes are coordinated, as they are in Mexico, where there is only one tax, the federal VAT collected by the states and shared with them.

taxes. In short, the coordination problem would seem to involve meshing the Canadian system of federal VAT and provincial RSTs with the U.S. system of state RSTs and no federal sales tax (and perhaps eventually with the Mexican unified VAT system).

The combination of free trade, the adoption of the Canadian GST, and the continued absence of a federal sales tax in the United States is likely to aggravate existing problems of cross-border shopping. Canadians living near the U.S. border can be expected to shop increasingly in the United States for certain goods and services that are taxed in Canada, but not across the border. (The same problem exists along the U.S. border with Mexico, but in attenuated form, both because the population of Mexico is less concentrated near the U.S. border and because U.S. and Mexican income levels are quite different.) This effect will be experienced more strongly in some sectors than in others, depending on the tax saving involved, the convenience and expense of conducting and concealing cross-border shopping, tax treatment under RSTs in the United States, and existing treatment under the Canadian MST. Especially heavily affected will be such relatively "big-ticket" and essentially undetectable "importable" activities as domestic air transportation (e.g., flying to Vancouver from Detroit, instead of from Toronto) and automobile repairs. (International air transportation, including flights to the United States on tickets not purchased in Canada and domestic connector flights, is tax exempt. The law requires self-assessment of services imported for use in Canada; in many cases of services provided to households this provision will be impossible to enforce.) Of course, this point has greater implications for some parts of Canada (and the contiguous parts of the United States) than for others. In addition, there will be increased pressure on enforcement of rules relating to declaration of values and payment of tax on mail-order sales from the United States to Canadian households. (At present, no tax is due if the value is less than $40 and the tax and duty due would be less than $5.) There seems to be little likelihood that these problems can be avoided, as long as the United States has no federal sales tax and the state RSTs do not exceed the provincial ones by enough to offset the Canadian federal VAT.

If the United States adopted a federal sales tax, it would be desirable for the two nations (three, with Mexico) to engage in some sort of coordination that would reduce the need to implement BTAs on cross-border shipments. Otherwise, progress in achieving the administrative objectives of the free-trade area by eliminating customs duties would be largely nullified. (This problem will arise once the Canadian VAT is introduced. It generally does not arise under the state and provincial taxes. If Mexico were to join the free-trade area its VAT would raise the same issues.) There are two obvious alternatives. One is to adopt the restricted-origin principle under the VAT: origin principle for trade between Canada and the United States (intra–North American free-trade area trade) and destination principle for trade with other (nonmember) nations. The other is to adopt a clearing house for tax payments among the two (three) nations (see Cnossen 1983, 1990a; Poddar 1990). The former approach has the disadvantage of requiring the same tax rate in both (all three) countries. The loss of fiscal sovereignty this entails has caused the European Community to delay its implementation since it was first recommended by the Neumark Committee in the early 1960s. (In addition, it is not clear that there is much administrative benefit, given the need to value exports.) The clearinghouse technique may be more promising, but the lack of trust that has caused its implementation to be resisted in the EC creates some doubt. It might be noted that such an approach would be somewhat simpler to operate if both (all three) countries had RSTs, rather than VATs. Presumably it could be operated if one or two had VATs and one a RST.

10.9   Concluding Remarks

The Canadian experience provides several types of lessons for the United States. For convenience, I distinguish between lessons on general issues and lessons on special questions. These are simply stated, with no further documentation or argumentation.[37] I conclude by noting that the Canadian model is not the one to follow if the United States is to consider adopting a federal sales tax.

10.9.1   General Issues

First, if the United States considers a federal sales tax, of whatever type, the tax should extend through the retail level.

Second, if relief is to be provided from the regressivity of the sales tax, it should be through explicit transfers or refundable credits, rather than through exemption or prorating of selected goods and services.

Third, it seems unwise, even so, to gamble that the Congress would apply one rate to virtually all consumption, especially if the tax is to be used to raise substantial revenue. Thus, the BTT should not be considered seriously. This view would be strengthened if it were thought that a joint federal-state BTT were under consideration.

Fourth, the credit-method VAT has considerable advantages over the RST, despite the relative simplicity and familiarity of the latter.

Fifth, there is no good answer to the problem of intergovernmental competition and coordination in this area. The two most promising approaches seem to be: a federal credit-method VAT with a clearing-house arrangement to

37. I do not bother to discuss issues about which there is neither much disagreement nor much Canadian debate, such as the superiority of the consumption base and the destination principle and the inferiority of the addition method. See, however, McLure (1987). It should also be noted that several features of the Canadian proposals reflect the prior existence of the MST. These include the decision not to zero-rate the activities of nonprofit organizations. Such considerations are not relevant for the United States and are not discussed. In addition, I do not discuss transition issues, which would not arise in the United States.

channel revenues to the state of destination of revenues; and a federal RST with state piggybacking. It appears that there would be considerable loss of state fiscal autonomy under any administratively feasible system.

Sixth, it is essential that taxpayers be prepared to implement any new federal sales tax.

Seventh, the introduction of the Canadian GST will aggravate problems of cross-border shopping and stymie efforts to allow trade to cross the international border with a minimum of delay. Adoption of a sales tax in the United States would reduce the first of these problems but would increase the need for administrative coordination between the two countries.

10.9.2   Special Questions

Food. One can only look to the proposed Canadian treatment of food with amazement. Rather than following the lead of New Zealand in introducing a relatively "clean" VAT, and after explicitly acknowledging the benefits of such a system, the government proposed a needlessly complicated form that zero-rates basic groceries. The United States should not follow Canada's lead.

Housing. The taxation of housing is problematic. Taxing the first sale of all housing is preferable to taxing new housing, but is politically difficult. If rebates for taxes on housing are to be provided, they should be designed with more attention to detail than the Canadian scheme exhibits.

Financial Institutions. As is well known, the taxation of the financial sector is extremely difficult. It might be better to zero-rate the sector than to exempt it, as Canada proposes.

Nonprofit Organizations. Rather than simply zero-rating the charitable activities of nonprofit organizations and the MUSH sector, Canada proposes to exempt them and pay partial rebates of tax. This seems to be needlessly complicated.

Small Business. The treatment of small business seems relatively generous by world standards. Such an exemption may not be needed in the United States.

Agriculture. That most agriculture will be zero-rated in Canada should have little relevance for the United States, since that feature of the proposal reflects primarily the decision to zero-rate basic groceries. If groceries are taxed, as is proper, agriculture should also be taxable.

10.9.3   Whose Lead to Follow

Despite the defects identified in this paper, Canada's VAT may not be markedly worse than those of the European Community. At least it has only one positive rate, and most exempt sales (residential sales, day care, education, health and dental services, etc.) are by those like the MUSH sector, who sell mostly to final consumers and make few taxable sales. Yet the Canadian VAT seems to be the wrong standard for comparison. It is decidedly inferior to the New Zealand tax, which is a more appropriate benchmark—and is the system the United States should emulate.

References

Aaron, Henry J., ed. 1981. *The Value Added Tax: Lessons from Europe.* Washington, D.C.: The Brookings Institution.

Barham, Vicky, S. N. Poddar, and John Whalley. 1987. The Tax Treatment of Insurance under a Consumption Type Destination Basis VAT. *National Tax Journal* 40(2): 171–82.

Brashares, Edith, Janet Furman Spreyer, and George N. Carlson. 1988. Distributional Aspects of a Federal Value Added Tax. *National Tax Journal* 41(2): 155–73.

Carlson, George N. 1980. *Value Added Tax: European Experience and Lessons for the United States.* Washington, D.C.: Government Printing Office.

Carlson, George N., and Charles E. McLure, Jr. 1984. Pros and Cons of Alternative Approaches to the Taxation of Consumption. In *Proceedings of the 77th Annual Conference,* National Tax Association-Tax Institute of America, pp. 147–54. Nashville, November 25–28.

Changes to Capital Cost Allowance Rate Announced for Electronic Point-of Sale Equipment. 1989. Ottawa: Department of Finance, Government of Canada. August 8.

Clarkson Gordon. 1989. *Sales Tax Reform and Financial Institutions.* Toronto. April.

Cnossen, Sijbren. 1983. Harmonization of Indirect Taxes in the EEC. In *Tax Assignment in Federal Countries,* ed. Charles E. McLure, Jr., pp. 150–68. Canberra, Australia: Centre for Research on Federal Financial Relations.

———. 1990. Interjurisdictional Coordination of Sales Taxes. In *Value Added Taxation in Developing Countries,* ed. Malcolm Gillis, Carl S. Shoup, and Gerardo P. Sicat, pp. 43–57. Washington, D.C.: World Bank.

———. 1991. Design of the Value-Added Tax: Lessons from Experience. In *Tax Policy in Developing Countries,* ed. Javid Khalilzadeh-Shirazi and Anwar Shah, pp. 72–85. Washington, D.C.: World Bank.

Committee for Economic Development. 1966. *A Better Balance in Federal Taxes on Business* New York.

Culp, Christopher L. 1989. Harmonizing the European Economic Community's VATs through the Market. *Tax Notes International* 1,(1): 8–12.

Dodge, David A., and John H. Sargent. 1988. Canada. In *World Tax Reform: A Progress Report,* ed. Joseph A. Pechman, pp. 43–69. Washington, D.C.: The Brookings Institution.

Due, John F. 1959. *Government Finance.* Rev. ed. Homewood, Ill.: Richard R. Irwin, Inc.

Ernst and Young. 1990. *Goods and Services Tax.* January 26.

Gillis, Malcolm. 1985. Federal Sales Taxation: A Survey of Six Decades of Experience, Critiques, and Reform Proposals. *Canadian Tax Journal* 33(1): 68–98.

Henderson, Yolanda. 1988. Financial Intermediaries under Value-Added Taxation. *New England Economic Review* (July/August): 37–50.

Hoffman, Lorey Authur, S. N. Poddar, and John Whalley. 1987. Taxation of Banking Services under a Consumption Type, Destination Basis VAT. *National Tax Journal* 40(4): 547–54.

Homma, Masaaki. 1992. Tax Reform in Japan. In *The Political Economy of Tax Reform*, ed. Takatoshi Ito and Anne O. Krueger. NBER–East Asia Seminar on Economics, vol. 1. Chicago: University of Chicago Press.

Kesselman, Jonathan R. 1986. Role of the Tax Mix in Tax Reform. In *Changing the Tax Mix*, ed. John G. Head, pp. 49–94. Sydney: Australian Tax Research Foundation.

McLure, Charles E., Jr. 1973. A Federal Tax on Value Added: U.S. View. In *Proceedings of the 66th Annual Conference*, National Tax Association-Tax Institute of America, pp. 96–103. Toronto, September 9–13.

———. 1987. *The Value Added Tax: Key to Deficit Reduction?* Washington, D.C.: American Enterprise Institute.

———. 1988. State and Local Implications of a Federal VAT. *Tax Notes* 38 (13): 1517–35.

———. 1989. Alternative Policies for the Future in Light of the Current Economic and Budget Outlook. *Journal of Accounting, Auditing and Finance* 4 (3): 388–403.

Noguchi, Yukio. 1992. Aging of Population, Social Security, and Tax Reform. In *The Political Economy of Tax Reform*, ed. Takatoshi Ito and Anne O. Krueger. NBER–East Asia Seminar on Economics, vol. 1. Chicago: University of Chicago Press.

Poddar, Satya N. 1990. Options for a VAT at the State Level. In *Value Added Taxation in Developing Countries*, ed. Malcolm Gillis, Carl S. Shoup, and Gerardo P. Sicat, pp. 104–12. Washington, D.C.: World Bank.

Sandford, Cedric, and Michael R. Godwin. 1990. VAT Administration and Compliance in Britain. In *Value Added Taxation in Developing Countries*, ed. Malcolm Gillis, Carl S. Shoup, and Gerardo P. Sicat, pp. 207–15. Washington, D.C.: World Bank.

Sandford, Cedric, Michael R. Godwin, Peter J. Hardwick, and M. I. Butterworth. 1981. *Costs and Benefits of VAT*. London: Heinemann Educational Books.

Tait, Alan A. 1988. *Value Added Tax: International Practice and Problems*. Washington, D.C.: International Monetary Fund.

U.S. Department of the Treasury. 1984. *Tax Reform for Fairness, Simplicity, and Economic Growth*. Washington, D.C. November.

U.S. General Accounting Office. 1990. *State Tax Officials Have Concerns about a Federal Consumption Tax*. Washington, D.C. March.

U.S. Internal Revenue Service. 1986. *Implementation and Administration of the Business Transfer Tax*. February.

Whalley, John. 1989. The Economics of the GST Proposal. Paper presented at annual meetings of Canadian Tax Foundation. Toronto, November 27.

Whalley, John, and Deborah Fretz. 1990. *The Economics of the GST Proposal*. Toronto: Canadian Tax Foundation.

Wilson, Michael H. 1987. *Tax Reform 1987: Sales Tax Reform*. Ottawa: Department of Finance, Government of Canada. June 18.

———. 1989a. *The Goods and Services Tax*. Ottawa: Department of Finance, Government of Canada. April 27.

———. 1989b. *Goods and Services Tax: An Overview*. Ottawa: Department of Finance, Government of Canada. August.

———. 1989c. *Goods and Services: Tax Technical Papers*. Ottawa: Department of Finance, Government of Canada. August.

Wilson Announces Sales Tax Reform Agreement with Quebec. 1990. Ottawa: Department of Finance, Government of Canada. August 30.

11

Subnational Tax Harmonization, Canada and the United States: Intent, Results, and Consequences

François Vaillancourt

The U.S. and Canadian tax systems are often compared, particularly in Canada. The comparison is usually made between the two federal tax systems, and little attention is paid to subnational–provincial/state and local—tax systems in that context. Yet subnational tax systems collect an important share—40 to 50%—of overall tax revenues in both countries and are, therefore, likely to have an impact on economic choices. Accordingly, this paper presents the subnational tax systems of the two countries and, in particular, examines the degree of harmonization within and between countries, for recent years. This project should be of interest, since there has been little, if any, comparative quantitative assessment of the degree of harmonization of subnational tax systems in Canada and the United States.

The paper is divided into five parts. In the first, we address some definitional and methodological issues. In the second, we present the key features and importance of subnational tax revenues in Canada and the United States. In the third, we examine for three major taxes—personal income, corporate income, and retail sales—the nominal tax rates, an important dimension of the intended degree of tax harmonization. In the fourth, we turn to the evidence on the effective tax burdens for these three taxes, as well as for the property tax and all taxes, and examine the resulting degree of tax harmonization. In the fifth, we reflect on the causes and consequences of the existing degree of harmonization.

François Vaillancourt is professor of economics and fellow at the Centre de Recherche et Développement en Economique, Université de Montréal.

The author wishes to thank the conference participants, particularly Jonathan Kesselman, Richard Musgrave, John Shoven, and John Whalley, participants in a workshop at the Université de Montréal and colleagues Leonard Dudley and André Raynauld for useful comments on a first version of the paper, the Sloan and Donner foundations for funding this research, and Paul Butcher and Martine Hébert for able research assistance.

11.1 Subnational Tax Harmonization: Definitional and Methodological Issues

As indicated above, the issue of measuring quantitatively the degree of tax harmonization between two or more sets of subnational governments does not appear to have been addressed before. Thus, there is no standard definition of harmonization or measurement technique. In this paper, harmonization is measured using coefficients of variations of tax rates. The smaller the coefficient, the more harmonized through uniformization are the tax rates with zero (which implies zero variance in tax rates), the limiting case. Such an approach to tax harmonization has the benefit of being operational, but suffers from its simplicity. A more comprehensive and correct definition of tax harmonization would require that the treatment of taxpayers by the tax system in terms of deduction, credits, and other tax factors be examined. In that case, harmonization would mean that taxpayers in the same economic circumstances face the same tax circumstances across jurisdictions.

Having attempted to define measurement of tax harmonization, we are faced with two additional questions: How does tax harmonization interact with benefit harmonization? Should tax harmonization be measured for the overall tax burden or for each tax taken separately? With respect to the first question, one should note that in this paper we do not address the issue of the use of tax revenues. This is a common convention in tax papers, which implicitly avoids the issue of the role of government. It was particularly appropriate here, given the data available. Ideally, one would calculate the net (benefits minus taxes) incidence of government budgets for representative taxpayers for the appropriate set of governments, and calculate the variation in those amounts. These calculations should account for the economic incidence of taxes rather than for their legal incidence (such an accounting is not done here). With respect to the second question, the answer depends on how one expects taxpayers to behave. If they correctly calculate the overall tax burden they face and are not confused by the instrument substitution governments engage in, then we should examine the overall tax burden. But if there is some fiscal illusion, it is then appropriate for us to examine the harmonization of specific taxes, since it will affect individual behavior.

Finally, one should note that the degree of tax harmonization between subnational governments in a federal state will be influenced by the actions of the federal government. The amount of influence will vary between the countries, depending on the nature of fiscal arrangements such as tax collection arrangement, sharing of revenue sources, and tax/transfer mechanisms. As shown by Boadway and Bruce (ch. 1 in this volume), Canadian institutional arrangements are more conducive to harmonization than those in the United States.

11.2   Subnational Tax Systems in Canada and the United States: Key Features and Importance

In this section, we examine the key features and importance of the U.S. and Canada subnational tax systems for the year 1986. In the other sections of the paper, we also report results for 1976. The choice of these years reflects the availability, at the time that data collecting and analysis was initiated (1989), of data sets yielding comparable information for both countries for two years.

Table 11.1 presents evidence on the main structural characteristics of the subnational tax system in Canada and the United States. One can draw several conclusions from it:

1. Subnational governments in the United States and Canada make use of the same tax instruments, with differences resulting from different assignments of jurisdiction between federal and subnational governments (e.g., for unemployment insurance) or the nonexistence or smaller importance of government intervention (e.g., for public health insurance).
2. Canadian provinces are more likely all to make use of a given tax than U.S. states (e.g., personal or corporate income taxes).
3. Canadian provinces that make use of a given tax instrument are more likely all to make use of the same specific provision than U.S. states (e.g., capital gains and food-consumed-at-home taxation).

Thus, while the same taxes are commonly used in both countries by subnational governments, the degree of harmonization appears lower in the United States than in Canada. The importance of subnational taxes can be ascertained from various angles. In table 11.2, we report evidence on the importance of specific subnational taxes with respect to GDP and to all subnational taxes for 1986. In table 11.3, we examine for 1976 and 1986 the importance of subnational taxes with respect to all taxes, so as to ascertain the level of, and changes in, their importance for both governments. Finally, in table 11.4, we examine the share of four specific taxes—personal income, corporate income, retail sales, and property—in subnational government revenue for each of the sixty such governments, as well as for the nine U.S. regions commonly used for economic analysis.

Table 11.2 shows that subnational taxes are almost twice as high in Canada as in the United States, when their importance is measured as their share of GPD. This differential is highest when direct, indirect, and payroll taxes ("All Taxes II") are used for this measurement and smallest when property taxes are also used ("All Taxes III"). The disparity is thus greater at the state/provincial level. Table 11.2 also indicates that, while the three main sources of subnational government revenues are the same—personal income tax, retail sales tax, and property tax—their relative importance is not the same. In Canada the main source of revenue for both provinces and all subnational (including local) governments is the personal income tax, while in the United States the main source for states is the retail sales tax and for all subnational governments it is the property tax.

Table 11.3 shows that the importance of subnational governments, measured by their share of subnational and federal taxes, is higher in Canada than in the United States. This also holds when provinces are compared to states. The importance particularly of states and provinces has increased from 1976 to 1986, but more so in Canada. Finally, these results indicate that part of the difference between the shares of GDP of Canadian and U.S. subnational governments is the result of their higher share of governmental activity in Canada.

The difference between Canada and the United States in the importance of subnational taxes is even more important than as shown in table 11.3, if one takes into account the deductibility of property and sales taxes (before the tax reforms of 1986) in calculating federal taxes in the United States, and the absence of such deductibility in Canada. As a result, the cost of one dollar of subnational taxes is higher in Canada than in the United States.

Table 11.4 presents data on the share of total tax revenues of four taxes by subnational government. The main finding is the high degree of variation among subnational governments in the relative importance of the four main taxes. More industrialized units (Michigan, Ontario, etc.) rely somewhat more on the corporate income tax. Differences in the share of total taxes may reflect, in part, the differences among the tax systems of subnational governments, which can be the result of choices as to the imposition, base, and rate of a given tax. This last point is examined in the next section.

11.3   Intended Harmonization: Statutory Tax Rates

In this section, we examine the statutory tax rates, in 1976 and 1986, of three taxes—personal income, corporate income, and retail sales. The absence of a statutory rate at the state/provincial level precludes the examination of the property tax. In the case of the personal income and corporate income taxes, both the first non-zero (minimum) and highest (maximum) rates are presented in tables 11.5 and 11.6, while the standard retail sales tax rate is presented in table 11.7. To facilitate the analysis, the coefficients of variation associated with these various sets of rates for a year, as well as the intertemporal correlation between 1976 and 1986, are presented in table 11.8.

Examining first the level of statutory tax rates found in tables 11.5, 11.6, and 11.7 for 1976 and 1986, one notes that the mean level is always higher in Canada than in the United States. Differences are larger for personal income tax rates (reflecting, in part, the use of tax points to effectuate federal–provincial revenue transfers), with the Canada-U.S. ratio of means ranging from 2.55 to 3.23, than for corporate income tax rates, with a ratio ranging from 1.65 to 2.21, or for retail sales tax rates (1.8 to 1.9). Mean personal income tax rates remained unchanged or declined from 1976 to 1986 in the United States, while they increased in Canada. Mean corporate income tax rates and retail sales tax rates did not decrease, and often increased, from 1976 to 1986.

With respect to variations, an examination of table 11.8 shows the following:

1. In both 1976 and 1986, the variations in the minimum and maximum personal and corporate income tax rates are greater for subnational governments in the United States than in Canada, with the exception of the minimum personal income tax rate in 1976. In the case of retail sales taxes, they are of the same order of magnitude.
2. If one regroups U.S. subnational governments into nine regions, then the difference between the U.S. and Canada coefficients of variation for personal and corporate income taxes are greatly reduced, but these coefficients are still higher for the United States. In the case of minimum personal income tax rates and retail sales taxes, the U.S. coefficients are smaller than the Canadian ones.
3. The coefficients of variation for minimum tax rates are always larger than those for maximum tax rates, except for personal income tax rates in the United States in 1976, where they are equal or almost equal. This may reflect the higher mobility of high-income earners (than low-income earners) and of larger corporations.
4. The coefficients of variation from 1976 to 1986 have decreased (personal income tax, particularly in Canada), remained roughly unchanged (retail sales tax), or increased (corporate income tax, particularly in Canada). The main change is in the coefficient of variation for the minimum rate for corporate income taxes, due to an important change in Quebec (from 12% to 3%). Except for these tax rates, the intertemporal correlation between the various sets of tax rates is quite high, ranging from 0.80 to 0.98.

These differences in statutory tax rate do not necessarily imply, however, that the effective tax burden varies to the same degree, since other features of the tax code (e.g., tax exemptions, deductions, etc.) and differences in the incomes of economic agents affect this burden. This is examined in the next section.

11.4   Resulting Harmonization: Effective Tax Rates

In this section, we examine the effective tax rates for 1976 and 1986 of four specific taxes—personal income, corporate income, retail sales, and property—as well as of all taxes. One should note that, while effective tax rates are defined as the ratio of taxes paid divided by the tax base, in this paper we calculate effective tax rates both with respect to the relevant tax base, when possible, and with respect to GDP. Thus, we calculate the ratio of personal income and of retail sales taxes to personal income and the ratio of corporate income taxes to profits, as well as their ratio to GDP. In the case of property taxes and all taxes we calculate ratios only with respect to GDP, since for property taxes we do not know the tax base by state, while for all taxes there is no tax base common to all taxes. One should also be aware that these are average and not marginal effective tax rates. Hence, they indicate what tax burden is faced, on average, by existing taxpayers, but not what the marginal tax burden of a new taxpayer is.

Tables 11.9–11.13 report the effective tax rates and their means for the four specific taxes and for all taxes, while coefficients of variations and of correlation for Canada and the United States are reported in table 11.14.

A study of the mean effective tax rates with respect to GDP, reported in tables 11.9–11.13, shows that, except for property taxes in 1976, mean effective tax rates are always higher in Canada than in the United States. Once more, differences are largest for personal income taxes, with the Canada-U.S. ratio of means equal to 2.67 in 1976 and 2.87 in 1986, while similar ratios are smaller for corporate income taxes (2.25, 2.0), retail sales taxes (1.88, 2.0), property taxes (0.87, 1.15) and all taxes (1.49, 1.51). Except for corporate income taxes, mean effective taxes increased from 1976 to 1986.

There are several conclusions to be drawn from table 11.14:

1. Coefficients of variations calculated using either GDP or specific tax bases for the four main taxes are higher in the United States than in Canada for every tax, in both 1976 and 1986. If one regroups U.S. states into regions, however, one observes a reduction in these coefficients. Effective retail sales taxes are now less dispersed in the United States than in Canada, while both personal and corporate income taxes remain more dispersed in the United States than in Canada.
2. Coefficients of variations, calculated using either GDP or specific tax bases for personal income and property taxes, decreased in both Canada and the United States from 1976 to 1986. In the case of retail sales taxes, they decreased in the United States and increased in Canada, while for corporate income taxes they increased in both countries. This last result could reflect increased tax competition.
3. Except for corporate income taxes in Canada, there is a strong intertemporal correlation between 1976 and 1986 effective rates calculated using either GDP or specific tax bases, with the correlation coefficient always above 0.66 and, in most cases, above 0.8.
4. Coefficients of variations of effective tax rates are lower than coefficients of variations calculated for the minimum statutory personal income tax rate, and higher than those calculated for the minimum and maximum corporate statutory income tax rates.
5. The coefficients of variations for all taxes are smaller than each tax-specific coefficient in 1976 and 1986, for both Canada and the United States. Thus, the overall tax burden is more uniform than specific tax burdens.

We will now examine three specific questions: (1) Do proximate states and provinces have more similar tax policies than all states and provinces? (2) Are effective tax burdens correlated together? (3) Are nominal and effective tax rates correlated together?

The results presented in table 11.15 allow us to examine the degree of variation between state and provincial effective tax rates for the six north-south regions that we created. Looking first at the combined sixty subnational governments, one finds that the degree of tax harmonization is lower than at the national level (shown in table 11.14). Thus, pressure for harmonization between subnational governments appears to be stronger within countries than between countries. The main result that emerges from regional calculations is that the coefficients of variation for the Ontario/Middle Atlantic-East North Central region are always smaller (16 of 16) than those of all states and provinces. This degree of intraregional harmonization contrasts strongly, for example, with the relative lack of harmonization in the Foothills and British Columbia/Pacific regions, for which respectively 12 out of 16 and 10 out of 16 coefficients of variations are larger than those for all states and provinces. This may reflect the fact that Ontario is the most important recipient of American investment in Canada, and thus is in more direct competition with U.S. states. A second interesting result is that, for most specific taxes (with respect to GDP), there is a fair amount of intraregional variation, with the notable exception of property taxes, where the regional coefficients of variations (11 out of 12) are almost always smaller than all the state and province coefficients. This may perhaps reflect a greater sensitivity of individuals and businesses to this tax. Finally, the overall tax burden varies much less within regions than specific taxes, indicating that there are compensatory differences in tax burdens.

The results presented in table 11.16 allow us to assess the interrelation between the various effective tax burdens measured with respect to GDP. The main result from table 11.16 is that the degree of correlation between the effective tax rates for the four main tax rates is not very high either in Canada or the United States for 1976 or 1986, but that there are some compensating differences in tax burdens. In the United States, the most striking finding is the recurring negative correlation between the retail sales tax and the three other taxes, indicating perhaps that it is a substitute for these three taxes. One also notes the positive correlation between personal income and corporate income taxes and between these two taxes and all taxes. In Canada, there is substitution between personal income taxes and corporate income taxes.

Finally, table 11.17 indicates that there is a correlation between statutory and effective tax rates in both the United States and Canada. It is a fairly strong (> 0.5) correlation in most cases, the exceptions being observed in Canada in the case of the personal income tax/maximum statutory rate correlation and in the case of the corporate income tax correlations.

11.5 Tax Harmonization: Causes and Consequences

The results presented in the preceding two sections can be examined from two perspectives. One examines what factors explain the dissimilarities between tax burdens, both within each country and between them. The second examines the impact of these dissimilarities on the behavior of economic agents and the appropriateness of these dissimilarities.

11.5.1   The Causes of Dissimilarities

Given the importance of the dissimilarities in state and provincial tax structures, we can only agree with Elder and Misiolek (1988, p. 1) that "there has been surprisingly little research directed towards explaining the wide differences which exist among the tax structures of state governments in the United States"; with Hunter and Nelson (1989, p. 41) that "there has been very little research on the political determinants of the structure of tax systems"; and with Inman (1989, p. 454) that "in contrast to our understanding of local government spending, however, we know surprisingly little about how cities and states set taxes." Indeed, these three papers appear to be the only body of recent empirical work on the specific issue of tax structures in the U.S. states. No comparable study appears to have been carried out for Canadian provinces.

The main findings of these studies are that tax structures are influenced both by interest groups, who shift taxes away from themselves (Hunter and Nelson 1989; Inman 1989), and by the structure of the economy (Elder and Misiolek 1988). Presumably, these factors also explain the differences between U.S. states reported here.

As to the differences between Canada and the United States in the coefficients of variations, the key factor in explaining them is the larger number of subnational governments in the United States. As a perusal of table 11.14 shows, calculations made using nine regions yield substantially smaller coefficients of variations, indeed, sometimes smaller than their equivalent Canadian coefficients of variations.

11.5.2   The Consequences of Dissimilarities

As Oates and Schwab (1988, pp. 333–34) stated, "The literature on local public finance contains two sharply contrasting themes. The first views interjurisdictional competition as a beneficent force . . . . however, a second body of literature contends that interjurisdictional competition is a source of distortion in public choices." As a result, it is difficult to assess whether the degree of variation in tax burdens among subnational governments is, in some sense, optimal. What can be said is that these differences in taxes probably affect, to some degree, the locational decisions of economic agents, given the recent findings of Newman and Sullivan (1988) and assuming that there is a relationship between effective average tax rates and effective marginal tax rates. Such a result, if it reflects the preferences of local residents, is an appropriate one.

11.6 Conclusion

The purpose of this paper is to draw attention to the subnational level of government in the ongoing debate on tax harmonization between Canada and the United States. This topic is of interest, since these governments account for an important and slightly growing share of taxation revenues in both countries. As a result, differences in their tax systems have an effect on locational decisions and thus on the efficiency of the national economy as a whole. The empirical findings of tables 11.8 and 11.14 show that there was a greater level of harmonization in Canada than in the United States on a tax-by-tax basis, using either statutory or effective tax rates, but that the effective overall tax burden (in table 11.14) was more harmonized in the United States than in Canada, indicating a greater degree of instrument substitution in the United States. Thus, a complete harmonization of Canadian and U.S. federal tax systems, something which is neither considered nor advocated here, would not lead to a complete harmonization of the overall tax burden in both countries. As a result, locational decisions would still be influenced by tax considerations. Indeed, one result of the 1986 U.S. tax reform, which eliminated sales tax deductions and made deductions for income and property taxes less valuable, due to lower marginal tax rates, will be to make subnational taxes more salient in individual choices (Courant and Rubinfeld 1987). Hence, we believe that more attention should be devoted both to the determinants (perhaps making use of the approach put forward by Hettich and Winer 1988) and the consequences of tax differentials at the subnational level—in both Canada and the United States, taken separately, as well as in a second step, jointly.

References

Courant, Paul N., and Daniel L. Rubinfeld. 1987. Tax Reform: Implications for the State-Local Public Sector. *Economic Perspectives* 1:87–100.
Elder, Harold W., and Walter S. Misiolek. 1988. Determinants of State Government Tax Structures: A Theoretical and Empirical Analysis. University of Alabama. Manuscript (March).
Hettich, Walter, and Stanley L. Winer. 1988. Economic and Political Foundation of Tax Structure. *American Economic Review* 78: 701–12.
Hunter, William J., and Michael A. Nelson. 1989. Interest Group Demand for Taxation. *Public Choice* 62: 41–61.
Inman, Robert P. 1989. The Local Decision to Tax: Evidence from Large U.S. Cities. *Regional Science and Urban Economics* 19: 455–91.
Newman, Robert J., and P. H. Sullivan. 1988. Econometric Analysis of Business Tax Impacts on Industrial Location: What Do We Know and How Do We Know It? *Journal of Urban Economics* 23: 215–34.
Oates, Wallace E., and Robert M. Schwab. 1988. Economic Competition among Jurisdictions: Efficiency Enhancing or Distortion Inducing? *Journal of Public Economics* 35: 333–54.

Table 11.1   **Main Structural Characteristics of the State and Provincial Tax Systems, Canada and the United States, 1986**

	Fraction of Total Jurisdictions	
Tax/Characteristic	Canada	U.S.
Personal Income Tax:		
Existence in	10/10	40/50
Use of federal income base or income tax for calculation of liabilities in	9/10[a]	34/40
Inclusion of interest income in	10/10	40/40, but some have exclusions
Inclusion of capital gains in	10/10	40/40, but various bases are used
Corporation Income Tax:		
Existence in	10/10	45/50
Sales Tax:		
Existence in	9/10	45/50
Food consumed in the home taxed in	0/9	17/45
Specific Public Health Insurance Premiums or Payroll Tax	4/10	0/50
Unemployment Insurance Payroll Tax	0/10[b]	50/50
Public Worker Compensation Financed by Payroll Tax	10/10	21/50[c]

Sources: Canada: Canadian Tax Foundation, *Provincial and Municipal Finances, 1987.* U.S.: Advisory Commission on Intergovernmental Relations, *Significant Features of Fiscal Federalism, 1987.*

[a]Quebec has its own income tax code, which is similar but not identical to the federal one.

[b]A federal responsibility in Canada.

[c]States with some or only public coverage are included in the 21 states. Other states require private insurance. See *Social Security Bulletin,* January 1986, p. 29.

Table 11.2 Subnational Government Taxes, Amounts, Percentage of GDP, and Percentage of All Taxes, Canada and the United States, 1986

Taxes	Amounts (thousands of $)		% of GDP		% of State/Provincial Taxes Collected[a]					
					Canada			U.S.		
	Canada (C$)	U.S. ($)	Canada	U.S.	I	II	III	I	II	III
(1) Personal/Individual Income Tax	24,456,200	67,469,000	4.8	1.6	46.4	40.8	31.9	29.6	26.6	18.5
(2) Corporation Income Tax	3,924,000	18,462,000	0.8	0.4	7.4	6.6	5.1	8.1	7.3	5.1
(3) Retail/General Sales Tax	12,916,000	74,927,000	2.6	1.8	24.5	21.6	16.8	32.7	29.5	20.5
(4) Motor Fuels Tax	3,290,300	14,101,000	0.7	0.3	6.3	5.6	4.3	6.2	5.6	3.9
(5) Alcohol and Tobacco Tax	1,996,800	7,511,000	0.4	0.2	3.8	3.3	2.6	3.3	3.0	2.1
(6) Other Sales and Excises Taxes	726,600	15,814,000	0.1	0.4	1.4	1.2	0.9	6.9	6.2	4.3
(7) Motor Vehicles Tax	509,000	8,372,000	0.1	0.2	1.0	0.8	0.7	3.7	3.3	2.3
(8) Other Tax Revenue	4,819,300	21,639,000	1.0	0.5	9.2	8.0	6.3	9.5	8.5	5.9
(9) Unemployment/Worker's Compensation/Health Insurance Payroll Taxes	7,295,600	25,258,000	1.4	0.6	—	12.2	9.5	—	10.0	6.9
(10) Property Taxes	16,840,400	111,711,000	3.3	2.7	—	—	21.9	—	—	30.5
(11) All Taxes I[b]	52,638,200	228,295,000	10.4	5.4	100.0	—	—	100.0	—	—
(12) All Taxes II[c]	59,933,800	253,553,000	11.8	6.0	—	100.0	—	—	100.0	—
(13) All Taxes III[d]	76,774,200	365,264,000	15.2	8.7	—	—	100.0	—	—	100.0
(14) GDP	506,103,000	4,191,705,000	—	—	—	—	—	—	—	—

Sources: Canada: (1)–(4), (8)–(9)—CANSIM MATRIX series D460885, D460886, D460887, D460888, D460889, D460891 and D460894, D460889, and D460890; (5)–(6)—CANSIM D467535, D467536; (7),(14)—Statistics Canada, *Provincial Economic Accounts: Annual Estimates, 1976–1987* (13–213), tables 10 and 1; (10)—Statistics Canada, *Consolidated Government Finances* (68–202). U.S.: Bureau of the Census, *Statistical Abstract of the United States, 1989*, (1)–(8)—table 441 ((6) equals [total sales and gross receipts] minus [general sales and gross receipts + motor fuels + alcoholic beverages and tobacco products]; (8) equals total revenue minus [sales and gross receipts + individual income + corporation net income + motor vehicle and operator's license]); (9)—table 453 (insurance trust revenue minus employee's retirement); (10)—table 457; (14)—table 697.

[a]Calculated using line (11), (12), or (13).

[b]Sum of lines (1)–(8).

[c]Sum of lines (1)–(9).

[d]Sum of lines (1)–(10).

Table 11.3   **Subnational and Federal Taxes, Amounts and Shares of All Taxes, Canada and the United States, 1976 and 1986**

	Canada				United States			
	1976		1986		1976		1986	
Taxes	C$[a]	%[b]	C$[a]	%[b]	US$[a]	%[b]	US$[a]	%[b]
Subnational Taxes:								
(1) Province/State	21.7	35.0	64.4	39.4	89.3	24.9	228	27.0
(2) Province/State + Local	28.5	45.1	81.1	49.8	156.8	43.8	373	44.1
Federal Taxes	32.3	—	81.8	—	201.4	—	472	—

Sources: Canada: Statistics Canada, *National Income and Expenditure Accounts* (13-201), tables 45, 46, and 47, pp. 50–53. U.S.: 1976 Bureau of the Census, *Statistical Abstract of the United States, 1977,* table 477, p. 293; *1978,* table 484, p. 299; *1986—1989,* tables 446, 457, and 461.

[a] Billions of current dollars.

[b] Percentages are calculated as: subnational tax (line (1) or (2)) /line (2) + federal taxes.

Table 11.4   Share of Four Main Taxes in Total Tax Revenues, United States and Canada, 1986

	Total Tax Revenue					Total Tax Revenue			
	PIT[i] (%)	CIT[ii] (%)	RST[iii] (%)	PT[iv] (%)		PIT[i] (%)	CIT[ii] (%)	RST[iii] (%)	PT[iv] (%)
U.S. STATES:									
Maine	20.3	3.1	23.1	33.8	North Carolina	28.5	6.6	17.9	21.6
New Hampshire	2.0	7.9	0.0	60.7	South Carolina	23.6	3.9	28.9	22.9
Vermont	20.0	3.9	12.3	37.5	Georgia	24.9	5.3	21.0	25.7
Massachusetts	32.1	9.5	15.3	31.1	Florida	0.0	3.3	33.8	32.2
Rhode Island	19.2	4.6	19.5	40.8	Kentucky	19.9	5.7	21.4	17.6
Connecticut	4.8	9.9	26.2	37.5	Tennessee	1.3	5.2	36.1	21.9
New York	25.7	4.2	10.5	29.5	Alabama	18.3	3.8	20.2	11.6
New Jersey	14.4	6.7	18.4	40.5	Mississippi	10.8	3.8	40.7	22.9
Pennsylvania	15.3	5.6	18.7	26.6	Arkansas	21.3	4.7	29.1	18.0
Ohio	18.3	3.1	20.9	27.9	Louisiana	8.1	4.7	20.1	15.1
Indiana	19.6	2.7	32.0	32.1	Oklahoma	16.2	2.5	15.5	18.2
Illinois	14.8	4.8	18.8	34.8	Texas	0.0	0.0	20.1	40.0
Michigan	20.9	9.3	17.2	38.2	Montana	15.3	5.2	0.0	47.3
Wisconsin	27.0	4.9	18.6	34.7	Idaho	24.2	4.1	23.7	28.4
Minnesota	27.0	5.1	18.8	30.8	Wyoming	0.0	0.0	13.8	44.7
Iowa	21.4	3.4	19.0	38.4	Colorado	19.7	2.4	15.2	35.1
Missouri	19.1	3.0	26.2	21.1	New Mexico	5.6	3.9	34.1	11.5
North Dakota	8.4	6.4	20.3	28.3	Arizona	14.3	3.5	29.8	28.6
South Dakota	0.0	3.0	24.6	41.8	Utah	21.0	3.1	26.0	28.4
Nebraska	16.5	2.6	16.4	43.3	Nevada	0.0	0.0	34.6	21.8
Kansas	17.0	4.5	16.4	38.2	Washington	0.0	0.0	43.9	27.8
Delaware	37.4	8.5	0.0	13.4	Oregon	30.8	4.2	0.0	45.3
Maryland	24.8	3.2	15.3	25.1	California	24.4	8.2	22.3	26.1
Virginia	26.8	3.5	12.6	28.2	Alaska	0.0	7.4	0.0	24.2
West Virginia	20.6	3.8	34.8	16.7	Hawaii	24.7	2.3	39.4	17.6
					Mean:	18.1	4.9	20.1	29.9

(*continued*)

Table 11.4 (continued)

U.S. REGIONS:	PIT[i] (%)	CIT[ii] (%)	RST[iii] (%)	PT[iv] (%)
		Total Tax Revenue		
New England[a]	20.8	8.5	18.2	35.5
Middle Atlantic[b]	21.2	5.0	13.8	30.9
East North Central[c]	19.2	5.3	20.3	33.7
West North Central[d]	20.3	4.0	20.3	32.2
South Atlantic[e]	18.7	4.2	22.8	26.4
East South Central[f]	12.0	4.7	28.9	18.3
West South Central[g]	4.9	1.4	20.1	31.6
Mountain[h]	14.1	2.8	23.1	30.3
Pacific[i]	2.1	6.8	23.1	27.2
Mean:	18.1	4.9	20.1	29.9

CANADIAN PROVINCES:	PIT[i] (%)	CIT[ii] (%)	RST[iii] (%)	PT[iv] (%)
		Total Tax Revenue		
Newfoundland	27.3	5.6	42.3	9.9
Prince Edward Island	29.5	6.0	41.1	15.5
Nova Scotia	36.0	5.8	30.2	17.9
New Brunswick	31.3	5.9	36.0	16.1
Quebec	45.5	2.1	22.2	18.8
Ontario	30.4	8.3	22.1	27.2
Manitoba	22.3	6.4	21.5	29.8
Saskatchewan	29.6	5.5	16.3	30.0
Alberta	37.1	14.5	2.6	41.4
British Columbia	29.8	6.7	23.5	27.4
Mean:	34.8	6.4	21.7	25.2

Sources: U.S.: Bureau of the Census, *Statistical Abstract of the United States, 1988,* table 445; *1989,* table 457. Canada: Statistics Canada, *Provincial Economic Accounts, Annual Estimates, 1976–1987* (13-213), tables 5, 6, 9, 10.

[i]Personal income tax.

[ii]Corporate income tax.

[iii]Retail sales tax.

[iv]Property tax.

[a]Maine, New Hampshire, Vermont, Massachusetts, Rhode Island, and Connecticut.

[b]New York, New Jersey, and Pennsylvania.

[c]Ohio, Indiana, Illinois, Michigan, and Wisconsin.

[d]Minnesota, Iowa, Missouri, North Dakota, South Dakota, Nebraska, and Kansas.

[e]Delaware, Maryland, Virginia, West Virginia, North Carolina, South Carolina, Georgia, and Florida.

[f]Kentucky, Tennessee, Alabama, and Mississippi.

[g]Arkansas, Louisiana, Oklahoma, and Texas.

[h]Montana, Idaho, Wyoming, Colorado, New Mexico, Arizona, Utah, and Nevada.

[i]Washington, Oregon, California, Alaska, and Hawaii.

Table 11.5   Statutory Personal Income Tax Rates, United States and Canada, 1976 and 1986

	Statutory PIT Rate 1976		Statutory PIT Rate 1986			Statutory PIT Rate 1976		Statutory PIT Rate 1986	
	Min.[a]	Max.	Min.[a]	Max.		Min.[a]	Max.	Min.[a]	Max.
U.S. STATES:									
Maine	1.0	8.0	1.0	10.0	North Carolina	3.0	7.0	3.0	7.0
New Hampshire	0.0	0.0	0.0	0.0	South Carolina	2.0	7.0	2.0	7.0
Vermont	3.5	17.5	2.9	13.2	Georgia	1.0	6.0	1.0	6.0
Massachusetts	5.0	9.0	5.0	10.0	Florida	0.0	0.0	0.0	0.0
Rhode Island	2.4	11.9	2.4	11.1	Kentucky	2.0	6.0	2.0	6.0
Connecticut	0.0	0.0	0.0	0.0	Tennessee	0.0	0.0	0.0	0.0
New York	2.0	15.0	2.0	13.5	Alabama	1.5	5.0	2.0	5.0
New Jersey	2.0	2.5	2.0	3.5	Mississippi	3.0	4.0	3.0	5.0
Pennsylvania	2.0	2.0	2.16	2.16	Arkansas	1.0	7.0	1.0	7.0
Ohio	0.5	3.5	0.855	8.55	Louisiana	2.0	6.0	2.0	6.0
Indiana	2.0	2.0	3.0	3.0	Oklahoma	0.5	6.0	0.5	6.0
Illinois	2.5	2.5	2.5	2.5	Texas	0.0	0.0	0.0	0.0
Michigan	4.6	4.6	4.6	4.6	Montana	2.0	11.0	2.0	11.0
Wisconsin	3.1	11.4	5.0	7.9	Idaho	2.0	7.5	2.0	7.5
Minnesota	1.6	15.0	1.0	9.9	Wyoming	0.0	0.0	0.0	0.0
Iowa	0.5	13.0	0.5	13.0	Colorado	3.0	8.0	3.0	8.0
Missouri	1.5	6.0	1.5	6.0	New Mexico	0.9	9.0	1.8	8.5
North Dakota	1.0	10.0	2.0	9.0	Arizona	2.0	8.0	2.0	8.0
South Dakota	0.0	0.0	0.0	0.0	Utah	2.75	7.75	2.25	7.75
Nebraska	2.1	10.5	2.1	9.5	Nevada	0.0	0.0	0.0	0.0
Kansas	2.0	6.5	2.0	9.0	Washington	0.0	0.0	0.0	0.0
Delaware	1.6	19.8	1.2	9.7	Oregon	4.0	10.0	4.0	10.0
Maryland	2.0	5.0	2.0	5.0	California	1.0	11.0	1.0	11.0
Virginia	2.0	5.75	2.0	5.75	Alaska	3.0	14.5	0.0	0.0
West Virginia	2.1	9.6	2.1	13.0	Hawaii	2.25	11.0	2.25	11.0
					Mean:	1.7	6.9	1.7	6.4

(*continued*)

Table 11.5   (continued)

U.S. REGIONS:[b]	Statutory PIT Rate				CANADIAN PROVINCES:	Statutory PIT Rate			
	1976		1986			1976		1986	
	Min.[a]	Max.	Min.[a]	Max.		Min.[a]	Max.	Min.[a]	Max.
New England	2.0	7.7	1.9	7.4	Newfoundland	2.5	19.3	3.6	20.4
Middle Atlantic	2.0	6.5	2.1	6.4	Prince Edward Island	2.2	16.9	3.1	17.8
East North Central	2.5	4.8	3.2	5.3	Nova Scotia	2.3	18.1	3.4	19.2
West North Central	1.2	8.7	1.3	8.1	New Brunswick	2.4	19.1	3.5	19.7
South Atlantic	1.7	7.5	1.7	6.7	Quebec	11.44	16.72	11.62	21.6
East South Central	1.6	3.8	1.8	4.0	Ontario	5.8	14.3	8.0	17.5
West South Central	0.9	4.7	0.9	4.7	Manitoba	2.5	24.0	3.2	22.0
Mountain	1.6	6.4	1.6	6.3	Saskatchewan	7.6	20.7	8.5	19.0
Pacific	2.0	9.3	1.4	6.4	Alberta	4.9	12.2	7.4	14.8
					British Columbia	1.9	14.8	2.8	17.8
Mean:	1.7	6.6	1.8	6.1	Mean:	4.6	17.6	5.5	19.0

Sources: U.S.:1976—Advisory Commission on Intergovernmental Relations, *Significant Features of Fiscal Federalism, 1976*, tables 64, 106, and 113; 1986—1987, table 51. Canada: 1976—Canadian Tax Foundation, *The National Finances, 1976–1977*, table 4.8; 1986—1986–1987, table 7.9.

Notes: The means are simple unweighted means of the data in the subtables. Rates of zeero indicate the absence of a tax; these rates are included in the calculation of the means and of the results reported in table 11.8.

[a]The first non-zero rate where income is broadly taxed. For Canadian provinces other than Quebec, it was calculated by multiplying the minimum federal rate by the provincial rate, which is a percentage of federal taxes. Quebec's rate is adjusted downward to account for the 16.5% federal personal income tax abatement available only in that province.

[b]As defined in table 11.4.

Table 11.6 Statutory Corporation Income Tax Rates, United States and Canada, 1976 and 1986

| | Statutory CIT Rate | | | |
| | 1976 | | 1986 | |
	Min.	Max.	Min.	Max.
U.S. STATES:				
Maine	5.0	7.0	3.5	8.93
New Hampshire	7.0	7.0	8.25	8.25
Vermont	5.0	7.5	6.0	9.0
Massachusetts	8.33	8.33	8.33	8.33
Rhode Island	8.0	8.0	8.0	8.0
Connecticut	10.0	10.0	11.5	11.5
New York	10.0	10.0	10.0	10.0
New Jersey	7.5	7.5	9.0	9.0
Pennsylvania	9.5	9.5	9.5	9.5
Ohio	4.0	8.0	5.1	9.2
Indiana	3.0	3.0	3.0	3.0
Illinois	4.0	4.0	4.0	4.0
Michigan	7.8	7.8	2.35	2.35
Wisconsin	2.3	7.9	7.9	7.9
Minnesota	12.0	12.0	6.0	12.0
Iowa	6.0	10.0	6.0	12.0
Missouri	5.0	5.0	5.0	5.0
North Dakota	3.0	6.0	3.0	10.5
South Dakota	0.0	0.0	0.0	0.0
Nebraska	3.75	4.125	4.75	6.65
Kansas	4.5	4.5	4.5	4.5
Delaware	7.2	7.2	8.7	8.7
Maryland	7.0	7.0	7.0	7.0
Virginia	6.0	6.0	6.0	6.0
West Virginia	6.0	6.0	6.0	7.0
North Carolina	6.0	6.0	6.0	6.0
South Carolina	6.0	6.0	6.0	6.0
Georgia	6.0	6.0	6.0	6.0
Florida	5.0	5.0	5.5	5.5
Kentucky	4.0	5.8	3.0	7.25
Tennessee	6.0	6.0	6.0	6.0
Alabama	5.0	5.0	5.0	5.0
Mississippi	3.0	4.0	3.0	5.0
Arkansas	1.0	6.0	1.0	6.0
Louisiana	4.0	4.0	4.0	8.0
Oklahoma	4.0	4.0	5.0	5.0
Texas	0.0	0.0	0.0	0.0
Montana	6.75	6.75	6.75	6.75
Idaho	6.5	6.5	7.7	7.7
Wyoming	0.0	0.0	0.0	0.0
Colorado	5.0	5.0	6.0	6.0
New Mexico	5.0	5.0	4.8	7.6
Arizona	2.5	10.5	2.5	10.5
Utah	6.0	6.0	5.0	5.0
Nevada	0.0	0.0	0.0	0.0
Washington	0.0	0.0	0.0	0.0
Oregon	6.0	6.0	7.5	7.5
California	9.0	9.0	9.6	9.6
Alaska	5.4	5.4	1.0	9.4
Hawaii	5.85	6.435	5.85	6.435
Mean:	5.2	6.0	5.2	6.6

(*continued*)

Table 11.6   (continued)

U.S. REGIONS:[a]

	Statutory CIT Rate			
	1976		1986	
	Min.	Max.	Min.	Max.
New England	7.2	8.0	7.6	9.0
Middle Atlantic	9.0	9.0	9.5	9.5
East North Central	4.2	6.1	4.5	5.3
West North Central	4.9	5.9	4.2	7.2
South Atlantic	6.1	6.1	6.4	6.5
East South Central	4.5	5.2	4.2	5.8
West South Central	2.2	3.5	2.5	4.7
Mountain	4.0	5.0	4.1	5.4
Pacific	5.2	5.4	4.8	6.6
Mean:	5.3	6.0	5.3	6.7

CANADIAN PROVINCES:

	Statutory CIT Rate			
	1976		1986	
	Min.	Max.	Min.	Max.
Newfoundland	14.0	14.0	10.0	16.0
Prince Edward Island	10.0	10.0	10.0	10.0
Nova Scotia	12.0	12.0	10.0	15.0
New Brunswick	9.0	12.0	9.5	15.0
Quebec	12.0	12.0	3.2	13.63
Ontario	9.0	12.0	10.0	15.5
Manitoba	13.0	15.0	10.0	17.0
Saskatchewan	12.0	14.0	10.0	17.0
Alberta	11.0	11.0	5.0	11.0
British Columbia	12.0	15.0	8.0	16.0
Mean:	11.4	12.7	8.6	14.6

Sources: U.S.: 1976—Advisory Commission on Intergovernmental Relations, *Significant Features of Fiscal Federalism, 1976*, table 113; 1986—1987, table 57. Canada: Canadian Tax Foundation, *Provincial and Municipal Finances, 1987*, tables 5.6 and 10.8.

Notes: The means are simple unweighted means of the data in the subtables. Rates of zero indicate the absence of a tax; these rates are included in the calculation of the means and of the results reported in table 11.8.

[a]As defined in table 11.4.

Table 11.7   Statutory Retail Sales Tax Rates, United States and Canada, 1976 and 1986

	Statutory RST Rate			Statutory RST Rate	
	1976	1986		1976	1986
U.S. STATES:			North Carolina	3.0	3.0
Maine	5.0	5.0	South Carolina	4.0	5.0
New Hampshire	0.0	0.0	Georgia	3.0	3.0
Vermont	3.0	4.0	Florida	4.0	5.0
Massachusetts	5.0	5.0	Kentucky	5.0	5.0
Rhode Island	5.0	6.0	Tennessee (July 1)	3.0	5.5
Connecticut	7.0	7.5	Alabama	4.0	4.0
New York	4.0	4.0	Mississippi	5.0	6.0
New Jersey	5.0	6.0	Arkansas	3.0	4.0
Pennsylvania	6.0	6.0	Louisiana	3.0	4.0
Ohio	4.0	5.0	Oklahoma	2.0	3.25
Indiana	4.0	5.0	Texas	4.0	5.25
Illinois	4.0	5.0	Montana	0.0	0.0
Michigan	4.0	4.0	Idaho	3.0	5.0
Wisconsin	4.0	5.0	Wyoming	3.0	3.0
Minnesota	4.0	6.0	Colorado	3.0	3.0
Iowa	3.0	4.0	New Mexico	4.0	4.75
Missouri	3.0	4.225	Arizona	4.0	5.0
North Dakota	4.0	5.0	Utah	4.0	4.5938
South Dakota	4.0	4.0	Nevada	2.0	5.75
Nebraska	2.5	4.0	Washington	5.0	6.5
Kansas	3.0	4.0	Oregon	0.0	0.0
Delaware	0.0	0.0	California	4.75	4.75
Maryland	4.0	5.0	Alaska	0.0	0.0
Virginia	3.0	3.5	Hawaii	4.0	4.0
West Virginia	3.0	5.0	Mean:	3.5	4.2

(*continued*)

Table 11.7 (continued)

U.S. REGIONS:[a]	Statutory RST Rate		CANADIAN PROVINCES:	Statutory RST Rate	
	1976	1986		1976	1986
New England	4.2	4.6	Newfoundland	10.0	12.0
Middle Atlantic	5.0	5.3	Prince Edward Island	8.0	10.0
East North Central	4.0	4.8	Nova Scotia	8.0	10.0
West North Central	3.4	4.5	New Brunswick	8.0	11.0
South Atlantic	3.0	3.7	Quebec	8.0	9.0
East South Central	4.2	5.1	Ontario	7.0	7.0
West South Central	3.0	4.1	Manitoba	5.0	6.0
Mountain	2.9	3.9	Saskatchewan	5.0	5.0
Pacific	2.8	3.0	Alberta	0.0	0.0
			British Columbia	7.0	7.0
Mean:	3.6	4.3	Mean:	6.6	7.7

Sources: U.S.: 1976—Advisory Commission on Intergovernmental Relations, *Significant Features of Fiscal Federalism, 1976*, tables 96, 106, and 113; 1986—1987, tables 51, 57, 58, and 61. Canada: 1976—Canadian Tax Foundation, *Provincial and Municipal Finances, 1977*, table 5.6; 1986—1987, table 10.3.

Notes: The means are simple unweighted means of the data in the subtables. Rates of zero indicate the absence of a tax; these rates are included in the calculation of the means and of the results reported in table 11.8.

[a] As defined in table 11.4.

Table 11.8   **Variations of Statutory Tax Rates, United States and Canada, 1976 and 1986**

	PIT		CIT		RST
	Min.	Max.	Min.	Max.	
		U.S.—50 States			
Coefficients of Variation:					
1976	0.72	0.72	0.53	0.46	0.43
1986	0.75	0.65	0.55	0.47	0.40
Correlation: 1976–1986	0.89	0.81	0.82	0.88	0.89
		U.S.—9 Regions[a]			
Coefficients of Variation:					
1976	0.28	0.29	0.37	0.27	0.21
1986	0.36	0.21	0.40	0.25	0.17
Correlation: 1976–1986	0.86	0.87	0.98	0.92	0.89
		Canada—10 Provinces			
Coefficients of Variation:					
1976	0.72	0.19	0.14	0.13	0.42
1986	0.56	0.11	0.29	0.16	0.46
Correlation: 1976–1986	0.98	0.80	−0.06	0.86	0.97

[a]As defined in table 11.4.

Table 11.9 Effective Tax Rates: Personal Income Taxes as a Percentage of Personal Income and GDP, United States and Canada, 1976 and 1986

	PIT			
	% of Personal Income		% of GDP	
	1976	1986	1976	1986
Maine	0.9	2.2	0.8	1.9
New Hampshire	0.1	0.15	0.1	0.14
Vermont	2.3	2.2	1.9	1.9
Massachusetts	3.2	3.5	2.8	3.1
Rhode Island	1.6	2.0	1.5	1.9
Connecticut	0.2	0.5	0.2	0.4
New York	3.1	3.8	2.5	3.2
New Jersey	0.2	1.4	0.2	11.3
Pennsylvania	1.4	1.6	1.2	1.4
Ohio	0.7	1.9	0.6	1.6
Indiana	1.2	1.8	1.0	1.6
Illinois	1.5	1.5	1.2	1.3
Michigan	1.8	2.4	1.5	2.1
Wisconsin	3.3	3.4	2.7	2.9
Minnesota	3.5	3.1	2.7	2.6
Iowa	2.1	2.3	1.6	2.0
Missouri	1.2	1.6	1.0	1.3
North Dakota	1.7	0.9	1.1	0.7
South Dakota	0.0	0.0	0.0	0.0
Nebraska	1.1	1.6	0.8	1.3
Kansas	1.3	1.6	1.0	1.4
Delaware	3.4	4.1	2.7	3.4
Maryland	2.7	2.6	2.5	2.5
Virginia	1.9	2.4	1.6	2.1
West Virginia	1.4	2.4	1.1	2.0

	PIT			
	% of Personal Income		% of GDP	
	1976	1986	1976	1986
North Carolina	2.0	2.8	1.5	2.2
South Carolina	1.7	2.4	1.4	2.0
Georgia	1.5	2.4	1.2	1.9
Florida	0.0	0.0	0.0	0.0
Kentucky	1.6	2.0	1.2	1.5
Tennessee	0.1	0.1	0.1	0.9
Alabama	1.2	1.6	1.0	1.4
Mississippi	1.0	1.1	0.8	8.6
Arkansas	1.4	1.9	1.1	1.6
Louisiana	0.6	0.9	0.3	0.6
Oklahoma	1.3	1.7	1.0	1.4
Texas	0.0	0.0	0.0	0.0
Montana	2.3	1.8	1.7	1.4
Idaho	2.1	2.3	1.6	1.9
Wyoming	0.0	0.0	0.0	0.0
Colorado	1.9	1.9	1.5	1.6
New Mexico	1.0	0.6	0.7	0.4
Arizona	1.2	1.6	1.0	1.3
Utah	2.1	2.5	1.6	1.9
Nevada	0.0	0.0	0.0	0.0
Washington	0.0	0.0	0.0	0.0
Oregon	3.2	3.3	2.5	2.9
California	1.9	2.5	1.5	2.1
Alaska	3.7	0.0	1.9	0.0
Hawaii	3.0	3.0	2.2	2.4

U.S. REGIONS:				
New England	1.8	2.1	1.6	1.9
Middle Atlantic	2.0	2.6	1.7	2.3
East North Central	1.5	2.0	1.2	1.7
West North Central	1.9	2.0	1.5	1.7
South Atlantic	1.5	1.8	1.2	1.6
East South Central	0.9	1.1	0.7	0.9
West South Central	0.4	0.5	0.3	0.4
Mountain	1.5	1.5	1.1	1.2
Pacific	1.9	2.2	1.4	1.9
Mean:	1.5	1.7	1.2	1.5

CANADIAN PROVINCES:				
Newfoundland	3.6	4.2	3.6	4.1
Prince Edward Island	3.0	3.9	3.0	4.0
Nova Scotia	3.5	5.1	3.4	4.9
New Brunswick	3.7	4.7	3.5	4.3
Quebec	7.1	8.2	6.0	7.1
Ontario	2.6	4.8	2.1	4.1
Manitoba	3.5	3.6	2.8	3.2
Saskatchewan	4.0	4.4	3.1	4.0
Alberta	2.7	3.7	1.6	2.6
British Columbia	3.3	4.5	2.7	3.8
Mean:	3.7	4.7	3.2	4.3

Sources: U.S.: Bureau of the Census, *Statistical Abstract of the United States, 1988* (for 1986 taxes), p. 270; *1977* (for 1976 taxes), p. 295; *1988* (for 1986 revenues), p. 416; *1977* (for 1976 revenues), p. 436; Bureau of Economic Analysis, *Survey of Current Business* (for GDP), May 1988, table 1. Canada: Statistics Canada, *Provincial Economic Accounts, Annual Estimates, 1976–1987* (13–213), (for personal income), table 9, line 6; (for personal income tax), table 16, line 9; Statistics Canada, *Canadian Economic Observer, 1987* (11–210), (for GDP), table 12-1.

Notes: In calculating personal income taxes for Quebec, we subtracted from reported personal income taxes an amount equivalent to the 16.5% Quebec abatement, as follows: 1976—opting-out option, $252,603,000, from Canadian Tax Foundation, *The National Finances, 1976–1977*, table 10-1, p. 144; 1986—contracting-out tax transfers, $1,431,200,000, from *The National Finances, 1986–1987*, table 16-3, pp. 16.24, 16.25.

ªAs defined in table 11.4.

Table 11.10   Effective Tax Rates: Corporation Income Taxes as a Percentage of Profits and GDP, United States and Canada, 1976 and 1986

CIT

	% of Profits		% of GDP	
	1976	1986	1976	1986
U.S. STATES:				
Maine	2.9	1.4	0.5	0.3
New Hampshire	2.4	2.3	0.4	0.5
Vermont	2.5	1.5	0.4	0.4
Massachusetts	4.5	5.0	0.7	0.9
Rhode Island	3.3	2.6	0.6	0.4
Connecticut	3.0	4.6	0.5	0.9
New York	4.0	2.7	0.7	0.5
New Jersey	2.0	2.8	0.4	0.6
Pennsylvania	3.8	2.7	0.7	0.5
Ohio	1.5	1.2	0.3	0.3
Indiana	0.9	1.0	0.2	0.2
Illinois	1.5	1.9	0.3	0.4
Michigan	2.1	4.9	0.4	0.9
Wisconsin	2.6	2.4	0.5	0.5
Minnesota	3.2	2.4	0.6	0.5
Iowa	1.3	1.4	0.3	0.3
Missouri	0.9	0.9	0.2	0.2
North Dakota	1.7	2.1	0.4	0.5
South Dakota	0.2	1.2	0.04	0.2
Nebraska	1.0	1.0	0.2	0.2
Kansas	2.1	1.6	0.5	0.4
Delaware	2.4	4.6	0.4	0.8
Maryland	2.1	1.7	0.3	0.3
Virginia	1.8	1.2	0.3	0.3
West Virginia	0.5	1.4	0.2	0.4

CIT

	% of Profits		% of GDP	
	1976	1986	1976	1986
North Carolina	2.0	2.2	0.4	0.5
South Carolina	2.5	1.6	0.5	0.3
Georgia	1.8	1.7	0.4	0.4
Florida	1.8	1.3	0.3	0.3
Kentucky	2.2	1.7	0.5	0.4
Tennessee	2.0	1.5	0.4	0.4
Alabama	1.3	1.2	0.3	0.3
Mississippi	1.3	1.0	0.3	0.3
Arkansas	1.9	1.3	0.4	0.4
Louisiana	0.8	1.1	0.3	0.4
Oklahoma	1.0	0.8	0.3	0.2
Texas	0.0	0.0	0.0	0.0
Montana	1.6	1.7	0.4	0.5
Idaho	2.4	1.5	0.5	0.3
Wyoming	0.0	0.0	0.0	0.0
Colorado	1.7	1.0	0.3	0.2
New Mexico	1.1	1.1	0.3	0.3
Arizona	1.5	1.4	0.3	0.3
Utah	1.4	1.1	0.3	0.3
Nevada	0.0	0.0	0.0	0.0
Washington	0.0	0.0	0.0	0.0
Oregon	1.6	1.7	0.4	0.4
California	3.6	3.2	0.6	0.7
Alaska	2.1	2.7	0.4	0.9
Hawaii	2.5	1.0	0.4	0.2
Mean:	1.8	1.8	0.4	0.4

U.S. REGIONS:				
New England	3.7	4.0	0.6	0.8
Middle Atlantic	3.5	2.7	0.6	0.5
East North Central	1.7	2.2	0.3	0.5
West North Central	1.7	1.5	0.4	0.3
South Atlantic	1.8	1.6	0.4	0.4
East South Central	1.8	1.4	0.4	0.4
West South Central	0.4	0.4	0.1	0.1
Mountain	1.3	1.0	0.3	0.2
Pacific	3.0	2.7	0.5	0.6
Mean:	1.8	1.8	0.4	0.4

CANADIAN PROVINCES:				
Newfoundland	6.7	13.3	0.7	0.8
Prince Edward Island	7.9	13.2	0.5	0.8
Nova Scotia	9.8	14.5	0.6	0.8
New Brunswick	9.0	16.0	0.7	0.8
Quebec	9.5	3.8	0.9	0.3
Ontario	9.3	10.3	1.0	1.1
Manitoba	14.4	13.7	1.1	0.9
Saskatchewan	12.2	13.8	0.9	0.7
Alberta	8.5	10.5	1.6	1.0
British Columbia	14.6	12.6	1.4	0.9
Mean:	10.2	12.2	0.9	0.8

Sources: U.S.: Bureau of the Census, *Statistical Abstract of the United States, 1988* (for 1986 taxes), p. 270; *1977* (for 1976 taxes), p. 295; Bureau of Economic Analysis, *Survey of Current Business* (for capital charges and GDP), May 1988, table 1. Canada: Statistics Canada, *Provincial Economic Accounts, Annual Estimates, 1976–1987* (13-213), (for corporation income), table 1, line 2; (for corporation income tax), table 5, line 2; Statistics Canada, *Canadian Economic Observer, 1987* (11-210), (for GDP), table 12-1.

^aAs defined in table 11.4.

Table 11.11   Effective Tax Rates: Retail Sales Tax as a Percentage of Personal Income and GDP, United States and Canada, 1976 and 1986

	RST					RST			
	% of Personal Income		% of GDP			% of Personal Income		% of GDP	
	1976	1986	1976	1986		1976	1986	1976	1986
U.S. STATES:									
Maine	2.6	2.6	2.2	2.2	North Carolina	1.6	1.8	1.2	1.4
New Hampshire	0.0	0.0	0.0	0.0	South Carolina	2.6	2.9	2.1	2.5
Vermont	1.1	1.4	0.9	1.1	Georgia	2.2	2.0	1.7	1.6
Massachusetts	0.9	1.7	0.8	1.5	Florida	2.4	2.9	2.2	2.8
Rhode Island	1.9	2.0	1.7	1.9	Kentucky	2.2	2.1	1.6	1.7
Connecticut	2.4	2.6	2.0	2.3	Tennessee	2.4	3.2	1.9	2.6
New York	1.7	1.6	1.4	1.3	Alabama	2.1	1.8	1.7	1.5
New Jersey	1.6	1.8	1.4	1.7	Mississippi	3.9	4.0	3.0	3.2
Pennsylvania	1.8	1.9	1.6	1.8	Arkansas	2.2	2.7	1.8	2.2
Ohio	1.5	2.1	1.2	1.8	Louisiana	2.0	2.3	1.2	1.5
Indiana	2.7	3.0	2.1	2.5	Oklahoma	1.2	1.6	0.9	1.3
Illinois	2.0	1.9	1.6	1.6	Texas	1.9	1.9	1.3	1.4
Michigan	1.7	2.0	1.4	1.8	Montana	0.0	0.0	0.0	0.0
Wisconsin	2.0	2.3	1.7	2.0	Idaho	1.9	2.2	1.4	1.9
Minnesota	1.8	2.2	1.4	1.8	Wyoming	3.1	2.8	1.7	1.6
Iowa	1.9	2.0	1.5	1.8	Colorado	1.8	1.5	1.4	1.2
Missouri	1.9	2.2	1.5	1.8	New Mexico	4.0	3.7	2.8	2.7
North Dakota	3.1	2.1	2.1	1.6	Arizona	3.3	3.3	2.7	2.7
South Dakota	2.8	2.4	2.1	2.0	Utah	2.9	3.1	2.2	2.3
Nebraska	1.7	1.6	1.3	1.3	Nevada	2.2	3.5	1.6	2.7
Kansas	2.0	1.6	1.6	1.3	Washington	4.1	4.6	3.2	4.0
Delaware	0.0	0.0	0.0	0.0	Oregon	0.0	0.0	0.0	0.0
Maryland	1.4	1.6	1.3	1.6	California	2.4	2.3	1.9	1.9
Virginia	1.2	1.1	1.0	1.0	Alaska	0.0	0.0	0.0	0.0
West Virginia	4.1	4.0	3.1	3.4	Hawaii	5.1	4.7	3.7	3.9
					Mean:	2.1	2.2	1.6	1.8

U.S. REGIONS:[a]				
New England	1.5	1.9	1.3	1.7
Middle Atlantic	1.7	1.7	1.4	1.5
East North Central	1.9	2.1	1.5	1.8
West North Central	1.9	2.0	1.5	1.7
South Atlantic	2.0	2.2	1.6	1.9
East South Central	2.5	2.7	1.9	2.2
West South Central	1.9	2.0	1.3	1.5
Mountain	2.5	2.5	1.8	2.0
Pacific	2.5	2.4	1.9	2.1
Mean:	2.1	2.2	1.6	1.8

CANADIAN PROVINCES:				
Newfoundland	5.8	6.6	5.7	6.3
Prince Edward Island	4.0	5.4	4.0	5.6
Nova Scotia	3.4	4.3	3.3	4.1
New Brunswick	3.4	5.4	3.3	5.0
Quebec	3.6	4.0	3.1	3.5
Ontario	3.0	3.5	2.4	3.0
Manitoba	3.3	3.5	2.6	3.0
Saskatchewan	3.0	2.4	2.3	2.2
Alberta	0.1	0.3	0.1	0.2
British Columbia	3.5	3.5	2.8	3.0
Mean:	3.3	3.9	3.0	3.6

Sources: U.S.: Bureau of the Census, *Statistical Abstract of the United States, 1988* (for 1986 taxes), p. 270; *1977* (for 1976 taxes), p. 295; *1988* (for 1986 revenues), p. 416; *1977* (for 1976 revenues), p. 436; Bureau of Economic Analysis, *Survey of Current Business* (for GDP), May 1988, table 1. Canada: Statistics Canada, *Provincial Economic Accounts, Annual Estimates, 1976–1987* (13-213), (for retail sales tax), table 10, line 16; (for personal income), table 16, line 9; Statistics Canada, *Canadian Economic Observer, 1987* (11-210), (for GDP), table 12-1.

[a]As defined in table 11.4.

Table 11.12 Effective Tax Rates: Property Taxes as a Percentage of GDP, United States and Canada, 1976 and 1986

	PT as % of GDP			PT as % of GDP	
	1976	1986		1976	1986
U.S. STATES:					
Maine	4.7	3.2	North Carolina	1.8	1.7
New Hampshire	5.2	4.1	South Carolina	1.9	2.0
Vermont	4.8	3.5	Georgia	2.5	2.0
Massachusetts	5.7	3.0	Florida	2.8	2.7
Rhode Island	4.3	4.0	Kentucky	1.4	1.4
Connecticut	4.3	3.3	Tennessee	1.8	1.6
New York	4.8	3.7	Alabama	0.91	0.87
New Jersey	5.4	3.7	Mississippi	1.8	1.8
Pennsylvania	2.3	2.5	Arkansas	1.6	1.4
Ohio	2.8	2.4	Louisiana	1.0	1.1
Indiana	2.8	2.6	Oklahoma	1.6	1.6
Illinois	3.1	3.0	Texas	2.3	2.8
Michigan	3.8	3.9	Montana	4.5	4.4
Wisconsin	3.8	3.7	Idaho	2.5	2.3
Minnesota	3.2	2.9	Wyoming	2.9	5.1
Iowa	3.4	3.5	Colorado	3.2	2.9
Missouri	2.5	1.5	New Mexico	1.4	0.89
North Dakota	2.7	2.3	Arizona	3.9	2.6
South Dakota	4.4	3.4	Utah	2.4	2.5
Nebraska	4.0	3.5	Nevada	2.7	1.7
Kansas	3.4	3.1	Washington	2.7	2.5
Delaware	1.5	1.2	Oregon	4.1	4.3
Maryland	3.2	2.6	California	4.4	2.3
Virginia	2.3	2.2	Alaska	5.1	2.0
West Virginia	1.5	1.6	Hawaii	1.9	1.7
			Mean:	3.1	2.6

U.S. REGIONS:[a]		
New England	5.1	3.3
Middle Atlantic	4.2	3.4
East North Central	3.2	3.1
West North Central	3.2	2.7
South Atlantic	2.4	2.2
East South Central	1.5	1.4
West South Central	1.9	2.3
Mountain	3.0	2.6
Pacific	4.2	2.4
Mean:	3.1	2.6

CANADIAN PROVINCES:		
Newfoundland	0.89	1.5
Prince Edward Island	2.0	2.1
Nova Scotia	3.0	2.4
New Brunswick	2.3	2.2
Quebec	2.8	3.0
Ontario	3.2	3.6
Manitoba	4.0	4.2
Saskatchewan	2.9	4.1
Alberta	2.1	2.9
British Columbia	4.0	3.5
Mean:	2.7	3.0

Sources: U.S.: Bureau of the Census, *Statistical Abstract of the United States, 1989* (for 1986 property taxes), p. 274; *1978* (for 1976 property taxes), p. 299; Bureau of Economic Analysis, *Survey of Current Business* (for GDP), May 1988, table 1. Canada: Statistics Canada, *Consolidated Government Finance, 1976* (68-202), (for 1976 property taxes), table 7, line 7; *1983* (for 1986 property taxes), table 7, line 4; Statistics Canada, *Canadian Economic Observer, 1987* (11-210), (for GDP), table 12-1.

[a]As defined in table 11.4.

Table 11.13 Effective Tax Rates: All Taxes as a Percentage of GDP, States and Provinces, United States and Canada, 1976 and 1986

	AT[a] as % of GDP			AT[a] as % of GDP	
	1976	1986		1976	1986
U.S. STATES:					
Maine	10.5	9.6	North Carolina	7.4	7.7
New Hampshire	8.6	6.7	South Carolina	7.9	8.6
Vermont	11.4	9.3	Georgia	7.7	7.6
Massachusetts	11.9	9.8	Florida	8.3	8.4
Rhode Island	10.3	9.8	Kentucky	7.4	7.7
Connecticut	9.2	8.8	Tennessee	7.0	7.2
New York	13.2	12.4	Alabama	7.2	7.5
New Jersey	9.6	9.2	Mississippi	8.2	8.0
Pennsylvania	9.0	9.5	Arkansas	7.4	7.6
Ohio	7.3	8.6	Louisiana	6.8	7.6
Indiana	7.3	8.0	Oklahoma	7.0	8.5
Illinois	8.3	8.5	Texas	6.3	7.1
Michigan	8.9	10.2	Montana	9.1	9.3
Wisconsin	10.4	10.8	Idaho	7.8	8.0
Minnesota	10.4	9.6	Wyoming	7.1	11.4
Iowa	8.5	9.2	Colorado	8.6	8.2
Missouri	7.4	7.0	New Mexico	8.0	7.8
North Dakota	8.3	8.1	Arizona	10.1	9.2
South Dakota	9.2	8.2	Utah	8.2	9.0
Nebraska	8.2	8.1	Nevada	8.2	7.7
Kansas	8.0	8.1	Washington	8.5	9.1
Delaware	8.7	9.0	Oregon	8.6	9.4
Maryland	10.8	10.2	California	10.3	8.7
Virginia	8.0	7.8	Alaska	9.3	12.2
West Virginia	8.1	9.7	Hawaii	10.0	9.8
			Mean:	8.7	8.8

U.S. REGIONS:[b]			CANADIAN PROVINCES:		
New England	10.7	9.2	Newfoundland	14.2	14.9
Middle Atlantic	11.3	10.9	Prince Edward Island	11.9	13.6
East North Central	8.3	9.1	Nova Scotia	13.3	13.6
West North Central	8.6	8.3	New Brunswick	12.6	13.9
South Atlantic	8.3	8.3	Quebec	18.0	15.8
East South Central	7.4	7.5	Ontario	12.8	13.3
West South Central	6.5	7.4	Manitoba	13.8	14.2
Mountain	8.7	8.7	Saskatchewan	12.0	13.5
Pacific	9.9	8.9	Alberta	7.7	7.1
			British Columbia	13.9	12.8
Mean:	8.7	8.8	Mean:	13.0	13.3

Sources: U.S. Bureau of the Census, Statistical Abstract of the United States, 1989 (for 1986 all taxes), p. 274; 1978 (for 1976 all taxes), p. 279; Bureau of Economic Analysis, Survey of Current Business (for GDP), May 1988, table 1. Canada: Statistics Canada, Consolidated Government Finance, 1976 (68-202), (for 1976 all taxes), table 7, line 20; 1983 (for 1986 all taxes), table 7, lines 3, 4, 9, and 11; Statistics Canada, Canadian Economic Observer, 1987 (11-210), (for GDP), table 12-1.

[a]All taxes.

[b]As defined in table 11.4.

Table 11.14   **Variations of Effective Tax Burdens, United States and Canada, 1976 and 1986**

	Specific Tax Base			GDP Tax Base				
	PIT	CIT	RST	PIT	CIT	RST	PT	AT
	U.S.—50 States							
Coefficients of Variation:								
1976	0.69	0.56	0.53	0.69	0.49	0.51	0.41	0.16
1986	0.63	0.65	0.50	0.64	0.57	0.50	0.38	0.14
Correlation: 1976–1986	0.78	0.73	0.94	0.87	0.71	0.94	0.79	0.66
	U.S.—9 Regions[a]							
Coefficients of Variation:								
1976	0.36	0.52	0.18	0.38	0.42	0.16	0.36	0.17
1986	0.37	0.56	0.15	0.39	0.48	0.13	0.24	0.12
Correlation: 1976–1986	0.96	0.93	0.94	0.97	0.90	0.93	0.82	0.89
	Canada—10 Provinces							
Coefficients of Variation:								
1976	0.35	0.26	0.41	0.37	0.37	0.47	0.34	0.20
1986	0.28	0.28	0.45	0.29	0.25	0.49	0.31	0.18
Correlation: 1976–1986	0.89	0.12	0.92	0.92	0.37	0.95	0.83	0.88

[a]As defined in table 11.4.

Table 11.15   **Variations of Effective Tax Rates, United States and Canada, 1976 and 1986**

	Specific Tax Base			GDP Tax Base				
	PIT	CIT	RST	PIT	CIT	RST	PT	AT
All States and Provinces (60)								
Coefficients of Variation:								
1976	0.72	1.06	0.54	0.76	0.66	0.58	0.40	0.25
1986	0.71	1.22	0.56	0.74	0.59	0.60	0.37	0.23
Correlation: 1976–1986	0.88	0.90	0.94	0.93	0.76	0.96	0.77	0.88
Atlantic/New England (10)								
Coefficients of Variation:								
1976	0.64	0.55	0.67	0.67	0.19	0.71	0.42	0.16
1986	0.60	0.81	0.66	0.62	0.35	0.70	0.29	0.25
Correlation: 1976–1986	0.96	0.97	0.97	0.96	0.73	0.97	0.87	0.90
Quebec/New England-Middle Atlantic (10)								
Coefficients of Variation:								
1976	1.06	0.57	0.57	1.05	0.28	0.56	0.24	0.25
1986	0.89	0.40	0.52	0.88	0.39	0.52	0.14	0.24
Correlation: 1976–1986	0.98	0.41	0.97	0.97	0.08	0.97	0.62	0.95
Ontario/Middle Atlantic-East North Central (9)								
Coefficients of Variation:								
1976	0.60	0.83	0.26	0.61	0.49	0.24	0.28	0.22
1986	0.48	0.86	0.28	0.46	0.51	0.26	0.19	0.18
Correlation: 1976–1986	0.81	0.90	0.92	0.81	0.69	0.91	0.76	0.95
Prairies/West North Central (9)								
Coefficients of Variation:								
1976	0.66	1.29	0.28	0.67	0.74	0.26	0.19	0.22
1986	0.65	1.28	0.25	0.68	0.55	0.28	0.27	0.27
Correlation: 1976–1986	0.95	0.99	0.69	0.95	0.95	0.79	0.64	0.96
Foothills (6)								
Coefficients of Variation:								
1976	0.81	1.34	1.16	0.82	1.24	1.21	0.30	0.09
1986	0.86	1.54	1.15	0.85	1.02	1.23	0.32	0.16
Correlation: 1976–1986	0.95	0.99	0.99	0.95	0.96	0.99	0.62	−0.15
British Columbia/Pacific (6)								
Coefficients of Variation:								
1976	0.55	1.30	0.85	0.54	0.87	0.84	0.32	0.20
1986	0.83	1.29	0.85	0.83	0.71	0.85	0.31	0.17
Correlation: 1976–1986	0.44	0.99	0.99	0.75	0.69	0.99	0.52	0.64

Notes: U.S. regions are as defined in Table 11.4. "Atlantic" includes Newfoundland, Prince Edward Island, Nova Scotia, and New brunswick. "Prairies" includes Manitoba and Saskatchewan. "Foothills" includes Alberta, Montana, Idaho, Wyoming, Washington, and Oregon.

Table 11.16   **Correlation between Effective Tax Burdens (with Respect to GDP, Canada and United States, 1976 and 1986**

		PIT		CIT		RST		PT		AT	
		1976	1986	1976	1986	1976	1986	1976	1986	1976	1986
U.S.—50 States:											
PIT	1976										
	1986				0.35		−0.19		0.02		0.34
CIT	1976	0.59									
	1986						0.37		0.15		0.34
RST	1976	−0.31		−0.23							
	1986								−0.34		−0.10
PT	1976	0.15		0.32		−0.35					
	1986										0.51
AT	1976	0.56		0.47		−0.05		0.69			
	1986										
U.S.—9 Regions:[a]											
PIT	1976										
	1986				0.79		−0.10		0.68		0.87
CIT	1976	0.82									
	1986						0.04		0.52		0.63
RST	1976	−0.06		−0.01							
	1986								−0.62		−0.32
PT	1976	0.82		0.82		−0.31					
	1986										0.80
AT	1976	0.89		0.92		−0.14		0.91			
	1986										
Canada—10 Provinces:											
PIT	1976										
	1986				−0.86		0.31		−0.19		0.65
CIT	1976	−0.48									
	1986						−0.26		0.15		−0.57
RST	1976	0.44		−0.74							
	1986								−0.69		0.71
PT	1976	−0.11		0.38		−0.42					
	1986										0.10
AT	1976	0.83		−0.39		0.57		0.20			
	1986										

[a]As defined in table 11.4

Table 11.17   **Correlation Between Effective and Nominal Tax Rates (with Respect to Specific Base), Canada and United States, 1976 and 1986**

Effective Taxes	Nominal Taxes				
	PIT		CIT		RST
	Min.	Max.	Min.	Max.	
U.S.—50 States					
PIT 1976	0.67	0.81			
1986	0.63	0.76			
CIT 1976			0.77	0.78	
1986			0.59	0.50	
RST 1976					0.57
1986					0.71
U.S.—9 Regions[a]					
PIT 1976	0.56	0.73			
1986	0.47	0.64			
CIT 1976			0.89	0.86	
1986			0.72	0.77	
RST 1976					−0.47
1986					−0.33
Canada—10 Provinces					
PIT 1976	0.73	0.19			
1986	0.65	0.41			
CIT 1976			0.25	0.71	
1986			0.82	0.27	
RST 1976					0.92
1986					0.97

[a]As defined in table 11.4.

12   Reflections on Canada-U.S. Tax Differences: Two Views

Richard A. Musgrave
Thomas A. Wilson

Richard A. Musgrave

It is not surprising that tax reform has followed rather similar patterns in the United States and in Canada. Geographic proximity and trade involvement alone prohibit extreme divergence, as do shared traditions of tax thinking. At the same time, important differences remain. Canada, as a relatively small and open economy, cannot afford strategic departures from U.S. practices, and quite different structures of fiscal federalism impose constraints on both settings. Nevertheless, common patterns dominate, and future reforms will also be subject to similar trends.

1940–1990: The Age of Income Tax

My comments will be directed at these common patterns, but first a word about what has happened in the past. The history of tax reform over the past half-century, from about 1940 to 1990, has been that of income tax. The central image has been one of personal taxation based on ability to pay and measured in terms of a comprehensive income concept, providing for horizontal equity and a progressive burden distribution. The vision began with Henry Simons's writing of 1938 and reached full bloom in the Canadian Carter Commission Report of 1967.[1] Before the Canadian Political Science Association that year, I assessed the Carter Report as follows:

Richard A. Musgrave is H. H. Burbank Professor of Political Economy Emeritus at Harvard University and adjunct professor of economics at the University of California at Santa Cruz.

1. Canada, *Report of the Royal Commission on Taxation* (Ottawa, 1966).

The Report is indeed as orthodox as it is novel and revolutionary in its conception. It is orthodox in that it follows the basic structure of tax reform first laid down by Henry Simons thirty years ago and expounded since by many if not most academic students of taxation. It is revolutionary in that these proposals, in their sweeping totality, are ingeniously applied to the Canadian setting and are made the content of a public document, presented by practical men for summary enactment. After sharing in many an effort to inch our own (U.S.) tax structure in this direction, I can only marvel at the courage of this frontal assault and wish it good-speed.[2]

What has happened since? I begin with the Canadian side, where the Carter Report opened (or hoped to open) the gate to conclusive income tax reform. At its center was the call for uniform taxation of all income sources, including those from extractive industries and from capital gains. The top marginal rate was to be cut to 50 percent, the corporation tax was to be integrated, and, reaching beyond income tax reform, Canada's manufacturing tax was to be converted into a retail sales tax. The framework of base broadening, equalization, rate cuts, and approximate revenue neutrality was thus set, to be followed twenty years later by the U.S. reform of 1986 and by reform in other countries. But Canada soon faltered in its pioneering role. The Carter Report was met by almost universal opposition (academics excepted) and got nowhere in application. It was watered down in a subsequent White Paper and once more in the 1971 legislation; the extractive industries, supported by their provinces, prevailed, and little of the original message remained. Instead, a decade of income tax deterioration and base loss followed. Only in 1987, and following the U.S. reform of 1986, did the Carter spirit revive. Substantial income tax reform was achieved, but the proposed overhaul of commodity taxation—with VAT in the place of retail tax—is still unresolved.

The story of reform in the United States is essentially one of income taxation. Ever since the elevation of the income tax to a mass tax at the outset of World War II, the U.S. personal income tax has provided the core of the federal tax system. Over most of the period, the system featured steeply progressive nominal rates which, combined with a deficient base, yielded a much flatter pattern of effective rates. Occasional attempts at improvement were made, but they were exceptions. In the early 1960s, for example, the investment tax credit was included in place of accelerated depreciation as an incentive device. Loopholes widened, and the inflation of the 1970s brought new distortions, with unfair taxation of purely nominal gains. A Carter-style Treasury document (referred to as *Blueprints*) appeared in 1977 but failed to gain official status.[3] Instead, the supply-side-inspired reform of 1981 reduced the top personal rate from 70 to 50 percent and added a distorting pattern of highly accelerated depreciation.

2. R. A. Musgrave, "In Defense of an Income Concept," *Harvard Law Review* 81, no. 1 (1967): 42–62.

3. U.S. Treasury Department, *Blueprints for Basic Tax Reform* (Washington, D.C., 1977).

A change in direction began with the Treasury study of 1984 (referred to as *Treasury I*) and its comprehensive approach to income tax reform.[4] In Carter-like fashion, the goal was to combine base broadening, especially in relation to capital income, with a flattening of bracket rates. The number of brackets was to be reduced to three, with rates of 15, 25, and 35 percent. There was also to be a substantial increase in personal exemptions, so as to offset erosion by inflation since the late 1970s. In combination, the reform proposals would be essentially revenue neutral. Effective rates would be reduced at the lower end, but their pattern over the middle and upper range would be left more or less unchanged. The net outcome would be to improve horizontal equity and to reduce distorting effects. Indexing of rate brackets would protect against inflation.

Treasury I was followed by the administration's official recommendations (*Treasury II*), which offered a watered-down version, and then by the actual legislation of 1986.[5] The top rate was reduced to 28 percent, but capital gains were included in the base. Though falling far short of *Treasury I* or the Carter model, the legislation was nevertheless a major overhaul and was a high point of income tax reform, as was its Canadian counterpart of the following year. We now turn to consider whether this reform trend may be expected to continue or whether it will be followed by a change in direction, based on changing economic conditions, social climate, and new patterns of tax analysis. As in the past, any new trends affecting tax reform are likely to be shared by Canada and the United States.

The 1990s: New Patterns of Reform?

Among major elements of change, I will note (1) the emergence of consumption as a respectable tax base, (2) a flattening of upper-income progression, (3) a new perspective on corporation tax, (4) the rise of the payroll tax, and (5) adaptation of tax design to an open economy setting. These developments may have substantial bearing on the role of income taxation.

(1) I begin with the emergence of consumption as a respectable tax base. Ever since John Stuart Mill, economists have faulted the income tax base for penalizing late consumers and discriminating against saving. The optimal-taxation literature of the 1970s further stressed this point. At the same time, the consumption base gained in repute by a change in its image from an in rem commodity tax to a personalized expenditure tax. This helped to overcome earlier, equity-based objections. The case for the consumption base was strengthened by the compounding difficulties of income taxation. Many of these, especially those relating to the taxation of capital income under conditions of inflation, would be bypassed by an expenditure tax.

---

4. U.S. Treasury Department, *Tax Reform for Fairness, Simplicity , and Economic Growth* (Washington, D.C., 1984).

5. *President's Tax Proposals to the Congress for Fairness, Growth, and Simplicity* (Washington, D.C., 1985).

All this added to the attraction of the consumption base, but the case for a personalized and progressive expenditure tax was too novel to seriously enter the public discussion. Instead, the love affair with the commodity base focused on the value-added tax, which would serve as a superior replacement for the turnover tax and a more practicable alternative to the retail sales tax. At the same time, it would retain traditional support from some quarters as preferable to progressive income taxation, while gaining new support from others as a politically feasible, if second-best, way of sustaining public services and social programs. As a result of these arguments, the United States may well follow Canada in adding a value-added tax to its federal revenue system.

Whereas a progressive expenditure tax would remain within the family of direct taxation, the trend toward VAT implies not only a change in base, but also a change from visible and personal to hidden and in rem taxation. It is this latter shift that is especially unfortunate. This trend is supported also in the context of optimal commodity taxation, with its focus on selected commodities as appropriate tax bases.

(2) Support for progressive rates had eroded with the shrinking of the tax base, and it took a drastic plunge in the reforms of the 1980s. Various causes may be noted. At the academic level, the case for rate progression was weakened by allowance for deadweight loss and its compounding burden as marginal rates rise. For any given social welfare function, the pattern of nominal rates needed to minimize aggregate welfare loss is thus flatter than had been concluded previously. Argued less rigorously, but more important in practice, was concern over detrimental effects of high marginal rates on growth and the dynamics of enterprise. In addition, reduced concern with progressivity received support from a change in political climate, reflected in a flattening of the social welfare function as perceived by the voting public. While effective rate progression over the lower-middle range of the income scale retained acceptance, support for extension over the middle-upper range fell off. With lower-end progressivity provided for by a personal exemption or credit (a better alternative, used in Canada), a more or less flat nominal rate would take care of the remainder.

To be sure, the steeply rising nominal rates that had prevailed previously in many countries were largely ineffective in application, offset as they were by an imperfect base. The reforms of 1986 and 1987, with their offsetting rate and base adjustments, thus had little effect on the pattern of effective rates over the middle-upper range. The U.S. cut in effective rates had been made in 1980. Nevertheless, it was the U.S. reform of 1986, with its drastic cut in the top bracket rate to 28%, that marked the strategic turning point. In order to verify the preexisting pattern of effective rates to some degree, the reforms might have combined base broadening with retention of some nominal rate progression. This would have given some credence to the previously existing pattern of nominal bracket rates. Instead, their failure was ratified, and the principle of effective rate progression was withdrawn.[6]

Whether the flat-rate perception of vertical equity is here to stay, time will tell. If so, the question arises whether there remains a raison d'être, under a flat-rate system, for a personalized income tax. The inevitably cumbersome and complex process of personal taxation was the inevitable price of a system seeking (even if not reaching) to extend effective rate progression over the upper range. Without this goal, a flat-rate tax on income at source, combined with a flat transfer, would be much the simpler solution. The same holds for the consumption base. Under a VAT, lower-end protection might again be built into the base or be provided via transfers. Needless to say, impersonal flat-rate and invisible taxes are not my dream of responsible taxation in a democratic society, but such may be the course of events.

(3) No major reform changes were made in the treatment of the corporation income tax, but recent proposals for a cash-flow type business tax fit the above pattern. As part of a withholding system for the purpose of a flat-rate income tax, the cash-flow tax is inadequate, since the larger part of capital income or its interest equivalent is excluded. Only rent and excess profits remain in the base. As a withholding tax on wage income, noting that a consumption tax is essentially similar to a tax on wage income, it may be seen as "prepayment" of a flat-rate consumption tax.[7] The idea of a consumption tax has appeal, but its shadow image as an income tax on wage income only will hardly pass congressional muster, and perhaps for good reason.

(4) It might be argued that transition from general and personal income taxation to wage income taxation is nothing new, but has been in process over the decades, based on the growth of social security finance. Perhaps so, but I feel uneasy viewing the payroll tax as part of the general tax system without also allowing for the benefits financed thereby. To the extent that the payroll tax is linked to social security finance, which is more strictly the case in the United States than in Canada, its otherwise objectionable nature as regressive and in rem gives way to its more meaningful role as an intergenerational benefit tax.

(5) Finally, there is the growing importance of open economy considerations. As initially visualized in the Tiebout model, a marketlike mechanism of voting by feet could be relied upon to secure an optimal adjustment among fiscal jurisdictions; this vision still underlies much of the discussion.[8] The

---

6. R. A. Musgrave, "Short of Euphoria," *Journal of Economic Perspectives 1*, no. 1 (1987):59–71.

7. Charles E. McLure, Jr., J. Mutti, V. Thuronyi, and G. R. Zodrow, *The Taxation of Income from Business and Capital in Colombia* (Bogotá: Ministerio de Hacienda y Credito Publico, 1990).

8. Charles Tiebout, "An Economic Theory of Fiscal Decentralization," in *Public Finances: Needs, Sources, and Utilization* (Princeton: Princeton University Press, 1969).

model, when presented in my Michigan seminar of 1955, was ingenious and later became the basic theorem of fiscal federalism. Nevertheless, its power rested on a set of rather restrictive assumptions, assumptions which do not readily permit transfer from the local to the international setting. Among the premises are that all factors are equally mobile and that all taxes are paid on a strictly benefit basis. As to the former, capital is vastly more mobile in the international setting than is labor. As to the latter, a case can be made that public services should be financed on a benefit basis, but they are not, and even if they were, distributional objectives of the fiscal system would still need to be accounted for. Their disregard may have justification at the level of local finance but becomes unacceptable at the national level.

For these and other reasons, the Tiebout model and its invisible-hand solution to tax coordination does not resolve the international setting. A statutory arrangement has to be provided for to secure an efficient and equitable solution. Such an order may take the form of equalization, in which each jurisdiction remains free to have its own system, but differentials are neutralized. Forced uniformity, in this as in other contexts, is to be avoided, so the coordination technique should be preferred. I was surprised, therefore, to find primary concern with equalization in the conference papers.

The principle of coordination is straightforward, requiring the country of residence to credit source-country withholding. But difficulties remain. Crediting does not apply to retained earnings, sources may be difficult to identify, choice of residency permits tax avoidance, and so forth. These difficulties do not arise with the consumption base. A destination-based value-added tax is neutral, and even a personal expenditure tax is less open to avoidance by foreign consumption than is an income tax by foreign investment. Once more, income taxation seems to be at a disadvantage.

There is, however, an important reason for its retention. A good system of international taxation should be not only efficient and equitable as applied to the particular taxpayer, but also equitable between jurisdictions. The principle of international equity should be observed, entitling the country of source to a share in the income tax base that originates within its borders but accrues to foreign-owned capital.[9] Considerations of benefit taxation aside, such an entitlement arises as a matter of fairness, based upon a concept of international property rights agreed to by the participating jurisdictions. The legal property order, in an increasingly open world economy, cannot be written in national terms only. Implementation of such an entitlement, unnecessary to add, is of particular importance to capital-importing developing countries.

Suppose first that the countries concerned do not impose a classical corporation tax. They nevertheless agree on a mutually acceptable sharing rate and impose a corresponding withholding tax as profits are repatriated. To assure

---

9. P. B. Musgrave, "Interjurisdictional Coordination of Taxes on Capital Income," in *Tax Coordination in the European Community*, ed. S. Cnossen (Antwerp: Kluwer Law and Taxation Publishers, 1987).

neutrality, the country of residence will then grant a credit against the shareholder's income tax. The same principle applies in a regime of classical corporation tax. A sharing rate will again be agreed upon, with the withholding rate now equal to the excess (plus or minus) of the sharing rate over the source country's rate of corporation tax. Once more the country of residence will credit the withholding tax against its own corporation tax. In this way, considerations of both neutrality and equity are reconciled, while each country retains the freedom to choose its own rate of corporation tax. Contrary to the so-called nondiscrimination rule, setting the sharing rate becomes independent of the countries' own rates. Whether or not a classical corporation tax is applied, it remains necessary to determine taxable profits to which the sharing rate applies. Such remains the case even if domestic taxation is placed on a consumption base. While a VAT automatically permits the country of residence to tax the consumption of its foreigners, this is hardly an adequate allowance for base sharing.

Other elements of change might be noted, which may condition the tax climate of the 1990s and shape future tax reform. In both Canada and the United States, the reforms of the late 1980s may well have marked the end of a period. The traditional focus on income, on horizontal equity, and on effective rate progression may yield to new directions. Only time will tell whether they will bring reform or deform.

Thomas A. Wilson

This paper presents a brief comparative review of the tax systems of Canada and the United States. Although I will emphasize the differences, it should be borne in mind that the two countries' fiscal systems have many features in common, and that the Canada-U.S. tax treaty effectively harmonizes the treatment of most cross-border income flows.

I begin with a broad overview of the relative importance of the major taxes, and then examine how the two systems deal with several key issues: the treatment of income from equities; the treatment of savings and investment; rate schedules; and federal/provincial arrangements. The final two sections of the paper review the effects of recent and proposed tax reforms in Canada and consider possible future fiscal developments as the Canada-U.S. free-trade agreement is phased in.

The "Tax Mix": The Role of Major Taxes as Revenue Sources

Table 12.1 compares the relative importance of the major revenue sources—personal income taxes, corporate income taxes, indirect taxes,

Thomas A. Wilson is professor of economics and director of the Policy and Economic Analysis Program of the Institute for Policy Analysis at the University of Toronto.

Table 12.1   **Relative Importance of Major Taxes, 1987**
                   (Tax Revenues as % of GDP/GNP)

Tax Source	Canada	U.S.	OECD Average
Personal Income	13.4	10.9	12.0
Corporate Income	2.8	2.4	3.0
Indirect (Sales & Excise)	10.0	5.0	11.8
Social Security (Payroll)	4.6	8.6	9.5
Wealth	3.2	3.1	2.1
Total (Excluding Social Security)	29.9	21.4	29.3
Total (Including Social Security)	34.5	30.0	38.8

Source: David Perry, "International Tax Comparisons," *Canadian Tax Journal* 37, no. 5 (1989): 1347–57.

wealth taxes, and social security taxes—for Canada, the United States, and the OECD, on average. These data are revenues for all levels of government in each country, expressed as percentages of GDP/GNP.

Two striking differences between the U.S. and Canadian revenue systems appear. Indirect taxes are twice as important in Canada as in the United States, reflecting the absence of a federal sales tax in the United States, and somewhat higher provincial retail taxes in Canada relative to state retail taxes in the United States. At 10 percent of GDP, the role of indirect taxes in Canada is somewhat below the OECD average of 11.8 percent.

On the other hand, payroll taxes to finance social security programs are much more important in the United States than in Canada. At 8.6 percent of GDP, U.S. social security taxes are close to the OECD average (9.5 percent), and well above the Canadian level.

Both Canada and the United States rely on the personal income tax (PIT) as a principal revenue source, with Canada collecting somewhat more than the United States and somewhat more than the OECD average. The relative importance of the PIT has increased in recent years in both countries. Currently, the effective PIT burden in Canada is almost 25 percent higher than in the United States.

As for corporate income taxes, in recent years this revenue source has been declining in relative importance in most countries, including the United States and Canada. Current effective rates in Canada and the United States are 2.8 and 2.4 percent of GDP, respectively, just below the 3.0 percent OECD average.

Wealth taxes are surprisingly similar as a revenue source in the two countries. Canada has no estate tax, and U.S. estate taxes are not an important source of revenue, yielding only 0.2 percent of GNP. In both countries, the most important wealth taxes are taxes on real property, with revenue yields of 2.7 percent in Canada and 2.8 percent in the United States.

It is also apparent that the overall tax burden is higher in Canada than in the United States, particularly if social security taxes are omitted.[10] Without social security taxes, the total tax burden in Canada is 29.9 percent of GDP, just above the OECD average and well above the U.S. level of 21.4 percent of GNP.

When social security taxes are included, the gap between Canadian and U.S. tax burdens is narrowed. Canada is then 4.5 percentage points below the OECD average, but still 4.3 percent above the U.S. level. I shall return to the issue of overall burdens after review of certain key differences in the tax structures of the two countries.

The Treatment of Income from Equities

As is well known, the United States has a "classical" corporate income tax—a separate tax on corporate income that is generally not integrated with the personal income tax.[11] The Canadian system, by contrast, involves partial integration of dividend income (and full integration of dividends from small firms). This integration is effected by a "gross-up and credit" applied to dividend income. At the present time, dividend income is grossed up by 25 percent before calculating tax and is subject to a 25 percent credit. This effectively reduces the marginal rate of tax on dividend income, providing partial relief from the corporate taxes presumably borne by that income.[12]

Of course, dividend income is not the only component of income from equities. The other major component is capital gains on sale of shares. In the United States, since the 1986 tax reform, capital gains are subject to tax on realization at full marginal rates. In Canada, a lifetime exemption was introduced prior to the 1987 tax reform. Under tax reform, the exemption was limited to $100,000, and the inclusion rate for other capital gains was raised in two stages to 75 percent.[13] Effective marginal tax rates on capital gains are therefore three-quarters of the rate applicable to other income.

Overall, it is clear that Canada treats income from equities of Canadian firms considerably more favorably than other income under its PIT. This is a difference between the Canadian and U.S. tax systems that has persisted over time. It represents a deliberate use of the tax system to encourage equity investment in Canadian companies by Canadian residents, perhaps as an out-

---

10. Some would argue that, since social security taxes pay for identifiable benefits, they do not constitute a burden (or at least as large a burden) as do other taxes. See Boadway and Bruce (ch. 1 in this volume).

11. The exception is the tax on small corporations when all stockholders elect partnership treatment under Subchapter S.

12. For example, an individual with a combined top marginal rate of 48 percent would pay approximately 35 percent on dividend income. Since the dividend gross-up and credit mechanism applies to *any* dividends paid by Canadian corporations to Canadian residents, dividends from corporations that do not pay tax get a credit for "phantom" corporate tax.

13. Capital gains on shares of small business corporations and capital gains on the sale of family farms receive an exemption of $500,000. Prior to the 1987 reforms, the inclusion rate for capital gains was 50 percent; this was increased to 66 2/3 percent for 1988 and 1989, and to 75 percent in 1990.

growth of public concern about the role of foreign ownership and control of Canadian enterprises.

Tax Treatment of Savings

The double taxation of savings, like the double taxation of equity income, has long been an issue in the public finance literature. Indeed, proponents of consumption-based taxes rely heavily on their advantages in avoiding this double taxation and thereby reducing the dead-weight losses associated with taxation.

Both the Canadian and U.S. PITs involve significant departures from the Haig/Simons definition of income as a base. Some of these departures—the omission of imputed rental income from the tax base and the deductibility of contributions to pension plans—move the PIT in the direction of a direct tax on consumption.

Overall, the Canadian PIT has moved further in this direction than the U.S. PIT has, although some of the recent "reforms" in Canada have moved the Canadian system back toward an income base.

Both systems exclude imputed income from owned consumer assets from the tax base, as is appropriate under a consumption-based tax. However, the United States, by permitting deduction of interest paid to acquire these assets, effectively encourages acquisition of consumer assets relative to other assets, moving the U.S. system away from a pure tax on consumption.[14]

Both systems also allow for favorable treatment of retirement savings, but the Canadian RRSP deductions are more generous and more widely available than U.S. IRA deductions, and Canada allows deductions for individual contributions to pension plans, whereas the United States does not.

Although the 1987 tax reform moved the Canadian PIT away from a consumption base, it nevertheless remains closer to a consumption base than its U.S. counterpart.[15] It is fair to conclude that the marginal rate of return earned by many savers in Canada is the before-tax rate of interest, whereas the typical saver in the United States earns the after-tax rate of interest.[16]

Tax Treatment of Investment

In recent years, both countries have moved (unwisely, in my opinion) to eliminate or reduce many of the incentives for investment that had previously been introduced. The course of corporate tax reform in Canada was charted in a White Paper issued in 1985, which proposed the phaseout of the general

14. Although currently the deductibility of interest on loans to finance personal assets is limited to mortgages or housing equity loans, it is nevertheless relatively easy for U.S. residents to finance acquisition of consumer durables, as well as housing, through such loans.

15. The most important 1987 Canadian change in this respect is the elimination of the $1,000 investment-income deduction. Other measures have limited the ability to defer receipt of interest income (e.g., by the purchase of deferred annuities).

16. Canadian taxpayers who have mortgages on their residences typically earn the before-tax rate of interest when they pay down their mortgages. Furthermore, many Canadian taxpayers have not reached their RRSP contribution limits.

investment tax credit over a three-year period, reductions in capital cost allowance rates, other base-broadening measures, and substantial reductions in statutory rates.[17] The first step was implemented in the 1986 budget, and subsequent steps were included in the 1987 tax reform package.

In the United States, the 1986 tax reform act swept away the general investment tax credit and sharply limited allowable depreciation rates. Coupled with other base-broadening measures, these changes permitted substantial reductions in statutory rates.

Both countries have probably somewhat reduced the interindustry and interasset distortions under their corporate income taxes, but at the cost of increased intertemporal distortions. As I noted in a previous paper[18] the tax reforms shifted the tax burden from old capital to new capital, thereby increasing the effective tax rate on investment.[19]

Tax Treatment of the Family

A salient difference between the two personal income tax systems is the definition of the taxpaying unit. In the United States, because of income splitting through joint returns, the basic unit is effectively the nuclear couple; in Canada, the personal income tax is largely on an individual basis.[20]

Taxing income on an individual basis can reduce tax disincentives for the lower-income spouse. Canada's recent tax reform, by replacing the spousal exemption with a credit, has further reduced such tax disincentives. Under the current Canadian tax system, the "secondary" earner faces tax initially at the lowest bracket rate. In contrast, under the U.S. system, the effective marginal rate of tax for the lower-income spouse is the appropriate marginal rate on the couple's combined income.

Like many issues in taxation, this advantage to the Canadian system entails a cost in the form of extraordinarily complex "attribution" rules to prevent shifting of property income from the higher to the lower-income spouse. The obvious solution is to combine the best features of the two systems. For example, earned income could be taxed on an individual basis, as in Canada, and property income on a pooled basis, as in the United States.[21]

The two countries have also adopted very different treatments for dependent

17. Hon. Michael Wilson, *The Corporate Tax System: A Direction for Change* (Ottawa: Department of Finance, Government of Canada, 1985).

18. Thomas A. Wilson, "The Corporate Income Tax Proposals: Reform or Retrogression," in *Report of the Policy Forum on Reform of the Corporate Income Tax System*, ed. Jack M. Mintz and Douglas D. Purvis (Ontario: Queen's University, Nov. 1985).

19. This is strictly true for investments made by taxable firms. For risky investments by firms who are, or may be in tax loss positions, the reduction in statutory rates may outweigh the removal of tax credits. See Vijay Jog and Jack Mintz, "Corporate Tax Reform and its Economic Impact: An Evaluation of Phase 1 Proposals," in *The Economic Impacts of Tax Reform*, ed. Jack Mintz and John Whalley, pp. 83–124. (Toronto: Canadian Tax Foundation, 1989).

20. The Canadian PIT is no longer strictly on an individual basis. Certain credits are transferable between spouses, and the child tax credit is clawed back on the basis of family income.

21. An alternative method would be joint returns, coupled with adequate earned-income credits for the lower-income spouse.

children. The U.S. PIT provides the same exemption for a child as for an adult. Until recently, the Canadian PIT provided a much smaller exemption for a child, coupled with refundable tax credits and taxable transfers (family allowances). Following tax reform, the Canadian system now provides a mixture of nonrefundable tax credits, refundable tax credits that are clawed back, and taxable transfers that are proposed to be clawed back.[22]

The Canadian system clearly delivers better child benefits for lower- and lower-middle-income families than does the United States system. But as income rises, at some point middle-income families find their benefits beginning to be clawed back, and at a higher income level, all child benefits except the nonrefundable tax credit would be totally clawed back.[23]

Rate Schedules

Following the 1986 and 1987 tax reforms, both countries reduced the number of rate brackets and lowered their top marginal rates. In the United States, what appears on the surface to be two brackets, with a top rate of 28 percent, is in reality four brackets with a top rate of 33 percent (applied to the third, but not the final, bracket). In Canada, what was proposed to be three rate brackets has since become four brackets (because of the high-income surtax). Furthermore, effective marginal rates in the Canadian system are also affected by the various clawbacks of refundable credits and transfer payments, so that the number of true tax brackets is even larger.[24]

Providing fewer brackets has been justified on grounds of tax simplification, but I do not accept this argument. While there is no denying that a single rate would permit a vast simplification of the system, two brackets imply almost the same degree of complexity as fifteen! The problems of tax shelters, income splitting, and income averaging arise as soon as there is more than one effective marginal rate.

The top marginal income tax rate has been lowered significantly over the past ten years. Currently, the top U.S. federal rate is 33 percent, and the top Canadian federal rate will soon be 32 percent. Although the top marginal rates of the federal PITs are quite similar, significant differences emerge when state and provincial income taxes are taken into account. Data provided in Vaillancourt (ch. 11 in this volume) indicate that the typical top marginal rate for U.S. state income tax is 6.6 percent (deductible from federal tax), whereas

22. For a detailed discussion of the Canadian and U.S. treatments of dependent children, see Kesselman (ch. 3 in this volume).

23. A measure in the 1990 federal budget would claw back family allowances at a 15 percent rate, starting at an individual income level of $50,000 for the higher-income spouse. A single-earner family with two children would see its family allowance payments totally clawed back at an income level just above $55,000.

24. The refundable sales tax credit is clawed back at a 5 percent rate, starting at a family income level of $18,000. The refundable child tax credit is also clawed back at a 5 percent rate, but the clawback begins at a family income of $24,750. OAS and family allowance payments are proposed to be clawed back at a 15 percent rate on an individual basis, starting at an individual income of $50,000.

the typical top marginal rate for provincial income tax in Canada is 17 percent. As a result, the combined marginal rate of federal plus provincial tax in Canada is typically much higher than the combined rate in the United States. Indeed, in most provinces the combined top marginal rates approach 50 percent, whereas the highest combined marginal rate in the United States is about 42 percent.[25]

Federal/Provincial Fiscal Arrangements

There are two features of the Canadian federal tax system that have no counterpart in the United States. First, the federal government has entered into collection agreements with nine of the ten provinces for personal income taxes, and with seven provinces for corporate income taxes. This has led to much greater subnational harmonization of the income tax systems in Canada than in the United States. It may also have lowered the political cost of raising provincial taxes, since individuals see only one line for income tax withheld on their payroll statements and write only one check to settle their balances each April.

Second, and more important, are the equalization arrangements, under which the federal government equalizes the revenue yield of taxes in lower-income provinces up to the average yield of the five richest provinces; seven out of ten provinces currently receive equalization payments.[26] Equalization clearly reduces the cost of public goods relative to private goods in those provinces.[27]

Effects of Recent Proposed Tax Reforms in Canada

The income tax reforms of the past four years have moved the Canadian income tax system somewhat away from a consumption-based tax and have removed or lessened tax incentives for investment. It is reasonable to conclude that the net effect of the income tax reforms has been an increase in the tax burden on savings and investment.[28]

Phase II of tax reform was originally designed to do two things: to replace the antiquated manufacturers' sales tax with a new consumption-based value-added tax; and to shift the tax mix from direct to indirect taxes by reducing personal income taxes and increasing sales taxes.

---

25. For 1990, the combined top marginal rate equaled or exceeded 48 percent in all provinces except British Columbia, Alberta, and Nova Scotia.

26. *Provincial and Municipal Finances, 1989* (Toronto: Canadian Tax Foundation, 1990), table 13.2.

27. The provision of certain public goods has been encouraged under federal/provincial shared-cost programs. However, the most important of these—medical care and higher education—have been subsumed under the "Established Programs Financing Arrangements," under which they have, in effect, become unconditional transfers.

28. For an analysis of the economic effects of the income tax reforms, see Peter Dungan and Thomas Wilson, "Macroeconomic Effects of Tax Reform in Canada," *Canadian Tax Journal* 36, no. 1 (1988): 110–24.

In fact, the government has implemented the second objective by successive increases in sales taxes, without reducing income taxes. The current plans for the new Goods and Services Tax (GST) entail no significant income tax reductions, aside from the sales tax credits needed to offset the regressivity of the GST. The proposed new sales tax system, on balance, will bring in the same net revenue as the old, but the burden will be shifted from investment and exports to consumption.

The government's tax reform proposals have therefore worked at cross purposes, by increasing the tax burden on savings and investment through the income tax reforms of Phase I, and by reducing the tax burden on savings in the sales tax reforms of Phase II. We might have done as well with a simple reform of the sales tax system alone.

One other issue, incorporated in the 1981 U.S. tax reforms but ignored under the Canadian proposals, is adjusting the tax system for inflation. Up to 1985, the Canadian tax system incorporated more complete adjustment to inflation than did the U.S. system, as income tax brackets and exemptions were fully indexed to the CPI.[29] Although asset values were not indexed, it was possible to get indexed treatment of equity investment by holding equities in registered plans (ISIPs). The only assets for which the U.S. system provided better adjustment for inflation were inventory investments, since LIFO valuation provided near-complete exemption of phantom inventory profits.[30] In Canada, a 3 percent inventory allowance provided only partial relief from the impact of inflation on inventory profits.

In 1985–86, the positions were reversed. The Canadian federal budget of 1985 limited the indexation of brackets and exemptions to the rate of inflation less 3 percent, and the ISIPs were abolished. The 3 percent inventory allowance was eliminated in the first phase of corporate tax reform the following year. In the United States, on the other hand, full indexation of exemptions and rate brackets came into effect in 1985.

As neither Canada nor the United States indexes asset values or capital cost allowances, inflation will continue to affect the incidence of the tax system on capital income in both countries.

Issues for the Future

The key issue is whether the phase-in of the Canada-U.S. free-trade agreement (FTA), prospective lowering of trade barriers with other countries, and increased "globalization" of financial and product markets will necessitate increased harmonization of tax systems. This, fortunately, is an area in which public finance theory provides useful insights. The key is the mobility of the factors bearing the tax.

---

29. During the federal government's "6 and 5" program of public-sector wage restraints, the indexation factors were limited to 6 percent for 1983 and 5 percent for 1984.

30. If inventories are financed by debt, LIFO valuation is an overly generous offset to inflation.

Factors of production that have perfect international mobility can in the limit be taxed on a benefit basis. Where similar public benefits are provided to such factors in two countries, we should expect tax rates to be similar, if not the same. Less mobile factors of production can be taxed more heavily than the rates consistent with benefit taxation, and perfectly immobile factors can bear tax as if they were located within a closed economy.

The above remarks apply to the direct taxation of factor incomes at source. Increased tax harmonization will therefore likely occur for those factors that become more mobile as a result of globalization and the FTA. As capital was already highly mobile between Canada and the United States, there would appear to be little that the FTA could do to increase capital mobility. However, when the mobility of intangible assets is taken into account, the FTA should increase, or at least protect, the cross-border mobility of business enterprise. The one area in which international capital mobility has clearly been less than perfect is foreign direct investment (FDI). FDI is associated with technology transfer and with the earning of returns on intangible assets. FDI has also been subject to government controls, generally in Canada and in selected sectors in both countries. The FTA, by limiting general government intervention in Canada and preventing it in the United States, should increase the cross-border mobility of FDI. Furthermore, since the FTA increases the cross-border mobility of certain individuals, the mobility of enterprises as "going concerns" should also be increased.

What one would predict is that the FTA and globalization will serve to reinforce the trend toward harmonization of corporate tax systems. The harmonization of corporate systems is not a new phenomenon. It is noteworthy that effective corporate tax rates are much more equal both internationally and within the Canadian and U.S. federations than are the other major taxes.[31] Given the importance of cross-border direct and portfolio investments, the governments of Canada and the United States should consider more effective coordination of taxes bearing on these investments, for the reasons stated by Gordon (ch. 2 in this volume).

My final comment has to do with indirect taxation. Typically, sales taxes are established on a "destination basis." However, such taxes are avoided by cross-border purchasing. Within a country, it is virtually impossible to prevent some leakage from high-tax to low-tax jurisdictions. Between countries, cross-border purchasing can be better controlled at border-entry monitoring points. Nevertheless, the cross-border mobility of buyers remains important.

Harmonization of VATs has become an issue in Europe, where it is recognized that the dismantling of internal border controls would permit wide-

31. Corporate taxes within the OECD countries range from 1.3 to 7.5 percent of GDP. By contrast, the range of personal income taxes is from 5.7 to 25.6 percent of GDP; social security taxes from 0.0 to 22.2 percent of GDP; and indirect taxes from 3.9 to 19.4 percent of GDP (David Perry, "International Tax Comparisons," *Canadian Tax Journal* 37, no. 5 [1989]: table 2, p. 1352). For Canada and the United States, see the data in Vaillancourt, (ch. 11 in this volume).

spread cross-border shopping. This is not yet an issue in the North American context, since the FTA falls short of a common market or even a customs union. But with the increased mobility of individuals, and with the proposed extension of the Canadian federal sales tax to services, the degree of tax harmonization of indirect taxes may yet become important.

Contributors

William T. Alpert
University of Connecticut
Department of Economics
Scofieldtown Road
Stamford, CT 06903

Alan J. Auerbach
Department of Economics
University of Pennsylvania
3718 Locust Walk
Philadelphia, PA 19104–6297

Robin Boadway
Department of Economics
Queen's University
Kingston, Ontario K7L 3N6
Canada

Neil Bruce
Department of Economics, DK-30
University of Washington
Seattle, WA 98195

James B. Davies
Department of Economics
University of Western Ontario
Social Science Centre
London, Ontario N6A 5C2
Canada

Roger H. Gordon
Department of Economics
University of Michigan
Ann Arbor, MI 48109

Jonathan R. Kesselman
Department of Economics
University of British Columbia
997–1873 East Mall
Vancouver, BC V6T 1W5
Canada

Laurence J. Kotlikoff
Department of Economics
Boston University
270 Bay State Road
Boston, MA 02215

Kenneth J. McKenzie
Department of Economics
University of Toronto
150 St. George Street
Toronto, Ontario M5S 1A1
Canada

Charles E. McLure, Jr.
Hoover Institution
Stanford University
Stanford, CA 94305–6010

Jack M. Mintz
Faculty of Management
University of Toronto
246 Bloor Street West
Toronto, Ontario M5S 1V4
Canada

Richard A. Musgrave
Department of Economics
University of California
Santa Cruz, CA 95064

James M. Poterba
Department of Economics
Massachusetts Institute of Technology
50 Memorial Drive, Room E52–350
Cambridge, MA 02139

John B. Shoven
Department of Economics
Stanford University
Encina Hall
Stanford, CA 94305–6072

Joel Slemrod
Director, Office of Tax Policy Research
School of Business Administration
University of Michigan
Ann Arbor, MI 48109–1234

Michael Topper
Department of Economics
College of William and Mary
Williamsburg, VA 23185

François Vaillancourt
Department of Economics
University of Montreal
CP 6128, STN A
Montreal, Quebec H3A 2T5
Canada

John Whalley
Department of Economics
University of Western Ontario
Social Science Centre
London, Ontario N6A 5C2
Canada

Thomas A. Wilson
Institute for Policy Analysis
University of Toronto
140 St. George Street, Suite 707
Toronto, Ontario M5S 1A1
Canada

Author Index

Subject Index